*Both Sides of the Ocean*

# *Both Sides of the Ocean*

## A BIOGRAPHY OF
## HENRY ADAMS
## HIS FIRST LIFE
## 1838 - 1862

## EDWARD CHALFANT

*Archon Books*

*1982*

© 1982   Edward Chalfant   All rights reserved
First published 1982 as an Archon Book,
an imprint of The Shoe String Press, Inc.,
Hamden, Connecticut 06514

Printed in the United States of America

**Library of Congress Cataloging in Publication Data**

Chalfant, Edward, 1921-
    Both sides of the ocean.

    Includes bibliographical references and index.
    1. Adams, Henry, 1838-1918.    2. Historians—United
States—Biography.    I. Title.
E175.5.A2C46    973'.072024 [B]     82-6805
ISBN 0-208-01901-4                           AACR2

*in memory*
for Aileen Tone

*"Through this labyrinth of difficulties he still managed to guide himself with a discretion that is astonishing. . . . "*

Henry Adams, 1861

# Contents

# *Preface*

Henry Adams was set apart from other human beings mainly by having always known he mattered. Beginning no one knows exactly when, perhaps at a moment so early as to be lost in the oblivion of childhood, he learned he was important. He also knew his life would be important. Wanting to live up to what he was, he assumed that his life, when lived, would have meaning and value for other Americans and possibly for all mankind.

Proverbially, life is difficult. No one escapes the necessity of making efforts. Willing to make an exceptional effort, Adams started life in earnest at eighteen, while in college. Within the span of a mere five years and some odd months, he met with a kind of success he could not have anticipated. When not yet twenty-four, he discovered that he had completed one life and would have to start a second. This instructive turn of events permitted him to suppose that radical self-renewal—passing onward from one life to another—could be planned and voluntary as well as unplanned and obligatory. Thirty years later, at fifty-four, having completed a second life, he deliberately began a third. A phase at a time, he completed his third life, too. Thus, when he died at eighty, he died three times fulfilled—a consummation beyond his dreams.

To his biographers and others who wish to know about him, his having lived three times is a great convenience. Because his story falls of itself into three stories, each of which can make up the contents of a single book (this one is the first of a trilogy), a chance exists that his immensely eventful, threefold triumph can be brought within the compass of readability. But there is an interesting complication.

The more one studies the three lives that Adams managed to fit within the space of his eighty years, the more his lives reveal themselves as coming, not one after another, like the acts of a play, but one above another, like the tiers of arches in a Roman aqueduct. The direction of his life was upward. The man was not content to live. He aspired to live and then live better. Each time he started over in life, he again pursued his former objects—but in ways so improved and different as to effect a transformation.

It is far from easy to write about such a person. His first life was exceedingly ambitious; his second was meant to be an unqualified advance upon his first; his third was meant to be an equal advance upon the second; each of his efforts gave rise to a different style; and the challenge presented to his biographers by his efforts—a challenge never slight—becomes extremely difficult to meet as Adams moves upward from his first effort to his last.

In this preface, as little as possible should be said about the phenomenal American's improved existences, each of which, when the time comes, will require a preface of its own. Here attention should be concentrated on Adams's first life—on the lowest arches of the aqueduct, formed, one notices, of large stones, roughly hewn.

What did Adams make of his early years? The question is a good one, and the answer is not as well known as it ought to be. To his astonishment, fright, and even horror, his first life acquired the shape of a strenuous and extremely dangerous adventure—an adventure which some readers may feel ought properly to have been his undoing, and which other readers may feel was unmistakably his salvation.

There could be no better way to get to know him than to go with him step by step into the exertions and perils of that horrific experience; to endure with him what he endured when the crisis at last arrived; and to emerge, as he emerged, prepared for a new effort and willing to take new risks, having already won a sense of high achievement. To meet Adams in this way admittedly is to meet him only as he was when young. Yet it is also to learn what a truly gifted and willing young American could do; and, beyond that, what young human beings generally can do, if they will listen to the better angels of their natures.

At present, young people do not have many young models to imitate who deserve much imitation. It is more than possible that Henry Adams, between the ages of eighteen and twenty-four, presents just such a model. The best judges of the degree to which he deserves imitation will not be older readers but younger ones, in the universities or not long out. It is to them that the following narrative has been tacitly addressed.

# Acknowledgments

Research biographers accumulate debts beyond all possibility of fair acknowledgment. My debts are great and cannot be fully listed, but I shall mention enough of them to indicate how little the merits of this book, whatever they are, can be attributed to myself.

I owe special thanks to Thomas Vance, who, in 1941, by urging me to read Brooks Adams, put me on the track of what became an interest in Henry Adams. Stringfellow Barr, during a chance meeting, confirmed me in the interest.

During World War II, the U. S. Army Air Force made me a historian and placed me in such advantageous circumstances in Nevada and on Guam that, after working hours, I was able to study Adams concentratedly.

In 1946, the U. S. Government financed my buying much-needed Adams books under the G. I. Bill; and, in 1947, Vernon Loggins did me the inestimable favor of making me rewrite an overambitious master's essay on Adams at Columbia University after it was "finished." New York bookmen, Charles Everett, Peter Lader, and the "Seven Book-hunters," supplied me Adams books I sorely lacked; and a distinguished publisher, Charles Scribner, showed me how willing people are to furnish sincere inquirers with recollections and hard-to-get information.

Dartmouth College, by adding me to its faculty as an instructor in English, put a two-year stop to my Adams work, yet taught me how indispensable it is to get away from a difficult subject at intervals, as a means of getting close to it in the long run.

The University of Pennsylvania gave me a Harrison Fellowship and freed me to study Adams full time for a year. Roy F. Nichols helpfully challenged my ideas concerning Adams; and Robert E. Spiller and Sculley Bradley condoned my writing my dissertation (*Henry Adams and History*, 1954) in the near-absence of supervision and then permitted me to rewrite it voluntarily after it was accepted, as a step towards attempting harder tasks. In Boston, Stephen T. Riley, then librarian of the Massachusetts Historical Society, had meanwhile begun to acquaint me with its fathomless resources; and in Cambridge, William Jackson, head of the Houghton Library at Harvard University, had told me the secret of his authorship of a list of Adams's writings published under another author's name—a list which identified most of young Adams's unsigned early reports to Boston and New York newspapers.

At the suggestion of a friend, Paul Rockwell, and with the express encouragement of a friend of his, Benjamin Tone, I telephoned the latter's great-aunt, Aileen Tone, was invited by her to visit, and was at once accepted as a friend—thanks in great measure to my wife (born Eleni Petrou), for whom Miss Tone felt an immediate strong affection. Elizabeth Grinnell alerted me and my wife to the availability of an apartment across the street from Miss Tone's; we moved into it; and Miss Tone introduced us to Mrs. Ward Thoron (born Louisa Chapin Hooper). Since Miss Tone and Mrs. Thoron were the two persons still living who had known Henry Adams very well and lived with him for long periods, their approbation and friendship were decisive for me. Herself a researcher, Mrs. Thoron opened for my use her (and her husband's) entire collection of Adams materials, including some evidence of the first importance.

A publisher, Charles "Cap" Pearce, hearing about my dissertation from a stranger on a commuting train, called me into his office, offered to publish any book I would write for his firm about Adams, and did not renege when I said it would have to be a one-volume biography for general sale, not a critical biography or critical appreciation. In company with Frank and Elsie Meyer, and Richard Corneille, Pearce arranged my applying to the Volker Fund for a direct research grant to myself as a writer and biographer—quite apart from my attachment to Hofstra College as an assistant professor of English. The Volker grant permitted my working on Adams full time continuously for thirty-two months, starting in June 1956; and Hofstra was later good enough to rehire me when I ran out of funds; but, by attempting to write one, I learned I could *not* fit Henry Adams into a one-volume biography. The evidence itself suggested a new idea for a three-book biography—a large work made up of three independently readable but interrelated narratives, each telling the story of one of Adams's three lives; and, shifting to this idea late in 1957, I started over.

Earlier, in 1955, the Adams Papers had been opened to scholars at the Massachusetts Historical Society, at least in the sense of no longer being completely closed. I applied to Thomas Boylston Adams, president of the society, for permission to see a portion of the papers not impounded for editing and microfilming purposes: the separately boxed papers of Henry Adams in the period 1890-1918. My wife and I studied this huge collection in the summer of 1955. I did not then know it; but that experience gave me, at least in outline, the story I shall want to tell in the *third* book of this biography. Also it prepared me to discern the outlines of the stories I have to tell in the *first* and *second* books. I wish now to express in the strongest terms my gratitude to Mr. Adams for that early access, and to his valued associates, Stephen Riley, Lyman Butterfield, Malcolm Freiberg, and others, for repeated and thoughtful assistance of many kinds, both then and later.

When I returned to teaching early in 1959, very few details concerning the three-book biography were settled; but it was clear that the chapters would be written in short episodes; two episodes—one about Adams's birth and another about the death of his father's eldest brother—had taken fairly satisfactory forms; many others were drafted; and I had faith that the needed hundreds of additional episodes could eventually be written. That autumn at Hofstra, Raymond W. Short arranged that I begin to teach two upperclass courses every year in American Literature and Shakespeare, an unusual privilege and one immensely helpful to a person anxious to complete in good form a biography of an American whose claims to attention include his being a great writer. In 1960, Ginette Courchet offered my wife and me the use of her Paris apartment during every summer we might wish to use it; in 1961, Thomas Marriner extended the same munificent favor to us in connection with his London apartment; so I was free for nine summers to write successive drafts of this book and the first half of the second book of the biography in Paris and London—cities propitious to writers; and I freed time in the winters to type revisions of each summer's work.

To my and others' great advantage, the microfilm edition of the Adams Papers through 1889 had meanwhile been completed, and Columbia University allowed me full access to its set. The staff of Houghton Library helped me obtain additional Adams materials of great value. Private owners, notably Mrs. Thoron, Miss Tone, Mr. and Mrs. Henry S. Sherman, Mr. and Mrs. Harold Landon, and Mr. Samuel Reber, gave me books, photographs, and manuscripts. In connection with this first book, I was particularly assisted by the staffs of the Harvard University Archives, the Boston Public Library, the

Boston Athenaeum, the New York Public Library, the Library of Congress, the National Archives, and, in England, the British Library and the Historical Manuscripts Commission.

Louis Auchincloss, to whom I was introduced by Aileen Tone, took a generously supportive interest in my project. In person, three other writers well-informed about Adams—R. P. Blackmur, Harold Dean Cater, and William H. Jordy—provided information and encouragement. Through their writings, a long chain of persons—most notably Charles Francis Adams, Jr., Brooks Adams, John Franklin Jameson, William Roscoe Thayer, Worthington Chauncey Ford, Ephraim Douglass Adams, Ward Thoron, and Ernest Samuels—aided me with source materials, information, and ideas concerning Adams. Henry Adams II replied to questions which only he could answer. Leon Edel, whom I met through the kindness of Frederica Landon, accepted me as a fellow biographer, gave me needed documents, and set me an example of biographical mastery and self-respect. Martin Brunor, ethnologist and polymath, in addition to needling me about my own and Adams's insufficiences, provided insights no other human being could have offered.

Miss Tone and Mrs. Thoron, while helping me defray my research costs, read and constructively reacted to the early drafts of this book as fast as I could complete them. Relatives and friends—Allan B. and Ruth Chalfant, Nancy Davis, Patricia Murray, Richard Norton, and George James Grinnell—also read drafts and made detailed criticisms.

In 1969-1970, the "university crisis" put a second two-year stop to my Adams work by bringing disturbances to the Columbia and Hofstra campuses which, for me, made writing momentarily impossible; but the interruption may have helped. When I got back to my manuscripts, I saw them differently and realized that the exhilarations of starting the project had given way to the myriad exactions and pains of completing it. Not always difficult to draft, biographies can be extremely difficult, perhaps impossible, to perfect; and the fact that Adams himself wrote well made it imperative that I remove from the first and second books as many blemishes as I could. Except to say that I completely re-researched a great many portions of Adams's experience, and that I was much helped by working on the first and second books in alternation, I want not to explain how I went about the lifting of the present book to its current, decidedly improved condition. I wish instead to say that, in the process, I contracted additional obligations.

Extraordinary assistance by Harley P. Holden, curator of the Harvard University Archives, together with his aides, greatly augmented my store of information concerning Adams's college years. Stephen Riley and Charles Vandersee alerted me to the availability of crucial new materials. Additional friends—Richard A. G. Dupuis, Dennis Flynn, Frances Sicari, Margaret Hofeller, Domenica Barbuto, Andrea Tobias, Betty Barthelme, Joseph Cardello, Jocelyn Weston Krug, and Linton Thorn—read the first book and helped with detailed suggestions. Louis Auchincloss read a near-final version and prevailed upon me to change a climactic passage. At intervals, Hofstra University had meanwhile granted me two paid semesters' leave of absence to work on Adams; and American "high technology," by revolutionizing the copying and typing processes, had revolutionized biographers' methods, permitting me to work with much-diminished irritations and to face the necessity of repeated revision and correction with easier equanimity.

Timely advice by Michael Steinberg and the positive intervention of Robert L. Gale resulted in my agreeing to an appeal by Gale to the Shoe String Press on my behalf about the chance that my biography of Adams might be of interest to the firm.

Three of the editors of the forthcoming, definitive Harvard University Press edition of the *Letters of Henry Adams,* J. C. Levenson, Charles Vandersee, and Viola Hopkins Winner, in recent days have glanced through the final draft of the manuscript, caught two misspellings of names, and, by giving me free access to their notes concerning Adams's early letters, enabled me to catch myself in, and correct, an oversight in my research concerning one of Adams's early letters in the *Boston Courier.* Such outright blunders, the terror of biographers and historians, are certainly still lurking in the book; they always are; but the editors spared me those, and I shall never cease to thank them.

All extracts from the Adams Papers (AP) and Henry Adams Papers—1890-1918 (HAP) are quoted by permission of the Adams Manuscript Trust. All extracts from Henry Adams associated material in the Harvard University Archives are quoted by permission of the Harvard University Archives. The extracts from letters by Charles Sumner in the Theodore F. Dwight Papers, the extract from an inscription in the copy of Macaulay's *History of England* in the Henry Adams Library, and the extracts from notes taken by Harold Dean Cater from an unpublished journal by Benjamin W. Crowninshield and preserved in the Cater Papers are quoted by permission of the

Massachusetts Historical Society. The extracts from letters by Lord John Russell in the Palmerston Papers are quoted by permission of the Trustees of the Broadlands Archives Trust. The extracts from the letter from Henry Adams to Charles Sumner dated March 22, 1861, and the message written on it by Sumner to William Henry Seward are quoted with the permission of the Rush Rhees Library, University of Rochester. The extracts from the letter from Henry Adams to Henry J. Raymond dated January 24, 1862, are quoted with the permission of the New York Public Library, Manuscript Division. The extract from the letter from Henry Adams to William Henry Seward dated August 25, 1864, is quoted with the permission of the National Archives, Washington, D.C. The extracts from the letter from Henry Adams to Horace Gray, Jr., dated June 17, 1861, and the extracts from the letter from Henry Adams to Charles Sumner dated January 30, 1862, are quoted with the permission of the Houghton Library—Harvard University Library.

# PART ONE

# 1 / A Fine Boy

In mid-February 1838, Charles Francis Adams was living in Boston in a house he had rented at the top of Beacon Hill, at No. 3 Hancock Avenue, facing the Massachusetts State House. For the present, his efforts were divided between two unobtrusive pursuits. As a rule on weekday mornings, he walked to his office on nearby Court Street and gave some time to managing his investments. Then he walked back to the house and devoted several hours to rigorous self-education. His study schedule currently required that he master the last play of Sophocles, *Oedipus at Colonus*—in which Oedipus, no longer king of Thebes, and overtaken by age, finds his fated resting place near Athens and very strangely vanishes.[1] Mr. Adams was reading the Greek original. To his annoyance, while he tried to concentrate, his wife distracted him. Mrs. Adams had earlier borne three children without important mishap. Now the birth of a fourth child was at hand, and she seemed needlessly alarmed, even despairing of her survival.

Nothing calamitous took place. On February 16, 1838, a Friday, at three in the morning, C. F. Adams was wakened by his wife and sent to get Dr. Bigelow. The doctor came as needed. After breakfast, the husband learned that a "fine boy" had been delivered with "less suffering than on former occasions." Recording the event in his diary, Mr. Adams was moved to note that he had gone out into the darkness "in the midst of a snow storm and in the extraordinary silence of the streets." The experience had been new and instructive. "No wonder that thieves select this period as their most favorable time."

The mother's forebodings proved to have some warrant. She recovered slowly, and her "fine boy" endured a month of difficulties and discomforts. The father meanwhile continued his reading of Sophocles' great play. On March 18, he was able to record, "My wife now gains steadily and the baby improves. . . ." He added three days later, "The baby grows."

Mrs. Adams's maiden name had been Abigail Brown Brooks. She had married Charles Francis Adams in 1829. As a wife, she had taken a positive interest in her husband's family but also had maintained her fond attachments to all her many blood relations. Her love for the Brookses became entwined with her hopes for her newest child. During that hard first month, while she was recuperating, her new boy was "in a way given to his mother." Urged to choose for him any name she might prefer, she decided to name him after a favorite brother, Henry Brooks, who had died not long before. The resulting name, Henry Brooks Adams, was duly affixed to the infant at a christening by the minister of Boston's First Unitarian Church, Nathaniel Frothingham—the husband of Ann Brooks, one of the infant's mother's sisters. The moral of these developments appeared to be that the child, while of course an Adams, would be called upon in time to be very much a Brooks.[2]

The center of the Adams family's activities had always been their property in Quincy, then a country town, seven miles south of Boston, on low hills overlooking the Atlantic. The family owned a dwelling there called the Old House, originally an undistinguished structure, but expanded and improved until it turned into a mansion. At the time of Henry's birth and christening, the mansion was the home and summer residence of his paternal grandparents, John Quincy Adams and Louisa Catherine Adams. When he was less than three months old, infant Henry was taken to stay in Quincy. There he was quartered with his parents, his elder sister, and two elder brothers, not in the Old House, but instead in a separate house which his father had recently caused to be constructed on the family's property. Located on President's Hill, this separate house commanded a wide view of the sea. It entered into the family's calculations as a mere annex to the larger building, from which it was about an eighth of a mile distant.

For the baby, the move to Quincy in the spring of 1838 was the beginning of an experience of alternation. Such were the wishes and habits of his parents that he was destined to live part of every year in Boston and most of every year in Quincy for an indefinite period. Of the two places, only Quincy would afford the child a sense of home, and for him the sense would be strongest within the walls and on the immediate grounds of the Old House. All the same, he would in one way be deeply affected by living in the new, subsidiary dwelling "on the hill."[3] Returning there every spring, he would seize the opportunity to feel and feed a passion which would never afterwards desert him: love and hunger for sight of the open ocean.[4]

When he was three, growing Henry was supplanted as the family's youngest child by a fourth son, Arthur Adams.[5] This disturbance went hand in hand with others. That autumn, when the family returned to Boston, Henry knew that he and his relations would soon be moving from their winter house on Hancock Avenue to a new winter house around the corner, at No. 57 on steep Mount Vernon Street. The new house would not be rented. It had been given to Henry's parents by his other grandfather, Peter Chardon Brooks— known to everyone as the richest man in New England.[6] And, as things fell out, the prospective move coincided for Henry with a fearful illness. On December 3, 1841, he came down with scarlet fever. For a time his recovery was doubted. He was carried to the new house while still unwell.[7]

Although in later life he would retain no memory of his ailment, the sufferer would come to believe that the dreaded fever had shocked his nerves, checked his growth, and prevented his resembling the standard family type. In regarding himself as nervous, Henry possibly was right. He may have seemed exceptionally sensitive even when an infant. More than other children, he reacted to fluctuations in the weather. On sunny days, he shone. On wet or gloomy days, he fell silent and desponded. His idea of bliss was Quincy in the springtime. His horror was late November, when it rained and the family went back to hated Boston.[8] Yet no outward difference existed between himself and his male relations. All the Adamses had been small. As a man, the third son would be shorter than his brothers but taller than his father. He would stand about five feet four.[9]

Being small, Henry was sometimes tempted to think he was not strong. When leaving college, he would write about himself, "I never was strong enough to fight, along with other boys, though my health has always been excellent, so long as I can remember." He ought instead to have written that he was never big enough to fight.[10] Very strong in proportion to his size, he also was well-coordinated, agile, and extremely energetic.[11]

Henry's mother used to say how astonishing it was that one woman, herself, could have so many clever children.[12] The four elder children comprised a coherent group. The eldest, Louisa Catherine Adams II, had been born in 1831. John Quincy Adams II and Charles Francis Adams, Jr., were born in 1833 and 1835. Arriving in 1838, Henry came along sufficiently soon to think of himself as belonging with the others, rather than apart.

All the elder children were self-asserting. Louisa—often addressed as "Loo"—set an example of ceaseless vivacity. John and Charles were muscular and athletic. They liked Henry well enough but sometimes, when tired of tormenting and pounding each other, instead tormented and pounded him. One day in Quincy, learning in the orchard behind the Old House that their younger brother was overfond of fruits and berries, they raised a taunting cry, "Henry greedy, cherry-eater!"[13] Acting as they did, they often drove him for protection to fiery Loo, and she accepted their victim as her friend and favorite.

Sheltering the child, Louisa brought herself into close relation with a being capable of profound and permanent attachments. Henry was very loving. He loved his elder brothers. Loo he loved extremely, and he did not hide his feeling.[14] With her as with others, his manner was direct and uninhibited. In everything he did there was always something hearty. Nature had formed him in such a way that his emotions and responses were pronounced and forceful. His appetite was keen. His walk was rapid.[15]

All the same, the amount of notice given to Henry at first was comparatively slight. Among the older children when very young, Loo and John attracted the most attention. Both were considered very promising and certain of high achievement. Much time went by before the parents realized that their fourth child, after all, was the cleverest of their brood.[16] When this knowledge dawned upon the parents is now uncertain. It may have stolen into consciousness when father and mother agreed that Henry was never any trouble. He seemed to raise himself.[17]

Some human beings, it would be hard to say how many, more or less unconsciously give their lives the shape of a story—or, as happened in the case of Henry Adams, a succession of stories. How Henry set this process in motion is a subject for intelligent and well-informed conjecture.

He began, it seems, during the winter hours he spent indoors in Boston in the early 1840s, when he was not yet old enough to go to school. Apparently someone read him Aesop's fables.[18] He reacted by forming a passionate attachment to all the kinds of animals. Once possessed of their names and images, he continued to value them extremely. His conduct showed that, more than anything, he loved vitality. He saw in pictured and imagined animals precisely what he felt in himself: an impulse to be always active, inventive, and up to something. In this way, he became self-consciously a doer.

Evidence of his having taken this first step may be found in certain things he did at later times. While in college, wanting to write, he introduced one of Aesop's fables and several imagined animals into his fledgling articles and essays.[19] Thereafter, he herded an enormous train of imagined animals—ants, mules, rabbits, whales, fleas, camels, coons, beavers, elephants, and bees—through the many pages of his published works and private letters. He went so far as to describe himself as "a modern Noah."[20] These actions were not extravagances or follies. They expressed his superactive makeup.

In Boston, the new winter house on Mount Vernon Street boasted a large room on the second floor, overlooking the front yard. C. F. Adams had appropriated the room for himself as a library and study in which to talk with his political allies. The room was warmed with fires at either end and filled with sun through three tall windows. The children were not barred from going into it, but the three eldest stayed away. To Loo, John, and Charles, the "Governor"—as they often called him—seemed unfriendly. He unintentionally shut them out.[21]

Where the three eldest felt unwanted, younger Henry entered and remained. On brighter days, of course, he ran down the stairs, out the door, across the street, and two blocks downhill to Boston Common, to play with the other children of the neighborhood. He went many times to a house on Beacon Street, No. 45, to see a boy his own age, his special friend, George Harrison Otis.[22] But on wet or cloudy days, forsaking the other children, Henry was likely to be found among the books in his father's library, shifting for himself while C. F. Adams studied, wrote letters, talked with visitors, or rode his hobby of collecting and comparing a hoard of gold and silver coins.

At Quincy, Henry discovered another library, belonging to his father's father, on the second floor of the Old House. John Quincy Adams may have himself precipitated this all-important discovery by giving his little grandson a present, inscribed in his own hand, a book of nursery rhymes.[23] The book, and possibly other kindnesses on the grandfather's part, was evidently construed by Henry as an invitation to assert in Quincy the rights he had acquired in Boston. Entering J. Q. Adams's study when the old man was there, the grandson began a systematic handling and examination of his grandfather's many books, papers, purses, coins, canes, pistols, and similar possessions, the accumulated paraphernalia of an unparalleled career in politics, stretching back to the earliest years of the Republic. One might think that intruding Henry in this way must have made himself a nuisance, but J. Q. Adams seemed not to mind. Though nearing eighty, the grandfather kept a pliancy and sparkle looked for in persons half his

age. He took pleasure in Henry's reappearances. In time, the statesman and his marauding visitor grew "almost intimate."[24]

Starting possibly in November 1843, the grandson was sent to a
school on Kitchen Lane in Boston.[25] When the family returned in the
spring to Quincy, he was enrolled at a second school there. This
arrangement strained his youthful patience beyond its breaking point.
One morning at the Old House, he rebelled and told his mother he
would not go to school. The sound of his voice carried up the stairs to
the president's study. J. Q. Adams came down the stairs and inter-
vened. Without a word, he took the rebel by the hand and conducted
him to his place in the schoolhouse a mile or so away. The episode had
two fateful effects. Despite an irremovable and growing aversion to
schools and schoolteachers, Henry thereafter went regularly to school
and did his lessons. Perhaps because John Quincy Adams held his
hand, he presumed that he and the president were joined by common
interests and concerns.[26]

Both in Quincy and Boston, observing the actions of his grandfather and father in their respective dens, Henry witnessed a phenomenon which was fully as attractive to him as school was repulsive.
J. Q. Adams and C. F. Adams were tirelessly devoted to self-directed
study. They were alike as well in writing never-ending letters and
keeping diaries. They also were perpetually reading newspapers.
Henry watched their behavior with interest and supposed that he, too,
would become a possessor of shelves of books, would teach himself all
sorts of things he wished to learn, would keep a diary, write letters, talk
with visitors, and rifle newspapers.

Thus his boyhood assumed a very regular pattern. Part of his time
he yielded to mere school and schoolwork. In all seasons, he played,
sometimes with other children, often with his brothers. In the city, in
winter, he hurled snowballs, sledded, and skated; in the country, in the
spring, summer, and autumn, he walked the hills, rode horses, fished,
swam, went out in boats, and sailed. Wherever he was, and as much as
he could, he practiced self-education. He pored for endless hours over
pictures, maps, books, magazines, newspapers, and government documents. He loved geography. Reading whatever pleased him, he gravi-
tated towards biographies, histories, novels, poetry, and accounts of
travel. In imagination, he began to go on long, rewarding journeys to
Europe, Tahiti, China, Egypt, and Central Asia.[27]

Arthur, a handsome boy, died at five. Consolations for his loss
were found in the birth of a second daughter, Mary Adams, in 1846

and a fifth son, Peter Chardon Brooks Adams (invariably called "Brooks"), in 1848. No other children followed.[28]

Unavoidably, each of the six children who survived, Louisa, John, Charles, Henry, Mary, and Brooks, had to grapple with the challenging information that a great-grandfather of theirs, named John Adams, had been the second president of the United States; that one of their grandfathers, John Quincy Adams, had been the sixth president of the United States; and that their father, Charles Francis Adams, was the only living citizen of the Union whose father and grandfather had both been presidents. The burden imposed upon the children by such data should not be underestimated. There was never a time when Henry, his brothers, and his sisters could escape being scrutinized by other people and by each other as heirs and heiresses of America's most distinguished political family. But Henry had to grapple with the additional information that his mother, from the time he was born, had wished him to attach himself to *her* relations and grow up a virtual Brooks, although in name an Adams.

His mother's hopes in this respect were disappointed. Her fourth son wholly failed to become a Brooks.[29] Taken as a child to live for a time at the home of his mother's father, Henry grew "so violently homesick" that he had to be brought back at once to the surroundings with which he was familiar.[30] His way of dealing with his Brooks relations was always cordial, even friendly, but objective. He respected his mother, became her invaluable confidant, helped her in innumerable instances, but never felt or behaved as if his life were fundamentally connected in any way to hers. In old age, he would be acutely embarrassed to find that, on one occasion, under sudden stress, he could not remember—had entirely misplaced—her name.[31] The lapse was hardly accidental. In his heart, Henry was not his mother's son. Were he to become indissolubly linked to any woman, it would not be as a son, and it would have to be to a woman not a Brooks.

Oppositely, Henry succeeded altogether in feeling himself an Adams. In fact, he should be counted as one of the greater Adamses, of whom there were only three, among the males. Yet his experience in one respect was unprecedented and wholly new. Long before, John Adams had thrust a duty upon his eldest son, John Quincy Adams: to make himself as great a man as his father, perhaps a greater. The idea conveyed to Henry Adams in boyhood was very different: that he was great already; it had been given to him to be so; and his problem would be to live up to a stature and importance known to himself as real from the beginning.[32]

As was manifest in their behavior, his elder sister and elder brothers also felt the challenge of the family's history. Louisa, being female, was admittedly not obliged to dress herself in the costume of manly heroism. Nonetheless, combative and headstrong, Loo showed a sort of courage and moved with energy towards negation. She reacted against the increasing provincialness of Massachusetts, against democracy, against America. For decades after she said it, people in New England would remember her declaring that she would have "married a blackamoor" to get away from Boston.[33]

John Quincy Adams II chose a different path. The eldest son felt the honor of his name and seemed certain to make a bid for political advancement; but, until that time arrived, he intended to relax. Rather than make himself a slave of duty, honor, family, and country, he proposed to be a good fellow, sociable, gregarious, and never in a hurry.[34]

Charles Francis Adams, Jr., was prey to inner conflicts. Seldom completely happy, the second son contrived to be both likable and hard to get along with. On one day, he might be companionable and overbearing; on the next, cooperative and envious. While he was struggling to resolve his doubts, he sometimes became pugnacious. Later, when they were in their twenties, Henry at last would tell him, " . . . you used to box my ears because your kite wouldn't fly. . . ."[35]

Henry Brooks Adams reaped the benefit of the eldest children's bad examples. He acted in ways directly opposite to theirs. Where Loo's responses were dominantly negative, his from the outset were dominantly positive.[36] Where John relaxed and held back, Henry went forward and speeded up. Where Charles was indecisive, the third son made decisions promptly.

Still, there was one respect in which Henry did resemble his elder sister. He and Loo felt uprooted. In his most famous book, *The Education of Henry Adams*, first distributed in 1907, he would point to the fact of his own uprootedness, saying that, through all the early years he passed in Quincy and Boston, he had experienced the strange sensation of really being "somewhere else; perhaps in Washington with its social ease; perhaps in Europe." Especially he would describe how, from the Quincy hills, he had watched the smoke of the Cunard steamers leaving Boston and disappearing beyond the horizon.[37]

In another respect, Henry stood completely apart, not only from his brothers and sisters but also from his parents. He far outran them in ability. The younger children, Mary Adams and Brooks Adams, stood in the best positions for observing this all-important difference. In later life, Brooks published his opinion that Henry alone, among the latter-day Adamses, could measure up to the family's presidents. According to the youngest son, the gap in ability between the greater and lesser Adamses was wide. Brooks believed that the eldest brothers, John and Charles, and also their father, C. F. Adams, had been "ordinary lawyers or men of affairs," while Henry, in contrast, had been a phenomenon worth careful scrutiny. In this connection, Brooks's judgment should be respected. What he recognized in his best brother was a human being both "powerful and original."[38]

The J. Q. Adams whom Henry knew had been repeatedly re-elected to Congress by his neighbors in the Third Massachusetts District surrounding Quincy. The only former president ever to accept election to the House of Representatives, he was one of the most distinguished members that body had ever had. In Boston late in 1846, he suffered a stroke and was partly paralyzed. He made a fair recovery and resumed his place in Congress, but the following winter in Washington he was one day taken suddenly ill at his desk in the chamber of the House. Moved to the speaker's room, he lingered two days, regained consciousness at the close, and died saying, "I am content!" His grandson Henry on that day, February 23, 1848, was ten years and one week old.

The death of the sixth president was a national event. In halls and churches, in legislatures and in Congress, the nation gathered into crowds to commemorate his worth. Preparations were made in Quincy for a great funeral service. On March 11, Henry waited with his relations at the Old House to march in the procession. Dignitaries, admirers, and friends had come to Quincy from many societies and institutions, from Harvard College, from the towns and cities of Massachusetts, from all the states and territories of the Union, from everywhere, it seemed. The cannons boomed, the procession formed, and all moved slowly from the Adams house to the First Church. Once inside and seated, Henry saw a familiar figure in the pulpit, the local minister, William P. Lunt. No ordinary preacher, Lunt had known John Quincy Adams well and was unafraid to describe his qualities, including his ferociousness in debate. The eloquent clergyman spoke frankly about the departed stateman's "dreaded controversial skill," which, he said, "like the mill-stone in Scripture, was fatal to those on whom it fell, and to those who fell upon it."

In the course of his funeral sermon, Lunt told his hearers that the modern Adamses were descendants of a certain Henry Adams, a vigorous Englishman, who, in the 1630s, had fled the dragon of religious persecution in Devonshire, crossed the Atlantic with eight sons, and alighted in Massachusetts near Mount Wollaston. Methodically, Lunt unfolded the story of the family through six generations in America, ending with the life of the man whose body lay coffined in the church. The sermon nonetheless was not historical. Its exclusive purpose was to impart a moral lesson concerning the rewards stored up for those who unfailingly did their duty. Its text was a line from Revelations, which Lunt repeated as he closed: "Be thou faithful unto death, and I will give thee a crown of life."[39]

Henry never forgot the experience it was for him to listen while such words were being spoken. For him, the service, and especially the sermon, was "overwhelming."[40] But the great occasion at Quincy became for him only half of a twofold experience, the other half of which soon began in Boston. The Massachusetts legislature had requested Edward Everett, the famous orator, to write and deliver a fitting eulogy on the life and character of John Quincy Adams. Everett chanced to be the husband of Charlotte Brooks, the second of Henry's mother's two sisters. The orator consented to appear on the appointed day, April 15, 1848, at Faneuil Hall. The surviving Adamses, Henry among them, attended the meeting as the legislature's guests. Everett delivered a polished eulogy which, at least in Henry's view, belittled the man it was advertised to praise.

J. Q. Adams had first been elected to Congress in 1830. Shortly after taking his seat in the House, he had started to insist upon discussion of an obnoxious question: civil rights. His fellow congressmen had realized that he meant to force debate concerning slavery. A "gag" rule had been quickly passed to silence him, but he had turned about and attempted to get the rule repealed. At every session, growing always more skillful and successful, he had convulsed his enemies with new expedients of argument and procedure. Several members of the House, previously timid, had come to his support. In this way, at an age when such a feat seemed hardly possible, the embattled former president had created an antislavery faction within the federal government.

At Faneuil Hall, eulogizing the antislavery leader, Edward Everett avoided all mention of his subject's antislavery triumphs. J. Q. Adams had won his campaign to force the repeal of the "gag" rule. The deciding vote, 108 to 80, had been cast by the House in December 1845. Everett, in April 1848, spoke neither of the passage of the rule nor its reversal. Yet his audience for the most part applauded enthusiastically. The better citizens of Boston, whether Whigs or Democrats, were agreed that the exertions of J. Q. Adams as a foe of slavery were a dangerous precedent best forgotten. Henry's uncle-by-marriage had said exactly what the crowd had wanted him to say.[41]

The living Adamses could not evade the challenge implicit in the crowd's applause. C. F. Adams was himself a well-known antislavery advocate. While J. Q. Adams had tried to form a national coalition of antislavery leaders, C. F. Adams had tried to effect important changes locally. By serving in the Massachusetts legislature, then by editing a small newspaper, the *Boston Whig*, Henry's father had attempted for several years to unite the Whig politicans in Massachusetts in support of a frankly antislavery doctrine. He and his allies had been dubbed the "Conscience Whigs" and were attracting wide attention. The position taken by C. F. Adams with respect to slavery was impossible to mistake. He was publicly committed in favor of its "total abolition" and the "eradication of the fatal influence" it was exercising in Washington.[42]

When J. Q. Adams died, C. F. Adams entered national politics at once. In the spring of 1848, at his office, the leading Conscience Whigs agreed upon a fighting strategy. Should the Whig convention that June at Philadelphia fail to choose a presidential candidate willing to speak out against the evils of slavery, they would immediately bolt the party. As it happened, the convention nominated a man without opinions, General Zachary Taylor, hero of the recently ended war with Mexico. The Conscience Whigs withdrew and issued a call to antislavery leaders across the North to attend a new convention in August in Buffalo. The new convention met. The delegates, a patchwork of disaffected Whigs and Democrats, named themselves the Free Soil Party. The former Democrats asserted a wish to select the party's presidential candidate, and the former Whigs reserved the right to build the party's platform. The ex-Democrats put forward a New Yorker, ex-President Van Buren, who was duly nominated. At the insistence of the Ohio delegation, C. F. Adams was chosen as vice-presidential candidate.

Henry, a ten-year-old adherent of the antislavery cause, watched the race that autumn with inexpressible concern.[43] He learned in November that the Free Soil candidates had received 300,000 votes across the North and more than a quarter of the vote in several states, including Massachusetts. For the Adamses, the result was mixed. The family had kept its fame and asserted its passionate support of freedom—at the cost of exile from the national government. It seemed possible that Charles Francis Adams would never win federal office. While he was running in vain for vice-president on the Free Soil ticket, the seat in Congress which his father had held since 1830 was given to a deserving aspirant, Horace Mann. So, for the Governor, the door to the House of Representatives in Washington seemed firmly closed. Entrance into the United States Senate seemed even less in prospect. In the long run, Henry's father might go to the capital as a political winner and office holder, but at the moment his future looked very doubtful.

Quite unexpectedly, one day in October 1848, during the campaign which drew so much attention to his father, Henry had learned that his intimate friend George Otis was dead. He and George had often played together in the yard of the Otis house on Beacon Street. Practically overnight, his playmate was carried off by a disease—apparently poliomyelitis. The shock for Henry was the greater because he had allowed himself the joy of dreaming that he and George might be friends and allies through life.[44]

The effects of the shock were far-reaching. After losing George Otis, young Henry formed many close acquaintanceships and near friendships in Boston and Quincy, mainly among his schoolmates, but apparently made no efforts to form real friendships.[45] In lieu of a new friend, he sought a more advantageous place—or rather several advantageous places—within the private world of his father's household.

Being the middle child in point of age, Henry had found it possible to declare himself the least responsible, least needed, and most expendable of the children, a declaration which masked his true feelings, exactly inverting them. And he did not mean to forego the advantage of pretended unimportance, whatever else he did.[46] Yet, in an effort to help himself, he acquired two added roles in the family. To do so, he simply divided the family's members into groups. In the one, made up of his parents and the older children, he took the role of youngest child and tried more than ever to be a lively competitor and friendly rival of Loo, John, and Charles. In the other, which would have consisted of his parents, Arthur, Mary, and Brooks if Arthur had lived, he took lost Arthur's place as the eldest of three children, became a surrogate parent of Mary and baby Brooks, and tried actively to help his mother, who had had too many children.[47]

This pattern of behavior may seem complex, and admittedly

Henry had never been simple. Still, the pattern was there and readily noticed. As his wishes might determine, or as the need arose, he by turns would be a middle, a youngest, and an eldest child. By the same token, he would become a conscious assumer of roles or identities. Entering into each of his changing identities with energy and in earnest, he would keep a good conscience. Shifting ceaselessly from one role to another would help him learn, grow, and improve.

Two exceptions must be noted to the rule that after losing George Otis he made no heartfelt friendships with boys in Quincy or Boston. Both exceptions were brothers. Henry was disposed to make a friend of his younger brother, if Brooks were willing, once the boy was older. Meanwhile, Henry made a friend of Charles. The change was the easier for Henry to bring about because he loved the second son and understood his problem. Yet their friendship—which would be life-long—could never be entirely happy. Charles did not love Henry; or, if he did, Charles could not always abide him. What was worse, Charles wanted to own him.[48] The elder brother regarded the younger with a jealously possessive eye, and, in his role as owner, favored the younger with advice. It helped, for the younger, while incomparably cleverer than the elder, was hardly perfect. Also the advice that Charles doled out in the course of their interchanges was sometimes just the advice his brother needed, and Henry would take it.

Peter Chardon Brooks died on New Year's Day, 1849. He left a will which affected Henry in two ways. The boy's parents became recipients of a fortune of about $300,000. Henry himself was advised that on coming of age ten years later, in 1859, *he* would receive an inheritance from his maternal grandfather. The sum would not be small. And, if well invested, it might suffice to provide the nucleus of a new, independent fortune.

Accustomed to wealth from birth, Henry's mother felt no change. Henry's father, always careful with money, was not likely to depart from habits of strict economy merely because his financial resources were greatly increased. One expensive temptation, however, proved too strong for him. C. F. Adams became a biographer. He began to write a full-scale life of John Adams and bring out an edition of his writings. Toiling at these new projects in his library at 57 Mount Vernon Street, the Governor found that busy Henry wished to use the room almost as much as he. The father accordingly gave the boy a writing table and a place of his own among the books in a sort of alcove.[49] Because the other sons were not given tables near their father in the library, criticisms of Henry by John and Charles were soon forthcoming. They began to speak of their father's favorite, and directly address him, as a "philosopher."[50]

Thoughtful Henry meanwhile had been put to work. The boy was required by his father to serve as a biographical and editorial helper. Nine volumes of John Adams's writings were in process of being selected, arranged, and published. Henry was given the task of reading volume after volume aloud, to assist in correcting proofs.[51] Performing this and other duties, he showed such aptitude as an aide to his father that a basis was laid for possible, later agreements between them that he should help his father on a more or less permanent footing. At the same time, Henry imbibed the spirit and made the close acquaintance of his presidential great-grandfather, bold irascible John Adams. In addition, Henry learned something of what it would involve, were he to become an author. He saw with his own eyes that multivolume books were not miraculous creations but things well within the power of human beings to write, and also read.

Any impression one might form that Henry's earliest years were consistently happy would be an error. All may have gone very well for him in infancy and early childhood, and his days thereafter were more often good than bad, from his own point of view; but beginning at some time after he started school, and continuing until he was fifteen or thereabouts, he was intermittently plunged into despondency so severe as to instill thoughts of suicide. Although it eased and eventually lifted altogether, this recurrent affliction left its marks, among them a sometimes mordant sense of irony and a conviction that he was fully prepared to kill himself at any time, should the need arise. He later expressed this conviction by saying, not without ironic humor: "... [I] long ago made up my mind that when life becomes a burden to me, I shall end it, and I have even decided the process. The only difficulty is that every year I live, I feel on the whole less of this despondency than formerly, and the worst time of all was the earliest; when a boy at school."[52]

The chief schools Henry attended while beset by this "melancholy disposition," as he also called it, were two.[53] In 1849, when he was eleven, he won a prize, two volumes of Macaulay's *History of England,* for "industry in Latin grammar" while under the tutelage of Mr. David B. Tower, master of the Park School, a private institution in the basement of the Park Street Church.[54] It was expected that, in 1852, following the steps of his elder brothers, Henry would enter the Boston Latin School. After being accepted for admission, he was barred from attending on the ground that his father paid the school tax in Quincy, not in Boston. Henry accordingly was enrolled instead in a private school newly established across the Common by Mr. Epes Sargent Dixwell, formerly the Latin School's headmaster.[55] Two years of recitations under Mr. Dixwell sufficed to ready Henry for admission to Harvard College. At sixteen, in July 1854, he went to Cambridge and took and passed the college's entrance examinations.[56]

During his two years as one of Mr. Dixwell's scholars, Henry was praised by his father. In the privacy of his diary, C. F. Adams noted that his third son was "a good boy, and so unassuming that he does not get half his merits."[57] Henry at the time appeared to be a docile scholar, disposed to do his lessons and anxious to pass his examinations. Appearances were deceptive. His old aversion to school had become a strong revulsion, which, if he were to do his schoolwork, he had first to repress, and which sooner or later would issue in some sort of fierce rebellion or carefully plotted vengeance.

Much more important than his seeming docility and smoldering hatred of school was the secret fact of his having experienced recurrent despondency and tempting thoughts of self-slaughter. The questions needed to be faced: why had he been despondent? why had he thought of suicide? and why had he gone so far as to consider the appropriate "process"?[58]

The questions can be answered with some assurance; but the answers can be learned only by looking a second time, in a different way, at the entire matter of his birth and upbringing. Some subjects do not yield their full meanings to mere casual inquiry. Persons interested in meeting Henry Adams, forming accurate judgments of his worth, and judging him in comparison with other Americans, or, more broadly, in comparison with other human beings, have no choice but to consider, at least in outline, the story of all the Adamses down to his time. The family he belonged to was ambitious and did such things that, in the 1840s, a place in the family was waiting for someone to fill it. The place could only be taken by a son of very unusual strength and ability. Henry Adams was recognized when a child as uniquely valuable—and took the place that was waiting to be filled. The person who recognized him and decided his course was not a man but a woman.

## 2 / Perilous Endurance

The Adamses had begun in America as ordinary farmers. The Englishman named Henry Adams who emigrated to Massachusetts in the 1630s made his home and farmed on the same hillsides south of Boston to which the infant named Henry Brooks Adams would be brought in the 1830s. Among the sons of the old Henry Adams, the eldest, Joseph Adams, farmed on the same ground, as did a son of his, also named Joseph.

The door to opportunity was opened when one of the sons of the second Joseph, named John, proved deserving enough, or fortunate enough, to marry Susanna Boylston, daughter of a leading Boston family. John and Susanna Adams had a son, also named John, born in 1735, who went to Harvard College and became a lawyer, a leader of the American Revolution, a chief architect of independence and union, a successful diplomat, first vice-president, and second president.

Like his father, the new John Adams married a daughter of a leading Boston family, Abigail Smith. The eldest child of John and Abigail Adams, named John Quincy Adams, was born in 1767. Intended for politics, he entered public life at ten when he went with his father as private secretary on a diplomatic mission to France. At fourteen, he accompanied Francis Dana on a diplomatic mission to Russia. His abilities attracted the notice of President Washington, who made the lad his protege and at the first chance sent him to Europe as a full-fledged minister. When John Adams succeeded Washington as president, the acknowledged attainments of J. Q. Adams excused his retention by his father on the federal payroll as a diplomat abroad. In 1800, the elder Adams was defeated at the polls by Thomas Jefferson. At the time, the younger Adams was serving as minister to Prussia, residing in Berlin.

During the last weeks of his administration, John Adams recalled his son from his post as minister. The younger man did not immediately leave Berlin. His diplomatic wanderings in Europe had earlier led him into the company of a young woman, half American, half English, named Louisa Catherine Johnson. Born in 1775 in London, she was in no way connected with Boston or its leading families. Her father, Joshua Johnson, a member of a family prominent in Maryland, had married an Englishwoman, Catherine Nuth, and spent much of his life abroad, as a businessman and as U. S. consul in the British capital. In the natural course of things, the consul's daughter and the younger Adams had met, fallen in love, and married—in London in 1797.[1] Four years later in Berlin, when J. Q. Adams was recalled as minister to Prussia, he and Louisa were awaiting the birth of their first child.

It proved a boy. The choice of a name for the boy became the prerogative of the retiring minister. In grateful memory of the first president, who recently had died, but with some trepidation, fearing that such a name might be a heavy one for the child to bear, John Quincy Adams decided to name him George Washington Adams. Writing to one of his brothers, the minister remarked: "My child was yesterday baptised by the name of George Washington; and may the grace of Almighty God guard his life and enable him, when he is come to manhood, to prove himself worthy of it!"[2]

The prayerful father traveled with his wife and baby to Boston but did not escape the toils of politics. In 1803, when only thirty-six, he was elected senator from Massachusetts. He went to Washington, took his seat in the Senate, and served capably for five years, but disagreed with his party colleagues, the New England Federalists. In 1808, cutting himself free of Federalism, he attended a meeting called by the Democratic Republicans, resigned his place in the Senate, and put himself in line for a diplomatic appointment by the incoming president, James Madison, one of his erstwhile opponents. Madison offered him, and he accepted, the post of minister to Russia.

Louisa Catherine Adams had meanwhile become the mother of two additional sons, John Adams II, born in 1803, and Charles Francis Adams, born in 1807. Required to accompany her husband to St. Petersburg in 1809, she was separated from her two elder sons, George and John, who stayed behind to go to school. She was permitted to take along her youngest, Charles; and at the Russian capital she later bore a fourth child, Louisa, named for herself. All the same, a tragic theme had been sounded. The minister's wife had begun to lose her children. As if to state the theme with perfect clearness, in 1812, her cherished Louisa died in infancy.

John Quincy Adams succeeded better as a diplomat than as a

senator. He won invaluable gains for the United States, not only at St. Petersburg but at Ghent, in Holland, where he headed the five-man diplomatic team which negotiated the treaty ending the War of 1812. He served two years as minister to England under President Madison and eight years as secretary of state under President Monroe. In 1824, after a fierce contest, he was elected president himself.

One of the features of his administration was the invisibility of his wife. A modern writer has said of her: " . . . Mrs. Adams received very little and went seldom into society. She kept silkworms, several hundreds of them; she derived keen enjoyment from music and books; she was an extremely retiring, scholarly person. She was also, and ever increasingly, in extremely delicate health."[3]

Her eldest son was never invisible. George Washington Adams had always been regarded as talented. In 1811, his grandfather, John Adams, had described him as a "Treasure of Diamonds." The second president had not been given to wasting compliments. Yet he had said that growing George had "a Genius equal to any Thing."[4]

It did not seem impossible that George would someday be elected president. He attended Harvard, became a lawyer, started to practice law in Boston, and seemed disposed to attempt a career in politics. He also was attracted towards literary objects. Whether he was torn by hurtful conflicts between a wish he felt to become a writer and an obligation thrust upon him to make himself a statesman would be difficult to say.[5]

One of young George's orations, given in 1824, said, "Heaven seems to strengthen the human faculties proportionably to the obstacles to be encountered. . . ." In a darker vein, the same oration added, " . . . undertakings of magnitude are accomplished only through toil, and suffering, and perilous endurance."[6] The son's expressions were apt. As he knew, he and his relations were engaged in an enterprise of exceptional magnitude which, although confined to a single family and bound up with the welfare of a single country, could not be completed within the lifetimes of his grandfather and father, and deserved to be continued—an enterprise, too, which might be growing more difficult as it proceeded, and more dangerous to its protagonists—finally, an enterprise which, being seriously intended to work profound, far-reaching changes helpful initially to Americans but ultimately to men and women in all countries and in many generations, could not lightly be broken off. A family had started something it could not stop but could only finish.

George Washington Adams had an attractive cousin named Mary

Hellen, his mother's niece. A quirk of fate brought George and Mary into close association. Orphaned, she was taken in by his parents as an added member of their household. The step led quickly to a very awkward consequence. Both George and his brother John became romantically inclined towards their charming relative. Prompted to choose between the brothers, she chose the younger, John Adams II, and married him at a White House wedding.[7]

While George in this way experienced defeat in love, his mighty father, John Quincy Adams, was losing in politics. The earlier division between Federalists and Democratic Republicans had given way in recent years to more confused divisions. President Adams was warring with many enemies in Congress and elsewhere, of whom none liked him less than the adherents of Andrew Jackson. A happy outcome of the hostilities seemed unlikely.

In the election of 1828, George's father was badly beaten by General Jackson. The result was not an easy pill for the Adamses to swallow. Until that time, only two presidents—John Adams and John Quincy Adams—had not won second terms. Fate, it appeared, had decreed that members of the Adams family in successive generations could indeed be elected president if they paid the penalty. The fated penalty seemed limited to political defeat. Having been elected, each Adams could expect to be "dis-elected." The family's enemies would drive each offending victor out of office. It had happened twice.

On the last day of his term, March 4, 1829, J. Q. Adams left the White House, giving way to General Jackson. Rather than go home at once to Massachusetts, the former president and his wife stayed for a time in Washington. The affairs of the family seemed in workable order. At sixty-two, scarred by more than fifty years of political exertion, the father was old enough to retire. At twenty-eight, George was old enough to draw continuous notice as the heir apparent of the family's political credit and influence. What seemed needed was an orderly transfer of responsibilities from the ex-president to his talented son.

In Massachusetts on April 29, intending to join his parents, George set out on a journey to Washington. His journey was an extremely anxious one. Behind him, a servant girl he had been involved with was pregnant through his fault. Awaiting him at the capital, ignorant of his misbehavior, were his sensitive mother, never strong, and his defeated but unconquerable father, not a person inclined to smile on moral errors. On arriving, George would have to tell them of his misconduct.

He journeyed safely to Providence, Rhode Island, and there took passage for New York on a steamboat, the *Benjamin Franklin*. Once aboard, he made the casual acquaintance of several passengers, who found him friendly and seemingly in good spirits. The day was clear. The steamboat took its usual course down Narragansett Bay, past Point Judith, and towards Long Island Sound. As the hours wore by, George lost his cheerfulness. Complaining of a fever, he went to his berth, but soon rejoined his companions. Agitated and upset, he informed them that someone had tried to break into his cabin. His assertion conceivably was true. All the same, his mental balance was unmistakably disturbed. He was experiencing delusions. Especially he believed that the noisy engine, levers, and paddlewheels were uttering a message intended for himself. He said they were endlessly telling him: "Let it be. Let it be."

After sundown, his companions retired and left him on the deck alone. Fearing that they were conspiring to murder him, and hoping to elude them and get to land, he found his way to Captain Bunker on the bridge and supplicated him to stop the boat. Just then, by purest accident, the captain hurt his foot. Himself upset, he gave the intruding passenger a scanty welcome.

The boat was midway on the Sound. George ceased attempting to get the captain's help and retreated from the bridge. What followed was never entirely determined. He could swim and possibly drowned while madly attempting to swim ashore through the cold April water. Or, just as possibly, the noisy mechanisms of the boat, repeating "Let it be," impelled him overboard in blind panic, when otherwise he might have calmed himself, stayed on the boat, and recovered.

News of the son's disappearance reached his parents in Washington on May 2. Its effects on John Quincy Adams were extreme. That day and for several days thereafter, he tried to learn in detail about his child's catastrophe. The more he learned, the worse became his own condition. The father wrote, "The overwhelming calamity which has befallen me, has in a great measure prostrated my faculties, both of mind and body." He almost seemed to feel that he himself was drowning. "Reason is infected, and nature sinks in the agony of imagination." The effects on his wife were possibly even greater.[8]

Throughout the remainder of 1829, John Quincy Adams felt cut off from every other human being—"deserted by all mankind." Like his son, he was tortured by an ever-repeating phrase. His mind obsessively went back to a song he once had heard in a French opera, Gretry's *Richard Coeur de Lion*. In the opera, the minstrel Blondel, standing beneath the walls of King Richard's prison, had sung with tragic force: *"O, Richard! O mon Roi! L'univers t'abandonne."* In the father's thoughts, the words returned incessantly: "The universe abandons you."[9]

The father did not emerge from despair. Instead, he learned its better uses. Himself replacing his vanished son, he became his own successor. In 1830, opportunely, his neighbors in Massachusetts elected him to Congress. Glad of their support but greatly changed in mind and feelings, he reentered public life.

Returning to Washington and taking a lowly seat in the House of Representatives, the elder Adams appeared content to remain a congressman, provided he could use the office as a means of starting the final overthrow of slavery in the Union. His progress as a friend of liberty and enemy of bondage was impeded by private difficulties. In 1834, he lost another son. John Adams II died amid a tangle of business embarrassments which brought the father to the verge of economic ruin. Charles Francis Adams, the one survivor among the ex-president's four children, did not approve the new career that the intrepid father had begun in Washington. Relations between the lone remaining son and the congressman at times grew very strained.[10]

John Adams and John Quincy Adams had both been assertive men, so much so that one of their enemies, John Randolph, had likened them to bears and complained that the "cub" was a "greater bear than the old one."[11] C. F. Adams might also turn out to be a bear, but he had begun by seeming unassertive, even recessive. In Russia when a boy, walking with his mother on the Nevsky Perspective, as it was known to Americans, Charles had several times met Czar Alexander, who, leaning down to shake hands, had tried to help the boy overcome his shy, defensive attitudes. Not that Charles could not talk; on the contrary, as would happen in St. Petersburg, a nurse taught him German; many people taught him Russian; his parents taught him English; and everyone combined to teach him French. In 1815, when he was seven, he traveled with his mother in a chartered carriage from St. Petersburg to Paris, an unforgettable experience; and during the Hundred Days, when all Europe was caught up in a paroxysm of excitement, he gazed a while at the Emperor Napoleon through a window of the Tuileries. Such preparations considered, he might fairly have been expected to seek a broad and varied pattern of experience.[12]

After returning to America with his parents, in 1817, Charles completed his course at Harvard at an unusually early age, studied law, and married. It said something about him that his wife, Abigail Brooks, was a daughter of a leading Boston family. It said something more, perhaps, that she was rich. And it may have said still more that the marriage occurred when the bridegroom was twenty-two. For Charles was nothing if not cautious and circumspect. Early marriage to an heiress permitted him to secure a safe position for himself, proceed with the necessary business of having children, and gradually make ready for an eventual entry into public life.

During the 1830s, reconsidering, the son withdrew his disapproval of his father's second career in politics. Going further, C. F. Adams became a fervent convert to the antislavery cause which J. Q. Adams was relentlessly advancing, against determined opposition, in the lower house of the nation's Congress. But the great undertaking shared by the successive males in the Adams family could only be continued by C. F. Adams; it could *not* be greatly re-energized, fundamentally renewed, or adaptively transformed—not by a person of his abilities. Although an Adams through and through, the younger man was built on too small a scale in mind and ability to sustain the full weight of the family's enterprise, still less improve and conclude it. A chance existed that a son of his might not have his limitations.

Henry Brooks Adams was born almost nine years after George Washington Adams disappeared from the *Benjamin Franklin.* From early infancy, Henry was required to adapt himself to the demands of *two* Adams households. One was his father's household, consisting of his father, mother, Loo, John, Charles, himself, Arthur while he lived, and later Mary and Brooks. The other was his paternal grandmother's household, consisting of his grandmother, his grandfather, and a widowed aunt.[13]

The second Adams household became much more meaningful and helpful to Henry than the first, but the story of his dealings with its members is shadowy and hard to reconstruct. For instance, late in life, writing the first chapter of what would become his most famous book, *The Education of Henry Adams,* he would look into the furthest recesses of his memory and recall that an "aunt" of his had brought him a baked apple when he, a small boy, still weak from scarlet fever, was recovering in his parents' new house at 57 Mount Vernon Street. Writing the chapter, he failed to specify which aunt. Theoretically, the person carrying the apple could be Ann Frothingham, Charlotte

Everett, or the aunt—Mary Catherine Adams, familiarly known as "Mrs. John"—who belonged to the second Adams household.

In a later chapter of his *Education,* Adams would again refer to his "aunt" without supplying a name, yet do so in such a way as to permit no doubt that the person meant was the one aunt he possessed on his father's side. Thus Mrs. Frothingham and Mrs. Everett can be tentatively ruled out and the interesting conclusion reached that Henry's earliest memory of another human being concerned a member of his grandmother's household, a woman *not* a Brooks, but instead an Adams twice over, first by adoption and then by marriage—the inconspicuous "Mrs. John," who evidently had been visiting or staying at Mount Vernon Street early in 1842, had helped nurse Henry back to health, and while so doing had brought him a baked apple so welcome that its fragrance, its taste, and the identity of its bearer never vanished from his mind.[14]

Among his problems when a child, none was more instructive to Henry than the problem of his name. From time to time, people asked him how his name originated. The inquiry was sometimes pressed insistently, for upperclass New Englanders paid inordinate attention to names and genealogy. Perforce, he grew prepared to explain—as he later wrote on one occasion—that "my own name, Henry Brooks," had been the name of one of his mother's brothers, who "died before I was born."[15]

The explanation was true but had the defect, or advantage, of making Henry thoughtful and inquiring. He knew his name had been chosen for him by his mother. The choice could hardly seem a good one. Compared to the names earlier chosen for the older children in his father's household, it was clearly inferior. Loo, John, and Charles had been named after living Adamses whom they would get to see and talk with. He, the fourth child, had been given a name which could only make him frame a question, fall silent, and keep the question to himself. In later life, he at last would state the question in carefully chosen terms, saying he had "always wondered why my excellent mamma thought proper to name me after a brother whom I should never see or hear of."[16]

The boy's predicament was even worse than the question indicated. From the beginning, the three words Henry Brooks Adams to his ears were an utter contradiction. To him, the Adamses and the Brookses seemed different beings, and he wished to be an Adams exclusively. In the long run, he would have to acquire an Adams name. What it might be, how he might get it, and who might give it to him were questions which kept him wondering fully as much as his mother's reason for having called him Henry Brooks.

The three elder children, Loo, John, and Charles, were comparatively unreflecting Adamses who took their membership in the family for granted. The problem of his name made Henry different. He was an Adams, too, but also he consciously wished to be one. He had an idea. Indeed he had a business. With all possible speed, he would become as much an Adams as his circumstances and talents would permit.

The means he used were two. During the winters in Boston, he sought the company of his father. During the summers in Quincy, he left the subsidiary residence at the top of President's Hill, walked down to the Old House, and—starting as soon as they arrived from Washington—sought the company of the persons in the other Adams household. Persisting in these courses, he became exceptionally well-acquainted with his father, grandfather, grandmother, and widowed aunt—and, further, through them and what they told him, also became exceptionally well-acquainted, at least in imagination, with his father's dead elder brothers; with his esteemed, long dead great-grandparents, John and Abigail Adams; and even with relations as remote as the earlier John Adams and his wife Susanna, not to mention the almost legendary Englishman who had crossed to America with eight sons.

As inquiring Henry learned to understand his family's history, the Adamses owed their preeminence in great measure to infusions of ability brought in by highly intelligent wives—Susanna Boylston, Abigail Smith, and Louisa Johnson.[17] Of the three, two were gone; but the third, his father's mother, while frequently quite unwell, was there at the Old House in the long green summers in rural Quincy; and Henry liked to visit her, bring her messages, sit with her at her breakfast table, and go about with her in her garden among the roses.

Originally, among his elders, the person who had most interested growing Henry had been his grandfather, John Quincy Adams, known to everyone as the "President." By degrees, the boy learned to take a still greater interest in his grandmother, addressed in Quincy as the "Madam." For him, the interest of knowing her was much increased by her being able to tell about places as far distant as St. Petersburg in Russia. Travel, it sometimes seemed, meant everything to him. But it also struck him very forcibly that she and the president owned a house in Washington which he was continually hearing about but had never entered. It also struck him that she was no New

Englander. Her Maryland patrimony could not be masked. Although half-English by birth, she was decidedly American in outlook, but Southern.[18]

As he continued to visit her, Henry became aware of something which affected him as quite unusual. Invariably when he approached her she would smile. If her expression had been a little different, he might have discounted her smiles as those of any grandmother when visited by any grandson; but he felt her smiles as meant; he remembered them all his life; and, when a man, he would not have discouraged inquiry into their significance.[19]

Such inquiry was needed, for the relationship that developed between the woman originally named Louisa Catherine Johnson and the boy disturbingly misnamed Henry Brooks Adams would be by far the most important relationship that the latter would ever enter into. It would settle the question of his place among the Adamses, the question of his rightful name, his sense of his role as an American, and his view of his essential identity.

Of course, any inquiry into the meaning of a woman's smiles is perilous, if not ridiculous; and any opinion that is offered may be scoffed at or contradicted. Here an opinion will be offered which has the advantage of simplicity. The reason Henry's grandmother invariably smiled when he approached her was that she recognized a startling physical resemblance between the child and her aged self and was deeply moved by the recognition.

Because the grandmother was old and ill, and the grandson was young and well, other people may not have been able to see the degree of their alikeness, or even notice its existence. But Louisa had been painted, in miniature, when she was twenty-two. If her grandson were painted or photographed when he neared the same age, and if the two images, hers and his, were held side by side, it could be predicted that the images would match remarkably.[20] (See pages 92-93)

Some such calculation, mixing memory of her own portrait with anticipation of his future appearance, must have gone forward to a conclusion in the grandmother's very capable mind. Her conclusion went beyond the physical. To the extent that a female and male could be the same, she and Henry were strangely one—a single creature. The boy perhaps was aware of it; the Madam was very strongly aware of it; and to see her replication in him gave her such solace and delight that, involuntarily, she would smile and let him know.[21]

Her doing so gave him the immensely welcome and deeply needed feeling that he mattered. She may have meant only that he mattered to her. If so, her meaning was one thing, her effect on him another; for she succeeded in teaching him that he mattered as an Adams. That much established, he would not be long in learning that he mattered, too, as an American. He would go on to know he mattered as a free human being—a child of the purported mysterious Creator who had made the world.[22] But what it all went back to was a grandmother and grandson's strange identity-and-equality. Recognizing its existence, she had placed him on her level, as herself in another form. He knew he had been so placed and accepted the consequences. And the transaction was completed when, at most, he was eight or nine.

After the president's death in 1848, the Madam chose not to return to Massachusetts. She soon was so stricken with illness that her traveling to Quincy would have been problematical, even if she had wished it. In her absence, after some hesitation, C. F. Adams and his dependents took the Old House for their own residence. Its rooms were so numerous that Henry, as his share, was given one as his own. His moving into it at twelve marked an era in his life, improving his sense of freedom and self-sufficiency.[23]

Early in 1850, when Henry had not seen his grandmother for more than a year, his mother went to Washington to visit the older woman. The grandson seized the occasion to write his mother a letter which— as he surely hoped—would be read in Washington when received by both his mother and his grandmother. Soon a letter came back, addressed to him at Mount Vernon Street in Boston and written by the Madam. Her letter said:

> I am so pleased with your Letter to your Mama that I write to request you to write a few lines to me occasionally when you have time.
>
> I at the same time send you a book for your Birthday which I hope you will like and tell me what you think of it when you have read it.
>
> I am so weak I cannot write any more except that I love you dearly for being a Good [Boy?] and hope you will live long to bless your kind Papa and Mama who do so much to make you happy—
>
> Give my best to your Brothers. . . .

The book she had sent him also arrived, *The Vicar of Wakefield*, by Oliver Goldsmith. He may be presumed to have read it and written to tell her what he thought of it, but whatever letters he wrote to her at the time, or later, have not been found. Likewise his initial letter to his mother is not in evidence. In fact, all his writings before he entered Harvard are now missing. Their disappearance lends added value to his grandmother's one surviving letter to him, written apparently in February 1850, when he was turning twelve. Conceivably it was the only letter she ever had strength to send him. He kept it, pasted into *The Vicar of Wakefield,* until his death, in 1918, when it was found among his other possessions in the famous house he built for himself and his wife in the mid-1880s, on Lafayette Square in Washington, directly opposite the White House.[24]

In June 1850, Charles Francis Adams made a trip to Washington, partly to visit his failing mother, and partly to be present at the Capitol when Congress would be debating a proposed new compromise on the slavery question. He took Henry with him.

The journey southward was the son's first escape from New England. It afforded him a wealth of new impressions. Yet the journey mattered less to Henry than his arrival in the national city—or village, for it seemed a village, and was as rural as Quincy. From the moment he saw it, the place was home. He knew, and never afterwards forgot the knowledge, that he was a Washingtonian. By some alchemy of the heart, perhaps by mere inveterate longing to be there, he had transformed himself into one of the capital's natives and proper residents. Very strangely, not Boston but Washington could now be counted as his birthplace, in spirit; and it was his spirit that mattered.[25]

In Boston, the third son of C. F. Adams had always had to struggle against compounding adversities. In Washington, Henry wonderfully prospered. He entered the Adams house at No. 1335 F Street which till then he had only heard of.[26] His Aunt Mary, who greatly liked him, gave him a hearty welcome.[27] Although paralyzed and exceedingly feeble, his grandmother was able to see him.

Very early the following morning, while his relatives were still in bed, Henry walked alone to the Washington Monument, then half-built, and inspected it carefully. Soon his father took him to the Capitol and introduced him to several members of the House and Senate. On Monday, June 3, 1850, he and the Governor sat together in the Senate gallery and heard speeches by three senators they regarded as mortal enemies: Jefferson Davis of Mississippi, Stephen A. Douglas of Illinois, and Daniel Webster of Massachusetts.

On Tuesday, at the insistence of the ladies among the Adamses at F Street, Mr. Adams took Henry to the White House and introduced him to General Taylor. As was only to be expected, Henry's father looked upon the presidential mansion with proprietary eyes. The mansion's first occupants had been President John Adams and the redoubtable Abigail, from 1799 to 1801. C. F. Adams had himself lived there during the presidency of J. Q. Adams, from 1825 to 1829. The effects of these associations could be discerned between the lines of the entry Mr. Adams made in his diary after he and Henry paid their call. The father wrote: "... I went for the purpose of showing to Henry, the President and his house. There were only two or three persons there. General Taylor is not a show man, still less a real President. Yet there is a simplicity and a modesty about him which is very taking."

Rather than stop with the White House, the Governor borrowed or rented a carriage and drove Henry down the Potomac to see Mount Vernon.[28] The expedition perhaps was suggested in part by the son's pre-breakfast walk to the Washington Monument the morning after their arrival, but the father was perfectly capable of taking Henry to see George Washington's house without other promptings than his own convictions. C. F. Adams was a believer in the notion that "the EXAMPLE OF WASHINGTON"—the capital letters were his own— was a supremely helpful one for "rising youth" to follow.[29]

Whether Henry responded to Mount Vernon quite in the way his father meant him to may be doubted. The things that most impressed the twelve-year-old son were the holes and bumps in Virginia's roads and some wild raccoons he spied in the great Virginian's trees. But going to George Washington's home, once tried, was something Henry knew he would want to do again. As he continued to think about it, the experience would affect him profoundly. For him even more than his father, the first president would become important, somehow still present, and even alive.[30]

Son and father traveled back to Massachusetts, there to learn almost immediately that President Taylor was dead and a new administration, less congenial to C. F. Adams than Taylor's, was being constructed in Washington. The news confirmed Mr. Adams in the grim expectation that for him the way to political victory, if indeed there were a way, would be long and hard. Henry's father did not intend to quit as a politican, but he told himself and others that he was not greatly ambitious and would be satisfied if he could just win election to Congress by his neighbors in his district.

Among the various Conscience Whigs in Massachusetts who had participated two years earlier in the effort that created the Free Soil Party, one of the ablest was Charles Sumner. Although only thirty-nine, Sumner had been put forward at the time as a candidate for senator. In those years, U. S. senators were elected not by popular vote but by the legislatures of their respective states. The candidacy of Sumner in 1848 had brought on a protracted contest. His antislavery views had stirred up such opposition—and such support—that the Massachusetts legislature deadlocked, both failing to elect Sumner and failing to elect some other person. Month after month, till years went by, the legislature voted without result.

The legislature met in the Massachusetts State House, just a few steps distant from the Adams house at 57 Mount Vernon Street. Feeling strongly about the contest, young Henry Adams had attached himself to Sumner as a volunteer watcher of the endless balloting. On April 24, 1851, listening for the winning vote, the watcher was in the State House gallery when Sumner was elected. Slipping through the crowd, he raced to the family's house, where the candidate was waiting anxiously for news. In the dining room, in front of everyone, Henry announced to Sumner that victory was his.[31]

A bachelor and a constant guest of the Adamses, the newly elected senator was friendly with all the family; but Henry, not wishing to be a mere casual friend of Sumner's, and adapted to forming close relationships with persons of either sex and any age, had been trying to draw his father's ally into a separate, two-person relationship with himself and had succeeded. No contemporary records of their first years of friendship have been found; but it seems impossible to doubt that, occasion permitting, Sumner and Henry were meeting and talking by themselves; and that, when Sumner went to Washington, they would begin exchanging occasional notes and even letters. Friends they were—and yet their Eden contained a serpent.

Earlier, young Adams had been very friendly with a congressman, old J. Q. Adams. Now friendly with a senator, Henry once again could feel a sense of near-participation in the affairs of the national government. He could feel as well that he was being taken seriously, at thirteen, by a high-ranking federal official *not* related to him by blood. Knowing that Sumner was in earnest about human freedom and the extirpation of slavery, he could admire and even love him. But the senator's friendship, as Henry had learned while getting it, could be won and kept only if paid for continuously in the false, expensive coin of flattery. Sumner demanded deference and was evidently prepared to relish it no matter how plentifully supplied. Henry was meeting the demand but might not forever do so.[32]

Louisa Catherine Adams died on May 14, 1852, in Washington. Her grandson Henry may have gone there to attend her funeral. First buried in the capital, her remains were later moved and reburied in the Quincy churchyard beside her husband's.[33]

In the same year, 1852, her valued grandson began his diary. He conceivably was moved to start it by her death. Later burned by its author, the diary may be presumed to have differed from other diaries kept by members of the Adams family, being more private and less adapted to preservation and eventual disclosure.[34]

That autumn, Henry saw his father go down to defeat by a narrow margin as a candidate for Congress in the district surrounding Quincy; and the following summer, in August 1853, in company with one of his uncles, Gorham Brooks, and a cousin, probably Shepherd Brooks, Henry was taken to Niagara Falls and then to Montreal—his first sight of a foreign city. His going to Canada was the occasion which moved his father to write in his own diary the interesting judgment that the third son and fourth child in the younger generation was "a good boy, and so unassuming that he does not get half his merits"—a judgment best taken as evidence that the "good boy" was often silent.[35]

Henry's trip with his Brooks relations, at fifteen, afforded him an unexpected experience on a steamboat which so impressed itself on his memory that, while in college, he would write an account of it—an account which, being part of a published essay, would escape destruction. With his uncle and cousin, he had boarded the steamboat at Niagara and slept while it proceeded eastward on Lake Ontario. His experience began in the early morning of the following day and was not made the less important by being extremely placid. It partly concerned a mistaken idea of Canada.

> ... going up on the deck of the steamer in which I had passed the night, [I] found myself in the midst of the 'Thousand Isles.' Light clouds of mist were just vanishing slowly before the warmth of the sun, so that the river presented a grand tableau, in which everything looked rich and fresh and exquisitely quiet. All day I watched the shores of that splendid river [the St. Lawrence], till towards evening we shot the last rapid, and saw the city of Montreal glittering in the sunlight. To say the truth, I had labored under a pleasing, though rather mistaken persuasion, that Canada was a cold and desolate region, mostly inhabited by bears, wolves, half-breed Indians, and savages, situated far in the North, and chiefly important on account of the beavers who were trapped there. It was a very pleasant surprise to see the queer

Canadian farm-houses which lined the shore, and the villages that appeared here and there. To me the whole panorama was new and striking; especially so, seen as it was on a summer's day, when all the clouds seemed to have migrated to the Antipodes, for not one appeared in the sky.[36]

C. F. Adams was at his weakest when attempting to judge the characters and behavior of his children. He had called his third son a "good boy" and said he was "unassuming." But, at fifteen, the son was not a boy. For at least five years, going back to the funeral of John Quincy Adams in 1848, Henry had been extremely old for his age and in most respects a man.[37] Also he was very assuming. In fact, of all the Adamses, dead and living, this particular Adams was far and away the most assuming.

Part of the reason was his name. All things considered, the name his mother had chosen for him was *not* an error. It had the twofold merit of permitting Henry to parade himself in early life as a Brooks, should the imposture be necessary or helpful, and, further, permitting him to consider a particular question. It had been impressed upon him repeatedly that the story of his family had had a beginning—the coming to America of a man named Henry Adams. The question was simple. Were he himself, the fourth child in the eighth generation of the Adams family in America, to drop the Brooks from his name, become Henry Adams, and thus take the oldest name in the family, what then? There was also a further question. If he did give himself that old name, would the family's story end?

Of course, there had been Adamses in England before the old Henry Adams had crossed the ocean, and there presumably would be children in a ninth Adams generation younger than Loo, John, Charles, himself, Mary, and Brooks. From one point of view, human life was infinitely extended in time; it had no beginning and no end. Yet, from another point of view, the story of the American Adamses had several beginnings: the labor of the earliest Adamses on their farms; the influx of talent and ambition traceable to Susanna Boylston; the model partnership of John Adams and Abigail Smith; the independent course steered by John Quincy Adams as a youthful diplomat; and the second career he launched after the death of his eldest son. The fourth child in the eighth generation felt the power of these accumulated beginnings. He could not propose to be another of the family's beginners. It was now too late for that. Neither could he be content to sustain the family's enterprise a few years longer. That role, it appeared, had been given to his father. Yet, for himself, a different, important role was waiting. Assured of his own significance and aware that his talents outran all usual measures, the new Henry Adams would willingly make extraordinary efforts but did *not* intend to continue the family's story. Just the reverse, in some good and positive way, he meant to end it.[38]

Assuming that he read it, Henry had encountered some words in the opening paragraphs of *The Vicar of Wakefield* which could almost seem to have been put into the book by Oliver Goldsmith long before with the object of making a certain American reader in 1850 stop and think. The words were, "Our oldest son was named George, after his uncle. . . ." Rather queerly, they brought together two facts of which Henry had become very conscious: first, that he had himself been named after one of his uncles; and, second, that his grandmother, who gave him the book, had had an eldest son named George.

Juxtaposed, these facts raised a further question concerning Adams names. If there were some necessity that occasional sons in the Adams family be named after uncles, including dead uncles, why had the third son of C. F. Adams not been named after his father's dead eldest brother, George Washington Adams? Or, to put the question more generally, why had *none* of the five sons of C. F. Adams been named after that dead uncle? The question cried for an answer. The pattern of avoidance was glaring.

It is not likely that the son named Henry Brooks Adams ever wished in any serious way that he had instead been named George Washington Adams II. He may be assumed to have learned so much so early about his uncle George from his father, grandfather, grandmother, and widowed aunt that he could himself conclude in silence that the name George Washington Adams had proved an unlucky one for its bearer and hence was a name best not given to any nephew. But the new Henry, in addition to being an important Adams from birth, or at least from boyhood, and in addition to knowing himself to be one, also knew himself to be an important American. He accordingly had had to consider his own relation to the person for whom his uncle George has been named—the relation, that is, between his growing self, Henry Adams, and the original president, George Washington.[39]

As if he found it acceptable, Henry would continue for many years to use the name given him at his christening, using it in three forms, Henry Brooks Adams, Henry B. Adams, and H. B. Adams, somewhat favoring the last.[40] When thirty-two, in 1870, he would quietly drop the Brooks and begin requiring others to know him as, simply, Henry Adams. But his decision to change his name in that way had probably been settled in his mind when he was half that old or younger, most probably when his grandmother died and he began his diary, at fourteen.

In 1880, when he was forty-two, Adams would anonymously publish a novel, *Democracy,* involving mention of the first president. In the novel's sixth chapter, the characters would board a steamboat in Washington and go down the Potomac to Mount Vernon. On the way, they would talk about the revered Virginian whose home and grave they would shortly see. One character, a young unmarried woman, Victoria Dare, would say forthrightly, "Oh! I know all about George Washington." She would then explain, "My grandfather knew him intimately. . . ."[41]

A second character, Lord Dunbeg, an impecunious Irish noble-man much interested in America, would remark in Victoria's hearing that he, given the choice, would rather be George Washington than an earl; and she would turn upon him with the unusual rejoinder, "You have not the air of wishing to be George Washington."[42]

This odd reference to an impulse to *be* the Virginian, published by Adams anonymously when he was forty-two, had as its basis a feeling he undoubtedly had harbored from an extremely early age—perhaps as early as five or even four, when he had just grasped what presidents might be, and why a first president might be even more imposing than a second or a sixth. But the full result of that feeling would not emerge till he was forty-nine. Something would happen in 1887 which would arise from occurrences dating as far back as 1843 or 1842. It would develop that Adams wanted to be a taker of *two* names.

Because what happened in 1887 could be described as something psychological, meaning the coming into the open of an impulse long kept hidden, the occurrence may best be presented apart from the passage of time, in the present tense. Also the occurrence may be best set forth as if it were a scene in a play—or rather in the form of a dry, factual summary of such a scene, followed by added information, pointed questions, and suggested answers.

The scene is a room in the house Henry Adams owns in Wash-ington, opposite the White House, on Lafayette Square. One of Mr. Adams's idiosyncracies is love of children, of whom he knows several very well, but none better than Martha Cameron. Much too little to come visiting by herself, she has been brought to see him by her mother, Elizabeth Cameron, wife of the senator from Pennsylvania.

To amuse his younger visitor, Mr. Adams holds Martha in his lap and shows her the picture of a man on a piece of paper—actually the picture of George Washington on a postage stamp.

Martha looks at the picture and spontaneously, of her own volition, identifies the man as "Dobbitt."

Hugely pleased to be told the man's name, which he says till then was unknown to him, Mr. Adams tells Martha that, come to think of it, he himself is Dobbitt, too!

In the course of a later visit by the little girl and her mother, Mr. Adams explains to Martha that, appearances to the contrary notwithstanding, he is her age. Really, he says, his name is Georgie Dobbitt. But being still too young to be able to pronounce so difficult a name, he can only call himself Dordy Dobbitt.

During the two visits, does Mr. Adams seem embarrassed or disturbed? No, he is his usual self, but pleased in an extreme degree, as if something unexpected but perfect has been done which he could not have done alone.

Does little Martha ever learn that the funny nickname she and Mr. Adams will now begin to use for him is an encoded form of George Washington? Possibly not. Her mother, present throughout the visits, is perfectly aware that the name has a hidden meaning but may always hold back from discussing with Martha what "Dordy" and "Dobbitt" stand for.[43]

Mr. Adams and Martha go on delightedly calling him by his nickname until their deaths in 1918. Other people, hearing them use it, sometimes feel shut out by a private joke whose meaning is far from clear.

Elizabeth Cameron, much younger than Henry Adams, knows very little about his early life. She grows old but never has a grandchild. It may never occur to her in any forcible way that Adams had a grandmother; that grandmothers now and then inadvertently call a grandchild by the name of a child; and that he might sometimes have been called George in error by his grandmother when a small boy, might have been struck by the error, and made to think.[44] If that happened, in the lost summers of 1843 and 1842, Henry would not have needed many weeks to lead himself to the fact that George, in his family, besides meaning a dead uncle, meant the greatest of all Americans.

When ready for college, at sixteen, Henry Adams was a fully formed young man already clear in his mind about his ambitions but not disposed to explain them more than necessary, or at all. His ambitions were four in number and complementary to each other. Born and raised a politican, he meant to be a politician second to none in his generation in America. Equally disposed to become a writer, he supposed he might best try to become a great writer, yet was sufficiently prescient to sense that the pathway forward to such a goal might be hard to find and harder to walk. As soon as possible, he intended to move permanently to Washington, make his home there, and look for chances to become the owner of a suitable house. As opportunity permitted, he meant to travel everywhere, even to such impossible destinations as Tahiti and Central Asia.[45]

One ambition he lacked. He felt no wish whatever to become the father of a family. For that matter, he did not seem much taken by girls. The one young woman he could care about profoundly was his elder sister Louisa, his grandmother's namesake. His deep affection for Loo rested partly on her qualities, partly on her being for him the living representative or symbol of the older woman. Because his sister was alive, their grandmother, for him, in illusion, was also in a measure alive. But were Loo to die, as might happen, the blow to Henry would be serious in the extreme.[46]

Other terrors could strike. It might appear that Henry could go ahead and become four things, a full-grown politician, an aspiring writer, a resident Washingtonian, and a tireless traveler, without great risk. But he knew better. The experience of his family had been an experience of ambition; and the experience had proved, at the cost of sons, that ambition was the twin of risk; when the first was born, the second was also. Inherently, each of his four ambitions was an invitation to trouble, and it would come.

As a child, he had been attacked by despondency so violent as to make him think he would kill himself; and he had wondered how— and would continue to wonder till he knew the means. Americans, being democrats, could fancy themselves immune to such princely diseases as the one he had suffered, like a recurrent Hamlet.[47] But presidencies and similar glories were things Americans would learn they had to pay for. He had paid, not in maturity but at the outset. His cost had been to endure the stress of inwardly knowing his own importance while outwardly playing the role of a child among the other children, a brother among his brothers, a lesser Adams and American when a greater.

Weathering his suicidal moments somehow, he had waited for sunshine. It evidently had come for him in abundance when he went down the St. Lawrence the previous summer and saw reflected evening light in the windows of Montreal. The omen seemed good. Perhaps his worst risk in life was already surmounted, and the future would never be as hard and desperate as the past. A child could be very strong. What had he, when a child, not endured?

# 3  /  *Politician and Writer*

When Henry matriculated in September 1854, Harvard College was the leading college in the United States but remained a small institution, very limited in educational resources and short of funds. The holdings of its libraries totaled less than 70,000 volumes, and the sums allotted annually for the purchase of books for the libraries averaged less than $500, a dismal figure.[1] Fewer than 400 undergraduates were in attendance. They succeeded in doing their lessons and attempting some slight supplementary study only because they themselves supplied much-needed educational helps, notably the libraries created and maintained by student societies and clubs.[2]

The undergraduates were required to wear black coats.[3] They voluntarily affected black silk top hats, which, combined with their black coats, and sometimes with moustaches, lent them an appearance of age.[4] Although they looked like men, they were judged by their mentors to be unready for independence. The president, the professors, instructors, and tutors imposed upon them a curriculum wholly prescribed throughout the first two years. Henry knew in advance that he would recite as a freshman in Latin, Greek, mathematics, religion, and history, and as a sophomore in Latin, Greek, French, mathematics, chemistry, botany, and rhetoric, meaning chiefly themes and Anglo-Saxon.[5] He knew in addition that he would be required to be religious; that twice daily he would appear at prayers, and twice each Sunday at services.

His brother John had already graduated. Charles was beginning his junior year. Henry was well-acquainted with several fellows from Boston and its environs who had been admitted with him to the Class of 1858 and might have been willing to room with him; but the third son preferred to accept a suggestion made by the second that they live together for two years in off-campus quarters at Mrs. P. L. Story's house on Harvard Street.[6] Henry's willingness to go along with this suggestion partly arose from his hatred of school. In later life, he said he had differed from his Harvard classmates chiefly in one respect: a mental habit he had of "standing outside the college."[7] He arrived in Cambridge half-inclined to fear that everything connected with Harvard might give him trouble. In this spirit, he took the precaution of holing up with his brother Charles, away from the dormitories, in a private house.

During his first two months of attendance, Henry faithfully appeared at all his recitations.[8] On Saturday, October 29, feeling unwell, he returned with Charles to the Old House in Quincy, and there, at tea time, threw the family into a fright by suddenly fainting. He was put to bed in his room. A doctor was summoned. It developed that Henry had an illness—possibly mononucleosis—which involved a fever, loss of vivacity, and great difficulty resuming his normal pursuits. Five weeks passed before he could return to the college.[9]

Such interruptions were very serious matters. Harvard imposed not only a prescribed curriculum for freshmen and sophomores but also an ill-considered grading system, interlinked with a disciplinary system and a phenomenon called the "Scale of Merit." The grading system awarded points to each student in separate, small amounts in proportion to the merits of each of his recitations, themes, oral examinations, and other required academic performances, as judged by the teachers and supplementary examiners. During his illness, Henry lost five weeks of points at missed recitations, a huge total; and, under the system, the lost points could not be regained.

The loss made him even more sensitive to the rules of the college than other students tended to be. The rules were exceedingly numerous. Many were intended to deter students from engaging in particular actions and activities. The usual penalties inflicted on undergraduates found guilty of misconduct were subtractions of points from the totals won by them while performing their academic duties. In practice, such subtractions could be maddening. Like Sisyphus, a fellow would laboriously roll his grades uphill, only to be told that he had called up to a dormitory window, smoked on forbidden ground, or taken part in a three-person conversation while standing still in the Yard, whereupon his grades would slide. Then there was the Scale of Merit. Points won by each student through academic achievement were continuously added. Points charged against him for misdeeds, if any, were continuously subtracted. Simultaneously, all the members of each of the four undergraduate classes were ranked in order of their points, from the member with the most to the member with the least. In this way, at the cost of perpetual record-keeping and calculation, the president and the faculty were able to know with nice exactness at any moment the rank currently held by any student on the Scale of Merit for his class; and the students could be, and were, kept apprised of their often-shifting ranks. The points Henry was able to earn by academic achievement during his first term rose to a mere 1647. He suffered no deductions at all for misbehavior. His rank at the end of the term was seventieth, in a class then composed of ninety-one scholars.[10]

The academic year at the college was broken by two vacations six weeks in length, one beginning in mid-January and continuing until the end of February, the other beginning in mid-July and continuing through all of August. For the students accordingly, going to Harvard was a process of passing through eight successive, distinctly separate experiences. Actually being at Harvard apparently transformed Henry's feelings about it. His fears of the college gave way to sad emotions which would have been hopes, if only he could have made them hopes. He thought a student should love the college he attended and rejoice at the sight of its buildings. To his dismay, his own affections were slow to awaken. He later wrote: "As I bade good by, at the beginning of my first winter vacation, to the College Yard, and looked back upon the buildings from a distance, they seemed to me dungeons and torture-cells. They looked, in the midst of the leafless trees over which I saw their roofs, like the fairy castle of the sleeping beauty surrounded by an impenetrable hedge of thorns." He was himself unable to see "whatever beauty might lurk dormant among them."[11]

Of the four ambitions he harbored, two, his ambition to become a distinguished writer, even a great one, and his ambition to become an unrivaled politician among his American contemporaries, could be pursued very actively on the Harvard campus by a member of Class of '58. To rise as a politician, he would need to meet many people and find allies. As it happened, the arrangement he had made to live with Charles afforded him doubled chances to be convivial. He could either stay at their rooms and help entertain his brother's friends or go out and make friends of his own. After returning from winter vacation, he apparently did both and convinced himself that he was going to have jolly times at the college after all.[12] Especially he sought the companionship and good opinion of freshmen from places outside of New England. One such classmate, Nicholas Longworth Anderson of Cincinnati, wrote in May 1855 to his mother in Ohio that Henry Adams was "a particular friend of mine."[13] Another, W. H. F. Lee of

Arlington, Virginia, known as "Rooney," with whom Henry from the first found himself on very good terms, had been elected president of the class.[14] With two such fellows to turn to, Lee from the South and Anderson from the West, Adams could feel he had made a great step forward. He was moving quickly towards a career in national politics.

By coincidence, when he entered Harvard, the undergraduates were launching a new periodical called the *Harvard Magazine*, to provide a vehicle for aspiring student writers. Because its six editors were freely elected, three by the seniors and three by the juniors, the magazine from its inception was democratic; its management was interwoven with other aspects of student self-government; and contributors were assured a fair reading before their pieces were accepted or rejected. Monthly issues were planned, and subscriptions sold at two dollars a year.[15] The founding editors hoped to prevent the issues from lapsing into dullness. At the end of their first year of labor, they boasted in their anniversary issue that their pages had not been thrown away on threadbare topics or blemished with worn-out allusions. "We have proved . . . the possibility of [students'] writing on various subjects without introducing Leonidas and the three hundred Spartans, the Pilgrim Fathers, or even George Washington."[16] The boasts of the editors were exaggerated and inaccurate. One of their first year's issues had contained an entire paragraph introducing George Washington. The offending passage had been written by Henry Adams, a freshman.

Ambitious Henry, in this instance the writer, not the politician, had evidently resolved to appear in print in the new magazine before his first year at college was over. He hit upon the idea that its editors and subscribers could not refuse to take at least passing interest in the history of Harvard's various buildings, surely not if an article about one of the buildings were so written as to be both sympathetic and amusing. Among the buildings, Holden seemed to him the best victim for an initial experiment. Built originally as the college chapel, but later remodeled and used as an annex to the medical school, it was the smallest of Harvard's buildings, one of the oldest, and the only one that seemed to him to be graced in any degree with beauty, charm, or mere good looks. The essay he wrote about it, titled "Holden Chapel," published in the issue of the *Harvard Magazine* for May 1855, was short, filling five and a half printed pages. The essay said that the buildings on the campus had not been intended to please the eye. ". . . as far as my acquaintance with architecture can inform me, [they do not have] the least aspirations to beauty or elegance. Such was not the taste of the time when they were built." Little Holden was an exception. He tried in his pages to account for its charm, which he attributed partly to the carved cherubs on its front and the carved shield over its door. He went on to say that the building had once served as a temporary meeting place of the colonial Massachusetts legislature and, during the Revolution, as a barracks for soldiers in General Washington's army. By dilating on these and other items of antiquarian lore, also by attempting to write lifelike descriptions of Washington, John Adams, John Hancock, James Otis, and Joseph Warren, entering the chapel or coming near it, he managed to swell the essay to publishable size. Probably the editors agreed to print it not so much for its contents as its manner, which combined something of the humor associated with Washington Irving and something like the evocation of former times associated with Nathaniel Hawthorne.

Nicholas Anderson read "Holden Chapel" when it was published and said it was "quite good."[17] Henry's feelings about it were not so simple. He was both pleased with and ashamed of his first publication. He later said he had "perpetrated" the thing and dismissed it as flimsy, which it certainly was.[18] Yet he realized that a writer had to make a beginning somehow, if he wanted to publish, and felt that a writer could be satisfied with any beginning that was practicable. He was lucky enough to get through "my Holden Chapel period," as he called it, when he was seventeen.[19] The acceptance of his sketch settled for him the question whether he might ever get started as a published writer. He already was one.

Having advanced that far, he stepped aside in favor of his elder brother. Charles, too, wished to be a writer and see his productions appear in the *Magazine*. About the time Henry's essay came out, the second son took up his pen and attempted a criticism of Hawthorne, which was published in the July issue. Once started as an author, Charles attracted admiration for his well-chosen sentiments and literary flair. His first admirer was himself. The pleasure he derived from his college publications stayed with him all his life. With unblushing self-importance, he wrote long afterwards: ". . . I was one of the recognized litterateurs of my time and class. In the [Hasty] Pudding Club, I was Secretary, Poet and Odist. . . . I wrote for the *Magazine*; there the articles—on Whittier, Hawthorne, Charles Reade, etc.—are yet, bound in my voluminous *Miscellanies*."[20]

If upperclassmen spoke to Henry when a freshman about his joining a Greek-letter fraternity or social club, he rejected their overtures. He joined no merely social organizations while at college, and he openly criticized them for exerting secret influences on student elections and resting upon a rotten principle of feigned, not actual, brotherhood and fellowship.[21] Somewhat similarly, he showed no disposition to become a student leader, in the sense of having followers. There were such leaders in the freshman class, but they evidently were so numerous that none could have as followers more than a handful of his classmates. In such circumstances, advantages were sure to accrue to any member of the class who formed cordial relations with many of its leaders without attempting to be one. This Henry did. By the time his first year had ended, he had established friendly ties with most of the leaders of his class.[22]

Literary clubs were another matter. Henry was anxious to join them. At the beginning of his sophomore year, in September 1855, he and forty-one of his classmates were elected to such a society, the Institute of 1770. In turn, at a meeting on the evening of September 14, he and three others were elected editors of the institute. One of the four elected was a student added to the class at the start of the term, William Gibbons of New York City. Gibbons had scarcely set foot on the campus when he was recognized as a luminary. It mattered to Henry that someone should come into his class whom everyone could look up to, and their common status as editors promised to bring them together.

Editors of the institute were recognized student writers. They were expected to enliven its regular meetings by writing and reading aloud to the members whatever their abilities might permit them to produce in the way of "fun, sense, and nonsense." They served in rotation, each being scheduled to perform every fourth Friday evening. Two weeks after being elected, Henry made his first appearance. The minutes of the meeting, written by the secretary, said in part:

> The society came to order at 8 o'clock, . . . [and] the president introduced Mr. Adams as the editor of the evening. Mr. Adams read but three pieces, one of prose, one poetical and an editorial.
>
> . . . these productions were excellent of their kind and were received by the society in a manner which must have been highly gratifying to the Editor.
>
> Especially we were pleased with the pure and elegant style of the editorial. Mr. Adams may certainly congratulate himself on his debut. . . .

At an October meeting, Henry renewed his success by reading an "Allegory." In November, according to the minutes, he offered an "Effusion," something called "Eating Houses," and a piece relating to "Old Massachusetts Hall."[23]

Gibbons all the while had been taking his own turns as an editor. On Saturday night, December 13, the New Yorker unluckily missed the last omnibus from Boston to Cambridge and had to walk the whole way to the campus, a distance of several miles, in a freezing rain. Another student might not have been hurt by the mishap, but Gibbons was. The next day he vomited a great deal of blood, and on Monday evening he died in his room.

The shock in Cambridge was great. Cases of students dying in their rooms were uncommon, and Gibbons had been very highly regarded.[24] His classmates held a special meeting and chose two of their number to write resolutions about him for adoption by the class and communication to his parents. The writers chosen were George E. Pond and Henry B. Adams.

As usual, the Institute of 1770 met the following Friday evening, December 19. The editor appointed to appear was Adams. Rather than put on another of his amusing performances, he introduced a motion "that all literary exercises be suspended for the evening," and a second motion "that all further exercises except the election of officers be given up for this term." Both his motions passed.[25]

A new set of four editors was elected by the Institute of 1770 at a meeting in January. Anderson was one of them. Adams spoke at length about Gibbons in the course of the meeting. His role in the society thereafter was mostly one of listener; but he was once called upon to appear again in a prominent way at a meeting, in April 1856, when he gave what the minutes described as "a manly and forcible lecture."[26]

When he wanted to be, Henry could be an excellent student. During his second term as a freshman, by making heroic efforts, especially in Greek and Latin, he had hoarded up 2573 points, a large total, and had again escaped penalties for misbehavior. At the same time, he had lifted himself from seventieth to forty-third on the Scale of Merit. He had continued to study hard, but not heroically, as a sophomore. Although penalized 24 points for cutting three recitations, he lifted himself during the fall term to thirty-fourth in a class expanded to ninety-six students. Unhappily, such successes involved a sad lesson. He might "pull up," as the students said, and gain a few more places on the rank-list; but he could never ascend into the top fifth or tenth of his class. The cumulative arithmetic of the system forbade it. For such a purpose, his illness as a freshman had finished him.[27]

About the time Gibbons died, Henry came around to the view that one's rank on the Scale of Merit did not matter. Also he decided he was not learning enough at college. He grew interested in three possible kinds of education: formal or academic education, self-education, and mutual efforts by students to educate one another. He asked himself how much he needed of each.

In February 1856, while at home in Boston during winter vacation, he made up his mind that during his remaining five terms at Harvard he would merely hurry through the work assigned him by his teachers and try to get a good education both by teaching himself and persuading other students to join him in schemes of mutual instruction. Looking ahead to his junior and senior years, when, his brother having graduated, he would either have to room alone in Cambridge or share some rooms with one or more of his friends, he made a careful plan.[28] The only surviving record of the plan was written not by Henry but by Nick Anderson, in mid-March 1856, when the spring term of their sophomore year was two weeks under way. By then, three conspirators, Adams, Anderson, and a classmate very close to Anderson, Hazen Dorr, of Boston, had agreed to live together as juniors and had reserved some off-campus rooms they expected would ideally suit their tastes. Nick wrote enthusiastically to his mother: "What a pleasant, social time Adams, Dorr, and I will have next term. The rooms are as nice and cozy as is possible, and of a winter evening, how comfortable it will be to cock our legs up on the mantel-piece, and study or talk or read."

Nick itemized the details of a philosophy of education which he, Hazen, and Henry were to carry into practice in September, when they started to room together. "There is to be no formality. We are to take such liberties as we choose, in fact, to do what we please. Moreover, we intend to pursue a course of [independent] reading, so as to keep up our knowledge of the Latin language as well as the French. We intend to have no idle hours; when not studying or reading some worthy work, we are to talk on various topics, and 'in primis' to argue and discuss all the subjects of the day, which, by the by, Adams is well qualified to do."

The chief inventor of their philosophy was clearly Adams. He had been able to prevail upon Anderson and Dorr to go along with it for one reason only: they shared his doubts about formal or academic education. Anderson warned his mother frankly: "I am going to put time into *learning,* not *studying.* . . . Undoubtedly there is need of study, but no need for studying for, hoping for, praying for *rank.* Rank is a shoal in the course of learning on which many wreck their future prospects of a good, virtuous, and happy life."[29]

Adams was not the only sophomore organizing friends. At the beginning of the same term, in March 1856, Rooney Lee induced seven of his classmates to join him in forming an eating table for the term. Half the group were fellows from Boston and thereabouts: Henry Adams, Josiah Bradlee, Benjamin Crowninshield, and Hollis Hunnewell. The other half were fellows from the South and West: Lee and James May from Virginia, Anderson from Ohio, and William Elliott from South Carolina. Nick Anderson thought their table "one of the nicest little assemblies in the city." Adams must have liked it equally, for it put into immediate practice his fond new ideas concerning mutual education.[30]

Henry believed that college students should transform themselves from boys into men in part by engaging in the lively give and take of adult conversation.[31] He was not averse to heated interchanges and—in the language of Anderson's outline of their intentions—was downright eager to "argue and discuss all the subjects of the day." If the conversations the eight members of the new table had together tended to bring their political differences into the open, Adams, for one, would be happy, and would expect no harm to result. He and his friends at college had all along disagreed with each other on political topics without becoming estranged.[32]

Unfortunately for Henry, 1856 was an election year. What was worse, the current of American politics had grown turbulent and at times seemed full of menace. A strange political whirlwind which had crossed the landscape a few years earlier, the Know-Nothing movement against Catholics and "foreigners," had not yet entirely spent its force. In the Northern states, the antislavery voters had been reorganized under a new name as the Republicans. Meanwhile, two distinct kinds of Democrats, those in the North and those in the South, were as often irritating each other as working together.

Some of the members of the table Lee organized held decided opinions or at least felt strongly about national issues. Nominally a Democrat, Anderson at heart belonged to the Know-Nothing movement, officially called the American Party. Nick had earlier written privately to his mother: "All my sympathies and hopes are with the

Know-Nothings, and I only wish I were a man and could stump the country for their benefit. . . . Down with all foreigners who dare molest the laws of our Country and oppose the rights of Native Americans.''[33] At a different extreme, Adams was a whole-hearted Republican and convinced believer in the rightness of the antislavery cause. He had never made it a secret that he was personally close to Charles Sumner, whose election to the U. S. Senate five years earlier had been the high point of success for the old Free Soilers.[34] Henry laid no claim to political originality. His principles were practically interchangeable, or so he thought, with those of Senator Sumner, not to mention those of C. F. Adams, which meant they were also the same as those enunciated twenty years earlier, in Washington and elsewhere, by J. Q. Adams.

Sometime late in March or early in April 1856, a falling-out occurred. The agreement Adams had made with Anderson and Dorr to live together as juniors was cancelled. Nick and Hazen made a new plan of their own and obtained assurances that they could occupy as juniors and seniors the very rooms in one of the dormitories, Hollis Hall, which Nick's father, Lars Anderson, had occupied a generation earlier.[35] Why the previous agreement with Adams was dropped is now unknown. It had enjoyed Nick's warm support for a few days at least and could not have been cancelled without serious cause. One imagines that the trouble was a passing but furious quarrel between Nick and Henry concerning the slavery question, or the rights of "niggers," as Anderson freely called them.[36]

Henry turned about and arranged to live as a junior and senior with Hollis Hunnewell. He and Hunnewell reserved good rooms— No. 5—on the third floor of Holworthy Hall. Their action was part of a movement among the students to make use of rooms in the college buildings. Still another member of Lee's assembly, Ben Crowninshield, reserved space in Holworthy near Adams and Hunnewell. The movement into the dormitories was mainly inspired by lower rents, but the would-be occupants of Holworthy had a special motive. Gas light would soon be installed in the building, for the first time in a dormitory. While they lived in the building, their windows would glow in the evenings as no students' windows in the Yard had ever glowed.[37]

In Washington and on the western frontier, current events grew suddenly lurid. News spread that Charles Sumner, on the Senate floor at the Capitol, had started a long antislavery oration on the "rape" of

Kansas by the slavepower. Holding the floor for five hours on two successive days, the orator spoke with unprecedented boldness against the friends of slavery, using strong language.[38] In Kansas immediately thereafter, on May 21, organized proslavery men sacked the town of Lawrence. In the Senate chamber on May 22, Congressman Preston S. Brooks of South Carolina assaulted Sumner at his desk with a cane. So severe were the senator's injuries that his convalescence and renewed participation in the affairs of the government reportedly could not be assured. Excitement mounted everywhere. On the night of May 24-25 in Kansas, fanatical John Brown and seven followers, four of them his sons, butchered five allegedly proslavery settlers as a reprisal for the Lawrence attack. In consequence, guerrilla warfare flamed throughout the territory.[39]

When he maimed Charles Sumner in Washington, Preston Brooks also rained ghostly blows upon a sophomore at Harvard College. Henry Adams was sufficiently a friend of the injured senator to feel vicariously, and almost physically, the whole ferocity of the South Carolinian's onslaught.[40]

Danger, manifest in the capital and in Kansas, showed itself as well in Cambridge. On June 6, Hazen Dorr went rowing on the Charles River and overtaxed himself. The day was very warm. That night, alone in his room, he died of what the doctors said had been "congestion of the brain." Previously shocked by the death of Gibbons, the Class of '58 was amazed and stunned by the loss of Dorr.[41] It was voted at a class meeting that resolutions about him should be written by Adams and Hunnewell.[42] Hazen's closer friends went to Mount Auburn Cemetery to witness the interment.

When the term ended in July and the sophomores were no longer sophomores, the eight members of Rooney Lee's table scattered to their respective homes. Theirs had been no ordinary assembly. Because students in their class from states other than Massachusetts numbered only one in five, the table had had an unusually national character.[43] In miniature, it had almost been a national student Senate, or another Union. With one exception, its members patched up their quarrels before leaving Cambridge. The exception, Billy Elliott, was leaving Harvard to complete his education at a school in the South. He had been the South Carolinian in their diminutive Union.[44] The implications of his departure could not have been lost on his seven associates. One of their company had seceded.

## 4 / Election

In late July 1856, at the outset of his summer vacation, Adams accelerated his progress. Spending part of his time in Cambridge, he moved his belongings from Mrs. Story's house to Holworthy. Perhaps an impulse seized him, or perhaps he had long been meditating the idea, but he immediately started drafting an essay called "My Old Room" with the object of reappearing at Harvard as a published writer. The *Harvard Magazine* was issued monthly during each term but not in February or August. Accordingly its September and March numbers, coming out at the beginnings of terms, had the aspect of fresh departures. Henry wanted his new essay to appear in the very next issue, the one for September 1856, and, after making successive efforts in Cambridge, Quincy, and possibly other places, he achieved his object. Soon after returning to the college as a junior, he had the pleasure of seeing "My Old Room" in print.

At first glance the new essay could seem very mild. Its author dwelt on the "romance" and "philosophy" of college rooms. Unashamedly imitating Hawthorne, he spoke about his own room which he explained was "in an old house." He said he did not know its history. "I cannot discover who has lodged under its roof, except for a few years back; but sometimes in winter evenings, when the clock strikes twelve, and I put out my light before going to bed, I have sat looking into the mass of glowing coals in the fireplace, trying to conjure up the faces of my predecessors, and imagining to myself a long procession of forgotten figures trooping through my room, like the old governors at the Province House, in 'Howe's Masquerade.'"

Looked at a second time, the essay was startling for its omissions. It omitted Charles. It omitted the Adams family—indeed all mention of families. Were its pages taken literally, its author had not had a brother at Harvard, nor a roommate, but had lived alone in the same room for a long time—"while years have passed by"—and had had many friends, all of whom had carved their initials with penknives in his chairs. Also he had greatly liked his room but now was leaving it for another. "... I have bidden my room good-by. I have spent my last evening there. I have studied my last lesson there. I have seen the pictures taken down from the walls, and the carpet torn up from the floor."

Contributions to the *Magazine* were published anonymously, but the authorship of each of the contents of every issue was advertised among the students by word of mouth. Reading "My Old Room" and hearing that it was written by Adams, some of the undergraduates may have asked Henry why he had eradicated his brother Charles and otherwise exchanged fact for fiction. To tell the truth, he had given more the appearance of being a senior than a junior, as if the current year were his last. But his essay in one way was really not fiction. It expressed what its author was feeling. Although chronologically younger than most of his classmates, Adams felt decidedly older. He may even have felt older than his older brothers. He had become rather fond of Cambridge and, at eighteen, felt as if he were freed from his family and standing alone.

The essay deserved still a third reading. It contained indications of a counterrevolution in Henry's attitude towards the Scale of Merit. He had decided, after all, to become extremely studious and "pull up" as far as possible. He said that he and his fellow collegians should turn away from "romance" towards "reality"—more particularly that they owed it to themselves to do their lessons "with the strong and steady effort of men who see that life is before them, and that they must struggle hard for an honorable rank." He confessed, "I have learned, too, however late, that College rank is *not* a humbug, as some pretend. ..."

During his fifth term, as a beginning junior, he evidently wanted to contribute to the *Magazine* "regularly."[1] Possibly he submitted pieces for every issue. If so, only two of the pieces were accepted, and both were mere brief notices of new books. The first, published in November, commended a political treatise, *The Conquest of Kansas by Missouri and Her Allies,* by William Phillips, and showed that Adams remained a faithful adherent of the antislavery cause but viewed the vicissitudes of the antislavery struggle with mingled hope and dread. The second, published in December, ridiculed a bad novel, *Paul Fane,* by N. Parker Willis, and showed that Henry wanted American novels to be realistic.

His meager success as a writer apparently resulted in part from very hard work in his courses. He was acting upon his idea that a college student should do his lessons with a "strong and steady effort." In the course of the term, he did outstandingly well on his themes. His absences from recitations, services, and prayers cost him only twenty-eight points. He added 3302 points to his academic treasury, the highest score he had earned till then in a single term. Yet, for purposes of raising his rank, the effort was wasted. After all his exertions, his rank when his fifth term ended, in January 1857, was thirty-fourth, the same rank he had held a year earlier, when a sophomore.

A somewhat parallel but much more serious problem for him related to the learning of languages. First as a schoolboy and then as a collegian, he had been studying Latin for more than eight years and Greek for four or five. The year before, he had studied French intensively and made a beginning in Anglo-Saxon. Allowed one elective course as a junior, he had chosen German, and as a senior he would similarly elect to take Italian. Thus he enjoyed a prospect of becoming more or less versed in six languages, other than English, before he should graduate. The cloud in the sky of this prospect was the sad truth that American scholars learned to read foreign languages at school and college, and made some efforts to write in them, but did not learn to speak them or comprehend them by hearing. Henry was no exception. His father over the years had attempted to teach him a good accent in French, perhaps with some success; but the son, as a Harvard junior, could not speak French in more than a very limited way, promised to succeed no better in German, and knew in advance that of all the languages he had studied he would feel secure at graduation from the college only in Latin.

To another student, these deficiencies might not have seemed deficiencies. On the whole, American undergraduates were quick to read difficult authors in their original languages and were proud of their triumphs. Even to Henry it meant a great deal to read Caesar, Cicero, Virgil, Livy, Horace, and Tacitus in Latin; Homer, Aeschylus, Sophocles, Euripides, Aristophanes, Herodotus, and Thucydides in Greek; Moliere and La Fontaine in French; and many others. But Henry's personal experience had been exceptional in relation to the speaking of modern languages. The two older persons whose company he had most sought in recent years, his father and Charles Sumner, both spoke French. Sumner also spoke German. Henry's grandmother, too, had spoken both French and German. In fact, Louisa Catherine Adams had spoken French so well as to be mistaken in France for a native.[2] Compared to her especially, Henry felt extremely disadvantaged and mute. In the light of her abilities, his education could only seem radically misplanned. The worry was growing constant with him that he would have to find a means of self-rescue and learn to speak several modern languages, the more the better.

After he was injured in May 1856, Senator Sumner stayed for many months in places not far from Washington, attempting to recover. He returned to Massachusetts in November in time to vote. Rather than arrive at the Boston station unanticipated and unnoticed, he made a gradual, triumphal entry into the city, with all possible ceremony. His popularity in Massachusetts had much increased, and he was greeted by large crowds.

The legislature enthusiastically reelected him to the Senate. In one sense, his reelection was conditional. Except for Sumner himself, who bravely kept faith in his power to recover, no one felt much confidence that he could recuperate. Pale, haggard, and unsteady, he seemed a different person. His first task would be to find better doctors, either in America or abroad.[3]

Sometime late in 1856 or early in 1857, Henry talked with his friend about the future. According to his own later testimony, he told the senator, " . . . you have Massachusetts under your hand and will have it so all your life."[4] The prophecy could not have been bettered. Sumner after his injury *was* irremovably secure as one of the state's two senators. But young Adams intended his comment as a probe as well as a prophecy. He wanted to find out whether Sumner, who was *not* well enough to perform his senatorial duties, would cling to office for the mere sake of remaining a senator in name. Henry sided with the minority among Sumner's friends who both thought and were willing to tell him that he should place his health ahead of all else, resign his place in the Senate, and give his whole time to recovery. How far Henry pressed his arguments is uncertain, but he learned what his friend intended: Sumner would not leave the Senate.

This news transformed their friendship. Outwardly, Henry and the senator seemed as friendly as ever, but Henry retained not a shred of confidence in Sumner as a force for good in American politics. Reacting to his injury, Sumner had undergone an astonishing metamorphosis. The human being had disappeared; and a statesman, the wounded hero of the Republican Party and the antislavery cause, had appeared in his place. So Henry saw the matter at least, and for him the change was oppressive. To know Sumner the man, Henry had had to humor and flatter him. To befriend the statesman, Henry would have to play the part of a young boy overtowered by a modern Cicero, an American political god.[5]

Henry took the necessary pose, but he secretly concentrated all his hopes for constructive leadership by Massachusetts Republicans older than himself upon one political aspirant, his father, whose chances of preferment had improved. Some years before, Horace Mann had resigned the place in Congress held still earlier by John Quincy Adams, and the place had been awarded to a Know-Nothing named Damrell. An egregious incompetent, Damrell could not be expected to keep the office long. Charles Francis Adams had claims to being the ablest politician in the District, and there seemed a good chance that he would be elected to Congress in 1858, the year Henry would graduate.[6]

The foremost student organization at Harvard was the Hasty Pudding Club. Much liked for its public theatricals, the club was sometimes criticized by the faculty for the alleged facetiousness and ribaldry of its members at their private meetings on alternate Friday evenings. The date of a student's election to Hasty Pudding, supposing he was elected at all, was viewed on the campus as an indication of his comparative popularity. Adams was elected on December 15, 1856, later than Nick Anderson and Ben Crowninshield but sooner than Rooney Lee. Apparently Adams's star had somewhat risen, and Lee's had considerably fallen.[7]

The club scheduled two farces, *Lend Me Five Shillings* and *In for a Holiday,* as a double bill to be performed early in January 1857. Adams was selected to manage the former, in which he would act the part of Captain Phobbs, and was given a female role in the latter as Mrs. Comfit. His performances in January were sufficiently approved to win him a more demanding part as the father, Sir Anthony Absolute, in Sheridan's *Rivals,* to be produced by Hasty Pudding the following May.[8]

He meanwhile contrived to step forward again as a prominent contributor to the *Harvard Magazine.* He used part of his winter vacation in late January and February to write a long article about college students free on vacation. Titled "Retrospect," it distinguished winter vacations, which he had not much enjoyed, from summer ones, in which he had reveled. Without giving their exact dates, or even their years, he remembered halcyon moments in his own past: an August day he had spent on a steamboat descending the

Hudson River and passing through the Catskills; a ramble he had taken "over the southeastern coasts and islands of Massachusetts," during which, from the sandy beaches, he had watched "the ocean that for miles and miles away foamed and boiled over the most dangerous shoals on our coast"; and an entrancing view he had once glimpsed from North Conway in New Hampshire, where, reading one day under a tree, he had looked up and seen "far off to the right the white peak of Mount Washington, hardly distinguishable from the thin cloud that lay behind it."

"Retrospect"—like "My Old Room"—appeared in the *Magazine* at the start of a term, in March 1857. It, too, reflected the feelings of its author. Henry said he had never yet been in love and was not sure he could ever become so. " . . . usually I despise sentimentality. Neither can I be fond of any pretence or appearance of sentiment in any form in public. . . . An affectation of love where none is felt is absurd. A display where it is real, is disgusting. In either case, it is out of place; or at least so it has seemed to me; perhaps for the same reason that the grapes seemed sour to the fox."

Although his newest essay was written in winter, all his thoughts in it pointed towards summer. He imagined an ideal vacation. The setting he chose for his vision, while not named explicitly, was clearly the Old House at Quincy. He described a collegian spending his summer vacation "at home in the country, with pleasant neighbors, pleasant guests, and pleasant occupations." His idyll made room for a young woman and possibly for love after all. "It is one of my castles in the air to imagine a parlor on a summer morning, its open windows surrounded by rose bushes covered with flowers and dew, and looking out upon a smooth green lawn, while within sits the student reading or working or talking with some angel in muslin. Sometimes the scene changes a little; the pair are evidently going to walk together, looking at the sunset, hunting four-leaved clover, or engaged in very deep and philosophical talk. I never in my dreams could distinguish their faces."[9]

Because of its variegated activities, Hasty Pudding had been found to need no less than ten officers. Management of the club was passed from the seniors to the juniors each year at the beginning of the spring term, when the junior members elected a new set of officers from their own number. Thus, at the election meeting on the evening of March 6, 1857, in addition to a president, a vice-president, a secretary, and a treasurer, the Pudding men of the Class of 1858 chose a property master, a librarian, a chorister, a poet, an orator, and an alligator. Anderson was made president, Crowninshield treasurer, and Adams alligator.[10] The place of alligator—also known as the "Kroko-deilos," or crocodile, or K. P.—was usually reserved for "the best and most humorous writer in the class."[11] It would be Adams's duty to regale the members at their private meetings with comical papers. He would be called upon to perform at no less than seven meetings between mid-March and early July.

Winning the office of Hasty Pudding Alligator was the turning point in Henry's undergraduate career, and he knew it. By electing him, the juniors had meant to serve their own interests. They had tasted some of the benefits of his sense of humor and wanted more. Perhaps they told him in advance that they would choose him. He attended the election meeting and after being chosen said he would serve, provided his papers met with no reprisals. He mentioned that jesters in the courts of the Middle Ages had been free to make fun of others without being made fun of themselves. His comment passed for a joke and an auspicious beginning, but his situation was not without perils. Custom required that alligators prepare and read papers which were not merely comical but scatalogical and obscene. The custom was reinforced by the preservation of some of their manuscripts for handing down from one alligator to another. After inheriting these documents, Henry found that they bore each other "a striking re-semblance" and described them as "repetitions of the same smut, forty or fifty times over." As a rule, his predecessors in the office had not given their papers even a pretence of finish, but they had created a tradition, and he was caught within it, with no apparent chance of escape.[12]

For him, the term then beginning would be excessively busy. He remained anxious to do well in his courses and raise his rank. He hoped not to disgrace himself in *The Rivals*. He was taking an interest in campus politics and the proposed abolition of Greek-letter frater-nities. He wished to read independently, apart from his courses, and write for the *Magazine*. All the same, he decided to become such an alligator as there had never been at the college, and might never be again, while Harvard endured.

Previous alligators had written some of their papers in the form of a periodical called the *Hasty Pudding Social Alligator and Gridiron* and had willed Adams a bound book with ruled, blank pages. He wished to improve upon the past periodical. Making use of his best penmanship, he wrote the final draft of his first paper in the book.

Intended for and evidently read aloud at the club's meeting on March 20, the paper mainly consisted of a pretended letter from a minister of religion to the alligator in which the minister defended his record of sexual misconduct; a pretended account of the formation of a club by the Harvard president and faculty for the purpose of promoting extreme filth and indecency; a pretended letter to President Walker from one of the professors, Cornelius Felton, written while on a visit to Washington, in which the Professor rejoiced at the opportunities for drunkenness and sexual licence in the capital; and a pretended poem by Lord Byron. Inherited, with acknowledgment, from a previous alligator, the poem concerned the "first grandparents" of the human race, Adam and Eve, especially Eve, and depicted the eating of the forbidden fruit in terms very nearly explicit, and descriptive of a particular sexual act.

The series of papers Henry had started bore the title *Hasty Pudding Social Alligator and Gridiron, Volume II*. If he went on in the same way, writing additional papers into the club's blank book in his attractive, superbly readable handwriting, he risked creating a sizable manuscript fifty or sixty pages in length which the club might never destroy. He went on. His next paper, written for the meeting of April 3, said, "*THE* Alligator regrets to learn that some little fault was found with the last number of the Social Gridiron by members . . . on account of the freedom of language which was made use of. . . ." He declined to answer such criticisms, except by reminding the members that he was an alligator and that the alligator was an animal unchangeable in his traits. " . . . creatures of his class are not naturally witty, and . . . it is their innate disposition to wallow in filth."

Genuine humor could be found in the papers. It partly arose from Adams's consistently speaking of himself in the third person singular—a device he returned to late in life in *The Education*. Also he worded all his pages as if he were indeed an animal with claws, jaws, fearful teeth, and a long tail. In his new paper, mitigating his bestiality, he promised that the alligator would not be offensive. "For once he will try to refrain from gross coarseness which has not at least some fun in it, to support itself." The new paper involved a pretended report received by the alligator from a French archaeologist. The report concerned some ruins in Egypt on the east bank of the Nile. As translated into English by the alligator, the report began:

"Above the ruins of ancient Thebes, above the Cataracts, where the foot of civilized man seldom penetrates, there stand, hard on the confines of the great desert[,] the remains of a splendid temple. At the grand entrance, four colossal kings sit, watching in everlasting repose, and gaze into vacancy, resting their huge hands upon their knees. Behind them stretches a long vista of heavy pillars and columns, while on the walls, and wherever a spot is to be found, are wrought long lines of pictured story, triumphs and labors, priests and holy men. From these rude hieroglyphics we gather that here, ages ago, stood the great temple of learning. . . . This in short was the Egyptian University."

The alligator's pretended translation of the pretended French report continued by describing places found among the ruins in Egypt which precisely resembled the rooms used at modern Harvard by the Hasty Pudding Club and the Greek-letter fraternities for their meetings. For the most part, Adams's paper became a sometimes indecent lampoon. Still, it was not without meaning. At least some of the Pudding men who heard him read it would know that the temple he spoke of in Egypt was something perfectly real, Abu Simbel, on the Upper Nile, above the last cataract; and a few would know that the lampoon more or less consciously expressed Henry's absorption in antiquity, a special fascination he felt in relation to Egypt, and his intense desire to travel.

Recently the seniors had met and passed a resolution concerning the Greek-letter fraternities: "Resolved, that, in the opinion of the Senior Class, nothing but good would result from the dissolution of them all, provided only that some provision shall be made to secure the use of their libraries to their present and past members."[13] Soon thereafter, the *Magazine* had offered to print any article a student might submit defending the threatened fraternities. Adams was far from wanting to defend them, and felt no strong urge to attack them, for to do so would only be to thrash a dying horse. Moreover, he was coming around to the view that literary societies were not much better suited to benefit students than the doomed fraternities, and generally he thought the time had come for new ideas. Perhaps by prearrangement with the editors, he wrote an article called "College Politics" for the May 1857 issue of the *Magazine*. It was printed as a lead article and set forth original views. Henry's new ideas undercut both the literary societies he had belonged to. " . . . we have seen enough of literary exercises among undergraduates," he said. "These are not what the students want."

He proposed the creation of a new kind of undergraduate club open to all upperclassmen, which they would join "for personal convenience, not for brotherly love." Such a club would be very large. It would *not* be exclusive. It would facilitate mutual student education. It would inherit the libraries of the doomed fraternities and consolidate them in one collection.

Of the four full-length articles Adams had published till then in the *Magazine*, "College Politics" was easily the most important. As persuasively as he could he extolled the merits of his grand design. "There is needed a Club," he wrote, "which shall be the rendezvous for the ability of three Classes. There is needed a centring point, around which to collect, day after day, and read the papers and the reviews, and form opinions, and mature the character by continual contact with minds of all casts, and tempers of every stamp. There is needed a handsome undergraduates' library, which shall not be confined, like the present Society libraries, to the use of a dozen or two. There is needed, in short, a Club, well appointed, well conducted, and handsomely supported."

Although he was descended from many distinguished American families in Massachusetts and elsewhere, and had been brought up to appear before the world as a gentleman, Adams was an authentic democrat, aspiring to leadership among democrats. Hence his interest in a club open to *all* upperclassmen who wanted to join it. He was also something of a radical and revolutionary. In April 1857, he stood on the brink of losing faith altogether in formal higher education in the United States. He was moving back again towards the idea that he would have to be his own teacher. It seemed to him that he and his fellow students at Harvard, so far as possible, should take charge of their own educations. The ready and easy way was to get ownership and control of sufficient instruments of learning, meaning chiefly books, and organize them for use. If his grand club could be formed, its leading officer might be its student librarian, not its student president. He said in "College Politics" that a "good librarian" could extract from the wreckage of the Greek-letter fraternities an "excellent collection of books"—and one to which, if Henry Adams had his way, no upperclassman would be too poor or too unpopular to have access.

One of the features of his design was magnitude. He was not stepping forward as a leader among the Harvard juniors. He meant to step forward as a leader among *all* college students in America. Were such a club as he designed actually started in Cambridge, similar clubs would spring into being at colleges everywhere in the Union. His ideas were national. He was attempting to change the mood of undergraduate life in the United States from one of boyish dependence to one of manly independence, self-reliance, and mutual assistance.

Adams's chance of getting his club created depended on a great many things but on nothing more than the opinion held of him by his classmates. As finishing juniors, the other members of the Class of 1858 were mostly agreed that he was smart, gifted as a writer, and funny. He perhaps was tempted at times to make them think of him as a mere comedian. At some moment now impossible to date, he started to wear an engraved ring, given him by his mother, which bore the device of a fool's cap and bells—copied, he said, from a picture of the Fool in *King Lear,* found in Retsch's *Outlines of Shakespeare.*[14] And he made such a hit as the angry father in *The Rivals* that he must have seemed a talented actor.[15]

The juniors were given many opportunities to make new judgments of him as the term went forward. Some may have begun to think of him as a person of considerable substance. Unwaveringly, at meetings of Hasty Pudding on April 17, May 1, May 15, June 5, and July 7, he continued and finished his service as alligator. The later numbers of his *Social Gridiron,* while not always up to, or down to, the level of the earlier, were far cleverer than the standard fare put before the Pudding men by usual alligators. In one number, he pretended to divulge the licentious conduct of the faculty while making a trip to Germany and back on broomsticks, to attend a world congress of witches on Walpurgis Night in the Hartz Mountains. In another, he pretended to quote from a news report in a Boston paper about an indecent meeting of the Hasty Pudding Club at Harvard College during which the reporter had seen the club's famous alligator. According to the newspaper, this celebrity was a "wonderful creature," and "just the very finest creature to be seen in these parts."

If one meaning came through in his alligator papers more strongly than any other, it concerned his ambition and his desire to be taken seriously by others. Repeatedly the papers suggested that the alligator was the chief officer of Hasty Pudding and the only officer who mattered. In "Social Gridiron No. IV," an original poem of twenty-six stanzas, the alligator was a king who ruled not only the club but the college and stood on terms of equality with persons distinguished in history and mythology. His greatness was assumed with all possible plainness in the two opening stanzas.

From his bed in the mud of the Charles one day
    A walking the Crocodile went,
To see how his snug little College came on
    And whether his boys were content.

Over the bridge and up the road
    With royal stride his carcass he bore,
And he carried his tail on a six-wheeled car
    That Daedalus made for the Minotaur.

One of the first of the juniors to give Adams his due was Rooney Lee. The Virginian felt out of place at Harvard, was falling behind as a scholar, wished to leave, and hoped to become a soldier like his father, Colonel Robert E. Lee, a noted officer in the regular army. Opportunely, Rooney was offered a commission by Lieutenant General Winfield Scott at the War Department in Washington. Rather than write his letter of acceptance himself, Rooney asked Henry Adams to write it for him; Adams did so; and Lee got his bars. Writing the letter cost Henry no great effort, and Rooney's request that he write it made Henry prouder than anything that had happened till then in his dealings with his peers.[16]

As a finishing junior, Adams studied hard enough to expect he might add about 2850 points to his hoard by the end of the term in mid-July. Until the third week of June 1857, his losses for misconduct during the term totaled only 34 points. Then one morning a teacher seized a chance to punish him severely, and other students viewed the punishment as gratuitous and outrageous.

Nick Anderson felt so strongly about the case that he wrote its history. The moral of the tale he told was that the teachers were less concerned that the students should learn than that they themselves should be free to rule as they pleased. "Rank at college," he told his mother, "is determined not by a uniform elegance of recitation or by a knowledge of the subjects in hand, but by a conformity to the college rules. I have heard of seven persons receiving a 'public' [meaning a deduction of 64 points] . . . for cutting more than 20 prayers. Many, innumerably many, have received smaller deductions for similar offenses, and last, most absurd, unjust of all, Adams received a 'private' [a deduction of 32 points] for *not wearing a collar to recitation*. Now this is absolutely tyrannical."

The irony of the story was intensified by its concerning a student who, if anything, was working too much at his studies. Anderson went on to say: "I am completely disgusted. Adams has been studying hard for the purpose of pulling up; he is one of the smartest men in the class. . . . A few nights since he sat up late to write a theme. The consequence was he did not get up the next morning until it was too late to dress himself completely for the 7 o'clk recitation. Accordingly he went without his collar and rec'd therefor a 'private.' *This private has counteracted the study of a whole term and he now stands 34.* What do you think of that?"[17]

It seems possible that Adams reappeared in Cambridge several times during his summer vacation in 1857. He was certainly in Cambridge on August 4, for on that day he borrowed seven volumes from the library of the Hasty Pudding Club and recorded the loan on his page in the library's ledger.[18]

Days spent in Cambridge, in turn, might possibly have increased his chances of seeing one of his classmates. Strange to say, this classmate was an Adams. Son of a Cambridge doctor, he was named Charles Adams Allen and shared—on his mother's side—direct descent from that Henry Adams who had founded the family in America. Charles Allen was proud of his blood relationship with the modern Henry Adams in his class and later drew attention to it in writing. Before coming to Harvard, Allen had served as school librarian at the Cambridge High School.[19] Now he was one of the editors of the *Harvard Magazine,* and as a senior, for practical purposes, would be editor-in-chief.[20] He had read Adams's "College Politics" in the May issue, shared Adams's interest in the question of better access for students to libraries, and wished to join with him in making a serious effort to bring about the creation of a grand new student club at Harvard, sweeping away many old ones.[21]

At a time now difficult to pinpoint with certainty, probably just after the Class of 1858 returned to Cambridge as seniors in September 1857, Adams drafted a student petition. Although he seems not to have known it, his doing so was a second turning point in his undergraduate career. He evidently drafted the petition with Allen's knowledge and encouragement. Its purpose was to rally support for their proposed club. Two changes had occurred in their thinking on the subject. They had decided that membership in the club would have to be limited to seniors and juniors only; and they had learned that a space suitable for the club could, in theory, be granted to its founders by the college, if the president and faculty were willing, in Holden Chapel, which, no longer needed by the medical school, was becoming available for other uses.

Adams wrote the petition at the top of a plain sheet of paper. He and Allen signed their names beneath it, at the heads of two intended columns of student signatures. Then Adams went in search of seniors willing to add their names to Allen's and his own. The proposal to which their classmates were asked to subscribe said:

> The undersigned, members of the Senior Class, wishing to found a Club that may supply a want which the experience of recent classes has shown to exist during the last two years of the Course; to furnish better advantages for literary pursuits; and to bring each Senior Class together more harmoniously before graduation, respectfully petition that the lower story of Holden Chapel, when no longer needed for its present use, be granted to the Senior Class, as a Reading Room, Club Room, and Undergraduates' Library, to be open in regular course to every member of the two upper classes.

The signatures Adams obtained included those of all the survivors of the table Lee had organized when they were sophomores, all but two of those who had been made officers of Hasty Pudding the previous March, and most of Henry's fellow actors and managers in Hasty Pudding theatricals. He persisted until, of the 87 or so of the class who remained in attendance, 53 had signed. Then, perhaps by calling on President Walker, he presented the petition to the college authorities.[22]

A new set of ten officers was elected to manage Hasty Pudding for the fall term. Probably at his own suggestion, Adams was elected librarian.[23] The duty of succeeding him as alligator fell to a luckless member named George Washington Copp Noble who could not remotely approach his performance.

Adams asked Anderson to join him as *de facto* co-librarian. The two took stock of the club's 6,000 books, which, when not stolen, were allowed to stand about on the shelves in poor condition and little order. Improvements seemed necessary. Anderson shortly wrote: "The Pudding [Library] catalogue needs revision. Adams and I, with public spirit and a laudable degree of self-denial, have undertaken the Herculean job. He is to rearrange the books, re-fit and repair those which are delapidated, and renovate the whole system. Being a modern Magliabecchi, he is well fitted for the task. I have the rewriting of the catalogue for my portion. . . . Guns and firecrackers! What an undertaking!"[24]

The work being done by Adams and Anderson was really part of a *three*-person effort. The third person involved was Allen, and the purpose of their joint effort was to show that the seniors were in earnest about the proposed club. As his share of the demonstration, Allen wrote a long paper titled "Considerations in Favor of an Undergraduates' Library and Reading-Room." His paper marshaled squads and platoons of acceptable reasons why the authorities should approve the club and grant it space in Holden Chapel. Significantly, the paper further narrowed the club's proposed membership to all the seniors plus only half, or slightly more than half, of the juniors. The change was ominous. Apparently the three partners, Adams, Allen, and Anderson, had realized that the college authorities stood in fear of *all* student organizations and feared them in proportion to their size. By reducing the suggested membership of their grand club, the partners attempted to allay the fears of the authorities—at the cost of calling attention to the very thing which the authorities would view as most against it, the club's unheard-of inclusiveness.[25]

In other circumstances, the seniors in favor of the club might have taken a different course, ignored the college authorities, and sought space for their new, unexclusive society in a building off the campus not owned by the college. Money would have been needed, on a steady basis, to pay rent; and much more money would have been needed to pay other expenses, were the club to be enlarged to its intended dimensions. Unfortunately, for fund-raising purposes, the present moment was the worst possible. A fearful panic was rushing through the nation's business community like a storm on the ocean, ruining innumerable enterprises and individuals in its path. Its effects were nowhere worse than in Massachusetts. Anderson wrote on September 17: "One of the strongest firms in Boston, that of Mills and Company, has gone by the board with liabilities of $2,000,000. People are in high excitement, and other suspensions are announced."[26]

At the beginning of every academic year at Harvard, the college published printed sheets of paper known as rank scales or rank lists. Folded once, such sheets had a left-hand page and a right-hand page. On the left-hand page of a list, all the students in the upper half of a particular class were listed in the order of their ranks, as calculated by the president and faculty. On the right-hand page, all the students in the lower half of the same class were listed alphabetically, in shared, equalized disgrace. In keeping with usual practice, at the start of the fall term in 1857, an "Annual Scale" of the Class of 1858 was printed and mailed to the seniors' parents. The document in one way was misleading and even dishonest. A student's actual rank at the college was determined by adding all points credited to him during all his terms. The list sent to the seniors' parents reflected only the points the seniors had earned as juniors. By virtue of his having scored 6040 points as a junior, Adams was ranked on the list as the twenty-sixth scholar in the Class of 1858, although he and his classmates knew that his actual rank for all his terms remained thirty-fourth, or very near that.

A few days later, a new scale went through the mail to the seniors' parents. The new scale was a forgery. It purported to be a General Scale of the Class of 1858, reflecting all the points earned by the seniors while they were freshmen, sophomores, and juniors. Based on the official Annual Scale, the forged General Scale turned the official one around. On the new list, all the better seniors, who earlier had appeared in order of rank on the left-hand page, were hurled together in alphabetical opprobrium on the right-hand page. All the worse students, who earlier had been massed promiscuously on the right-hand page, were given spurious ranks and raised to glory on the left-hand page. Two dunces in the class, Cobb and Eliot, were lifted in this way to eminence as co-holders of rank No. 1.[27]

News of the exploit spread and made a sensation. Who had performed it was a matter of deep suspicion, intense speculation, and varying conjecture. A senior, Gerard Tobey, later reminded the class of the exploit publicly, treated it as a principal event in the seniors' experience while in college, and attributed it to "a few members" of their own class, without naming names.[28] Also without naming names, Anderson attributed it privately to "some" of the lower-ranking seniors, who, he said, had resented the publication of their disgrace. At the same time, Nick described the forged list as "one of the wittiest burlesques" of academic proceedings that he had heard of, and "one of the most successful practical jokes I have ever known."[29]

As both Tobey and Anderson probably realized, the forged General Scale could not have been the work of any senior but a very talented one. Among the members of the Class of 1858, one only had the requisite combination of nerve, ability, and motive to carry it off. That was Adams, and the fact that he had authored the forgery was not concealed from the president and faculty. On the contrary, it was there before their eyes, in cold print.

If they would merely look at the forgery, persons at Harvard sooner or later could see that the forger, by alphabetizing the names of the *better* students and moving them to the right-hand page of his felonious General Scale, had, in effect, given them spurious ranks as well, and had given the first three ranks to Adams, Allen, and Anderson, in that order. Vertically arranged, the names stared at the reader from the forged sheet of paper:

Adams
C. A. Allen
Anderson

The chief gainer by the arrangement was Adams—raised on paper to the top of his class. Henry, in short, not only forged the General Scale but, in public, defiantly signed it.[30]

All the while, during recitations and at other times on the campus, he was plainly visible to the teachers, almost all of whom knew him, or knew who he was and a good deal about him. As the teachers could see, he was exhibiting a new kind of behavior. He had ceased doing his lessons with uniform care and attention. He was cutting recitations and prayers, especially prayers, at a rate which would earn him a phenomenal deduction of points. Soon his misconduct became consistently flagrant. He was "privately" admonished for "smoking in the Yard," for "calling up to a college window under aggravating circumstances," for "smoking in the Yard" a second time, and for "lounging in the Chapel."[31] If things went as they were going, he promised to drop before graduation from the enumerated upper half of his class to the alphabetized lower half. Were that to happen, the same transfer of his name from left to right which had occurred on the two scales mailed to the seniors' parents at the start of term would be repeated in the College's authentic scales for his class.

Henry was not accused of forging the criminal list. Among the reasons for the college authorities' failure to act, two could be conjectured with confidence. The forgery had been so contrived that the authorities could suspect that one student, Adams, or two students, Adams and Allen, or three students, Adams, Allen, and Anderson, had been its authors. Listed together in Henry's devilish burlesque, the three names made a difficult puzzle, and the authorities were wary of attempting to solve it. Moreover, were they to accuse all three, or just Adams and Allen, or Adams alone, and were the accused sufficiently brazen to claim total innocence, the accusation might be construed on the campus as part of a faculty attempt to dodge the still-unsettled question of a proposed, large student club—meaning also the question of Adams's petition with its fifty-three signatures and Allen's long paper titled "Considerations" with all its reasons.

The president and faculty at the same time were placed under the strongest pressure to act. The unpunished exploit had been conducted with almost revolutionary impudence and address. Not only had the forged General Scale been printed in such a way as to look absolutely authentic; it had been printed in Boston by a firm on Washington Street accustomed to doing work for the college; the firm had sent the bursar a bill for the job; and the gentlemanly bursar, not dreaming that the job had been foisted upon the printer by a marplot, had paid the bill as soon as rendered. The marplot, too, had brought about the publication of the General Scale in the Boston newspapers as if it were bona fide news. Worst of all, he had aimed his blow at a contrivance, the Scale of Merit, which the college authorities had been holding up to public notice for a generation as a proof of their competence as educators, although in the privacy of their own councils they had often suspected it of being a proof instead of their well-meaning folly. In the last analysis, the blow struck against the authorities had been justified; they knew it; and they were even said to admit it. President Walker was later quoted on the campus as having declared at the time that he "hoped the faculty would never again attempt to publish a rank list."[32]

The forged list was mailed to parents and the October 1857 issue of the *Harvard Magazine* was published at roughly the same moment. The lead article in the issue, titled "Reading in College," was written by Adams. With a perfectly straight face, in all his beginning paragraphs, Henry treated the curriculum and disciplinary system at Harvard as things sure to benefit every student, and treated himself as merely another college man—explaining, however, that college men were not men but "invariably most exceeding boys." He had prepared to write his newest article by studying "the entry-books of our various [student] libraries," presumably including the ledgers of the now-extinct Greek-letter fraternities' libraries. He thus was able to speak with assurance about what students at the college were actually reading, apart from readings assigned to them in their courses; and he proceeded to name the authors most turned to by students in their leisure hours.

In such an essay, before he was done, Adams was sure to come out in the open. Forthrightly, in his second-to-last paragraph, he criticized his fellow students at Harvard for failure to attempt anything serious in the way of self-education or even mere independent reading. "There are not . . . twenty students in College who ever read, of their own accord, fifty pages of Homer, or Euripides, or AEschylus, or Demosthenes, or Cicero, either translated or untranslated. The number of those who appreciate or even like the classics is absurdly small. It is so too with modern languages, or nearly so. English literature is the bound, and even in English literature, little except the lightest and the most common portion is at all known. The fishes all swim on the surface, and neither dare nor wish to go deeper.''

His classmates looked carefully at his "Reading in College" and told him he was conceited. Adams agreed. Alluding to such encounters, he wrote a few months later: "I have usually considered myself a conceited fellow. Every one told me so, and I believed 'em.''[33]

Since others had raised the subject, he wrote an article about conceited people which Allen and his coeditors published as the featured article in the *Magazine*'s December issue. Its Greek title could be translated as "The Vanity of Authors." Coolly facing his classmates Henry said, "Men take a natural, but a very malicious and ungenerous, pleasure in picking holes in each other's characters, and hunting for foibles, as trained dogs hunt for truffles.'' He ventured that there were instances in which conceit "may not only be pardoned, but admired; in which it shows proper confidence and dignity and loftiness of mind." Naming two famous scientists who had worked revolutions in human knowledge, Kepler and Buffon, he noted that both had been conceited, gave samples of their conceited writings, and suggested that the self-esteem of genius was "something that we dare not ridicule."

His December article, the sixth he had published, was probably intended by Henry to be the last of his writings to appear in the *Magazine*. Its essential subject was not conceit but greatness. He seemed to say that, if he had to choose, he would dispense with the company of his fellow students at the college, retain his self-esteem, and look for companions elsewhere, mostly among great minds. His pages were amusing, in places very comical, but laughter would only echo what he was driving at. He brandished an aphorism: "The defects of great men are the consolation of dunces." The dunces he was thinking of were his classmates, from whom he was drifting away.

The underlying meaning of his new behavior was double. He did not think himself educated, and he had adopted a settled philosophy of education from which he would never recede. His philosophy reflected his long experience as a would-be learner. School, including Harvard, had taught him comparatively little; his fellow collegians had taught him less than he had hoped and wished; independent inquiry had taught him relatively much; and, lead where it might, he had decided to follow the path of self-education. This did not mean he would leave the college. No, he would conform to the faculty's requirements sufficiently to graduate as expected. Neither did it mean that he would try to dispense with teachers; he would need and be glad to have them, in many instances; but he would try to take charge of his own education completely, including the finding of teachers.

Left to his own devices, he had tended to show certain peculiarities as a learner. One was willingness, even eagerness, to read the writings of women. The books he borrowed from the Hasty Pudding library in August had included George Sand's *Consuelo*, in French.[34] He owned and was intermittently reading the poems of Elizabeth Barrett Browning, in three beautifully bound volumes, given to him by Hunnewell as a present.[35] Another peculiarity of Henry's was eagerness to burden his memory. He learned Poe's "Raven" by heart—learned it so well that in later years, to the delight of his little nieces, he would recite the thing in its entirety without hesitation.[36]

As a supplement to their course work, seniors were permitted to attend lectures by members of the faculty on special subjects. Henry elected to hear a series of lectures on geology and palaeontology by Professor Louis Agassiz. Ironically, the lectures were given in Holden Chapel, perhaps in the same space fifty-three seniors had petitioned the faculty to set aside for a new, useful club. Professor Agassiz simply talked. He made no one recite, gave no examinations, meted out neither points nor deductions of points. He explained some original discoveries he had made about a great glacier, or series of glaciers, which in very ancient times had descended from the Pole and covered much of North America, including the site of Harvard College. Listening intently, one of Agassiz's hearers experienced something verging on revelation. Young Adams perceived with a jolt that, although he had taken courses on scientific subjects, he really knew nothing whatever of science—that an ocean of scientific inquiry lay open for him, onto which he never had sailed.[37]

In his time, John Quincy Adams had been deeply interested in the sciences. Learning in the autumn of 1857 that his third son, too, had grown interested in science, Charles Francis Adams thought of a way to help him. On New Year's Day, 1858, he gave Henry a magnificent set of the writings of Francis Bacon. No gesture by the father towards any of his children could have been more thoughtful and sympathetic.[38]

The college authorities evidently never responded to Adams's petition and Allen's "Considerations." While waiting for the answer that never came, Henry completed his labor as Hasty Pudding Librarian and again acted in a play.[39] At the club's semiannual celebration, on January 15, 1858, perhaps as a stand-in for another member who was intended to speak but could not do so, he gave the Oration. It was so well received by the members who heard it that Allen and his associate editors seized the manuscript and later published part of it in the *Magazine* under the title "The Cap and Bells."[40] Not oratorical in style, but instead relaxed and decidedly quiet, Adams's words took as their point of departure the device on the ring he was wearing and what the device meant to him. "This cap and bells," he said, "does not mean weakness of intellect, and it does not mean want of courage." Along the way in his speech, without clearly intending to, he showed he had been affected by his experiences reading Shakespeare, whose tragedies he seemed to feel he could understand. It was notable that he should speak of Hamlet's madness as "half-real." It was interesting that he should explain, "King Lear's jester was wiser than his master,—wiser than that train of one hundred knights who left their unhappy master to the mercy of the storm. . . ."

Except that he was part of the time at his parents' house on Mount Vernon Street, his whereabouts during the winter vacation in 1858 cannot be traced. After returning to Cambridge for their last term, on the afternoon of March 15, the seniors met to elect their class officers. Adams was not at the meeting. He had gone for some reason to Boston and did not return to the campus till evening.

According to some remarks later published in the *Magazine,* the senior elections "passed off with remarkable good feeling."[41] Allen, who was elected class secretary, kept detailed notes concerning the voting.

The chief officer to be chosen was the class orator. Five candidates for the place received votes on a preliminary ballot, a merely informal one. Adams led with twenty-nine votes, a strong beginning.

There were eighty-one seniors present, and forty-one votes would be needed to win. The first formal ballot gave Adams thirty-five votes. A second formal ballot, in which he seemed to have garnered forty-two votes, was declared illegal. More votes had been counted than there were seniors present.

A third formal ballot gave Adams thirty-nine. His nearest rival, George Pond, had risen to thirty-six. One other candidate was still in the race.

Four seniors left the meeting. When a fourth ballot was cast, Adams again received thirty-nine votes, and his supporters now made a majority. All his backers had stayed till the finish.

So, in Allen's words in the official record, " . . . Mr. Adams was declared elected."[42]

When he came back to the campus in the evening, Adams was told that he had been elected class orator. The news caught him unprepared, and he was staggered and overcome. He thought his election a "miracle."[43]

The place his classmates had given him was the highest distinction within the power of the Harvard students to confer on one of their own number. In the eyes of the students, their families, the faculty, and the public, it was the highest honor a student could win at the college.

Adams said in his later years that, of all the judges he ever faced, the surest and most impartial had been his college classmates.[44] The Class of 1858 was not distinguished. Adams excepted, it contained not one person who would be famous a century later. Nonetheless, its members were intelligent, and while in college they felt they could fairly evaluate each other as easily as they could look through windows. In his absence, they freely elected one of their number class orator at a meeting undisturbed by hostilities or rancor. Adams's election was not a miracle but a result of his classmates' best judgments.

His election was also a result of a three-and-a-half year campaign by one of the seniors to win the place, with the unusual difference that the campaigner, a member of a great political family, had campaigned without knowing that that was what he was doing. Yet, in the back of his mind, he must have known it. From the time he first heard of the office, when only a boy, he had wanted to be elected class orator at the college. One could almost say he had come to Harvard for no other purpose. In his second year, he had seen Gibbons die. In his third, he had witnessed the eclipse of Lee's popularity. Had the election meeting been held in March 1857, instead of March 1858, Anderson would have been a hard candidate to defeat. In the interval a shift had occurred, and it was probable that a Democrat could no longer have won. Anderson sensed it and said that his "ambition for such offices" had vanished.[45] Pond was a fine scholar, but class orator was not a scholarly, academic distinction. Political and literary, it perfectly corresponded to Adams's ambitions to succeed completely as a politician and succeed also, perhaps equally, as a writer. Possibly better than any other distinction then open to an American, in youth or age, this one distinction would confirm him in the faith that his ambitions were justified and should not be given up. His classmates had not known that he needed encouragement. He had needed it, almost desperately; and they, at the critical hour, had found a means to provide it.

## 5 / *Departure*

Adams's election had a saving effect on his life. No sooner was he elected, in mid-March 1858, than he decided what he would do after graduating in July. This decision was probably the most important he would ever make, for purposes of his own development.

Had he not been elected class orator at the college, he might have tried to do what he was wished to do by his father, and conceivably ruined himself and passed into oblivion. C. F. Adams wanted all his sons without exception to do what he believed he had done: gone to Harvard, qualified to practice law by clerking in a well-established law office in Boston, married, and demonstrated sound business habits. That the father could speak French and had spent parts of his life in Russia, France, England, and other foreign countries was immaterial and irrelevant, in his opinion. What Mr. Adams wanted— and he was willing to say so—was sons with good characters, good wives, and growing families.

His elder sons had obliged him. John was currently a practicing lawyer in Boston; that is, when he was not wandering off with a rod to go fishing. Charles would soon complete his clerkship and win admission to the Massachusetts bar. Henry came next, and what was right for his elder brothers was assumed to be right for him, but the third son was troubled by an obvious question.[1] Supposing that he did what the Governor wished, would there be room in Boston for three sons of the Adams family, all lawyers, each hanging out a shingle to attract streams of clients? In a boom town, room might be thought to exist for five or ten young Adamses who were lawyers. Boston at the moment was the very reverse of a boom town. Following the excitement of the Panic of 1857, the city seemed to be falling asleep.[2]

This did not mean that Henry would not study law in Boston. He would, just as soon as he could. But first he would do what he believed he *had* to do first: learn to speak fluently at least two languages other than English.

A sure way to learn to speak languages, it seemed, was to go to Europe and live on the Continent for a considerable interval. This way for Henry was impossible. His father would absolutely oppose it. The Governor liked to say that one of his classmates at the college, Alleyne Otis, had gone to Europe after graduating and had come home an ass. That Otis might also have been an ass before going to Europe was not an idea that Mr. Adams was willing to contemplate. For him, it was a fixed moral principle that, for Harvard graduates, travel and study in Europe were doorways to degeneration and incurable folly. He intended that his sons should stay home.[3]

Borne up by his election, Henry intended to do the impossible. He would go just where he was wished not to go. He foresaw a crisis, a moment when his and his father's conflict would come into the open and a contest of wills would occur. He expected that the crisis could be deferred until late July or August, in Quincy, after his graduation, when he would be back at the Old House. Meanwhile, in Cambridge, he would prepare for the critical moment with all possible thoroughness.

If the success of Henry's design were to turn upon his father's opinion of his character—and his father put much stock in rank at the college as an index of character— the third son would have done well not to think of his bold design in the first place; either that or reform. During the past term, as a starting senior, he had been awarded only 1792 points for academic achievement. From this total, the faculty had subtracted no less than 328 points for misconduct, leaving him with a net gain of 1464. And Henry did not mean to reform. He had embarked upon the interesting process of *lowering* his rank on the Scale of Merit and, having started, would not turn back.

The new term, his last, would show that Henry could lower his rank with remarkable sureness. For reasons now impossible to trace, he would twice be absent from a whole week of recitations. This would help him hold down the points he earned in his courses to 1673. He would carefully accumulate penalties totaling 280 points, including a "public," or 64 points, for cutting more than 20 prayers. By these means, he would reduce his rank to forty-fourth, out of 89 scholars. He evidently was aiming as a senior to reach the exact middle of his class, forty-fifth, and he would come close enough to that ideal not to be sorry he did not achieve it.

Among the living Adamses, there was one who might be sympathetic to Henry's design, his elder sister; but whether he and Louisa had been regularly in touch with each other is unknown, and whether he would tell her about his intention in advance of winning his contest with their father and getting permission to go abroad seems very unlikely. Loo had married in 1854, the same year Henry had started his course at Harvard. She had gone with her husband, a wealthy Philadelphian, Charles Kuhn, to live in New York. A child she had borne had shortly died, and the loss had aggravated her continual restlessness. In the winter of 1857-1858, she was contemplating a long stay with her husband in Europe, where she wanted to travel.[4]

Four weeks before Henry's election at the college, during his winter vacation, a party was given by Mrs. Charles Francis Adams in Boston "for her daughter Mrs. Kuhn." One of the guests that evening at the house on Mount Vernon Street was Henry's classmate Ben Crowninshield, who mentioned the party in his private journal.[5] What his brief entry in his journal failed to mention was that, although given for Louisa Kuhn, the party was held on Henry's twentieth birthday, February 16, 1858. The fact showed awareness among the Adamses that Loo and Henry, whatever their differences, were in some sense united and belonged together.

When he saw her in February, Henry and his married sister had taken extremely dissimilar paths. He had turned his life into a succession of complex plans and multiple efforts. Mrs. Kuhn had no apparent ambition except to enjoy being well-to-do. The Kuhns were much given to fashion and society. They presumably told him they were going abroad and may have known their itinerary. At the time, his own decision to go had not been made. A month later, when he made his decision, the prospect of their departure—they would be sailing in May—possibly seemed to him a portent of his own success.

The principal means Henry wished to use to overcome his father's resistance was to get his friends at the college to make plans to go to Europe and study languages, so that he could use their plans as justifications of his own. For social purposes, as a senior, he belonged to a group of nine classmates who habitually banded together. Eight of the nine came from Boston and nearby communities. In addition to Adams, Ben Crowninshield, and Ben's roomate Louis Cabot, the eight included Josiah Bradlee, Ozias Goodwin, John Homans, William Milton, and Daniel Payne. The ninth friend, and only representative of other parts of the country, was Anderson.[6] For ordinary purposes, the group's leaders were Adams, Anderson, and Crowninshield. Were he to wish it, for some exceptional reason, Adams could exert a subtle but controlling mastery over most or all of the fellowship.

The previous December, Anderson had mentioned in a letter to his mother, "Father says I should study law whether I practice it or not . . . . " Having repeated his father's opinion as something not to be challenged, Nick had gone on to explain that he seemed to face a three-way choice. "Shall I . . . enter the Law School [at Harvard], or shall I first study a year in an office [in Cincinnati], or shall I recruit for a short time my wearied mind?" His letter had said nothing about Europe or languages. Yet two weeks after Adams's election, on March 29, 1858, Nick would write very differently. He would tell his mother, "Quite a deputation will be sent from my class to polish off in the elegant cities of Europe, and obtain that knowledge of the modern languages so necessary in the present age." He might better have predicted that a large deputation would be sent to Europe by the informal fraternity he had helped to make up; for by then, of its nine members, no less than five—Adams, Anderson, Bradlee, Cabot, and Crowninshield—were thinking of learning languages by going to Europe.[7]

The invention of photography had encouraged recent classes to have themselves photographed and give each other prints, so that, before graduation, every senior could assemble a book of his friends' pictures, autographed. The Class of 1858 followed the precedent. At some moment during his last term, Adams submitted himself to the photographers, Whipple and Black, who took an excellent picture of him, the earliest that survives, and one of the best ever made. According to later evidence, his hair in early life was brown, perhaps with a trace of red or chestnut. In the photograph taken that spring, his hair looked dark. His expression could be described as watchful, resolved, and somewhat defiant. By any standard, he was good looking.[8]

Allen, as class secretary, was charged with the duty of assembling a "Life-Book" of the class, containing not only photographs of its members but also each member's brief autobiography. Written in the last weeks of the term, the autobiographies could be read for any evidences they contained of Henry's success in persuading his friends to go abroad.. On that score, their testimony remained very mixed. Cabot, for instance, said his plans were too "unsettled" for him to describe them. Crowninshield said only, "I have not yet decided what I shall do after leaving college. . . . " Anderson alone went so far as to outline a definite plan. "In September I leave for Europe to devote a year or so to the study of French and German." Adams himself, when he wrote his autobiography, a carefully worded statement nine paragraphs long, had no way of knowing whether he would go to Europe,

Henry's grandmother, Louisa Catherine Adams, at age twenty-two.
Painting by James Thomas Barber-Beaumont. *The Cincinnati Art Museum.*

Henry Adams as a senior at Harvard College

and, if he wished, could have thought of various reasons to believe his friends might go without him. He managed all the same to take a confident tone, as if his going were almost assured. ". . . it is probable that I shall soon go to Europe, where I hope and expect to work harder than I have ever worked at Harvard. My immediate object is to become a scholar, and master of more languages than I pretend to know now."[9]

Henry and Ben were studying Italian within the formal curriculum under one of the instructors, Luigi Monti. Of the modern languages he had studied, Henry evidently liked Italian the best. Had he been free to shape his future in any way he pleased, he probably would have wanted to learn *three* languages in Europe and would have gone first to Florence or Rome. To work well, such a plan would have required his staying abroad for three years. As he thought about his situation, he grew certain that the longest absence he could try for would be two years; and he resolved to get permission to be away every month of that time; but also he became interested in possible ways of fitting three countries, Italy, France, and Germany, into a well-planned two-year program.[10]

When Henry first decided to go abroad, he and Ben were far enough advanced in Italian to be anxious to study Dante. They were attending lectures on poetry given by a teacher recently added to the faculty, James Russell Lowell—lectures similar to those given by Agassiz in the fall term, at least in being outside the formal curriculum. A young man, Lowell was already a famous poet. As Harvard's new professor of Modern Belles Lettres, he felt his teaching responsibilities keenly and was partly meeting them in a novel way. He had invited some of the seniors to join him in his study at his home, Elmwood, near the campus. Adams and Crowninshield were invited and jumped at the chance to go. They went chiefly to read Dante in Italian under Lowell's friendly guidance.[11]

To suit himself for his post, Professor Lowell had tried to learn to speak modern languages by going to Europe. During the winter of 1855-1856, he had lived with a family in Dresden named Reichenbach. While staying at their house, he had written in his customary, humorous way to President Walker at Harvard: ". . . I get along slowly enough. I hope . . . to come home in the summer speaking English tolerably & four other languages like a native—of some other country." The four languages he had studied were German, French, Italian, and Spanish. His success in learning to speak them had been far from complete. He warned the president, ". . . I shall be able to read them all as easily as English, which is the most important thing for me, & I shall do my best not to disgrace a professorship in which I have been preceded by Ticknor & Longfellow."[12]

At convenient moments that spring, Henry talked with Professor Lowell not only about the difficulties Americans seemed to experience learning to speak foreign languages but also about Lowell's travels. It seems very probable, almost certain, that he learned directly from Lowell about a long journey he had made from Dresden to Naples and thence to Sicily. He confided to Lowell that he, too, wished to study languages and travel in Europe, beginning that autumn. Their conversations led to the professor's making the suggestion—which Henry till then had hardly considered—that a good plan might be to enroll at one of the German universities.[13]

As he thought about it, Henry saw that this unexpected advice involved an advantage. Because graduate schools in fields other than divinity, law, and medicine scarcely existed in the United States, American college graduates seeking careers in many professional fields almost had to attend schools in Europe, in the hope of getting properly started. By the same token, if a fellow could just think of a right career for himself, he could acquire a very logical and possibly plausible reason for leaving the country and remaining a long while abroad. It happened, too, that the German universities were numerous and very highly regarded. If it came to that, and he had to choose one, Henry wondered which it would be.

Class day at the college was understood by the students to be the chief occasion of their four-year course and the one day in the year when everyone on the campus was encouraged to have a good time.[14] The duty of the class orator was to speak that day before a large audience—the president and faculty, other dignitaries, the seniors themselves, and their families and guests—as the chief representative of the seniors, selected by them. Similarly, it was the duty of the class poet to read an appropriate original poem.

The great day in 1858, June 25, was distressingly hot. The temperature rose to 90 degrees in the shade, without a sign of a breeze. A large but suffering throng crowded into the Unitarian Church and listened while Henry Adams gave an oration which Ben Crowninshield thought "good" and George Noble read a poem which Ben pronounced "splendid."

With the help of engraved cards earlier sent to their families, young women they liked, and other persons, the nine members of the informal fraternity Ben and Henry belonged to served a lavish spread of refreshments after the ceremony, in the south entry of Hollis. An east wind came up at three in the afternoon; the temperature fell a little; and all the seniors and their feminine counterparts held a dance which Crowninshield remembered as a "good, simon pure, real" affair lasting as much as two hours. Then the seniors marched around the campus in front of everyone, cheered each of the buildings, and ended by singing "Auld Lang Syne." The festivities continued. In the evening, the Yard was "brilliantly and beautifully illuminated" with vari-colored lanterns. President Walker and Professor Lowell threw open the doors of their houses to all persons who might wish to enter.[15]

Compared to other class orations given at Harvard, the one Adams had given was perhaps no better than Crowninshield said it was. It was certainly striking. Speaking with calm self-possession, Henry had explained the history of class day. He had said that the Class of 1858 was thoroughly average and ordinary. He foresaw that its members would be satisfied in life if they could make some money and take respected places in their communities. ". . . we expect from the future none of those brilliant prizes that men talk of so much. We recognize in our ranks no Newton or Napoleon, no heroes or martyrs, no demi-gods and no demons."

Young Adams had so written the oration that he could speak in it for his class, for himself, and also for Gibbons, so that the dead New Yorker could live again, for a brief time, near the close of their course. Henry told the audience that thirty scholars who joined the class at one time or another had been unable to finish, and that two had died, including one who "should have been speaking to you at this moment."

As he brought his words towards their close, the orator reversed himself dramatically. He predicted, after all, that among the seniors a few would be extremely ambitious. ". . . these at least," he foretold, "will still have trust in what they were taught to think the noblest ambitions that are permitted to man. . . ."[16]

The class secretary had requested the seniors to include in their autobiographies statements concerning their ambitions in life. During the four-week interval between class day and commencement, the seniors, taking turns, were able to read one another's autobiographies in the large, bound "Life-Book" they had completed together and in the process learn one another's professed long-run intentions. Because he was manifestly the member of the class most likely to attempt something notable in the future, the statements written by Adams were among those most likely to read by the class with attention; and if there was one question his classmates hoped his statements would answer, it was probably whether or not he intended to go into national politics.

Three sentences in Adams's autobiography related partly or entirely to his long-run ambitions. The first of the three could seem thoroughly forthright. "My wishes are for a quiet and a literary life, as I believe that to be the happiest and in this country not the least useful." If the first appeared to be written by Adams the writer, the second could seem to be written by Adams the politician. It was half-composed of a qualified prediction and half-composed of an asserted fact. ". . . it is most probable that I shall study and practise law, but where and to what extent is as yet undecided." The two sentences would each be misleading unless they were read together. In one voice, Henry had openly said he would try to become a notable writer. In another voice, he had guardedly said he would probably become a notable politician. At least his second sentence would be taken that way, for in the United States the practice of law was the usual prerequisite and antechamber of a career in politics, and aspiring politicians were expected to speak of their ambitions in guarded voices.

His third sentence was possibly the most worthy of careful notice. It concerned both his recent past and his entire future. "At the beginning of the last term, my Class-mates elected me as their Orator for our Class Day; a compliment which pleased and gratified me more than any other which I ever received, or probably, ever shall receive."[17] Adams was not an unthinking writer, and he could not say anything suggestive, subtle, or enigmatic without knowing what he wished to imply. His last five words—"or, probably, ever shall receive"—could be taken to have four different possible implications. The words could be taken to mean that Henry the politician expected to seek *elective* offices but assumed that, when election days came, he would probably lose. They could be taken to mean that Henry the politician would seek *appointive* offices, which, in time, could include very high ones, such as those in the cabinet. And equally they could be taken to be a prophecy that he would seek a career in politics but would make it an unusual, wholly atypical one, which might be important but which would gain him small recognition, or none at all, while he lived. But also they could be seen to imply that, after all, he would avoid a career in politics and content himself with being a writer only, and perhaps a workaday lawyer. Which of these implications he had intended when he wrote the words, his other writings of the time did not make clear.

The only dependable guide to his meaning would be his actions, both in the near and the further future.

At commencement on July 21, Adams was awarded his degree as a bachelor of arts. He completed the removal of his possessions to the Old House at Quincy. Roughly at the same moment, he learned that his intention to go abroad would meet much stronger resistance from his father than he had previously estimated. Charles Francis Adams was far from being an easy man to oppose. Not impetuous like John Adams, nor aggressive like John Quincy Adams, he nonetheless could show phenomenal combative abilities when he thought he was being lied to, pushed, or otherwise obliged to fall back on defensive tactics.

Just then, the father's affairs were hanging in the balance. He was hoping to become the Republican candidate for Congress in the Third Massachusetts District, surrounding Quincy. If made the candidate, he would certainly be elected in November; but another able Republican in the district, George S. Russell, was also seeking the candidacy; and the issue remained in doubt.

Henry revised the plan he meant to propose. Also he decided to speak first to both his parents together. Their conversation, which presumably occurred in late July, was one of the most important Henry would ever take part in, for his own harm and good.[18] The things he told his father and mother can be reconstructed from later testimony with reasonable sureness. He explained that he wanted to go to Europe for two years and would need an allowance of $1,000 a year, which would cover all his expenses, including his passage both ways across the Atlantic.[19] He further explained that, after returning from Europe, he would study law for two years in an office, take the bar examination, and seek ways to practice his profession; but he emphasized that he wished to become a "jurist"—a learned expert and writer on legal subjects. It was with this eventuality in mind that he needed first to go abroad. While in Europe, he would study civil law, meaning chiefly Roman law, at three universities, at Berlin, Heidelberg, and Paris. Along the way, while attending lectures at the universities, he would improve his command of languages, expecially German and French.[20]

The conversation was so close a thing that Henry resorted to lies. He said he would go to three universities; but he knew he would not go to any—not to Berlin, nor to Heidelberg, nor to Paris. His patience with formal schools of higher learning had expired. Also deceptive was his failure to explain and emphasize that his controlling motive in going abroad was to learn to *speak* German and French. He failed entirely to mention that, in addition, he wanted to travel—to be in Europe just to be there, move around, and see as much of it as he could possibly manage. His statement that he aimed in the long run to become a jurist was a deception and subterfuge but could become a truth if he would someday learn so much about law as to be a jurist, self-taught, among his other accomplishments.

His lies were at least partly excusable as responses to extreme and unwarranted family pressure. In the crisis, when his fate was in his hands and a mistake would be disastrous, he would be asked by his father what he wanted to do in life. Silence would not be possible. The son would have to reply. He could *not* reply that he was extremely ambitious and wanted to succeed completely as a politician and very considerably as a writer. To do so would be to convict himself on the spot of harboring inappropriate wishes. Among the living Adamses, it was permissible for the Governor to have political hopes, and for his eldest son to have them also; but second, third, and fourth sons were expected *not* to have political hopes.[21] As for becoming a writer, in the sense of writing things the public would delight in, as well as find instructive, such an ambition, in the Governor's view, would only seem unbusinesslike and lacking in weight and sobriety. But Henry *could* say he was ambitious to become a jurist. The history of law was one of his actual interests. As soon as he could get around to it, he would learn a great deal about the subject, by teaching himself. Previous Adamses, conspicuously John Adams, had steeped themselves in the history of law. Roman law was a subject best studied in Europe, where one could get the requisite books; and courses on civil law *were* available at the universities Henry had listed—for persons willing to hear the lectures. Finally a preference for going first to Prussia to study for a while in Berlin had a sober, responsible sound.

A man of principle, C. F. Adams could be won away from his principles only if two conditions were met. One was the allegation of exceptional circumstances, and the other was discovery of a special reason. As things fell out, Henry was befriended by circumstances. It was a point in his favor that Loo and her husband were already in Europe and could help him on his arrival, if help were needed. It was even more in his favor that he had often been viewed by Bostonians as more a son of his mother's than his father's, and more a Brooks than an Adams. Apparently in this spirit, some of his classmates at the College had called him "Old Brooks," a nickname possibly learned from his mother.[22] Such a pattern of error was ironic but helpful; for the

Brookses, unlike the Adamses in recent decades, Loo excepted, were travelers when they could be, and currently were always rushing off to Europe, mostly in search of what they thought to be their elusive health.[23]

The disease of going abroad had luckily been contracted by Henry's father. Feeling somewhat unwell, the Governor had been talking of a curative trip of his own.[24] Then, too, Henry's mother had been horrified by a seeming near-complication between her cherished third son and a young woman his own age in Boston. Foolishly, for a long time, Henry had been going about with "Carry" Bigelow, who was of course a nice person, but who did not strike Mrs. Adams as a suitable person for Henry to marry by the wildest stretch of a mother's imagination. The boy admittedly was in the process of learning that he cared not a straw for Miss Bigelow, nor she for him; but Mrs. Adams meant to take no chances. Whatever dangers Henry might face in the allegedly depraved capitals of Europe seemed to her much less threatening than the peril of mistaken commitments at home. She wanted him to get away until he might be old enough to know whom to marry.[25]

Her husband for a time was adamant that Henry could not possibly go. There was a momentary impasse. Then the Governor himself discovered the special reason. He remembered his third son's character, which was good, and the boy's exceptional resolution. Thus the matter was settled. Henry would leave and be gone for two years. But the father remained aware that his rules had been broken. Later, remembering with a twinge of discomfort the moment in Quincy when his consent had been given, he would write to Henry in Europe, "Nothing but my confidence in your native uprightness [,] aided by my remembrance of your strength of will [,] would have induced me to vary from my former conviction so far as to let you go."[26]

The elder Adams was right in thinking Henry honest. In proportion to the depth of his passion to adhere to the truth, the son would be wounded by having lied—and to his father. He *was* wounded, very deeply; and, in the absence of anything positive being done to heal it, the wound seemed likely to rankle for an indefinite period.[27]

Having won his way, the son stayed quietly in Quincy through August and most of September. He kept in touch by mail with his Harvard friends who had said they would go to Europe. Soon four out of the five in their deputation—Adams, Anderson, Cabot, and Crowninshield—were agreed that they should go on the same ship. Bradlee planned to sail separately.

While waiting to depart, Henry used some of his days at the Old House to catalogue his own collection of books, which had grown to about 220 volumes, an exceptional number.[28] He and his mother looked into the problem of suitable clothes and a trunk. At last, on Monday, September 27, 1858, he walked with his parents to the Quincy station, said good-bye, and sped away on his train. With Nick, Ben, and Louis, he devoted Tuesday night in New York to last revels in America.[29] At noon on Wednesday, they sailed for Liverpool on the *Persia,* pride of the Cunard Line, the largest and fastest steamship afloat.[30]

## 6 / Siberia

Three days out from New York, the *Persia* was intercepted by a late-summer hurricane which accompanied the vessel most of the way to Liverpool. The ship docked at 2:00 A.M. on October 10. Crowninshield described the crossing as "rough and tedious." Adams remembered it all his life as his first experience of being continuously seasick. The four friends had divergent itineraries and, partly for that reason, made an agreement that they would meet six weeks later for Thanksgiving dinner, a plan they carried out at Magdeburg, Germany. Meanwhile, Anderson went at once to London and across the Channel. Adams, Cabot, and Crowninshield—together with Henry's cousin, Shepherd Brooks, who had chanced to be a fellow passenger on the ship—went only as far as Chester. At nearby Eaton Hall, a great English country house, Adams formed his first strong impressions of Europe.

A week in London multiplied his impressions. Separating from his cousin and Cabot, he and Crowninshield took the steamer *Baron Osy* to Antwerp, went by rail to Cologne, and thence to Hannover. There at midnight on Thursday, October 21, 1858, Adams started for Berlin alone. American students in Berlin tended to converge at banks, where they could get money and mail, and at the U. S. legation, where Minister Wright, a friendly man, encouraged them to read the legation's copies of American newspapers. By falling in with such students on reaching the city, Henry could easily rent a room near the university and hire a tutor to visit him and teach him German. He evidently made both arrangements immediately on arriving.

Much later, in his *Education*, he would say that his first lecture at the University of Berlin was his last, as if he had gone to one; but no contemporary evidence has been found that he ever set foot within the university's buildings. He left such diversions as much as possible to Anderson, who visited Berlin, and to a cheerful Boston friend of long standing, James Jackson Higginson, who was there and proved an invaluable help to Henry in combating low spirits.

By prearrangement Adams was visited in Berlin by Louisa and Charles Kuhn. Loo did not approve of her brother's behavior. She perhaps did not mind his having started a full beard on leaving Quincy—Higginson's beard was even fuller and longer; but she emphatically did not think that Henry belonged in Berlin. She and her husband took him to art galleries in the city and required him to appreciate engravings and paintings. The boy hardly knew what to think or feel in the presence of such masterpieces. "Lord! Such engravings!" was all he seemed able to say. The Kuhns were going to Dresden, then to Paris, and Loo in all seriousness invited Henry to join them. He had mentally prepared himself to stay in Berlin at least through the winter, had ordered some heavier clothes, and bought a good lamp. Still, he could not deny that the Prussian capital seemed inhospitable and forbidding. He looked at his chosen city through a gray November drizzle and wondered what he should do. Although sorely tempted to leave, he declined his sister's invitation, saw the Kuhns off on their train, and returned to his lodgings.

At some moment along the way, Adams and Anderson had quarreled again, or started to differ. In the future, they would still be friendly but would not try to do things together, even when opportunity offered. If one or the other were the more anxious to separate, it was Henry, who, in November, without giving reasons, said of Nick, " . . . I shall see very little of him."

Crowninshield and Cabot had planned to stay in Hannover for a time, then come to Berlin. Ben was an excellent fellow, a superb athlete, quick scholar, and fine cellist. He liked Adams, valued his company, and when without it in Europe became very unsettled. On that account, Adams could look forward to having Crowninshield with him more often than not in the months ahead, but Henry was drawing away from all his fellow passengers on the *Persia*. A time would eventually come when he and Ben would part, on good terms. Thereafter, Henry would be free to take a course all his own.

A week after Henry left the Old House, on October 4, Mrs. Adams wrote him a letter and promised to write regularly. John, too, sent him a fraternal note. Charles, who had been away from Quincy when Henry left, started writing to him; and the Governor himself wrote on October 25.

The next day, Mrs. Adams was heartsick that no letters had yet come from Henry. She wept, not to have one. Her husband also was much affected by their prodigal's vanishing. In his first letter to the absentee, the father confessed that he missed Henry "much more than I had anticipated."

During the past two years, Charles and Henry had drifted so far apart that the second son had not so much as learned of the third's plan to escape to Europe until after Henry was gone. Looking into the matter, Charles discovered that his resourceful brother had been granted permission to study for two years in Europe, and would soon begin hearing lectures on civil law at the University of Berlin, in German, all on the pretext of intending to become a "jurist." Charles was himself completing his servitude as a clerk in a Boston law firm and would soon need only clients and a busy practice to make him a success. Something apparently told him he would never get the requisite clients. He wrote to Henry in part with the object of trying to pick up and tie the broken thread of their old relation. In his first letter, the elder brother was honest enough to say that he envied the younger's departure.[1]

When he received it, Henry felt the letter his brother had sent him as trouble-making and hard to answer. Charles had asked him to write back a detailed account of his intentions, both immediate and long-range. In effect, Charles wanted him to pass again through the fierce ordeal he had gone through at Quincy. Also it was from Charles that absent Henry got the news of their father's long-delayed political breakthrough. Helped by the obliging withdrawal of Mr. Russell, the Governor had become the Republican candidate in the district and was assured of election to Congress. The news was the best possible, but it subjected the third son to severe emotional pressure.

Of all the many letters Henry wrote to his relations in America that winter, six survive. All six were written to Charles, and all were important, but Henry started to write them more because he felt he had to answer than because he wanted to. The first reply he sent to Charles, now lost, must partly have concerned their father's good fortune. Henry could be counted on to smile and wish the Governor's victory at the polls would be great. Yet the absentee was far from happy about the timing of the family's political comeback. It would have been easier for the sons of the family if their father had been elected to Congress ten years earlier, in 1848, before his elder boys were grown up and brought face-to-face with their own political hopes. As a winner in national politics, C. F. Adams was making a very late start.

In his next letter, written in November, Henry explained to his brother that he had *two* plans for the immediate future. One, the plan he had outlined at Quincy, was to "accustom myself to the [German] language; then to join the University [of Berlin] and systematically attend lectures on the Civil Law, at the same time taking a Latin tutor and translating Latin into German; and to continue this course in Heidelberg or in Paris or in both." The other, which he told Charles had been the "original" plan, was confined to mere residence in Europe with the object of learning to read, write, hear, and speak as many languages as two years' effort might permit. Henry implied he would lean towards his original plan. ". . . I tell you now fairly," he burst out, "that if I return to America without doing more than learn German and French, I shall have done well, and these two years will be the best employed of my life."

As for eventual ways of making a living, the third son was not so obliging. Ironically, he said that his intentions were simple. "Two years in Europe; two years studying law in Boston; and then I propose to emigrate and practice at Saint Louis. What I can do there, God knows; but I have a theory that an educated and reasonably able man can make his mark if he chooses, and if I fail to make mine, why, then—I fail and that's all. I should do it anywhere else as well. But if I know myself, I can't fail." The statement that he would be a lawyer in far-off Missouri, of course, was Henry's way of saying that there was no place for him as a lawyer in Boston, and possibly no place for Charles.

Even more ironically, the third son touched upon the Adamses in relation to politics. Henry said that "all" the men in the family shared a "continual tendency" to become politicians and seek public office. "For my own ideas of my future," he added, "I have not admitted politics into them." But he further added that he might shift from a career as a practicing lawyer to a career as a public servant and office-holder if moved to do so by "irresistable [*sic*] reasons." In short, within the space of single letter, he both denied and predicted that he would someday be a politician.

The only plan of Henry's that greatly mattered was the one he was carrying out. It was not simple or long-range, but multiple and short-range. By coming to Europe, he was escaping the terrors of home, where too many Adamses, older and younger, all wanted to pass through too few political doors. He was seeing the world, indeed had seen more of the world in six weeks since leaving Quincy than in all his earlier years. He was learning to speak foreign languages, or at least was attempting to make a start. More generally, he was beginning an experiment in self-education. He fully intended to learn Roman law. He meant to learn whatever else might appeal to him, such as Heine's poetry, or Goethe's poetry and philosophy. The only limit on what he might learn would be imposed by lack of time, but two years would serve as four if he worked with a vengeance, as he wanted to do.

Walking one day on the Linden, in early December 1858, Henry was startled to see Charles Sumner riding by in a cab. Chasing after the statesman's vehicle, he succeeding in stopping it. Quickly he and Sumner exchanged accounts of themselves. The senator had recently tried to take up the full burden of his official duties and had suffered a relapse. He accordingly had come abroad for rest and strenuous medical treatments, administered by a doctor in Paris. That evening he was well enough to permit his and Henry's dining together and attending the opera. In the course of the evening, responding to the older man's inquiries, young Adams confessed that his progress learning to understand and speak German was alarmingly slow. They parted, and Sumner traveled to Montpelier in southern France. There he soon wrote a few lines of encouragement to Henry in Berlin, and asked him to convey a message to a Bostonian, a gentleman named Mr. Apthorp, who was passing the winter in Berlin for the sake of its music.[2]

Henry's meeting Sumner by chance on the Linden coincided with the arrival of the expected news from Massachusetts that the voters in the Third District had elected C. F. Adams to Congress and that the ten-year exile of the Adamses from public office had ended. The queer coming together of the meeting and the news threw Henry into a vortex of uncontrollable emotions.

The note Sumner had written to him from Montpelier reached Henry in Berlin. Young Adams's oldest feelings for his one-time friend revived. Yielding to his feelings, he tried a second time to do what he had failed to do two years earlier: persuade the antislavery hero to retire for a period from public life. He wrote outspokenly to the statesman in Montpelier, ". . . if you can recover in no other way, why not resign your seat and leave public life for two years; five years; ten years, if necessary, and devote your whole time to recovery[?]"

Young Adams suggested, moreover, that he and Sumner take a long, curative journey together. "If you will go and travel in Siberia," he offered, "I will leave German, Law, Latin and all, and go with you. . . ." In the same breath, he cried out against American national politics and "that bar-room of a Congress." He seemed to think of

Washington as a "City of Destruction" from which sane men would wisely flee. " . . . I might have supposed that [politics] . . . have done enough harm in destroying your health and happiness, but here is my father rushing into them and bent upon ruining not only our family comfort, but his own health in the pursuit." Lest Sumner think his offer to travel was not an earnest one, he insisted: " . . . I repeat my offer to you to go to Siberia. The climate, it is said, is remarkably fine and some of the scenery must be superb. I have got several thousand miles away from home orders, and might be in Tartary before my family knew I had left Berlin. That would be a journey worth making."[3]

Contrary feelings were driving Henry this way and that. He was elated by his father's election; he regretted his father's election; he was glad of being an Adams; he would have been happier to be anything else; he was thankful he was in Berlin; he wanted to go to the ends of the world. He knew perfectly well—and in his letter even implied— that Sumner would keep his place in the Senate and go on as before. Yet he failed to realize until after the letter was mailed how the senator might easily take it. Sumner could even construe it as evidence that the Adamses wanted his place! Were he to resign his seat in the Senate, some other Massachusetts Republican would be needed to fill it, and who would be quicker to seek it than Charles Francis Adams? Henry may have helped himself by *writing* his letter to Sumner, but he very possibly erred when he mailed it.

He had lied in Quincy and perhaps committed an error in Berlin but all the same was making an effort such as he had never made to feel, think, and do the right things. The idea had seized him that he should help the weaker members of his family. Being so far away did not mean that he could not exert an influence at home. He mentioned to Charles that before he left, at the Old House, he had had "two or three long talks" with their mother. Since then he had proposed to John, and was now proposing to Charles, that the three of them were "grown up and independent or nearly so," and therefore owed "a certain amount of respect and affection to our mother." " . . . it is not enough to merely *have* this affection; we ought to *show* it. . . ."

There was also the problem of the way the three older brothers habitually treated ten-year-old Brooks. The lad had been much more troublesome than Adams children tended to be. Just for that reason, Henry was the more anxious to say: " . . . we ought to try our hardest to tolerate the child, who is really a first-rate little fellow, apart from his questions, and we ought not to snub him so much. . . . Perhaps our influence . . . might give him a start and keep him straight."

Mary's case seemed less open to correction. According to usual norms, she had nothing the matter with her. Worried Henry could only lament: "It seems to me that she'll be a great, strapping girl, with as little consciousness of what God made her for, or what she wants to do besides getting a husband, as any of our other friends. Her manners too will never be good, I'm afraid. She has too many brothers."

The spirit in which the third son was speaking, while partly familial and affectionate, was mostly religious. The ordeals he was surviving had forced him to pray. He very openly said to Charles that crossing to Europe had made him strangely aspiring and drawn "more and more to a love of what is pure and good." He tried to make a joke of his feelings. "I should become a fanatic, I believe, and go into the pulpit if I remained here long." Yet he earnestly promised he would love and help all his relations. " . . . it was an entire mistake for me to suppose that I had only myself in the world to care for. . . ."

The New Year came, 1859. He shifted to cheap rooms a half-hour's walk removed from the university. Simultaneously, he acknowledged to himself that his efforts to learn to speak German had failed.

In a "fit of despair," he resolved to "dismiss teacher and exercise book, and break out a new road for myself." He remembered the Bostonian gentleman, Mr. Apthorp, to whom Sumner had asked him to relay a message. The man was a stranger, but Henry arranged to see him and explain that he had been trying to learn to speak German, had grown completely discouraged, and needed help. Apthorp had solved the same problem years before by attending a German high school. He told young Adams about his experience, and Henry said he was willing to try any expedient, even a high school. His admission to such a school—the Friedrichs-Wilhelm-Werdersches Gymnasium—was immediately arranged for him by Apthorp and the school authorities, who kindly led their visitor to a seat in an exceedingly dingy, unventilated, malodorous classroom, in the midst of forty-odd boys, adolescents mostly aged about fourteen.

Henry sat down on the third bench and returned the curious looks of his ill-fed, unlaundered classmates, most of whom, he soon discovered, came from good homes and were sons of respectable tradesmen.[4] He knew his troubles had ended. His fellow pupils could speak no English; their performances in Latin and Greek were remarkably advanced; and he could talk to them only in their own tongue. He exulted to Charles: "Here I pursue my original design. . . . Here is tremendous practice in hearing and talking and learning German. . . .

I've not as yet recited in Latin or Greek, but soon shall begin; to translate, that is, into German."

The term at the school would end in April. Since the Prussian capital was thought to be unhealthy in the warmer months, Henry, looking ahead, was required to make a plan for the coming seasons. He expected to leave the city about April 10, go to Dresden, and stay there for a while with a Saxon family as a lodger, in order to study independently. After that, in the summer, he would "wander far and wide," going as far south as the Austrian Tyrol, and perhaps to Switzerland, then as far north as Belgium and Holland.[5] In Berlin, meanwhile, four mornings a week at eight, he returned contentedly to the airless gymnasium. By reading Xenophon in Greek and Ovid and Cicero in Latin, and translating all three into German, he made steady gains. Hearing and speaking German continuously, he reinforced them. His stammerings gave way to active experimentation. Although sometimes tempted to "think I mustn't speak because I can't speak like a German," he mustered sufficient nerve to "talk with confidence."

Somewhat as a change from his other activities, he had gone one day to the Legation and paid his respects to the Minister, Joseph Wright. In response, in January, he received an invitation from Wright to join some other Americans in the city and meet Alexander von Humboldt. Born in 1769, and thus an exact contemporary of Napoleon I, the Prussian Baron was then in his eighty-ninth year and universally famous. Conveniently, he spoke many languages, including English.

Adams accepted the invitation, met the great scientist and explorer, and was much impressed. He described the occasion in a letter to his mother, now lost, to which she replied: "The old Baron is a rare curiosity, & one no one will be able to see much longer. Many persons have told me he bears a wonderful resemblance to Grandpapa Brooks."[6]

His minutes with Humboldt may have intensified Adams's interest in Russia. Only a month before, he had proposed his own departure for Siberia. The baron had won his extraordinary renown partly by conducting explorations in Central Asia. Possibly something said by him to Adams about Tartary, Siberia, or Russia affected Henry's thinking permanently. In later life, he would remember that it had been in Berlin that—in his own phrase—his eyes had first been opened to "the Russian enigma."[7]

There were two men in the United States whose current activities

Henry especially wanted to keep abreast of, if possible. One was the foremost leader of the Republican Party, Senator William Henry Seward of New York, a self-styled disciple of John Quincy Adams. The other was James Russell Lowell, who, in addition to being a poet and teacher at Harvard, was editor of the *Atlantic Monthly,* generally regarded as the country's best popular magazine. In one of his letters to his father, no longer extant, Henry had asked the family to have the magazine sent to him on a regular basis. Not sure that his request would take effect, he repeated and expanded it, saying in a subsequent letter to Charles: "Pray send the Atlantic Monthly . . . as I wrote papa, and if there's anything in the papers, like Seward's speeches, I'd like to see them."

The other Adamses fully shared Henry's interest in Seward, and Charles had already mailed newspapers containing two of Seward's recent speeches to the brother in Berlin. The newspapers were slow to arrive in the mail. That Henry should have wanted such things sent to him was hardly surprising to Charles, who could not have denied the truth of the third son's earlier declaration that "all" the men among the Adamses were unremitting politicians in intention, however they might talk. But Charles, in his own words, was "astonished" that his brother should "even want an Atlantic monthly." As soon as he recovered from his astonishment, however, he offered Henry a word of advice. As if the third son were incapable of having the idea himself, the second explained that Henry could "write some German letters or articles for the Atlantic." Charles promised to take the manuscript, or manuscripts, to Lowell for consideration and act as Henry's literary agent, if Henry would just busy himself and write the possible pages.[8]

Belatedly, the newspapers containing Seward's speeches were delivered to Henry's bank. He studied the speeches, which seemed to him "bold and straightforward."[9] The more striking was the one given in Rochester the previous October in which the Republican spokesman had said that the Union was moving towards an "irrepressible conflict." Also receiving his brother's friendly offer to take an article to Lowell for possible publication, Henry responded to Charles in friendly terms: " . . . I acknowledge gratefully your offer to negotiate for me about any article I may care to write. It has occurred to me that as I am here at school, it would not be impossible [for me] to write an article on the Prussian schools, which, if thrown into a sufficiantly [*sic*] conversational form, and hashed up with an intermixture of my own personal experiences, might be made as they say, at once readable and instructive. . . . You see, the subject, as I would treat it, offers a pretty wide surface for anything I should care to say, whether political, metaphysical, educational, practical. . . ."

The friendly offer Charles had made had been accompanied by unfriendly admonishment. On reflection, the elder son wanted the younger to become a writer—and *not* become a lawyer; also, by implication, *not* become a politician. In the letters he was continuously sending to Berlin, Charles suggested that Henry, being a genius, and therefore unsuited to law—meaning politics—should immediately and solely become a writer, both as a means of securing an income and as a means of having a creditable career.

Absent Henry, in response, flatly rejected the idea that he should depend on writing as a source of income. "I shall hesitate a very long time indeed," the third son explained, "before I decide to earn my living by writing for magazines and newspapers, for I believe it to be one of the most dangerous beginnings that a man can make." Yet he confessed that he was looking ahead to ambitious efforts as a writer. He even was willing to wonder aloud, in his replies to Charles, about the shapes his future writings would assume. " . . . how of greater literary works?" he asked rhetorically. "Could I write a history, do you think, or a novel, or anything that would be likely to make it worth while for me to try? This . . . has struck me as practicable."

Pursuing the question of his problematical future through a series of letters to Charles continued into March 1859, Henry discussed all sorts of careers which might possibly be suggested for himself, as scholar, journalist, editor of the family's not-yet-edited papers, even clergyman. The pursuit at times seemed to lead towards the fearful conclusion that he could not expect to have a career of any kind, nor any way of making money! His intuitions warned him naggingly that he would never succeed in becoming a lawyer of the usual sort, with a lucrative practice. " . . . I feel as certain that I never shall be a lawyer," he admitted to Charles, "as you are that I'm not fit for it." Indeed the prospect was alarming to Henry and growing more so. "I am actually becoming afraid to look at the future. . . . This is no new feeling; it only increases as the dangers come nearer."

While the brothers' transatlantic discussion was going forward, Henry turned twenty-one and came into an inheritance from his grandfather, Peter Chardon Brooks, of $9,193.53. The sum, which their father kindly rounded out to something more than $10,000, was sufficient to give Henry a reasonably dependable private income in excess of $500 a year. Such an income would not obviate the necessity of his making money in the future, and in his letters to Charles he

came back insistently to the fact. " . . . I *must* make some money . . . ,"
Henry said. "I hope your next [letter] will take a more practical view of
life."

Sustained discussion only confirmed Henry's long-standing pre-
dilections. He could not say to Charles in so many words that he meant
to succeed completely as a politician and considerably as a writer, any
more than he could have said so to their father at Quincy the previous
July, but he came so close to telling his brother as to leave almost none
of his meaning unspoken. To abandon hope of becoming a great
American politician, Henry knew, was for him unthinkable; and to do
so in order to become a writer pure and simple was worse. He told
Charles he would rather die. " . . . if it has come to that . . . , mediocrity
has fallen on the name of Adams." And he stuck to the idea that, once
done with his labors as a student of languages, he must move on to
becoming a lawyer. " . . . the law," the reiterated, "must be my ladder."
It would both give him an income and lead to political chances. The
best moment for starting really serious efforts to prove himself as a
writer would be after he had achieved "success in other respects."

In fact, it was Charles who was at a loss for a career. On that
assumption, Henry remarked sympathetically that the elder brother
had "struck on a snag." It was possible, he said, that their father's
election to Congress might help Charles by giving him "something to
think of and to do." He implied that the second son should go to work
as their father's aide or assistant. In that case, Henry would take a
course wholly separate from theirs. "My path," the family's runaway
concluded, "is clear to me for five years yet, and, I think, for any
number of years."

Becoming a successful politician in the future required the constant reading of newspapers in the present, partly in order to improve
one's skills in the difficult art of political prophecy. In the last
presidential election, in 1856, the Republicans had nominated a
soldier-politician, Colonel Fremont, and had been defeated. Henry
hoped that in the coming presidential election of 1860 the Republican
candidate would be Senator Seward. Indeed Henry expected it, but
also expected that the antislavery candidate would be defeated again—
that the Democrats would run Senator Stephen A. Douglas of Illinois
and win.

Earlier, in America, young Adams had studied with interest
published reports of a debate Senator Douglas had engaged in while
seeking reelection in Illinois. His opponent had been Abraham Lin-

coln, a Republican lawyer and former-congressman. Whether in Henry's opinion the winner of the debate had been Douglas or Lincoln was something Henry's extant writings did not say, but Senator Douglas had beaten Mr. Lincoln in the practical sense of remaining a member of the Senate, and had since gone on to greater ambitions. Looking at the tactics of the Illinois Democrat from a distance, Henry said, " . . . [Douglas] is playing a devilish hard game. . . ."

Adams was also watching the French emperor, Napoleon III, whose actions seemed "very strange and contradictory"—and thus in Henry's view, consistent with the overall political condition of Europe. Oddly, it was easier for him to predict the European future than the American. In his new surroundings, he seemed to feel he could know in advance exactly what was going to happen. He prophesied that, when summer came, Italy would be "the seat of war." Yet he said that the armies would not interfere with his plans. " . . . I doubt if the Tyrol feels it. . . ."

Henry could not like Berlin. He had never imagined a city so unsociable. In one of his bitterest paragraphs, he inveighed to Charles: " . . . Boston's a little place, but damn me if it isn't preferable to this cursed hole. . . . Society! Good God, a man might as well try to get into the society of the twelve Apostles. . . ." He usually despaired of making friends among the adult Prussian inhabitants. Prolonged residence in the city taught him that Berlin had other drawbacks. "The great difficulties here are really only three;" he concluded, "one that the weather is so bad; the second that the city and [adjacent] country is so flat and unpleasant; the last that one cannot get nutritious and healthy food."

While at Harvard, he had been a theatre-goer and an admirer of the acting of Edwin Booth in Shakespearean roles.[10] In Berlin, he went to plays, including a performance of *Hamlet* in German. He also attended operas but went with a feeling of being out of place. He had no ear for music. Such works as Mozart's *Zauberflote* and Beethoven's *Fidelio*, both of which he heard performed in December, seemed to him to lie completely outside the range of his talents. He called them things "which I can't appreciate."

Long-bearded Jim Higginson in this respect was Adams's opposite. The Boston Higginsons were a very musical family; and Mr. Apthorp, with whom Henry and Jim were becoming friendly, was musical as a vocation. It happened, too, that Higginson's talent for being agreeable had so won Adams's good opinion that they were seeing a great deal of each other and especially meeting for meals in a particular restaurant. They invited Mr. Apthorp to join them one day and sample "the style of our ordinary life." The older man may not have been fully prepared for the sort of entertainment they preferred, which was strenuous and involved an avoidance of taking cabs. Telling Charles about their diversions, Henry said: "Higginson and I went for [Apthorp] . . . at two o'clock and carried him off to our dirty little restauration [*sic*], and there dined him. . . . Then we went to a concert till six, and . . . walked down to a little theatre called Wallner's, a devil of a way off, and saw a drama. . . . Thence we walked back and sat till twelve o'clock in a wine cellar. . . . Here we . . . drank and talked and Hig and I smoked, and passed a very jolly evening, drinking two bottles and a half of Rhine wine. . . ."

After school, when the weather grew warmer, Henry went almost daily with his musically minded friends to concerts, often in beer gardens, and sat patiently while orchestras played Haydn, Beethoven, and Mendelssohn symphonies. Ben Crowninshield and Louis Cabot arrived from Hannover. Louis quickly departed. Ben wished to stay near Adams through the spring and summer. Soon Ben was allied with Jim Higginson and Mr. Apthorp in requiring that Adams listen to perpetual music, a pastime Henry regarded as burdensome and empty. In mid-March, seated one afternoon in a beer garden, Henry noticed with amazement that he was following and even enjoying one of Beethoven's symphonies. As if in an instant, he had become an understanding hearer and incipient lover of classical music. It hardly seemed possible. A Henry Adams who *cared* for music? In Ovid's *Metamorphoses*, which he was rereading in Latin and translating into German at the gymnasium, there were few transformations to surpass it.

The possibility that a single human being could have time and muster ability to become simultaneously a great politician and a great writer was a possibility not often thought of in any country, but the failure of the world to think much about such combined potentialities did not mean that they were never realized. In an earlier century, a German born in Nuremberg, Baron Gottfried Wilhelm von Leibnitz, had combined a great career as a practical politician with a career as one of history's greatest philosophers. Leibnitz had done so because he could—because his interests, talents, opportunities, and indefatigable industry had made it feasible.

While in Berlin in the early months of 1859, a young American perhaps almost as talented as Leibnitz felt that compound success was possible for him but also felt that, to assure it, he had better hurry. It was not enough for young Adams merely to keep up the continual efforts he had been making since the summer of 1856, previous to his junior year at Harvard. He would have to use *all* his time, every waking minute, to lasting advantage. His letters bore marks of his haste. "I seldom do nothing." " . . . I never feel thoroughly jolly anywhere till my whole time is employed." " . . . now I am hurried; I must work, work, work; my very pleasures are hurried. . . ."

When the other Adamses called Henry a philosopher, they were responding to something actual. In a commonsensical way, he was one. Leibnitz had been the philosopher who had tried to inform his fellow human beings that they were living in the best of all possible worlds, an idea which succinctly expressed what he felt was his positive knowledge of the omnipotence and goodness of the Creator. A somewhat parallel optimism could be found in youthful Adams's writings. He said in one of his letters sent from Berlin, in connection with people wanting careers, "It's been a great consolation to me to know that these things will work themselves out for us. . . ." He said, too, that instead of worrying about the degree of his abilities, he would continue by "leaving that to develop itself." The two statements expressed unusual, wholly assured, religious composure. At or near the center of his philosophy, at twenty-one, was the sense that, in addition to being important among his relations and fellow Americans, he was one of the sons of the Creator and thus in good hands.

He fully intended to write an article about the Prussian schools for the *Atlantic Monthly.* He was only hesitating over the question whether to base the article on his personal experiences or make it an authoritative paper, providing information about the Prussian school system that would require some trouble to get. While he was debating which course to take, he formed an impression that the teachers at his gymnasium had begun to dislike him. He could not tell how much, but they seemed to be tired of his presence, which had stirred up excitement among their regular pupils, who talked so much about their American visitor that Henry felt he had "caused some noise in Berlin" and grown "quite famous."

Sensing opportunity where another person might have felt discomfort or embarrassment, he planned a maneuver with the object of getting a supply of valuable information about the schools. The maneuver involved two possible outcomes, both favorable, and was an instance of his exceptional ingenuity in human dealings. Pleased with his stratagem, he explained it to Charles:

> . . . the masters don't like me. My own master behaves with the most perfect regularity, and they are all very polite, but naturally they find it very hard to know how to treat me. Tomorrow evening I am to call on Schwarz, the Ordinarius of my Class . . . and I mean to find out what the difficulty is. Of course, you know, if I find I am giving trouble, I shall withdraw [from the school] at once . . . for, you see, by doing this in a polite manner, I can get some claim on Schwarz's gratitude, and make him a friend instead of a master. Now, I want to visit several of the schools here, and also to obtain a large amount of information that I should perhaps not be able to get except through him. So . . . I shall strike while the iron's hot and do my best to turn the trouble to my advantage. On the other hand, if I am mistaken, and have imagined all this, I shall hold on at the school . . . and try to get what I want gradually.

He learned the following evening that dislike for him among the teachers was not strong enough for him to exchange a polite withdrawal from the school for a large fund of usable data. So he did what he could to assemble a small fund of data. After getting from Schwarz whatever information the Ordinarius could give him, he arranged to see a Prussian aristocrat, Baron von Ronne, author of a standard work on the schools, and have "a quite long conversation." The fact emerged that the school system in Berlin—not to mention in Prussia generally—was vast, intricate, and rapidly changing. All notions about an authoritative article had to be dropped. Henry began to draft an informal one, only to find that his manuscript was growing to "an enormous length." He wanted to revise it, could not begin the revision at once, and expected to do the needed work in Dresden. He supposed the revision might have the form of "three or four" pretended letters from himself to an interested friend at home. Such a form seemed best because the article, as it came from his pen, was becoming more and more an expression, not merely a reflection, of what had happened to him in Berlin.

In his opinion, based on first-hand experience of both, American and Prussian schools were extremely different. Education in Massachusetts schools and at Harvard had done him no harm, or none he could not counteract by self-education. He had grown freely into a person consciously individual and unlike all other persons—except unforgotten Louisa Catherine Adams, whose having been in Berlin sixty years earlier must often have been in his mind. The German boys he was going to school with, contrariwise, would grow up all alike. They were not free. Thanks in great measure to the school they were attending, they were mentally uniform and would stay so. Although "quite pleasant" for a visitor, the Prussian gymnasium, as he saw it, was worse than unpleasant for its regular pupils. He called it a "mill." Perhaps he was thinking of a machine for making identical objects out of wood or metal, or possibly a factory where identical patterns were printed on cloth. In either case, his young friends at the gymnasium were seen as opposites of himself. "The mill . . . is forming their minds," he said about them—in a letter to Charles, not in his article— "but my mind is already formed in a very different way. . . ."

What his article would say, when finished, was that he had learned something important to him about freedom. But time had sped by, and the term was over. He left the gymnasium and felt relieved. His days there had served their object admirably. He *was* speaking German. Also, in odd hours, he had bought a large number of books in Berlin's excellent bookstores. One book he mentioned to Charles, written in German and Latin, was by a learned author named Puchta. Henry meant soon to read it. "You don't know Puchta," he wrote to his brother, then explained, "Well, he's a cussed old jurist."

## 7  /  *An Absolutely Cloudless Sky*

Adams left Berlin with Higginson and Crowninshield on April 12, 1859, and in his letters shortly wrote a history of their peregrinations. After making a "pilgrimage to the shades of Luther" in Wittenberg, they hurried to Dessau and slept. With the object of doing homage to Goethe and Schiller, they proceeded next day to Weimar. There they encountered another native of Boston and graduate of Harvard, John Bancroft, son of George Bancroft, the foremost living historian in the United States. Bancroft consented to join them for a while on the understanding that they would make an effort to do something out of the ordinary. The four youths went to Eisenach, a place adapted to Henry's wishes. "The old Wartburg above it is covered with romance and with history. . . . The walks and views are charming and I would willingly have remained two or three days, but the next morning [,] . . . taking an open carriage [, we] rode through a heavy rain down to Waltershausen . . . where we proposed to begin— what! Why a walk in April through the Thuringian Wood."

They walked three hours that afternoon up wooded hills. Halting for a night at Georgenthal, they slept in "two most romantically large, rickety, cold and ghostly chambers, with the wind outside blowing like fits and creaking the dismal old sign in the most pleasing manner." After breakfast, their march became strenuous. They ascended a valley, "stopping once at a little dorf where we had a glass of beer and smoked a cigar and Bancroft sketched a dog." Five added hours of upward tramping brought them to Oberhof. There it was still "dead winter." Bowls of spicy *gluhwein* and sleep prepared them for a last day's exertions. Their steps would take them "over a mountainous country," on snow-swept roads. ". . . we set off again [in the morning] at eight o'clock in a snow-storm. . . . You may think this wasn't much fun, and indeed I believe I was the only one who really enjoyed it, but . . . the freedom and some wildness after six months in Berlin, made it really delightful to me."

Their three days' walk returned them to Weimar, as it happened, but they had not planned such an outcome. A mere sequence of whims had prevailed.

Bancroft left. Adams, Higginson, and Crowninshield journeyed to Dresden in Saxony, where Jim had made an arrangement for Henry to rent a room for nine or ten weeks in a house owned by a Saxon civil servant. Jim's plans took him to Bonn, and Ben remained near Henry in Dresden.

As rapidly as he could, once established in his room, Adams finished his article on the Prussian schools. He gave it the form of two letters only, each beginning "My Dear ———." He preferred not to give it a title. Written in an informal style, it revealed a change in his ideas. He had said two years earlier, in the *Harvard Magazine*, "Human nature is the same yesterday and to-day and to-morrow."[1] In the interval, he had come around to the practically opposite idea that human natures were different in every instance, deserved to be developed as different, and could be made the same only by willful effort. His article showed, in vivid detail, that the Prussian school was a horror. The vaunted Prussian system of education was basically a system of teaching. Its stress was not mainly on memorization, as many people supposed, although it was true that feats of memorization were required. Instead the stress was on the pupils' paying attention. The teachers were interesting and alert; the pupils responded and learned enormous lessons at high speed—at the desperate cost of losing their individual traits. The teachers succeeded in stamping a uniform character, a sort of new human nature, on all the boys in their charge.

Witnessing the tragic process had determined Henry afresh to go his own way in the world, whatever might be the resistance. The force of his strengthened determination was evident in his language. Repeating the word he had used in Berlin, he said in his finished article: "The school was a mill, and out of it men were produced with certain characters, or rather a certain character, that had been ground into them for eight years, until it could never come out. The fact that human nature varies, that one sort of development suits one mind and a wholly different one suits another; the fact in short, which I believe is in all the world only in America practically carried out, that each individual ought to walk that path for which God has best fitted him, and not that which man's regulations have planned out for him; this was wholly ignored."[2]

Charles had been prodding Henry to forward the manuscript to

Boston for consideration by Lowell. The younger brother had declined to send it, saying he no longer wanted it published. " . . . I write only to keep my hand in . . .," he had told the elder. "Don't suppose that this is affectation. . . ."

Now Henry said also that the article as finished was "very poorly written and excessively stupid." The phrase was designed to block effective protest by Charles. Actually, the manuscript was thoroughly intelligent and very well written, as the elder brother had been wise enough to assume. Its defect was that it revealed Henry's need to escape family pressures entirely and reconsider his course while standing wholly alone. He accordingly stowed it in his luggage, kept it more or less hidden for many years, and at some time in later life took it to his summer home in Beverly Farms, Massachusetts, where it was found long after his death and promptly published.

The article being out of the way, Henry proposed to open Puchta. He explained to Charles in a willing spirit, " . . . I shall set to work to try and make something out of old Herr Justinian's Institutions. . . ." It seemed that the absent brother at last was studying law, for his letters home spoke of "a few pages of Roman law every day." His reported studies were largely imaginary. He was looking each day at a single page of Roman law, only to put down the book without a notion of what he had read. Most of the time he lounged outdoors in the sun, took pleasant walks, or slept in his room.

Spring had come. The Dresden newspapers had grown extremely interesting to him. Napoleon III was poised to storm into northern Italy, and the Austrian army was actually on the march. "Extras are out tonight," he wrote from Dresden, "which indicate that the Austrian troops are preparing to cross the Rubicon. . . ."

More letters came from Charles, as much as ever full of advice. He suggested that, having time to spare, Henry should obtain and read Edward Gibbon's *Autobiography*.[3] The advice was inspired—could not have been bettered; yet indolent Henry replied that the book could not be purchased in Dresden. "I've looked for Gibbon but can't find him. . . ."

The War of Italian Liberation broke out. The clashing armies of France and Austria were almost five hundred miles away, across the Alps to the south, but alarm in the Saxon metropolis mounted feverishly and made the war seem quite real.

Henry studied German newspapers continuously and, wanting to follow the movements of the armies with precision, bought a map and kept it at hand in his room. His military researches became a virtual occupation. He said that the fighting occupied "a very large angle in our thoughts and talk."

The Austrian Tyrol, where he had proposed to go on vacation, appeared destined, after all, to be part of the battle zone and was better avoided. His plan for the summer needed modification. It occurred to him that Loo and her husband, who were momentarily in Rome, might be persuaded to share an interval with him in neutral Switzerland. Charles Kuhn liked Henry and enjoyed vigorous walking. So Henry wrote to Loo explaining that "if she'd settle anywhere in Switzerland I'd bring my books down and walk with her husband."

That Dresden was a likable place had not been part of Henry's idea in coming there. " . . . after my Berlin experience," he admitted, "I've become confoundedly skeptical about all places. . . ." Still, he could not help noticing that the city, being "full of strangers," was helpful to a student of languages. "One hears Russian on one side, French on the other, English everywhere, German occasionally and samples of every other tongue at intervals."

He had supposed that Dresden's main attraction for him would be the collection of paintings in the royal museum, but he had arrived just in time for Holy Week and found that its doors were shut. The Saxons, "thanks to their idiot of a King's being Catholic," had closed every place of amusement. When the museum's doors were opened at last, he entered and fell mildly in love with the painted image of a young woman in one of the pictures. The woman was the Virgin, and the painting was Raphael's *Sistine Madonna*. What there could be in the picture that should so affect him was a conundrum he did not try to solve; but for him the imaged woman, holding her infant Son and walking with easy grace on a cloud, was ravishing to behold. He often went back to the gallery to see her. Also he inquired about engraved reproductions, hoping to buy and keep an especially good one.

Without telling anyone very loudly, on leaving Berlin, he had started to lead a new sort of existence based on the principle of obeying his spontaneous likes and dislikes. Its results were surprising. He formed an affection for Dresden that put all skepticism to rout. In early June, he wrote to Charles: " . . . I begin to appreciate what the beauty of European life is. In Berlin I had no idea. . . . From five o'clock . . . till nine we are usually walking or at concerts. Sun doesn't set till after eight and I tell you . . . that a sunset concert on the Bruhlsche Terrasse at Dresden, sitting under the trees and smoking with a view down the Elbe at the sunset, and a view up the Elbe to the pine hills above, is something jolly."

His fluency in German seemed to double. Going about the city, he realized that he was "far enough along in the language to be able to feel at my ease among the people." To accelerate his improvement, he kept clear of involvements, when he could, with other American travelers he met. Crowninshield, he said, was "the only American I see much of."

The civil servant in whose house Adams was lodging had a son, a lieutenant about to be married. Lieutenant Strauss invited Adams to the wedding and a subsequent feast. Getting ready for the occasion, Henry noticed that his dress coat, a relic from his Cambridge years, was frayed by hard use. In a letter about the feast, he mentioned that he had worn his old dress coat, which had "seen so many experiences on both sides of the ocean."[4]

Although not put forward with any insistence, the phrase aptly expressed another important aspect of his new behavior. In the same letter, directly adverting to his altered conduct, he wrote, "The difference is that the whole ground has changed." The ground of his old existence had been America, past, present, and future. The ground of the new was both America and Europe, past, present, and future. He regarded himself as belonging within a great loop that enclosed all the countries of the North Atlantic world. Thus, when in Dresden, he was not away from his proper sphere; he was in it.

Napoleon I had fought a great battle at Dresden fifty years earlier, at the summit of his career. One day Adams walked over and carefully studied the battlefield, which he said was "almost under my window." The act was not a matter of looking at something distant or foreign. For Henry, the field had personal, immediate meaning.

He had no intention of becoming an uncritical enthusiast about all things European. As much as before, he regarded Europeans as denizens of a backward, unreformed region. Their political parties and "party fights," to his mind, were "matters of the last century." Only a handful of republicans could be found in Dresden. His host, the lieutenant's father, was one of them. Such republicans in Saxony were effectively silenced by the great mass of educated persons, who abhorred republics and regarded democracy as an inversion of natural law. Very explicitly Adams wrote home about Dresden: " . . . an American is not the thing here. America is much disliked now in Europe and no one will believe anything good of it. I never allow myself . . . to get into a discussion on the subject [,] for they [the vast majority of the Saxons] are wholly incapable as a rule of understanding our ideas. . . ."

In his view, the great exceptions to the rule of European political backwardness were the Liberals in England and Italy. The latter, under the leadership of Count Cavour, were struggling to bring about the unification and modernization of Italy along quasi-republican lines. They hoped to merge all its petty principalities and place them under a constitutional monarchy. The War of Italian Liberation could perhaps be discounted as a mere collision between the French and Austrian Empires, using hapless Italian territories as convenient battlegrounds, but Napoleon III had committed himself fairly deeply as a friend of Cavour and the new movement in Italy. Thus a victory for the French in the war could theoretically usher in a partial victory as well for the Italian *risorgimento*.

Henry admired neither Napoleon III nor Napoleon I. For years he had nourished a prejudice against the French.[5] Since he also nourished an across-the-board disdain towards Austria, he had begun by looking on at the war in a neutral spirit, without taking sides. Crowninshield had done the same. Yet he and Ben could not hold out very long against the seductions of Count Cavour's politics and the prospect of a future United States of Italy. Out of sympathy with the Italian Liberals, they grew hopeful of French advances and Austrian retreats.

Much excited, on June 7, 1859, Henry's host "bolted into my room in his shirt sleeves with a telegram that the French had entered Milan." The "Herr Secretar," as Henry called him, wished to consult his lodger's war map. While Adams watched, the Saxon civil servant went to the map and determined the distance separating Milan and Dresden. His action gave Henry a new idea of the underlying meaning of life in Europe. The people of Dresden were even more frightened than an observant American onlooker might have supposed. They were in dread that Napoleon III, like his uncle before him, would march an army over the Alps and into their midst, wreaking whatever havoc he wished. The same was true, Henry believed, of the citizens of other German states. " . . . they've lost all presence of mind," he said. "Prussia alone keeps cool. . . ."

The new Napoleon subjected the Austrians to a series of sharp defeats. Henry and Ben grew more and more "Italian," and less and less willing to stay among the unenlightened Saxons. They ceased discussing the war with anyone but each other. It did Adams's temper no good to keep silent at such a time, when Cavour seemed on the verge of securing Italy's independence and union. He wrote home, "I'd like to . . . express to assembled Saxony that I, H. B. Adams, consider them a pack of cowardly, stupid, idiots." The energy he would have liked to use to denounce the Saxons he used instead to cheer the French victors. "Ben and I have regular old hallelujerums together every night when a fresh battle's won."

Being in Europe seemed to lead to one's having almost excessively meaningful experiences. Once in a Dresden theater, Henry borrowed a playbill from a young man seated next to him, and was politely but silently offered his neighbor's opera glasses. When Adams made some remarks to his neighbor in good German, they met with no reply. He told himself that the young man possibly wasn't a Saxon and thus wasn't "up to Deutsch." " . . . I wracked my brain to invent a French sentence but all my small stock of French was long since driven out of my head by German. So finally I addressed him in English. It turned out that he was an American, a young fellow named Storrs, from near Worcester in Massachusetts. . . ."

To that point, the story was merely amusing, but its ending was ironic. Storrs was not a member of Massachusetts' most famous family, was not descended directly from *two* Presidents of the United States, and, for that matter, was not a grandson of rich Peter Chardon Brooks. Lacking such supposed advantages, he had been free, as Adams had not, to begin by going to Italy. As if nothing could be easier, Storrs had been staying there and had "left Milan in the last train that came through."

One day at nearby Konigstein, where they had gone to see a great fortification, Adams and Crowninshield turned back towards Dresden. Their steamer had not yet arrived. The two Americans exchanged sufficient words with some other persons at the landing to learn that one, a Russian who lived in Sweden, knew six languages but did not know English. The man's daughter, Henry discovered, did know English. Attracted by her good looks and evident cultivation, he contrived when the steamer came to get a seat directly beside her, and, pretending his German was poor, engaged her in a long conversation in English about traveling, art, poetry, and other matters. It developed that she had "just come from Italy and was strong Italian. Spoke pretty English. Was a little taller than I in figure; slim; light eyes; distingue." But he was not anxious to extend their acquaintance. "We arrived at Dresden; left the boat; touched our hats; I never shall see the pretty Swede again, but that's a traveller's luck and God forbid that I ever seen enough of a woman in Europe to care for her."

A step at a time, Adams was learning that, for a long while to come, he would have to dismiss all idea of love between himself and young women.[6] In Berlin, he had said about "women's society" that he felt its lack and would "give something for it."[7] In Dresden, he decided emphatically that he would be wisest to do without it. He told Charles, " . . . I've made an oath that if I can help it I'll not fall in love until it's certain I can't get along any other way." Meant as a preventative and prohibiter of love, the oath would also be a safeguard against marriage. To the extent that solemn vows could make a difference, he had become an unavailable bachelor.

He would still be attracted to women. If anything, his susceptibility to feminine charm was growing. At moments he would talk as if his oath had not been taken or had not been meant. But it *had* been taken, and he had become that much more a personification of youthful ambition wedded to hurrying, increasing effort.

The oath, too, made it still more likely that his need to love and show affection would be directed narrowly towards his Adams relations, and most of all towards the youngest. As a means of helping unfortunate Brooks, he exerted himself in Dresden to find and buy some postage stamps which the boy might treasure. Whether Brooks had earlier started collecting stamps on his own or now began at Henry's urging is unclear, but the stamps the third son assembled for the fourth included some of a kind that would make any collector burn with enjoyment. Sending them to Brooks in care of Charles, Henry later noted that some of the French stamps were "rare and valuable." Meanwhile, attempting a second time to point Charles in the direction of a viable life, he suggested: "If you want to travel, . . . go off to the Rocky Mountains. That would pay well."

The weeks that Henry had allotted himself in Dresden had ended. Loo and Charles Kuhn were expecting him at Thun in Switzerland. He and Ben planned to travel a great deal during the summer, mostly together. They went first to Leipzig, turned south, changed cars at the Bavarian border, and passed the night economically on the seats of their compartment. In the morning at Bamberg, getting out, they washed, ate, and saw the cathedral, then proceeded to Nuremberg, where they intended a two-day stop.

While Crowninshield was taking a nap, Adams went for an evening walk alone through Nuremberg's winding, medieval streets. His emotions astonished him. He experienced a sort of sane and waking delirium. "I hardly know how to express it all . . .," he later wrote. " . . . there's no use talking about it."

Next day was the Fourth of July. He and Ben drank glasses of wine and water to "our grand American spread eagle" but otherwise did not celebrate. Instead they inspected medieval churches. When the long day was over and night had fallen, Henry sat down in their hotel room, minus his clothes, and wrote to Charles: "Think me spooney if you will; but last evening as I wandered round in the dusk smoking a cigar in these delightful old peaked, tiled, crooked, narrow, stinking lanes I thought that if ever again I enjoy as much happiness as here in Europe, and the months pass over bringing always new fascinations and no troubles, why then philosophers lie and earth's a paradise."

Traveling seemed to make him a better writer. "Ben and I," he continued, "have passed the day in a couple of great churches, lying on the altar steps and looking at the glorious stained glass windows five hundred years old, with their magnificent colors and quaint Biblical stories." His elation upset and embarrassed him. "If I go on I shall be silly. . . ." Yet he was anxious to say how he felt. " . . . tomorrow we bid good-bye to Durer and old Peter Vischer, the churches and the streets; the glorious old windows and the charming fountains. . . . The weather bids fair to last forever; we roast and broil in this absolutely cloudless sky, but sleep well and enjoy life. . . . Ben wants to get through. As I'm determined at any price not to return to Berlin before the November semestre begins, and hate the very idea of seeing that city, I'm in no hurry."

They advanced, by way of Munich, to Zurich. Henry took their heavy baggage to Thun and left it with Loo. She was pleased to see him again and soon wrote to their mother that he was "the same, dear, affectionate, amiable, clever, sensible boy he ever was, & I love him dearly. . . ."[8] Nonetheless, Mrs. Kuhn had never understood his exposing himself to the influence of the Germans, disliked his new German clothes, and loathed his combining a full beard with a short German haircut. On July 24, 1859, she confessed to their mother, "I can't bear to think of his going back to Berlin."[9]

Two weeks later, on August 6 at Thun, Henry summarized his latest travels by saying that every instant had been taken up with "mountains and general accelerated motion." He was leaving the Kuhns for a week to see Lake Geneva, Vevey, and Mont Blanc. He prayed that during the interval money would arrive from his father, £100.

Prayer was needed, for the son's personal finances had become a source of grumbling on the part of the Governor. The year before, the father had agreed to give Henry $1,000 a year while he stayed in

Europe—a sum more or less equivalent, probably, to yearly al-
lowances he was giving to John and Charles as well. In Berlin, finding
that the amount was insufficient, Henry had practiced harsh econo-
mies and had written to his father declining any increase in his
allowance but asking permission to spend beyond it, if necessary, and
make up the deficit when he came home. The degree of pinching he
had resorted to in Berlin had perturbed the family. His mother had
written to him in January: "...it does not seem to me that papa wishes
it, or at all ties you to a thousand dollars a year.... We hate to think of
you in such mean lodgings, & associating with third class persons. It is
not good for you & lowers your standard, of refinement & taste &
habits."[10]

More recently, in April, the "Chief," as C. F. Adams was also
called by his sons, had completed the last arrangements concerning
Henry's inheritance. Exactly what changes ensued in the amounts of
money that the son could treat as his own, to be spent at once, is
unclear; but the sum immediately available to him remained too
small. Writing confidentially to Charles from Switzerland, Henry
said: "I wish to God I was not the first of the family who had done all
this [,] for it renders necessary all sorts of carefulness and puts me as it
were under obligations and bonds for future conduct. Travel as
modestly, yes as meanly as I will [,] it is wholly impossible to keep
independent of the Governor's assistance and that will bring its
discount, I suppose, with it, if not in one way [,] then in another."

He went to Vevey and Geneva, saw Mont Blanc, and received the
£100. Loo had gone to Bern, and he joined her there. The war had
stopped. Napoleon III had made an unexpected agreement with
Austria permitting the latter to retain possession of Venetia. The
agreement perhaps had been unavoidable, for the Austrian redoubts
defending Venice—at that time part of the Austrian Empire—had
been considered impregnable; but the concession was a severe disappointment to the Italian Liberals. Their hopes of adding Venice to
their expanding, free Italian kingdom were cruelly deferred.

A plan had been brewing in Switzerland in recent days, the parties
to which were Henry, Loo, her husband, and Theodore Chase, a close
friend of Loo's, an excellent pianist, who had recently come from
Boston. One of the four, possibly Henry, or just as possibly Loo, had
suggested driving to Milan for a glimpse of the victorious French
army. Henry disavowed all responsibility for the project. "This is an
innovation on my original plan," he admitted, "but Loo wants me to
do it. ...."

They hired an appropriate driver and carriage, started on August 16, crossed the St. Gothard Pass, and easily drove to Milan. The city, in Henry's words, written much later, was "picturesque with every sort of uniform and every sign of war." In ways his companions could not share, their plunge into Italy precipitated interior changes in him, affecting his sense of himself and his potential abilities. Having come to Italy once, he was absolutely resolved to come again.

Loo took charge. The party intended to stay awhile at Lake Como, but Mrs. Kuhn decided that she and her three escorts should instead go through the lines separating the French and Austrian armies and inspect the defeated Austrian forces. That a chartered carriage bearing four Americans would be permitted to pass from one side to the other seemed very doubtful, but an armistice was in force, and Loo's mind was made up. In a trice, the adventurers were again in their carriage, advancing up the spectacular slopes approaching Stelvio Pass, on the way to Innsbruck, in Austria. No one along the road would promise that they would not be turned back at the military frontier, and they grew apprehensive of danger. Reaching the barriers on the road, they were momentarily stopped, then waved ahead, and went freely down the other side of the mountains to Mals, "swarming with German soldiers and German fleas, worse than the Italian; and German language, thought, and atmosphere."

His sister's behavior was a revelation to Henry, who could only admire her will. He shortly said they had had a good time together. "I liked her better this summer than I ever did before. She petted me and seemed to try hard to make everything pleasant as could be. On the Stelvio she behaved like a trump [,] under pretty rough trial too."

Lonely, angry, and bored, Crowninshield was waiting for Adams in Frankfurt and had no way of knowing that—thanks to Mrs. Kuhn's decision to go to Innsbruck—his arrival would be delayed a whole week. Henry at last appeared at Ben's hotel. They descended the Rhine and visited every city in Belgium and Holland, and many cities in Germany, before going east to Berlin. There on October 14, 1859, Ben wrote in his journal: "Henry is all the time occupied with new and stronger outbreaks against the cold, unfriendly, wet, sunless town. I am really sorry that on our arrival it was such rainy weather."

In a letter written at the same time from a hotel, Henry said he was going to concerts. "I am climbing up to John Sebastian Bach now [,] whose music few can play, and none can understand." Ostensibly, he and Crowninshield were waiting to enroll as students at the University of Berlin, and Ben shortly did so. In fact, Henry was waiting to do something else.

Among the Adamses, one only, the father, C. F. Adams, any longer believed that when the November semester began Henry might be found among the students attending lectures at the University of Berlin. The other members, or at least Loo, Mrs. Adams, and Charles, had been engaged for months in a charitable conspiracy to release Henry from all necessity of staying in Berlin, and also from any supposed obligations he had incurred to enroll at European universities. Moreover, Crowningshield, before coming abroad, had secured a letter of introduction—presumably from Professor Lowell—to the family in Dresden named Reichenbach with whom Lowell had lodged and boarded four years earlier. Henry, expecting that the conspiracy on his behalf would succeed, had asked Ben to write to Madame Reichenbach and ascertain whether a friend of his could lodge and board in her house through the winter.

In good time, a letter reached Henry in Berlin from his father in Quincy which, as understood by the son, gave him permission, or did not refuse him permission, to flee Berlin forever and be his own teacher in Dresden. By then, Ben had heard from Madame Reichenbach that the wanted room in her house had not been asked for by others and that Henry could have it. With the greatest relief, on October 29, 1859, Henry again left Berlin.

He felt he had dawdled in Europe and, once established again in Dresden, should set himself a hard course of "books and exercise and German." From what he had heard of Madame Reichenbach and her husband, a scientist, curator of the Saxon museum of natural history, residence in their house would impart large amounts of learning, all the more because he would be sharing the family's meals. "The Madame," he told his mother, "is I believe an aesthetical lady, given to Shakespeare, Goethe and Schiller. The Professor is devoted to Botany and [is] a shining light in it. There is a daughter, eighteen years old and pretty, whom I shall probably fall in love with if she gives me a chance. There are two sons, I think, but they are not always at home."

Adams appeared at the Reichenbachs' house, No. 4, Kleine Schiessgasse, was welcomed, shown to his room, and made to feel at home.[1] Madame Reichenbach seemed motherly and "benign." Her husband—"the Herr Hofrath," as Henry called him—was evidently "a good old soul and very kind." Indeed the amount of kindness shown to the guest was almost more than he knew what to do with. "Frightful kindness overwhelms me from all sides," he said, "and I am put to my trumps to be polite." Showing Henry through the natural history museum, the Herr Hofrath expressed a desire to improve the collection by obtaining American seaweeds and a stuffed American swordfish. Adams wanted to offer assistance but could not think "who to apply to." A letter to Professor Agassiz at Harvard College seemed to be called for, one would think; but in 1859 Henry's relations with scientists, including American scientists, remained very timid.

One of the family's sons was away. Augusta, the daughter, proved good-looking and in temper much like Loo. Adams wrote, "She's a will of her own and gives me the most immense delight." Theodore, the other son, a collector of coins, was "passionately fond of all sorts of antiquarian rubbish." With Theodore for a guide, while good weather continued, Henry renewed his explorations of Saxony, observing to Charles, "The neighborhood of Dresden is [,] as you know, remarkably pretty, and . . . Theodore knows every foot of it and its history. . . ."

Living five months with a family as a boarding guest was a serious venture, and Adams took pains that the experiment not miscarry. Talking seldom, repressing jokes, and wearing a cordial smile, he got off on the right foot. Free at last of schools, colleges, universities, teachers, and classmates, he could give all his time to self-education. The curriculum he devised was intended to improve body and mind. Early in the day, he usually avoided the Reichenbachs. Three mornings a week, he took fencing lessons, and on three others he took riding lessons. After one o'clock dinner with the family, he studied till five, then was summoned to a German lesson by Madame Reichenbach, who commonly required that her daughter and the family's guest read German plays aloud, the former speaking the lines of the women characters, the latter those of the men. Supper was served at eight, and Henry often rested afterwards by giving Augusta an English lesson. Then he returned to his room, his lamp, his books, and his pen.

The plan worked to perfection. Without wasting time, he exercised abundantly. His health remained admirable, and his spirits grew excellent. When the weather turned bad in December, he altered his schedule, increasing his hours of study. He wrote home that he was doing a "tremendous amount of reading and writing." His reading was concentrated upon German literature, including fiction, German history, German studies of art, and German treatises on constitutional law. " . . . I never was so quiet. I am laboring under a perfect avalanche of German books. . . ."

Word that he had returned to Dresden had meanwhile reached the Old House at Quincy. His father did not upbraid him. The deed was done; the boy had come of age; besides, a fearful outbreak had occurred which needed C. F. Adams's full attention. In an effort to incite a slave revolt, John Brown, helped by a band of his sons and followers, had seized, then lost, a federal arsenal at Harper's Ferry, on the Potomac not far from Washington. Brown had been captured and would soon be tried, and doubtless hanged, but public alarm throughout the Union was mounting to unheard-of proportions.

While the other Adamses left him in peace, Charles taxed the absentee in an accusing letter with having been a failure and a "humbug."[2] Henry could not deny that, two summers earlier in Quincy, he had claimed that he wanted to be a jurist; that, during his long first stay in Berlin, he had failed to enroll at the university; and that, the previous spring in Dresden, he had not really studied Roman law. But Charles was back at his game of telling Henry to become a writer and *not* become a lawyer—or a politican.

If there were any need to list them, the failures among the Adamses, in Henry's view, were three. There was Loo, who had made a less than congenial marriage; John, who seemed to have become a social butterfly in Boston; and Charles, who had completed his legal apprenticeship but whose only other claim to distinction was trying to limit the scope of the third son's future activities. Henry did not want to itemize the shortcomings of the elder children or indulge in counter-accusations. He mainly responded to Charles by saying, " . . . I do what I can."

Since the elder brother had again raised the subject of the younger's becoming a writer, Henry continued: "If I write at all in my life . . . it will probably be when I have something to say, and when I feel that my subject has got me as well as I the subject. Just now this is anything but true. . . . But you. . . . Why do you . . . recommend this to me when you yourself are smouldering worse than I. . . . Busy you are, . . . but physician, heal thyself."

As before, Charles particularly wished that Henry would write for the magazines. If that were a good thing to do, the younger brother asked, why had Charles not "broken the path yourself?" As a college junior and senior, the elder brother had thought of himself as a writer. Little or nothing had since come of the notion. Henry said, " . . . you have never published a word. . . ." Yet he was not proposing that either of them should alter his present ways. For his own part, he meant to go on as before. His immediate future was already decided. In the spring, leaving Dresden, he would hurry to Italy, do some exploring there, then go for the summer to Paris. When his permitted two years in Europe were over, in September 1860, he would cross the Channel to London, go to Liverpool, and start home. He believed his time abroad was being well spent. "So far as education goes, I consider these two years as the most valuable of my life."

His plans for the further future were changed only in that he was even less willing than formerly to explain what they were. He contented himself with saying: "I shall return and study law. . . . What I have learned here is a part of my capital and will probably show itself slowly and radically."

By writing to each other steadily for a year, Henry and Charles had restored their friendship of earlier times; either that or formed a very similar new one. During the foreseeable future, their friendship would be continued—whatever their protestations—within the matrix of their both possibly becoming writers and their both attempting to assert themselves as politicans. How well each brother would succeed in each role would depend upon a myriad of factors, including the activities of their father, the activities or inactivities of John, and the drift of events in America, which had taken directions very difficult for political prophets to analyze.

A factor immensely helpful to Henry was beautiful Dresden. A small city, and one which most Americans might want to view as a summer resort, a European counterpart of Newport or Saratoga, the Saxon metropolis was adapted to meet all his momentary needs and requirements. The letters he wrote to Charles and their mother during the winter of 1859-1860 reflected perfect prosperity. " . . . I see the New York [news]papers pretty often . . .," Henry said in one letter; and in another, " . . . I don't think I was ever in my life more thoroughly satisfied with my position." In a third: "I have retired into my eggshell . . . and potter till midnight over obsolete formalities of the Roman law. This life just suits me. It seems to me as if within this last year, 1859, I had become a wholly different person from what I was before. And it's true. There's hardly a subject on which my ideas, if I have any, have not more or less changed. And it's very enjoyable to carry on the process and study quietly by oneself in this little icicle of creation."

The coming year, 1860, he saw as the one in which the Adams family might "get its lease of life renewed." Mentioning to Charles that their father had "a good chance of living in the White House," Henry reasoned that their father's tenancy in the executive mansion was not a matter that would be decided one way or another at some future time so much as it was a matter to be decided in 1860. The elder Adams's prospects depended crucially upon "the ability he shows as a leader now."

Henry's wintry sojourn in Dresden coincided with C. F. Adams's first winter in Washington as a member of Congress. Had he wanted to do no more than imitate the overwhelming majority of his colleagues in the House of Representatives and the Senate, Mr. Adams would have left his dependents in Boston, gone unaccompanied to the capital, rented a room there in a boarding house, and subsisted until Congress adjourned on a diet of monotonous meals, tobacco smoke, Bourbon whiskey, and political talk. In opposite fashion, Congressman Adams rented a house, brought Mrs. Adams, Mary, and Brooks with him to the capital, and lived in Washington almost as if he were in Boston. Among the other Republicans in Congress, only one, Senator Seward, would similarly occupy a house that winter. Accordingly, for five months or thereabouts, two houses only would serve as social centers for Republican members; and, for purposes of entertaining, Mr. Adams would stand on a level with Mr. Seward. In the American capital, willingness and ability to make such a center available conferred inestimable advantages on the host, if not immediately, then within the fairly short run. Henry's guarded optimism about his father becoming president at some future time, say in 1868, had a social as well as political basis.[3]

In his extant letters sent that winter from Dresden, the third son never explicitly said that he had changed his ideas especially about the fast-approaching presidential election of 1860; but Henry's letters could be read to indicate that he was much less disposed to believe that the Democrats were sure to win, was thinking less about Senator Douglas, was even more inclined than before to hope that the Republican candidate would be Senator Seward, yet supposed that the man elected, whoever he was, would have to deal with Democratic majorities in both houses of Congress, and, above all, was governed by an irremovable intuition. Without being able to say how he had come by the knowledge, Henry somehow knew in advance that the election of 1860 would cause or be attended by a political earthquake which would rock the temple of the American Union down to its deepest foundations. Its tremors would begin, he felt increasingly certain, about the time he debarked from his ship at New York the following October and went to Quincy. Thus he was able to say, in a letter to Charles:

> It's my own opinion, believing as I do in an "irrepressible conflict," that I shall come home just in time to find America in a considerable pickle. The day that I hear that Seward is quietly elected President of the United States, will be a great relief to me [,] for I honestly believe that that and only that can carry us through. . . .
>
> But if . . . a few more Sumner affairs and Harper's Ferry undertakings come up, then adieu my country. . . .

Other Americans were staying in Dresden that winter, not many, but enough to have afforded Adams numerous social opportunities, had he wished to take them. Madame Reichenbach wished that he *not* take them, as a rule, suggesting that to do so would impair his speedy progress in German; and he agreed. Not more adept at first as a student of foreign languages than other Americans his age, he was learning to speak German correctly, rapidly, and without hesitation.[4] In the bargain, he had grown certain that he could learn to speak any foreign language within a reasonable time, if he would merely reapply and possibly improve his current learning methods.

He kept his oath not to fall in love. On first seeing Augusta Reichenbach, he had warned his mother that the daughter of the family was "a perfect duck." " . . . you'd better get me down into Italy pretty quick or there'll be trouble." But no trouble at all had arisen.

The guest seemed made of stone. If anything, Henry disappointed himself, failing to sense the least throb of passion. He wrote to Charles: " . . . the daughter . . . is a brick. She might be dangerous if—well, if it only weren't that to me she isn't. . . . One can't explain these things." Yet, to some extent at least, he *could* explain his unromantic responses. He told his mother in plain terms, " . . . I have other things to get which marriage will have to yield precedence to."

As the weeks sped by and he saw more and more of Augusta, he took an increasingly experimental attitude towards their association, thinking that her company might permit him to improve his skills in dealing with others. In one of his regular letters to his mother, he mentioned that Augusta was "amusing as usual."

> Such a child; splendid study of human nature. With a taunt I can drive her in any harness. She plays [the piano] to me sometimes now; a great triumph on my part for she would not play before to please even her father, but I told her that she was afraid of me and didn't dare to have me listen, and she bolted for the piano and hammered away till I was tired. Then I make her read English to me, and occasionally worry her to be really angry, but she's a good girl and is always pleasanter the next time we meet. It's amusing to sound the keys of a person's character in this way, and as I am particularly careful never to assume an intimate tone (except in matters of utter indifference) and never to intimate a hint at more than a fatherly interest and care, it isn't probable that either the Augusta or I will be seriously damaged in the process.

A possibly better study of human nature was Augusta's mother. He tried hard to like Madame Reichenbach and never lost sight of her virtues. He even defended her, saying, "She isn't selfish, and she believes in educating the mind." But the good lady had too little mind for much education to balance on without falling off. The longer he remained in her home, the more he was forced to recognize her extreme limitations. She had a penchant for capturing him in the parlor and talking to him about matters that did not concern him. In addition to being a talker, the "good old fat silly Madame" was almost a meddler. He once called her "that female Polonius." "I am of a patient and long enduring disposition . . .," he wrote home in exasperation, "but to have the mother alone for three or four hours is enough to make a marble statue tear its teeth and gnash its hair."

His trials worsened when he saw that eighteen-year-old Augusta was just as fatally caught in her home in Dresden as the fourteen-year-old boys he had known the previous winter had been caught in a gymnasium in Berlin. The Saxon family, in its insistence on the children taking a certain shape, was every bit as much a "mill" as the Prussian school. Augusta would not escape bad effects. Henry explained to his mother in Washington: " . . . you must know I like the little Princess; there's something in her, such as we call spirit and the Europeans call nobility because common citizens don't often have it. She's plucky and headstrong and will insist on running her head against all the walls that come in her way. But I can see how she's got to be kept inside the modelling machine till she comes out according to the rules. That's just the difference between America and Germany; we are all for standing on our own feet and not being like other people; at least that's what we ought to be for; but here an originality is a crime."

Whatever the merits of the view Charles had taken, that Henry should drop other things and become a writer exclusively, there was no denying that the prodigal son was a very good writer already, and was becoming a better one. The fact had impressed itself on their mother, who had been more than a little astonished and pleased by Henry's letters to her from Europe. " . . . you are a first rate correspondent. . . ," she remarked in one of her replies, and in another, " . . . your letter is far too good to be lost [;] it is admirably written, & extremely interesting besides. . . ."[5]

In addition to maintaining regular correspondences with Charles and their mother, the absentee was exchanging frequent letters with their father and Mary—also probably with Loo. Although he did not correspond with Brooks, thoughtful Henry renewed his purchases of stamps for his younger brother, bought enough "to fill a wheel-barrow," and sent them to the lad in weekly installments, to "prolong his pleasure." Such activities on Henry's part made memory of him and longing for his return very vivid and keen among his relations. The person who missed him most painfully was clearly his father. Two summers before, when the third son had just gone, Mrs. Adams had been struck by her husband's saying repeatedly, "I feel pretty blue [;] I did hate to have that boy go."[6] And time had not abated her husband's heartache. She had later reported to Henry: " . . . I feel your absence very much. This is natural & does not surprise me, but the manner in which it affects papa does surprise me. He thinks and speaks of you so often, with such feeling and tenderness, & watches so for your letters."[7]

Charles Francis Adams was the more likely to sense Henry's absence because of something profound and unspoken. As much as other social organisms, large or small, the Adams family depended for its prosperity on leadership, among other things. Also the family was so structured that someone in it, at any given moment, occupied a central position or place of comparative authority—at least that would have held true if persons had always been present who had the requisite ability, energy, and will. But the death of John Quincy Adams in 1848 had left the family without a leader. C. F. Adams was not a leader at all, but an exceptionally capable follower. Henry Adams was a leader to the farthest corners of his being. Starting in 1848, he had tended always to move into the central, authoritative position in the family.[8] This did not mean that John and Charles lacked initiative; they would sometimes show it; and Loo would become very willful. Neither did it mean that their father's *seeming* centrality in the family would be revealed for the hollow fiction it always was. But nothing was going to stand very long in the way of Henry's exerting his leadership and authority, both within the family and in other theatres of possible influence.

The other members of his father's household, Brooks and possibly Mary excepted, would bemuse themselves about the power asserted by Henry. Also Henry would confuse them by wearing the mask of the merely useful, considerate, obliging son, always ready to be of service. In consequence, ironic and anomalous occurrences would become a feature of the Adamses' collective experience. Simultaneously, quiet Henry, who liked few things more than he liked peace, would win the game of life as he liked to win other games, without hurting anyone's feelings. Meanwhile, far away in Dresden, he was safely playing an innocuous role, that of student, self-taught.

Half the cause of his satisfaction during the winter arose from the honesty of his position. He was even keeping his word about being interested in Roman law. Legal history was a subject most young men would shun as a great Sahara of dryness. Hour after hour, reading easily in German and Latin, Henry continued to march back and forth across the desert he had volunteered to explore, until he could truthfully say he had surveyed it. Except as a means of stilling his conscience and possibly strengthening his hand with the Governor, the effort seemed mostly wasted. Treatises relating to legal history, he ruefully noted, left "precious few ideas" in his mind, after he read them.

Hollis Hunnewell, too, had come to Europe. In Dresden, thinking about the journey to Italy he wished to take in the spring, Henry for a time imagined that one or another of his former intimates at Harvard—possibly Crowninshield in Berlin, or Bradlee or Hunnewell in Paris, or even Anderson in Munich—might be persuaded to accompany him on his travels, which promised to be ambitious. All his old friends turned out to have other plans, and it was just as well that they did, for he had outgrown his need for the sort of society they could provide him.

As he reviewed it, the prospect of making the journey by himself developed attractions. Well in advance of his planned departure, on January 31, 1860, he wrote to his parents asking for money and mentioning a new expense. The tone of his plea was rather crisp. He said to his mother: " . . . I begin tomorrow to take French lessons in preparation for my start in April. . . . This is . . . a new expense . . . but there are two things I must spend money on without being afraid; tuition and books." He continued by saying that his German was already as good as it was ever likely to be; and, cost what it might, he wished to advance an equal distance in French. " . . . please inform papa that I leave Dresden April First and on or before that day at latest, shall be obliged to him for more money. I shall not leave Dresden till I've received it."

His appeal omitted all mention of his also wanting to advance in Italian and said nothing about his itinerary, still less about the glories of the places he intended to visit. Young Americans abroad had learned from experience, and were likely to warn one another, that parents for some reason were inclined to believe that European wickedness and depravity were most virulent in Paris, but less so in Rome.[9] Henry appeared to be heeding the advice of his peers. In the weeks to come, while studying French with the greatest energy possible, he would fit in some study of Italian, keep quiet in his letters home about his redoubling exertions, and look forward to seeing both wicked cities.

Mrs. Adams, in her letters to Henry, was full of complaints about the practical difficulty of establishing her Washington menage and seemed to feel herself put to a great deal of trouble and sacrifice. As he considered her tribulations, he thought of his own worst misfortune, the seeming necessity of his passing his next two winters in Boston. He had recently dared to suggest in one of his letters to his father that an extension of his time in Europe would be advantageous educationally. Congressman Adams had not liked the idea. Henry therefore wrote musingly to his mother: "I wish I could help you in your troubles . . . but even if I were in America now, I couldn't be in Washington. Papa objects to my extending my absence . . . beyond the two years, so that I shall, under the same train of reasoning, have to be awfully good on my return. . . ." In the son's expectations, being good could mean nothing other than adhering to family rules, living in Boston, and showing perfect willingness to "lock myself day and night in a lawyer's office."

Instead of merely exchanging letters with his mother, her favorite son wrote a linked series of letters to her with the intention, as he said, of doing what he could to "fix her out." Two passages in the main letter of the series, written on February 13, 1860, suggested that Mrs. Adams take an active role in American politics.

> I wish you would make your "salons" the first in Washington. . . . Now papa has got to make himself indispensable; not only in the wild-beast pen [the House of Representatives], but out of it too. So far as ability, courage, strength and bottom goes, that is, so far as public business is concerned, we'll all bet heavy on him and give odds; but his weak point is just where you can fill it; he doesn't like the bother and fuss of entertaining and managing people who can't be reasoned with. . . . People can be lead by their stomachs as well as by their understandings, and the opening is now a magnificent one. I don't see why you can't make your drawing rooms as necessary and as famous as you please and hatch all the Presidents for the next twenty years there.

One day at her rented Washington house, Mrs. Adams had received unexpected visitors. Without waiting for the Adamses to leave their card at his house, Senator Seward—usually referred to as "Governor" Seward, because he had earlier been governor of New York—had appeared at her door, bringing with him his daughter-in-law, who, his wife being chronically ill and unable to come to the capital, was helping the Republican leader by acting as his domestic manager and hostess. In Henry's eyes, the visit was rich in significance. His chief letter to his mother contained the notable comments:

> . . . if [Seward] . . . went so far as to bring his daughter-in-law

to you without a previous call from you, all I can say is, the Governor knows what he is about and I believe in him more than ever.

You must mark what Seward says; he's the man of the age and the nation; he knows more in politics than a heap; he's a far-sighted man and yet he's got eyes for what's near, too. I aspire to know him some day. Pray tell him so.... Keep him allied with papa, the nearer the better. If he comes in as President in that case, we shall see fun. Don't scold because I advise so conceitedly.

Except that he was no longer studying German so much as French and probably Italian, Henry went on in his usual pattern in Dresden. His dealings with the Reichenbachs remained cordial and quiet. He wrote home, "I'm beginning to have great confidence in myself, really; I consider my tactics in this family to have been admirable...." Trying to teach Augusta chess, and playing also with her father, he beat them so easily as not to enjoy it and accordingly stopped. A gap had opened between his abilities and his occupations. Feeling ready for harder challenges, he shaved off his beard and started to grow gentlemanly sideburns. As if he were ruminating aloud, he told his mother, "It's time to begin to think of a new direction for my letters."

On Saturday night, March 3, 1860, he began to read a German book he had ordered, newly published in Leipzig. He read all night, and at six in the morning, when day was breaking, wrote to his mother: " . . . I've not been to bed, having just received a new book which interested me exceedingly. It is a volume of Humboldt's letters to a friend of his in Berlin.... The letters are personal to the tip-top.... Half the Princes in Germany are ridiculed in it [,] and Prince Albert of England comes in for a scorcher. All Berlin is ridiculed and abused, to say nothing of the very strong political opinions and religious ideas which will set the stupids into a howl. And yet it does more honor to Humboldt and shows more what he was than fifty biographies...."

Obvious reasons existed for his intense absorption in the great Prussian's letters. He had met the Baron and spoken with him; he had long been attracted to books of letters; he was attempting to become a writer of really excellent private letters; and he had given his buried essay about the Prussian gymnasium the form of two pretended letters to a friend. But the obvious reasons mattered little in comparison with a hidden reason, the main features of which can be pieced together with considerable assurance. Henry was in process of changing his ideas about his immediate future. Anticipating that very serious trouble would begin in America in the autumn, he had grown anxious to act upon his political and literary ambitions and move himself a great jump forward without delay. For some time, he had been on the lookout for ways of combining politics and writing, so that, by making single efforts, he could win double gains. Evidently the experience of reading the late Baron's letters crystallized for him an idea for just such a combination.

The same night, or within a day or two thereafter, he decided to write a book and get a foothold in politics by publishing the parts of the book in an American daily newspaper and thus put on the clothes of a journalist. The book he had in mind would be short, informal, and conversational. Its subject would be his impending journey, unaccompanied, from Dresden to southern Italy. It would take the form of a numbered series of letters from himself to his brother Charles. Each of the letters would be so written as to be publishable somewhat by itself. He expected that the series would be published, at least when it first appeared in a newspaper, without the names of either author or addressee. Since the Boston papers sometimes published letters relating to travel in Europe, it seemed entirely possible that one such paper would welcome and print his letters, and, while he wrote and mailed them in Europe, he could trust Charles in Boston to try to arrange publication. That the series would constitute a book was an aspect of the plan which Henry would keep to himself until the last letter of the series was written, or longer, if necessary.[10]

Until that time, not many Americans had written books, even short books, when only twenty-two. If young Adams merely succeeded in getting his projected book of travels onto paper and sent to his brother at home, he might consider that he had done well. Were he to do more, were his letters accepted and published, he would reappear in Quincy and Boston that autumn armed with two signal advantages. Right away, he would be able to show newspaper editors his published travel letters from Europe, explaining that he was their author.[11] At a later time, if it came to that, he might show the whole sheaf of letters to a publisher and explain that they had been intended from the outset to form the text of a salable book.

His eagerness to involve himself with the newspapers had nothing to do with making money. It was inspired by both literary and political ambition. The age was one in which the line separating politics from newspaper journalism simply did not exist. Most news-

papers in the United States were organs of political interests, movements, parties, party leaders, or party supporters and hangers-on.
Every American politican was in some measure a journalist, and every
American journalist was one of the country's *de facto* politicans.
Adams did not need reminding that his father for a time had edited a
paper, the *Boston Whig*. In common with numberless Americans, he
knew that the political activities of William H. Seward were being
coordinated systematically behind the scenes with the tireless activities
of a still older gentleman, quietly famous in America as a grand wizard
of politics, Thurlow Weed. Founder-editor of a newspaper, the *Albany Evening Journal*, Mr. Weed was the Republican boss in the state
of New York. He did not hold office, like Governor Seward. Instead
Weed dispensed offices to other persons, and otherwise arranged and
rearranged the furniture of American politics, or at least a significant
share of it, with an almost imperial hand. In appearance, he was a
mere newspaper owner and editor, king of the Albany press.[12]

The following Saturday, March 10, an acquaintance in Dresden,
Billy Howe, gave Henry the *Boston Daily Advertiser* for February 25,
just received from America. The newspaper contained a letter from
Washington—in effect a news report—signed "Pemberton," a manifest pseudonym. Henry took the report to be the work of one of the
newspaper's experienced correspondents. Among other things, the
report said that Congressman Adams had raised his voice in the House
of Representatives against what he considered dishonest dealings
between the House and its printer.

Mr. Adams till then had been silent in Congress, and his absent
son in Saxony had suffered in consequence. It was a hardship for
Henry to belong to a family which, in its latter days, seemed able to
proceed in politics only a mere small step at a time. But a beginning
was a beginning. Excitedly, Henry scrutinized the "Pemberton" letter
and collected all the other American newspapers he could find in
Dresden which mentioned his father. Such papers being few, he
imagined what the papers he could not obtain would have told him,
were he able to see them also. The more he thought about it, the more
he supposed that the rise of his father in politics was a phenomenon
which ordinary reporters in the United States would mostly fail to
anticipate and not know how to explain. He wrote to his mother: "So
far as I can judge from the various papers I've seen, the spectacle of an
honest man in Congress seems to be something wonderful and beyond
all calculation. No one seems to know what to say to it; whether to
praise or blame; and I think I can imagine the various newspaper
articles as clearly as if I had them here."

He seemed to think a great struggle was imminent, that his father would be in the thick of it, and that he himself should give his father every support he could manage. " . . . it must have come sooner or later," he told his mother, "and on this matter as well as another. We young ones don't count much now, but it may at least please papa to know that those who are nearest and dearest to him, go heart and soul after him on this path."

Because he was newly and secretly intent on gaining entrance to the American press very soon, first as a writer of harmless travel letters, but later, possibly, as a political reporter or correspondent, he invited his mother's particular attention to the recent "Pemberton" letter in the *Boston Advertiser*. He remarked, in the voice of a close student of political journalism, " . . . I see how very cautiously and treacherously the *Advertiser* correspondent expresses himself. . . ."

Two newspapers reached Henry from Boston, sent by Charles, evidently as companions to one another. The younger brother saw that one was the *Advertiser* for February 25 which he had already read. Opening the second paper, Henry saw that it, too, contained a letter by "Pemberton."[13] The meaning of the newspapers sank in. "Pemberton" was Charles. There could be no doubt of the fact, for the two "Pemberton" reports Charles had sent were both signed by him with the handwritten initials "C. F. A."

For ten days, Henry was silent. He had wrongly estimated his elder brother. What was even more instructive, he had learned that Charles, already a lawyer, in the sense of having a license to practice, wanted in some degree to become a journalist. Indeed he had made a beginning; small, but not to be sneezed at. The *Boston Daily Advertiser* led the newspapers of Massachusetts in circulation and was the principal paper in one of the larger cities in the country. Apparently Charles had arranged with its editors to supply one or two news reports from Washington for publication in Boston, when he went south to visit his relatives in February. He had written his "Pemberton" letters in a pretendedly objective style. Probably no one in Boston, other than their brother John and the paper's editors, knew their author's identity.[14]

At last, on March 25, Henry wrote to their mother in Washington. He touched a number of topics—an excursion he had taken to Meissen, the greatness of Governor Seward, the prospect of going to Italy by himself. The next day, writing to Charles in Boston, he fell into his brother's usual error of giving unneeded advice. Insinuating such letters into the press in support of their father's actions in

Congress was a dangerous game, Henry said, and Charles should "take care of your incognito." Yet Henry had the grace to add, " . . . your success [is] as decided as papa's." As a third success, he called attention to his studies in Dresden. "I've digged like a Freshman. . . ."

Having completed his winter's labors, the third son had packed and sent on its way to Boston a box of books, engravings, and other valued possessions, in care of Charles. Money had come from the Chief, but in a smaller amount than Henry had looked for. Assuming that the second son would relay the message to their father, Henry said, "I *must* receive another remittance by the 1st June at Florence." Very briefly, he added: "I've been trying this winter to make my path clear to myself but haven't quite succeeded. I still waver between two [paths] and shall leave fate to decide."

What the "two" paths were that Henry saw ahead, the choice of one to be left to fate, tempts speculation. Very possibly, both paths were upward ones, leading towards long-since-established objectives, complete success as a politican and as-great-as-possible success as a writer; but one of the paths was steep, risky, and dangerous, the other less so. He apparently—while denying it—had chosen between the paths, preferring the steeper.

Because it had always been a point in the Adams family that younger sons should defer to elder; and because Charles, in his role as "Pemberton," had perhaps meant to assert himself as an elder—hence superior—brother, Henry for the present was ready to give him a great deal of rope. Wording the idea as if his brother were really the one who had suggested it, subtle Henry proposed a very broad purpose. He told Charles that they could imitate Goethe, who, in Henry's words, had "always said that his task was to educate his countrymen; and that all the Constitutions in the world wouldn't help, if the people weren't raised." Educating one's countrymen was an object which could be shared by two persons or any number of persons. Such a process, too, could be continued regardless of the vicissitudes of so-called practical politics. " . . . our field of action remains about the same," the younger brother went on, "whether [the Union] . . . stands or falls."

Having posited this very large premise, Henry built upon it a seemingly small and offhand application. "Your Washington letters . . . have stirred me up," he said.

As you know, I propose to leave Dresden on the 1st of April for Italy. It has occurred to me that this trip may perhaps furnish material for a pleasant series of letters, not written to be published but publishable in case they were worth it. . . . Now, you will understand, I do *not* propose to write with the wish to publish at all hazards; on the contrary I mean to write private letters to you, as an exercise for myself. . . . On the other hand if you like the letters and think it would be in my interest to print them, I'm all ready.

Henry's announcement to Charles was as remarkable for what it did not say as for what it did. The younger brother did not tell the elder that his idea for "a pleasant series of letters" had antedated his learning about the two letters Charles had written for the *Advertiser* from Washington. The younger brother did not tell the elder that the series would be numbered, that the successive letters would grow towards a climax and conclusion, and would end in forming a book. He did not tell Charles that the letters would be the work of a potential newspaper reporter and correspondent. Above all, the third son did not warn the second that the letters, if successful, would have the effect of moving the third well ahead of both the second and the first, not only as a writer and journalist but also in relative preparedness for serious political responsibilities.

Henry had devised some tactics for use within his own family, mapping out a maneuver more intricate and far-reaching than any he had earlier tried. He was not expecting complete success. If it were true that he was being uncommunicative with Charles, it was also true that time had run out. The younger brother did not want to go into long explanations. Henry wanted to act. "This is my programme," he wrote to the elder. "You may therefore expect to receive from week to week, letters from me, beginning at Vienna and continuing so long as I don't get tired of it. What the letters will be about depends of course on circumstances."

Louisa and Charles Kuhn had taken an apartment in Florence and expected her brother to pause in his travels to see them there for a time. Henry postponed his departure from Dresden a day in order to attend an unusual concert. He later said he heard two pieces of music "so tremendously classic that it is as good as high-treason to say that the first one exhausted me so much that I could hardly enjoy the second; for the first was Mozart's Requiem, and the second was Beethoven's Ninth Sinfonie, chorus and all. Royal Orchestra, one of the best in Europe, and a chorus of between two and three hundred voices." The affair was a social success. The Saxon aristocracy attended in force, and the "miserable-looking old King" with his daughters could be seen in the royal box.

In the morning, April 2, 1860, bidding good-bye to the Reichenbachs, he took the train and began a long overnight push, by way of Prague and Brunn, to Vienna. The Austrian capital, where he meant to stop only briefly, was the place from which he planned to send the initial letter of his pleasant series. Before leaving the city, on April 5, he completed the letter and mailed it to Charles, carefully marked "No. 1" at the top of its opening page. In an easy, conversational style, the letter mentioned a variety of things—a concert Henry had gone to in Dresden, people he had met on the train to Vienna, the unlikelihood for the present of a new Hungarian revolution. As a means of making his paragraphs more amusing, he presented himself as an inquisitive tourist and "travelling philosopher." "So long as I have good health and am no misanthrope," he disclosed midway in the letter, "I mean to satisfy so far as I can a healthy and harmless curiosity."

He apparently had assumed that the best strategy he might use in his letters would be to make them descriptive of cities. He had been welcomed in Vienna by American acquaintances, with whose help he

had quickly visited the picture galleries, seen the more notable buildings and views, and ascertained that the city's reputation for gaiety was
not misplaced. He and his guides, however, going for a drive on the
Prater the day he arrived, saw something unexpected. In the words of
Adams's first letter: "It threatened to rain and we turned to go back. An
officer and a lady with four servants came by on horseback. As they
passed, the coachman turned round to us and said it was the Empress
and Graf Grune. We all jumped as if galvanised, [and] ordered the
man to turn and catch them. . . ." The coachman complied, and Henry
saw the Empress of Austria. "We followed them till they too turned
and came back. I'm not in the least ashamed to confess that I stared at
them with all my power to stare."

Seeing the empress reminded Henry of an obvious truth: letters
written for newspaper publication in America would be more eligible
for acceptance if they concerned personalities than if they concentrated on cities. Adapting himself to the fact, he included in his first letter
a full account of his hour on the Prater. The episode required no
special skill to exploit. The empress, he said, finding herself stared at
by a carriageload of Americans, had favored her watchers with an
imperceptible nod. He spoke of her "exquisite" figure and "pretty,
good-humored, girlish face," and remembered that she was wearing a
"simple black English riding-habit and little flat hat." "We followed
them slowly some distance; groups of people collected along the
course; she recognised them all as she had us; and the Graf still rode on
like a statue."

The disadvantage of starting a book with a person was that one
might have to end it with a person. And how was Adams to be sure of
finding a person in Italy who could equal or outdo an attractive young
empress of Austria? From the day he mailed his first letter, the
question hung over his mind like the sword of Damocles.

A second overnight railway trip—enlivened by some Hungarian
wine grudgingly doled out to him by an Austrian naval captain at the
insistence of his pretty young wife, a countess—took Adams over
Semmering Pass to the shore of the Adriatic. In dull Trieste, he waited
from seven in the morning till midnight for the steamer to Venice,
caught some sleep on the steamer, and awoke in the morning, Sunday,
April 8, just as the boat pulled up across from the Piazza San Marco.

The weather had grown excessively bad. He went ashore and was
cheated on the way by his gondolier to the tune of a doubled fare. It was
only with difficulty that he could believe the person who had landed to
be himself. "In all my travels I've never felt anything so strange as this

being in Venice." The strangeness was perhaps partly caused by the city's remaining in Austrian hands, a captive jewel in the midst of a captive province. Yet Venice was real even under foreign subjection, and Henry wanted to see it. "Here I am," he assured himself, "sure as eggs is eggs."

He hired a guide, visited churches, and tried other standard amusements. "I have gratified my ambition of going in a gondola under the Ponte Rialto, but it was in a driving rain, and I felt cross and dismal. I have wandered up and down the Place of St. Marc, and drank my chocolate at Florian's, under the arcades, but without a greatcoat and umbrella it was wet work." The storm continued for three more days, one of which was a holiday, so that many sights were closed. But gloom and rain, he had to admit, seemed appropriate to the city; for Venice was visibly losing its life. On every hand, sumptuous palaces were "half in ruins, all in decay." Priceless treasures were suffering total neglect. "... for instance, I visited the tomb of Paul Veronese, in a church filled with his works, ceilings, walls, altars, all covered with paintings from his hand, except one Titian at a side chapel, and all blackening, mouldering, and dropping to pieces in the cold, damp air, till now the greater part are valueless."

On April 12, the weather cleared, and Adams started his visit over again. "Early in the morning, that is, at ten o'clock, I took a gondola and went out over the lagoons to the little Armenian cloister on the island [of] San Lazarro, and thence over to the Lido to see the Adriatic, and to satisfy my curiosity as to whether the French in the last war would have been successful in an attack on these fortifications, if they had tried it. . . ." The expedition left his question about the forts unanswered, but the sun was warm, and he found it delicious to glide along in a gondola and gaze across the lagoons.

At midday, returning to the city in much better spirits, he climbed the stairs to "get the view from the Campanile, or the Church tower if you prefer the English, on the place of S[t]. Marc." The day was wonderfully fine. "The Tyrol mountains all along the North were covered with snow, and the atmosphere was clear, as the Adriatic was blue." Viewed from the dizzying tower, Venice seemed unenterprising but far from dead. "The city itself looked very ragged, and two solitary chimneys and one dyeing establishment were all that showed of any productive spirit. There are a tolerable number of coasters and one or two larger vessels at the quays . . . but the greatest life is in the gondolas [,] which looked pleasantly lively."

He descended the Campanile and walked on the Rialto, where

there was "always life and a stream of passers-by." At two in the afternoon, retracing his steps, he went back to the Piazza San Marco "to sit in the sun, and drink chocolate, and smoke cigarettes, and look at the people, and listen to the seventy-two musicians, a regimental band."

Studied again next morning from the window of his room in Danieli's Hotel, Venice confirmed its being a "great city." Probably there in his room, he finished letter No. 2 of his series, this one about a city, contrasting Venice in rain with Venice in sunshine. The new letter said:

A pleasant sun and a warm day does certainly make a wonderful difference in the appearance of things. Not only the piazza but the whole city looks gay. From my window which looks out over the whole length of the quay—the Riva dii Schiavoni—I can see nothing but a swarm of people, mostly sailors or beggars, or both, I suppose, on occasion. . . . Greeks in red caps and gondoliers in striped shirts; boys playing or sleeping on the stone pavement in the sun; here and there a uniform, [Austrian] army . . . [or] navy; people walking up and people walking down, and people occasionally scolding very shrilly in very choice Venetianish . . . and presently that eternal puppet-show will begin again, and there will be a swarm of people before it till nine o'clock at night, with intervals of juggling by a popular master a little way off. . . . It isn't the Venice of the fifteenth century, perhaps, but it is a very pretty Venice, and lively enough. . . .

The train from Venice towards Florence went only as far as Padua, "dark, dirty, flat and provincial." In Padua on April 14, 1860, at ten o'clock at night, the sole passenger, Adams clambered into a diligence, which swayed and rumbled till daybreak, stopping at last at Santa Maria Magdalena on the north bank of the Po. While he drank some coffee, several Austrian officers scrutinized his American passport in the early morning light, then "watched me into a boat." He was ferried across the river. Reaching the south bank, he was "snapped up by a Piedmontese officer before I had fairly landed, to make sure, I suppose [,] that I shouldn't attempt a counter-revolution in favor of the Pope." It had occurred to Adams that he might be arrested as an Austrian spy, but the officer allowed him to pass.

Safely arrived in renascent free Italy, Henry seized a lucky chance to hire a wagon and driver and thus advanced at once to Ferrara. Another lucky chance there enabled him to reserve the top of a diligence which was leaving for Bologna at eight. "Having half an hour to spare [,] I wandered about Ferrara. It's a strange old place and has a cathedral built before the flood, I believe; a most extraordinary piece of work." Later in the day on the road to Bologna, he glimpsed the free Italians building a system of fortifications to discourage threatened Austrian attacks. Sight of Bologna confirmed and heightened his sympathies with the Italian Liberals, or patriots, as he called them. Pleased with all he saw in the city, he imagined that Italian progress would continue apace. His third letter, sent from Bologna on April 16, predicted airily, " . . . the country . . . will soon be opened by rail-ways, and the population raised up by schools, a free press, and liberal institutions; the churches [,] of which there are or were a hundred and thirty [,] and twenty cloisters, will be shaved down, I suppose, and the restrictions on trade removed."

Ending letter No. 3, he promised that No. 4, to be written in Florence, would partly concern the most noted persons in Italy. "Tomorrow I go on to Florence," he wrote, "just missing the King's reception I'm afraid, but I never heard till yesterday afternoon that he was on his tour. Still, I shall see him [,] which is something, and Cavour too, I hope."

Very early next morning, climbing atop still a third diligence and seating himself behind the driver, he started over the Apennines. The trip was "among the stupidest I ever recollect to have made." Part of the way he walked, while oxen pulled the weighty vehicle up the slopes. "Morning, noon . . . evening came and passed; we saw the sun rise, and we saw him set, and it grew dark; but at last we cleared the final hill, and as we came down on the run on this side, the conductor turned . . . to me and pointed to some lights a long way off, with an *'Eccola Firenze.'* "

Loo and Charles Kuhn welcomed him as one of their household, and he was soon abed. He later said about the next day, "I felt as though I'd lived in Florence all my life. Half America is here, I believe, and a very pleasant half, at that." Besides the many Americans, there were numberless well-to-do Europeans—Polish countesses, Russian princesses, and scandals and tales in proportion. The Kuhns were immersed in pleasures and visits. Henry remarked about them, in a separate letter to his mother: "They've charming rooms, and seem to have acquaintances in abundance. I'd like to stay here with them and see a little society, something I've not seen for years, but I've no time and no money. I think I shall go down to Rome and take rooms till money comes as I hate to borrow of Kuhn and don't care to forestall at Baring's."

His plan to leave his sister and hurry south reflected his conclusions about her marriage and prospects. Telling their mother that Loo was her old impetuous self, hot-headed as ever, and "good-hearted as possible," he added that both the Kuhns had lost sight of any serious aims they might once have had for themselves and now seemed only suited for living in Florence. " . . . they will never be happy anywhere else," he explained, "and Loo's object in life is now [,] so far as I see, pretty much reduced to that of being happy." The warning, he knew in advance, would greatly dismay and alarm the other Adamses at home. He had prophesied that a member of the family would become an expatriate, and might soon be urged in reply to counteract the eventuality, if he could. Better than anyone, he understood that Louisa was throwing her life away; but he felt he would not, or could not, stop her. " . . . I will not put my finger in the matter at all. Let every man wear his own boots."

As expected, on April 16, King Vittorio Emmanuel had made a grand entrance into Florence. Henry had not reached the city until the following evening. Learning early on April 18 that *"il nostro Re"* would be at the races, reporter Henry went to the racecourse, squeezed through a crowd before the stands, and spied the king in civilian clothes, wearing "a sort of glossy shooting jacket." The sight was a disappointment. The monarch looked "like a very vulgar and coarse fancy man, prize fighter or horse jockey."

These impressions appeared, as promised, in Adams's letter No. 4, written in Florence on April 23. The completed letter also disclosed that its writer, while in the city, contrived to see the king no less than four times, most advantageously on the Corso, while riding in a carriage. "He came right by us, . . . and I had a chance to see him face to face. It was a great improvement. He did not look so rowdy. . . ."

If journalism required that a reporter hunt down celebrities by whatever means might offer, Adams would make use of the means. Kings were many, but of Count Cavours there was only one. The best Henry could do in Florence in the way of observing Cavour was to spy him one night in a theatre through opera glasses. " . . . I got [a] . . . view of Cavour across the theatre, and examined him through my glass for five minutes steadily, as I always wanted to do." Known to shun publicity, the count had turned his face "as much from the house and towards the stage as possible." To the eye, the Liberal leader seemed surprisingly ordinary—"a most quiet, respectable looking, middle aged gentleman." Henry said he could never have guessed from the statesman's mere looks that he was "the greatest man in Europe."

Adams did not get away from Florence without being affected, even jarred, by his sister. Mrs. Kuhn was not a liberal. Henry once said about her succinctly: "She was not meant for America. She ought to have been an English aristocrat. . . ."[1] Loo's intelligence was keen, her temper short, and her tongue frequently scornful. Indeed she was sometimes a terror.

Echoes of her conversation could be heard within the pages of her adored brother's developing book of travels. In its fourth installment, Henry listed the good qualities of the natives of Florence and surrounding Tuscany. He said they were the "pleasantest people I ever saw, and neither lazy, nor dishonest, nor revengeful, nor ignorant." Tuscans, he observed, "don't quarrel or fight." "Tuscans don't get drunk, are not rude or ill-mannered, are not restless or impatient, and are infinitely capable of being amused." The passage indicated that he had been listening daily to someone who knew more than he did of Florence, but who also was easily irritated by persons who drank, fought, quarreled, cheated, were lazy, unpleasant, revengeful, dull, ignorant, or hard to amuse. Mrs. Kuhn was often displeased.

For a year or more, Henry had been describing himself as a liberal.[2] His liberalism had required him to presuppose that the various Italian-speaking states and principalities would be better united. He arrived in Florence when an important step towards the unification of Italy had just been taken. Tuscany, earlier an independent duchy, had been annexed to Vittorio Emmanuel's prospectively national realm. By bringing his liberalism into Loo's salon in Florence at such a moment, Henry put it to an unintended but salutary test. According to his own confession, he had not been two days in her company before all his ideas about Italian unification and progress were "knocked in the head." Yet he did not go over to her point of view. Looking afresh at the problem of Florence, he decided that its politics were ironic.

The shift brought his writings into much better tune with his character. In his letter No. 4, with challenging candor, he explained: "Even the most patriotic Italians, so far as I've heard, agree that they have nothing against the Grand Duke [the former ruler of Tuscany] except that he was hopelessly stupid and behind the age. I rather fancy that the [ducal] Government was on the whole an exceptionally good one, and the people among the most happy and honest in all Europe. The annexation will double their taxes, if not still worse, and at the same time make them provincials. So that it could have been only pure patriotism which should induce them to give up their independence."

Henry was writing his travel letters in the tone of a person convinced that Charles would find them deserving of publication, that a Boston newspaper would accept and print them, and that a relationship of sorts had been formed between the traveling writer in Europe and readers in Massachusetts. Thus his letter from Florence ended with the breezy announcement, "I'm now going down to Rome and Naples, rather at the risk of getting my head knocked off, and shall see how it all looks there."

Rome and Naples had not yet been sewn into the quilt of united free Italy. The former city stood at the center of a considerable territory ruled by the Pope, in his temporal capacity as an earthly monarch. The latter was the capital of a miniature empire, embracing Sicily. Neither Rome nor Naples was friendly to liberals, but both were favorite resorts of American tourists.

The weather, briefly good, had turned consistently wretched. It hardly seemed sensible under such conditions, but Adams left Florence, went to Leghorn, and tried to take a steamer, the *Lombardo*, to Civita Vecchia, the port of Rome. A storm was raging, and the steamer had not arrived. Obliged to wait, he cast about for something to do in Leghorn. " . . . the only excitement which the city could furnish was a visit to the English burying ground [,] where I saw the first spring roses hanging over Smollett's grave, and then a walk along the seashore, where the gale was throwing the spray about like a fountain, and the sun was setting in grand magnificence."

Until that moment, he had repeatedly underestimated the cost of his absence in Europe, understated his needs and desires, and economized to the point of wearing the same clothes until the linings were gone. The reason had been fear of altercations with his father. Far from easing his difficulties with the Chief, all the son's efforts to conceal the cost of his enterprise had been greeted with increasing paternal protest, tending always towards a castigation. While waiting at Leghorn, Henry decided to revolutionize his attitude towards his expenses. He adjured the part of a miser. " . . . I get neither credit nor advantage from it." In its place, he took the part of a person of sense, willing to spend money whenever doing so might be required. The change insured that an explosion of some sort would occur, but he was ready to face it. "I expect to hear grumbling enough about me on my return; I may as well give some reason for it."[3]

Two days late, the *Lombardo* docked and threw out its gangways. Henry had booked first-class passage. Accordingly, that night on the ship, he was able to stretch out in the first-class cabin, alone except for an ancient Frenchman, and drop off to sleep. The storm had ended, and the sea was quiet. Sometime before daybreak, wandering out on deck, he saw "an island in the distance on our right, which, after a short search for some one awake enough to be rational, I learned from the man at the wheel, was Elba."

Having survived a collision with the customs inspectors at Civita Vecchia, in the afternoon on April 29, 1860, Adams arrived in Rome, checked in at his hotel, and went in search of an acquaintance—a woman he had met in Boston as Lizzy Winthrop. She was now Mrs. Hooker, having married an American businessman and resident in Rome. Henry knew little or nothing about her husband but had their address, a certain building on the Via della Croce. On inquiring there, he learned that Mrs. Hooker was momentarily out. Going back to his hotel, he was told that another couple, older people, also members of the Winthrop family of Boston, were staying there and that their daughter Fanny had died only moments before of tuberculosis. He sent up his card to the bereaved parents and went to bed.

Before he rose in the morning, the Winthrops left for Marseilles. He soon discovered also that Mr. Apthorp, his old friend in Berlin, had gone on the same boat. It was raining. Adams went a second time to the Via della Croce and found Mrs. Hooker in. They chatted briefly. He borrowed some books, took them to his hotel, ordered a fire, read for a spell, and started a letter to his mother in Washington. Lizzy Hooker, he said, was "jolly as ever." " . . . I thank my stars that she is here, for otherwise I should feel dreadfully adrift in this old grave-yard of a city. It's the mournfullest hole you ever conceived of, and at my table d'hote everyone is dying and talks about it, while in the hotel there have been four deaths in a month. . . . The city is colonised with consumptive people. . . ."

Loo had promised to forward his mail from Florence. For sheer lack of money, he would have to linger in Rome and its environs until a bank draft arrived from their father. The thought did not disturb him, even if rain continued to fall. The eternal city had not answered to his expectations but kept him very busy. First he tried "a few churches." Next, on May 1, a Tuesday, he went to the Vatican and in no time was "all up in a heap, hardly knowing what to make of it." "I felt all lost in the oceans of art there. I wandered into St. Peter's and never appreciated where I was, any more than if I were in Boston Music Hall. Indeed, St. Peter's in effect disappoints me. It doesn't approach in grandeur and dignity, to my mind, to any of the great Gothic cathedrals nor even to St. Marc at Venice."

While lost at the Vatican, he encountered a young lady from New England whom he had earlier met in Dresden. She was with two other young ladies, also New Englanders, to whom she introduced him. They were all odd, to his mind, but decent, intelligent, cultivated, and very religious. He soon called on them at their hotel and began to join them on sight-seeing ventures, each time with the feeling that they considered him "wicked or improper company." " . . . I find it rather hard work to know how to manage them and . . . I don't find that I get ahead much."

That Tuesday, calling on Mr. Hooker at his office, he was told that some rooms in the Hookers' building on the Via della Croce, really part of their apartment but always separately rented, were vacant. Henry instantly took them and shifted his things there from his hotel.

His new quarters consisted of "four or five small rooms and countless passages between them, on the third story and opening out onto the flat roof of a part of the house as a promenade, so that I can walk straight into the Hooker's [*sic*] and they right into mine. . . ." Since the custom in Rome was to have meals sent in, an agreement was made that an extra dinner should be ordered daily for Henry at his expense, so that he and the Hookers might eat together. " . . . I am in a manner taken into their establishment," he advised his mother, "and feel rather more at home, if anything, than I did at Florence, little as I ever [k]new Lizzie Winthrop and though I never saw Hooker till to-day."

The weather in May was sublime. He had never experienced anything that approached it. "I feel as if I were in the uppermost of the Heavens. The air is filled with the perfume of the roses, and that sort of Spring sensation that makes everything so delightful. . . . I wander about the city from noon till four o'clock seeing sights; then Lizzy Hooker usually picks me up to ride till six, and at half past six we dine. You can imagine what a life for the Gods this is. . . . There seems to be no hope of seeing all that I ought to see."

He called his days in Rome the happiest "known ever to have existed for a person who was neither in love nor given to over-drinking." His usual waking state seemed exchanged for continual bliss. " . . . gradually after . . . [the] first few days I became drunken with the excitement. . . ." Yet his condition appeared to be normal for a person in such a city in such a season. " . . . the sensation is no monopoly of my own, but a part of the land and of human nature."

Going to a reception with Mr. Hooker, he saw the College of Cardinals, the *corps diplomatique,* the Roman nobility, a crush of people, all very bored, it was true, "but curious to me and interesting to my philosophical train of mind." He went again to St. Peter's, this time during a service, and began to realize the building's splendors. After another tour of the Vatican museum, on Monday, May 7, he rode out with his three religious young ladies to see the Pamfili-Doria Villa, and that same night, at eleven o'clock, escorted them to the Coliseum in moonlight. "We went all over it with a guide and a torch, and stayed a long time up on the highest platform listening to an owl and some nightingales, and as the clock of St. John Lateran struck twelve, we watched hard to see the ghosts of the gladiators and of the old Roman crowds come out of the shadows and have a fight in the moonlight but it was no go. Everything was as still and peaceful as if the eighty thousand Jews who were killed in building the old place, had never had any ghosts."

Till then, as he had told Charles he would do, he had added a letter each week to his numbered series. Probably for many reasons, while in Rome, he stopped. The interruption must have been much on his mind, but so were additional matters, each of which tended to distract him from the others. He was much worried, for instance, about the nominating conventions in America. The Democrats had met at Charleston two weeks before and presumably had chosen their presidential candidate and adopted a platform, but news of the outcome had not yet arrived. Supposing that Douglas would be the choice and again extremely afraid that the resourceful Illinois senator would be impossible for the Republicans to beat, Henry told his mother that he was "watching from here with a sort of sickness at heart, the course of American politics." He stopped his letters, in other words, just when the Republican chance of capturing the presidency appeared to have vanished.

A letter came from Charles, not important, but requiring an answer. On May 9 and 11, Henry wrote an extended, private note to his brother, a few pages of family talk. Except that he had hired a horse and was riding out of Rome into the surrounding Campagna, he claimed to be doing "absolutely nothing." "One part of the day I amuse myself by making plans which during the rest of the day I don't carry out. I ramble about ruins and churches and galleries and talk Italian to shop-keepers and guides, and generally do a power of lounging. The hardest work I ever attempt is occasionally a chapter of Gibbon's Autobiography, which, after having searched for it at your recommendation over half Europe, I picked up the other day at a book-store here."[4]

Concealed within his casual expressions to his brother was another, possibly more important explanation of Henry's failure to continue the numbered letters of his pleasant series. The younger brother was *not* doing nothing in Rome; on the contrary, he was midway along in a complex experience. Apparently, on reaching the city, he had bought a standard English guide for tourists, Murray's *Handbook of Rome.* In it he had stumbled upon a quotation from Edward Gibbon's *Autobiography.* One effect of the quotation was to send Henry upon renewed searches for the latter book, with the result that he found a copy and started to read it; but meanwhile the quotation had also turned his feet towards a church. For the short excerpt that appeared in the *Handbook* told, in the English historian's words, how, in Rome in October 1764, Gibbon had gone to the Church of the Zoccolanti and, while listening to the Franciscans singing vespers among the ruins of the ancient Capitol, conceived the plan of a masterwork, a majestic unfolding of the decline of the Roman Empire and its conversion to Christianity.

Frequently in the evenings, in imitation of Gibbon, young Adams had been going to the same church, to sit on the steps and watch the sunset. At such hours, looking over the eternal city while the fading light slowly altered the appearance of innumerable buildings and ruins, modern, medieval, and ancient, he lost all sense of his ambition to become a lawyer-journalist-politican, ceased wanting to travel, and grew absorbed in the one idea that he himself would write a great book to rival Gibbon's *Decline and Fall of the Roman Empire.* His own would be called a *History of the United States of America* and would concern the consolidation and emergence in modern times of a vast democracy, beyond the Atlantic, in the New World.[5]

Among his preternatural abilities, Henry Adams had none more amazing than his ability to foreknow his own future. Of all his varied experiences in early life, the deepest was probably its stealing upon him in Rome not merely that he could write such a history, or would, but that he would *have* to write it, before he was done in life, or else not succeed in doing what he had been brought into being to do as a writer.

There was nothing optional about his future *History of the United States*. His preparing to write it, then performing the actual task, was always fated and compulsory. But his knowledge of his future, granted to him at twenty-two in Italy, went beyond the great book he would write in later years about his country to another book he would write, in still later years, about himself. If it were asked when he conceived *The Education of Henry Adams*—at first glance a very hard question—it could be answered with considerable assurance: why, of course, in May 1860, in Rome, just after he had conceived his *History* and while, a chapter at a time, he was slowly and thoughtfully reading Gibbon's *Autobiography*.[6] The best evidence that he was thinking of *two* books he would write in his older years was his complete inability to get on with *one* book in the present, his book of travels, which, if it had a title, would perhaps be called *A Journey to Italy*.[7] A very small book, almost too small, it was nearly half-finished but seemed likely to stay so. Big books, or rather mere ideas for big books, had momentarily crowded a little one into a back corner of Adams's mind.

If possible, he wished to make friends among the American artists then in Rome. The one he most wished to meet was a Bostonian gentleman, William Wetmore Story, a sculptor. When time permitted, he called on Mr. Story at his studio and watched him work. He also visited another American sculptor, Mr. Rogers, and soon was shuttling between the studios of several men, both Americans and Europeans, all more or less famous. Sitting one morning in the studio of Hamilton Wilde, he was startled by a middle-aged Englishman who rushed in, upset at having seen a guillotine near the Coliseum. The contrivance had been used an hour or two earlier to behead a criminal. Talk continued, and Henry realized that the other visitor was Robert Browning.

A guillotine seemed suited to current Italian politics. It was rumored that the papal domain had been invaded along its northern border by forces loyal to King Vittorio Emmanuel. The commander of the Vatican army, General Lamoriciere, was hurrying every man he could muster into the countryside to repel the rumored attack. Simultaneously, an amphibious expedition against Sicily had been launched by a revolutionary soldier, Giuseppe Garibaldi, leader of a unit called the Cacciatori which Adams had seen the previous summer on Stelvio Pass. Now General Garibaldi had reportedly gone to sea at the head of a makeshift army, three thousand strong, carried on several ships, with the object of wresting Sicily away from its ruler, King

Francis II of Naples. The issue that hung in the balance was not war or territory so much as revolution and freedom from wholly autocratic rule.

After he had allowed three weeks to pass without continuing his small book of travels, on May 17, Adams started his letter No. 5. He avoided politics in the letter and wrote mostly about his rides. The most beautiful of all things in Rome, in his opinion, was a ride on horseback across the Campagna. "There one has Rome and Italy, the past and the present, all to oneself. There the old poetic mountains breathe inspiration around. There one sees the aqueducts in their grandeur and beauty, and the ruins stand out on the landscape without being wedged in by a dozen dirty houses, or guarded by a chorus of filthy beggars. The whole country lies open, unfenced and uncultivated; and as one rides from hill to hill, the scene changes with the ground, and St. Peter's or the Lateran, an aqueduct or a tomb, Mt. Albano . . . or Soraete and Tivoli, almost bewilder one with their different charm."

His emerging letter No. 5 spoke also of some bronze doors Mr. Rogers was making for the chamber of the House of Representatives in Washington and more particularly of a marble statue of Cleopatra which Mr. Story had brought to completion.

> His statue represents Cleopatra seated; her head leaning on her hand. . . . She is meditating apparently her suicide. To me . . . there is a great charm in the expression that she wears; it seems to be the same old doubt of God's great mysteries of life and death; a scornful casting up of accounts with fate, and a Faust-like superiority and indifference to past, present or future. Mr. Story has tried to breathe the mystery and grandeur of the sad and solemn old Sphynxes and Pyramids into his marble. I shall not undertake to say whether he has succeeded or not. I only know that his Cleopatra has a fascination for me, before which all his other works, charming as some of them are, seem tame and pointless.

Adams stopped writing when his letter was almost, but not quite, completed. He was waiting in puzzlement for a response from his brother at home about letters Nos. 1-4—a response now much overdue. Also Henry was hearing and trying not to believe false reports and wild rumors about Garibaldi's army. It was said that there had been "a sea fight and two of his vessels and fifteen hundred men sunk." It was averred that the army would not invade Sicily but land instead near

Rome, "to revolutionize Rome and attack Naples." Henry wished extremely to know what was happening but had to wait. "News goes slowly in Rome," he said, "and perhaps we shall hear in time."

The response from Charles came at last, delayed in transit because the elder brother had very oddly addressed it to the younger at Dresden. It seemed that the elder might have a wrong idea of the timing of the younger's journey. Yet the response was welcome, for Charles was willing to take Henry's letters to a Boston newspaper. Charles only suggested that each of the letters be published with the author's initials.

The suggestion about initials seemed to make no practical difference. While meditating other things in Rome, Henry had had a chance to review in his mind the four travel letters he had mailed from Vienna, Venice, Bologna, and Florence. In retrospect, they seemed so poor that he could not believe they had been accepted for publication. In a private note he immediately started to Charles, he guessed that newspaper editors in Boston would "hardly be likely to publish them at all after once seeing them; certainly not without corrections and changes which I should have made myself if I'd had time."

Temperamentally, Henry was much better adapted to being published anonymously than otherwise. Trying to remember what he had said to Charles in March when writing to him from Dresden about the series of letters that would come to Boston, the younger brother half-believed he had specified that the letters, if published, should not be signed. He also half-believed he might have failed to make his meaning clear. So now he tried to be explicit, declaring in his note, "What I said to you at first is literally carried out; the letters are private letters which might be published, but anonymously."

His unfinished letter No. 5 seemed an improvement over its predecessors. Adding a few lines to complete it, he put both it and his private note into a single envelope and sent them to Charles. The note promised that letter No. 6, also to be sent from Rome, would follow in time. In addition, the note mentioned that Henry had been reading more of Gibbon. A change appeared to have taken place in the younger brother's attitudes concerning politics and writing. He seemed to imagine that his adulthood would consist of a storm of politics intermixed with writing, in a first phase, and a calm of writing intermixed with politics, in a second phase. He evidently was influenced in part by the likelihood that writing a great history of the United States would consume all a man's hours for many years and mostly bar him from other activities. Referring to Gibbon's behavior, he said: " . . . I too might come to anchor like that. Our house needs a historian in this generation and I feel strongly tempted by the quiet and sunny prospect, while my ambition for political life dwindles as I get older."[8]

The Hookers were to move to new quarters on May 26. When they did, Adams would be left alone on the Via della Croce, a change he took as a sign that his departure for Naples should follow. Not that he wanted to go; for he was more than ever at ease in Rome; the weather was as sublime as before; and his health had never been better.

The basis of his passionate attachment to Rome was partly the opportunity it afforded him to exert himself freely from early morning till very late in the evening. Some of his days were almost incredibly full. One day, May 25, became the subject of an informative letter he wrote to his mother, which read in part:

> . . . at eight o'clock in the morning I was on horseback and off for Frascati. It's twelve miles off across the Campagna, a ride all alone, but the weather was exquisite and the Campagna utterly beautiful. At Frascati I left my horse and took another climb up to Tusculum. . . . On the way I picked up my family of young women of whom I've spoken before. . . . We explored together all the ruins of Tusculum, which . . . I never should have recognized from that engraving of Cicero's Villa there, which hangs in the dining room at Boston. . . .
>
> We came back over the Campagna at sunset and I saw for the first time how it was done. But the sunset wasn't so pretty as I'd wished; it left the landscape cold and misty. . . . It was nine o'clock when we arrived in Rome. I had been on horseback about seven hours altogether, to say nothing of climbing about. But I rushed home, dressed, and before ten was at the Story's [*sic*]. Mrs. Story asked me to come up, for the Brownings were to be there. So up I went and found a mixed crowd, twenty perhaps, of poets and priests, English and Americans. I talked a little while with Mr. Browning; a quiet, harmless sort of a being. Mrs. B[rowning]. is a great invalid and I wasn't introduced. As I know how celebrities talk, I contented myself with looking, and didn't ask an introduction.

Cheering news had arrived from America. In Charleston at the Democratic convention, the Southern delegates had refused to allow the nomination of Douglas and no nomination at all had been made! The convention had merely adjourned. The Northern and Southern halves of the Democratic Party were evidently drifting away from each other towards separate, new conventions. As Adams described it, the development was "one of the pleasantest flavored nuts that ever Republicans had to crack." It seemed probable, even more than probable, that the Republicans would win the Presidency in November. Four years, it appeared, had been gained in the space of a month.

While he attuned himself to the change, Henry received a second response from Charles misaddressed to, and forwarded from, Dresden. It reported that Henry's travel letter No. 1, sent from Vienna, had been published in the *Boston Courier*, signed "H. B. A."

The idea that his letter had been thrust before the public at home as his own work, plainly acknowledged, chilled and froze Henry's spirit. He told Charles: " . . . [I] feel as if some one had poured a bucket of iced water over me. As I recollect my letters[,] they are not such as I should care to publish as mine, and I shall disavow all part and parcel in it."[9]

The cold feeling passed and gave way to ambition. Henry went to the other extreme and prepared himself for the smooth, signed publication of all his numbered series, including the letters he had not yet written. He asked himself what the unwritten letters should say. It seemed time for a mighty effort. Money had come from his father. The Hookers had moved.

Adams could not imagine what was happening to Garibaldi's expedition against the Neapolitan Empire. The European papers said the revolutionary army had effected a landing in Sicily on May 11 and marched towards Palermo, but all subsequent reports were palpable fictions. Rome seemed cut off from the world. "This has gone on for a week," Henry said, "and even what occurs within fifty miles of the city is a mystery." He therefore started letter No. 6 with a rueful outburst: "This is a great age. One may congratulate himself, I suppose, on living in stirring times; indeed, to a certain degree in heroic times. . . . And here I am directly in the center of it all, and what good do I get of it?"

Once committed to paper, the theme reiterated itself in his mind and grew louder. He felt excluded from the meaningful events of the time. " . . . I feel a sense of personal injury and wrong that everything here should be so quiet. One might just as well live on the Sandwich Islands; Garibaldi and his three thousand might just as well have fought at Thermopylae. Cavour and 'il nostro Re' might just as well have ruled a century ago, for all the part that we, who are right in the heart of the country, can take in their troubles or their efforts."

After reconsidering, Adams did not think the outlook for the Republicans was necessarily bright. In one of his private notes to Charles, he remarked that American politics were "funny," in the sense of being liable to unpredictable turns.[10] He now was waiting to learn the outcome of the Republican convention at Chicago. It seemed to him entirely possible that the Party might be foolish enough to nominate a candidate other than W. H. Seward and get him elected. Henry wanted nothing to do with such a victory. He privately exclaimed to his brother: " . . . damn the thing without Seward. I shall reserve all my penny-whistle for him."[11]

Thinking the Republicans a subject better avoided in his travel letter No. 6, he spoke in it about the alleged drunkenness that had prevailed at the Democrats' quarrelsome convention at Charleston, returned to the question of American sculptors in Rome, and seized an opportunity to praise Nathaniel Hawthorne. " . . . in my last letter . . . I mentioned Mr[.] Story's statue of Cleopatra. At that time I did not know that Mr[.] Hawthorne had introduced it into his new novel, and to this moment, in spite of all my efforts, it has been my misfortune not to have been able to get hold of that book [*The Marble Faun*]. . . . When Mr[.] Hawthorne describes or praises anything, it is time that other people should hold their tongues."

At the end of the letter, he confessed that his love for Rome had become very deep. " . . . I have been this evening to the fountain of Trevi and there in the moonlight, in solemn solitude, have drunk of the water and bathed my face in it, for the story goes that he who does that on the last night of his stay, will surely return some day to drink those waters once more."

On May 30, 1860, at Civita Vecchia, he caught the steamer to Naples. A heavy swell was running. As a means of preventing seasickness, which the Atlantic had taught him to dread, he went immediately to his cabin and slept. The first thing he heard in the morning was a woman's voice "calling some one on deck, as we were just passing Capri, and it was necessary to see it." Knowing geography, Henry leapt from his berth and dressed. If what the voice had said were correct and they were passing Capri, the steamer had already put in at Naples and gone on towards Sicily. On deck, he learned to his relief that imagined Capri was in reality something else, and his adventures returned to normal.

He found Naples an "agreeable surprise"—the "gayest and live-liest place in Italy." Long practice had turned him into an efficient tourist. " . . . I set to work and . . . went straight to the Royal Museum." The same afternoon, going up to the convent of San Martino for the view of the city and the bay, he became acquainted with a friendly young German clerk with red whiskers and green glasses. The German was alone and glad to find someone to talk with, knew Italian, wished to see all the sights, and liked making arrangements and haggling over Italian prices. They went together that night to the opera, evidently met again the following day, then left on an expedition. Their notion of sight-seeing bordered upon the heroic. On June 2, Saturday, they inspected Herculaneum and Pompeii. Also they climbed high enough on Mt. Vesuvius to look into the crater of an active volcano. Adams thought it a "horrible chasm." " . . . clouds of sulphur smoke driven about by the gusts of air, down in the deep hollow, gave me the first idea of a chaos worse than a Hell."

Descending the mountain, they hurried to Salerno, slept, and at five-thirty on Sunday morning set off again in a cart to visit the great Greek temple at Paestum. In Naples again on Monday, Adams wrote an amused letter No. 7, telling how he had reached the city and all that he and his German co-explorer had done since his arrival.

His thoughts in the instant were divided between his own experiences, American politics, and Italian politics. An unequal battle appeared to be in the making in Sicily between Garibaldi's small invasion force, estimated at 3,000 men, and the Neapolitan garrison at Palermo, which, partly made up of Swiss mercenaries, had grown to 23,000 men, well-trained and well-armed. To Adams, it seemed possible that a second battle of great importance might be fought right where he was. He said of the city of Naples in his newest letter: "It looks as if it had enough energy to rebel. . . . Indeed it seems to me as if it were all up . . . with the [Neapolitan] Government. . . . All the reports are exciting and disturbing and if Garibaldi is not soon driven out of the Kingdom, it's reasonably safe to believe that the King will be. Still, I will say that the [royal] army is a very good looking one and well dressed, if it will only fight; and I believe too that the Swiss guard [the part of it not sent to Sicily] is strong as ever."

He had no sooner written letter No. 7 when a report reached his ears that the momentous battle in Sicily had long since occurred. In some manner that was not yet clear, the royal garrison had been utterly defeated by Garibaldi's much smaller force, had surrendered Palermo, and, though intact, was waiting shipment back to Naples!

Reacting to the news in a spirit he had never earlier shown, Adams decided to go at once to Palermo. He thought the excursion a "glorious idea," a "most royal and magnificent lark." To secure transportation, he imposed upon a banker to whom he had been recommended by Mr. Hooker. The banker gave him a letter of introduction to Mr. Chandler, the American minister. He hurried with the letter to the legation, saw the minister, and asked to be entrusted with official, government despatches that might need to be carried to Sicily. An accommodating person, Mr. Chandler acceded to the request and gave Henry despatches to the American consul in Palermo and to Captain Palmer of the United States war-steamer *Iroquois* in Palermo Harbor. Commissioned a temporary courier in the national service, Henry passed an anxious night, rushed next morning through departments and bureaus of the Neapolitan government seeking clearance, and, his papers in order, boarded a flea-ridden transport, the *Capri*, about to sail for Palermo towing two other vessels, to bring back a contingent of soldiers and soldiers' wives from the defeated, disgraced, and strangely paralyzed royal garrison in Sicily. On the ship before it started, he added some excited lines to his letter No. 7, then jumped ashore for a moment to mail it. The lines said that he had thought of "something new, something splendid." " . . . I would see a great drama in the world's history; I would take at last a part in the excitement of the day," he explained. "I am going to Palermo. . . ." "You may hear again from me[,] for I must see something worth telling."

The naval captain in charge of the convoy was Prince Caracciolo, son of a famous old family. At sundown, after a three-hour delay, the prince came aboard and the convoy sailed. The sea was calm and the weather ideal. Adams later remembered, "Towards ten o'clock, when I went on deck to take a last look before going to bed, the moon was rising and I could see the island of Capri still on our left, and . . . behind us the great fiery blotch on the side of Vesuvius."

By then, he had talked with the prince and found him "as jolly a little fellow as I ever saw, flying about . . . all the time like a whirligig." Late the following afternoon, as they approached the Sicilian coast, he and the prince heard firing and saw the flash and smoke of cannon directly ahead. Adams grew somewhat alarmed. "The idea of being shot, occurred to me with new and unpleasant force." He discussed the prospect with the whirligig prince, who "consoled me with the assurance that Garibaldi had no cannon, and that this was probably an admiral's salute from the war-ships in the harbor. So we drank a bottle of beer together and told the anxious old gunner that he might leave those four precious six-pounders of his unshotted."

The *Capri* entered Palermo Harbor that evening, steered past a number of warships belonging to the great European powers, and anchored not far from the British flagship. Next morning, Thursday, June 7, 1860, Adams delivered his despatches to the American naval officers of the *Iroquois* and to the harried American consul, who had taken refuge with his family on an American merchant vessel. Asking questions wherever he could, Adams learned that General Garibaldi ten days before, in the early hours on Sunday, May 27, had alerted his red-shirts, a mere fifteen hundred men, it developed, and ordered them to race directly into the center of Palermo. The red-shirts did exactly what their leader required. "All Palermo rose at once. The street fighting and barricading lasted all that day, and that night Garibaldi slept, if he slept at all, in the Senatorial Palace, the very heart of the city. . . ."

Daring could have gone no further. "This was a real Garibaldian move," Adams wrote, "which ought to have cost him his life . . . but . . . put the whole game in his hands." True, for a while, the issue had seemed in doubt. The royal garrison retained the advantage of over-whelming numbers. For every red-shirt who had intruded into their midst, the garrison boasted fifteen soldiers, willing to fight and waiting for orders. But the garrison's commander, General Lanza, was perplexed. His units were scattered in different positions with Garibaldi's men between them and the city in revolt. In Adams's words: "The next day and Tuesday the barricading . . . continued. . . . On Wednesday the 30th, the Governor yielded to a cessation of arms, which, on Saturday, was changed into a capitulation [by General Lanza] and evacuation of the city [by the garrison]; a most ludicrously disgraceful proceeding, for which the King [of Naples] would, I think, be justified in blowing the General's brains out with his own royal revolver."

Adams wished to inspect Palermo. "I took a boat and landed." The waterfront was in confusion. "I passed barricade after barricade till I came to the Senatorial palace. . . . Before it, there is a small square, and what the [American] naval officers call the improper fountain, improper because there's half Lempriere's Classical Dictionary on it, but a copious insufficiency of costume. [There] . . . I found a still greater confusion and chaos, and crowds of desperately patriotic Sicilians were sleeping, eating, chattering, and howling under the windows of [Garibaldi] the General-in-Chief." Henry saw that the invaders, after all, had brought some odds and ends of artillery. "I stopped a minute . . . to look at [five] . . . cannon of all ages and sizes, mounted on wagon-wheels and looking like the very essence of revolution, rusty, dirty, and dangerous to the men that used them."

All things considered, the city was not as disrupted as it might have been. " . . . the dead bodies and disgusting sights had all been cleared away. After a long detour [away from the palace] and a very indefinite idea of my whereabouts, I made my way through all the particularly nasty lanes and alleys I could find, back to the Toledo. For dirt Palermo is a city equalled by few. I do not know whether I ran any danger of being robbed. . . . I never dreamed of going armed . . . and looked I suppose a good deal as if I had just stepped out of the Strand in London. . . . "

It was midday. Thanks to some words he had exchanged on the *Iroquois* with Captain Palmer, Adams expected that very evening to meet Garibaldi. Palmer had turned out to be a friend of one of Henry's maternal uncles, Sidney Brooks. The fact had made it easier for the visitor and the captain to discuss the situation. Apparently at Henry's suggestion, a plan had been made for him to join Palmer and some of the other officers of the warship at six that evening, to go to the Senatorial Palace.

In place of lunch, Adams ate ice cream. He went to the hotel, where earlier he had been lucky enough to get a room, though not a tub of water for a bath. He rested and, at four-thirty, joined a distinguished party and had a full meal. "The celebrated Colonel Turr sat at the head of the table, next to him the correspondent of the London *Times*, then another of Garibaldi's colonels, then the correspondent of the London *Illustrated News*, then I think Colonel Orsini, and so on."

At six, as agreed, he met Captain Palmer and the others and walked to the palace. Telling the story in a long letter No. 8, completed two days later on the *Capri* while returning to Naples, Adams said nothing about Sidney Brooks and suppressed the name of Captain Palmer. Indeed he neglected to explain that the "officers" with whom he went to visit Garibaldi were Americans from the rakish *Iroquois*, dressed in braided coats and wearing the eagles of the great Republic. Yet his letter was vivid, and said in part:

> . . . the crowd made way to the uniforms, and the sentries at
> the steps presented arms as we passed. It was nearly the same
> scene inside the palace as outside. One saw everywhere the

head-quarters of revolution pure and simple. On the staircase and in the ante-rooms there was a chaos broken loose, of
civilians, peasants, priests, servants, sentries, deserters from
the royal army, red-shirts, and the blue . . . of Orsini's
artillery, and all apparently perfectly at home. We had no
time to look carefully, however, but passed straight on, every
one showing us the greatest respect, until finally the third
door opened and there we were. . . .

Garibaldi . . . apparently [had] just finished his dinner. . . .
He rose as we came in, and came forward[,] shaking hands
with each of the party as we were introduced. He had his
plain red shirt on, precisely like a fireman, and no mark of
authority. . . . I was seated next him, and as the head of our
party remarked that I had come all the way from Naples in
order to see him, he turned round and took my hand,
thanking me as if I had done him a favor. This is the way he
draws people. . . .

But this was only half the scene. At a round table in the
middle of the room, a party of six or eight men were taking
dinner. These were real heroes of romance. Two or three had
the red shirts on; others were in civil costume; one had a dirty,
faded hussar jacket on; one was a priest in his black robes.
They were eating and drinking without regard to us, and as if
they were hungry. Especially the priest was punishing his
dinner. He is a fine fellow, this priest, a slave to Garibaldi
and a glorious specimen of the church militant. I have met
him several times, rushing about the streets with a great black
cross in his hands. He has a strange, restless face, all passion
and impulse. The others were Garibaldi's famous captains—
a fine set of heads, full of energy and action.

Here I was at last. . .face to face with one of the great events
of our day. It was all perfect; there was Palermo, the insur-
gent Sicilian city, with its barricades, and its ruined streets
with all the marks of war. There was that armed and howling
mob in the square below, and the music of the national
hymn, and the five revolutionary cannon. There were the
guer[r]illa captains who had risked their lives and fortunes
for something that the worst envy could not call selfish. And
there was the great Dictator, who, when your and my little
hopes and ambitions shall have lain in their graves a few
centuries with us, will still be honored as a hero, and perhaps
half worshipped—who knows!—for a God.

And yet Heaven knows why he, of all men, has been selected for immortality. I, for one, think that Cavour is much the greater man of the two; but practically the future Italy will probably adore Garibaldi's memory, and only respect Cavour's.

As he sat there laughing and chattering and wagging his redgrey beard, and puffing away at his cigar, it seemed to me that one might feel for him all the respect and admiration that his best friends ask, and yet at the same time enter a protest against fate.

As we came away he shook hands with us again, and took leave of us with the greatest kindness. As we made our way through the crowd across the square, we stopped a minute to take a last look at him. He was leaning on the railing of the balcony before his window, quietly smoking his cigar, and watching the restless, yelling crowd below.

After sleeping that night at the hotel, Adams drifted about Palermo the following day with American naval officers and British newspapermen, looking at things he had missed. Excitement was subsiding, and an arrangement was being made for a plebescite in Sicily concerning its annexation. Henry felt no wish to stay for the voting. ". . . to my mind [,] these European popular elections have a little too much demonstration in them. . . I do not pretend to be a philosopher, but I do know that if I were a conservative I should wish nothing better than these elections for an argument against and a sarcasm on popular governments in their whole length and breadth."

The previous spring in northern Italy, Louisa Kuhn had taught her brother a lesson: that having seen the French army, which he had favored, he needed also to see the Austrian army, which he had despised. The brother had not forgotten the lesson. In fact, he wished to apply it. He had come from Palermo hoping to see two men, one famous, the other not. The story of the second meeting—which took up all Henry's last hours in Sicily—was indispensable. Without it, the full sense of his Italian experience would be lost.

. . .I had brought with me from Naples a letter to an officer of the Swiss legion. . . . So, towards evening to-day I walked round the harbor to the quarters of the royal army. . . . The troops were just forming for the *rappel* as I crossed the great parade ground, so I delivered my letter to the officer, who was already at the head of his command, and sat down myself before the guard-house to watch the performances. The troops came on the ground with their music and all their equipments, looking as fresh. . . as any troops I ever saw. There seemed to be no end to the numbers. They poured in, thousands after thousands, and packed the whole great space. . . .

After about half an hour the troops were marched off again, and my friend came back to me and took me into his quarters. It is a queer place now, this city, for strange sights and scenes. Here was a battalion of foreign troops quartered in a Franciscan monastery, and the cloisters were all alive with busy, chattering German soldiers. We went up the staircase and into my friend's room, a monk's cell, furnished with half-a-dozen chairs, on which a torn and dirty mattress was laid, a table on which there were some lemons and oranges, and a lamp. A couple of glasses of lemonade were ordered, and we sat down and sipped it, and smoked and talked.

. . . I must say the general effect was gloomy to a degree. The evening was heavy and dull, with the clouds hanging low on the mountains, and as the little white-washed cell got darker and darker, and the hive of soldiers down in the cloisters grew more and more indistinct, while the officer was telling his story, full of bitterness and discontent, I really sympathized with him, and felt almost as gloomy as he.

The Swiss officer recounted his experiences as a soldier of fortune in the service of a foreign king, told of the capitulation by General Lanza, and said a chance still existed to retake Palermo, if only the garrison could get from its forceless commander permission to fight and redeem their disgrace. So long a story took time to tell.

Of course, one ought to hate a mercenary soldier, and especially one of the King of Naples. Very likely I should have hated him if he had been coarse and brutal, but . . . he was very handsome, young, and well-bred. . . . His ideas were just about what I had supposed they would be. . . . He had personally nothing to brag of and nothing to be ashamed at. But he declared solemnly, as his own belief and that of the whole corps, that the King had been betrayed; that the city might easily have been held. . . .

It was dark when I came away, and he came with me to the

shore, to see me on board a boat. . . . We shook hands on parting, and I wished him happily out of the whole affair.

"Yes," said he, "I think indeed the whole matter is now nearly ended; at least for us; and I am not sorry. I am tired both of the people and the service."

A tolerably mournful conclusion of ten years' duty, and a gloomy yielding up of a long struggle against fate. But we liberals may thank God if the battle ends so easily.

For Adams, the voyage back to Naples with Prince Caracciolo on the *Capri* was a terminus. Hoping not to be eaten by fleas, a hardship he had suffered many times in Europe since his first arrival in Berlin, he passed the night in the upper cabin, stretched on a sofa. The ship was rolling. Many aboard were seasick. He noticed in the morning that the "poor soldiers' wives on deck looked very unhappy," yet noticed too that some "looked so pale and patiently sad that they might have made beautiful studies for Magdalens or Madonnas." His reactions as he watched them revealed the truth of his ultimate sympathies. "Certainly sea-sickness is one of the trials of life which brings us all down soonest to our common humanity. . . ."

Rather than stay in Naples, he went around the bay to Sorrento, where he spent his last day and night in Italy "alone and in quiet among the orange and lemon groves." There he finished his letter No. 9, the last of his series. It rounded out the history of his week-long excursion to Sicily, amplified his protests about Garibaldi, and said that the general-in-chief might "do more harm than good by the whirlwind that he's riding." Near its close, Adams admitted: "This letter is rather more stupid than usual. You will excuse it, for it is the last. I've tried to show you Italy as I've seen it, and now I have finished it all."

His tone was strained, and no wonder. He had learned in Naples that Seward had been passed by. Instead, at Chicago, the Republicans had nominated Abraham Lincoln—the Illinois lawyer beaten by Douglas in 1858 in their race for the Senate. Adams wished no harm to Mr. Lincoln but thought the American people were political profligates. It seemed to Henry that democracies needed leaders and that Seward was one. Adding a paragraph about the Chicago convention to his last letter, he said, " . . . we have deserted our Cavour."

If he could ignore the American and Italian political ironies which had been its accompaniments, Adams could look back on his journey to Italy as a stunning success. Not only had he seen far more than he could possibly have hoped to see, and met persons he could not have thought to meet, but also his nine letters had fallen out as a tiny but actual book. Without insisting upon it, he glancingly mentioned the fact in the book's last sentence. Aimed directly at the reader, whether the reader were Charles or a stranger, the sentence read, "If you ever come here and smoke your last cigar and watch your last sunset with the waves of the bay breaking under your window, and take your final leave of a book of life that has been all rose-color, you will probably feel as solemn as I do, and will finish with Italy by reflecting that our good God is really good, but that we have ourselves something good and immortal in us, which Italy calls out and strengthens."

# Part Two

## 10 / My Small Services

Charles had understood well enough that Henry wished to send some letters that might be suitable for publication in a Boston newspaper and that he, Charles, was to read them, set them aside if they were bad, and arrange their being published if they were good. All the same, his grasp of his brother's intentions had been so imperfect that he had continued writing to Henry at Dresden after receiving letters sent by him from Vienna and Venice. When further letters arrived from Bologna and Florence, Charles realized at last that his brother was traveling. So he wrote to their mother in Washington asking for Henry's newest address. Mrs. Adams partly reacted by writing to the younger son in Europe that the elder in Boston was a "goose."[1]

Senator Sumner made a parallel criticism. When Henry's letter from Vienna was published in the *Boston Courier*, copies of the newspaper were read in Washington by his parents and the senator, with varied results. According to Mrs. Adams, Sumner was much provoked "that Charles should send your letters to such an unprincipled paper as that, & I confess we all wondered at the same fact." Not only was the *Courier* deficient in antislavery zeal; it lacked the influence and circulation of the *Boston Daily Advertiser,* to which, it seemed, the letters could just as well have been given. The choice of the mere *Courier* aside, Henry's readers in Washington were fairly well pleased. His mother said they all thought the letter from Vienna "very good." Still, she rather believed that his "easy chit-chat" letters to herself had been "far better." When a new *Courier* arrived from Boston containing a letter of Henry's from Venice, Congressman Adams approved—then disapproved. He wrote to the author in Europe: ". . . [your letters] are lively and cheerful, and show you contented in the sphere of your observation. But if you write for the press I recommend it to you to take a graver style and give attention to the more solemn changes that are in progress all around you."[2]

As nearly as his Washington readers could know, the letters were appearing in the *Courier* just as Henry had written them. In fact, they were being altered. Whether the alterations were being made by Charles, by the *Courier's* editor, George Lunt, by a possible assistant editor, or combinations of persons is now difficult to determine. Conceivably Mr. Lunt asked Charles to edit the letters, promising to publish the resulting texts. If that were what happened, the elder brother began by exercising his editorial prerogatives in two small but significant ways. One thing was added to the letter from Vienna, and one thing was taken away. What was added was Henry's initials. What was removed was the sign "No. 1."

When letter No. 2 came from Venice, not only its number but its first six paragraphs were excised. Letters Nos. 3 and 4, each deprived of its number and reduced in length almost by half, were so printed in the *Courier* (after a long delay and under a heading, "Letter from a Tourist," which would do Henry no good with his father) as to create an impression that their author had written one letter on different days from Bologna and Florence. The editing pattern perhaps suggested that willingness or even enthusiasm about the series at the outset had given way to a certain hesitancy. This change of attitude—if it occurred—may have been felt by all the Bostonians involved in the first installments' getting published.[3]

Congressman Adams did not go to Chicago to attend the Republican Party convention. He stayed at his tasks in Washington, where the House of Representatives remained in session. The news of Seward's overthrow reached the Capitol from Chicago at once, on May 18, by the electric telegraph. On the floor of the House, the news was discounted at first, the members mostly supposing that further telegrams would sing a more probable tune. Later, when it became impossible to doubt that Seward had lost the Party's nomination to Abraham Lincoln, several Republican Congressmen were heard to say that they felt relieved. They held that Seward's antislavery statements had been too emphatic and that Lincoln, being comparatively little-known, might better attract undecided voters. Mr. Adams could not agree. It seemed to him that the convention had committed an injustice. Next morning, in his diary, he wrote of Seward as the man "to whom the party owed the nomination." With respect to experience, no comparison could be made, in his view, between winner and loser. C. F. Adams said of Mr. Lincoln, "I believe him honest and tolerably capable; but he has no experience and no business habits."[4]

Stories spread in Washington about the tactics of Lincoln's managers. It was alleged insistently that Seward's defeat had been brought about by underhanded methods. Listening to rumors and reading the daily press, Congressman Adams grew so indignant that he simmered with pent-up anger and moral outrage. At the moment, Senator Seward was away from the capital at this home at Auburn, near Syracuse, in upstate New York. He, too, believed that he had been owed the nomination. Moreover, he remained convinced that he—in consultation with Thurlow Weed—could devise the policies and supply the leadership needed to guide the country through its newest difficulties. To Seward, it was only right and proper that many Republicans in various parts of the Union, including Charles Francis Adams in Washington, should send him messages of unabated admiration and regard.

It was imagined that Seward, in defeat, had three alternatives. He could retire from public life, try to prolong his tenure in the Senate, or seek a place in Lincoln's cabinet, if the Republican candidate should win the election in November. William Henry Seward was not a man who could content himself with any of the three. Also he was capable of daring strategies and large-scale deceptions. Immediately in Auburn, while pretending to take the third alternative of looking towards a place in a possible antislavery cabinet, he chose a fourth alternative. Deposed as leader of the Republican Party, he secretly shifted his attention from the Party, which had deserted him, to the nation generally, which had not. Secretly, he decided to save the Union.

His decision made, it was agreeable to him that lesser men— James Buchanan in the present, possibly Abraham Lincoln in the four years soon to start—should hold the position of president-in-name. He himself would serve as president-in-fact. Sensing that the danger to the Union had much increased, he began at once to perform his office. His first visible step was an effort to enlist as his willing adherent the one surviving son of John Quincy Adams.[5]

After advising C. F. Adams by letter that he was coming back to Washington, the famed New Yorker sped by train to the capital and slept at his house. In the morning, he rode in his carriage to Mr. Adams's residence, the so-called Markoe House, on I Street, near the three-way intersection of I Street, Pennsylvania Avenue, and 20th Street. He intended to offer the admiring congressman a ride across the city to the Capitol. The gesture, although unprecedented, seemed natural; and the Governor's manner as usual was sociable and kind.

C. F. Adams, found at home, was nearly bursting with emotion. He wished to vent his anger at the alleged malfeasance of Lincoln's managers. Seward's unlooked-for offer of a ride seemed adapted to the purpose, and the two statesmen soon were seated in the carriage.

As the vehicle rolled towards the Capitol, Mr. Adams inveighed against the methods the Lincoln men had used, but Mr. Seward changed the subject. According to the elder Adams's own account, the displaced party chieftain "calmly deprecated all similar complaints, and at once turned my attention to the duty of heartily accepting the situation." The New Yorker spoke especially about the new Chicago platform. The Republican Party's principles, he said, had been given a perfect shape; and it now became his friends "to look only to the work of securing their establishment." C. F. Adams was unforgettably impressed. In his opinion, a great leader, slighted and put aside, had shown his greatness more than ever by rising above defeat. To him, Seward's behavior seemed a rare example of "moral superiority."

There matters might have stopped, but the congressman was amenable to orders. C. F. Adams preferred obedience to leadership; W. H. Seward preferred leadership to anything. Moreover, the New Yorker was a penetrating observer of his fellow politicians. How long it took him to perceive that his prospective coadjutor would yield entirely to his direction was a secret the senator was keeping to himself, but he saw his opportunity and did not shrink from taking it. By abstaining from complaints and exhibiting a selfless attitude, he acquired a blind admirer and devoted follower. Permanently, he put an Adams in his pocket.[6]

In advance of her husband, on June 11, 1860, Mrs. Adams started for Quincy with Mary and Brooks. Earlier, the mother had heard frequently from Henry. In recent weeks, while adding letters to his travel series, he had written only scattered letters to her.

To the best of the mother's knowledge, a mere three travel letters had reached Charles from Henry, and all had appeared in the *Courier*. In Boston or Quincy, she may or may not have learned from Charles that no less than six letters, including two from Rome, had come from Henry for publication; that the two from Rome had not appeared in the *Courier;* that, all told, only half of Henry's lines had so far found their way into print; and that the author, in a note to Charles put in with the sixth letter, newly arrived, supposed that each of his letters was being published as written, when received.

Whatever Mrs. Adams learned or did not learn, her presence in

Quincy made a difference. Besides, a seventh letter reached Charles from Henry. Sent from Naples, it ended with an arresting announcement that the family's "tourist" was going to Sicily, where there had been a momentous battle.

In these altered circumstances, on June 29, Henry's letter No. 5, from Rome, was published in the *Courier,* minus its number and five of its paragraphs—appearing forty-three days after its author had sent it. A week later, on July 6, his other letter from Rome was published also, shorn only of its number and opening sentence, portions of the next few lines, then most of a paragraph, and finally an entire paragraph, including one of third son's broadest jokes: "I leave half Rome unseen, and go away half ruined."

Simultaneously, on July 5 or 6, a heavy envelope arrived from Paris. Charles opened it and learned that Henry in Sicily had witnessed the first effects of successful invasion and revolt in Palermo and had briefly talked with Garibaldi. He told the story of his exploit in two related, detailed letters, Nos. 8 and 9, dated respectively at Palermo and Sorrento. Because he had left Italy on the same steamer that would have taken the letters to Marseilles if he had mailed them, Henry had not mailed them in Italy but instead had carried them by sea and rail as far as Paris and mailed them there. He added to the last installment an apologetic note to Charles, saying: "I expect a letter from you soon, scolding me violently for the poverty of these letters. . . . I don't want to see or hear anything more about them."

Henry could deprecate his writing all he pleased, but Charles would have to make a few decisions. Three of the younger brother's letters were on the elder's hands, waiting for editorial treatment. From the three, Nos. 7, 8, and 9, Charles selected No. 8, dated from Palermo, and showed it to their mother.

Three days later, on July 8, Mrs. Adams wrote her usual Sunday letter to Henry, now in Paris, and told her son that he had greatly pleased her. She explained that Charles had received more letters in Henry's series. ". . . the one he showed me was from Paris, & contained a most exciting account of your trip to Palermo. It was extremely interesting & I enjoyed every word of it." Meanwhile, the last three letters were consigned to various fates. Letter No. 7, from Naples, was suppressed. No. 8, an extraordinary effort impossible not to publish, was cut down to the extent of its number, opening sentence, and enough lines to total about three paragraphs, but otherwise was published whole. Henry had dated No. 9 from Sorrento but had written its first part in Naples. As printed in the *Courier,* its place was

changed to Naples, its number removed, and the concluding paragraph—including the tell-tale phrase "a book of life"—dropped from
sight.

Altogether, the writer's nine letters had been given the appearance
of being seven. All but the last were printed on the *Courier's* front
page. The most conspicuous had been the first, captioned "LETTER
FROM AUSTRIA. A Concert at Dresden—A Day on a German
Railroad—Impressions of Vienna—Political Condition of Austria,"
and the second to last, captioned "LETTER FROM PALERMO.
Appearance of the City—The Barricades—The Revolutionary
Army—Interview with Garibaldi."

Henry was expected to reappear at Quincy in mid-October.
Believing himself destined to enter a Boston law office immediately
thereafter, he had earlier asked Charles to keep an eye out for an
opening in a good firm.[7] Sometime in June, the elder brother had
replied by suggesting a different scheme. Reminding Henry that their
parents would be going to Washington again for the winter, starting
in December, Charles theorized that, were Henry to study law on his
own for six weeks between mid-October and early December, he could
then proceed to the capital with their parents, Mary, and Brooks, in
order to seek an opening in a law office there. Charles also advised his
brother to write an article for the magazines on Italian politics.[8]

The third son seemed to welcome the former suggestion, for he
adopted and improved it. On the assumption that their father would
be returning every year to Washington, not necessarily as a member of
Congress but as a high-ranking federal offical, Henry decided both to
study law in Washington and to become a legal resident of the District
of Columbia, like "Mrs. John," his widowed aunt, who had quietly
continued to live there. Thus, on July 1, 1860, the absent son was able
to write to his mother: "I never knew before this how I liked Quincy
and Boston and how sorry I should be to cut loose of them. . . . I shall
make up my bed in Washington, and no doubt it will be just as
pleasant as anywhere else. At all events, whether it is or not, it's the
place my education has fitted me best for, and where I could be of most
use."

As for a magazine article, Henry would not comply. He had
already written an article—his two letters on the Prussian schools. He
also had written a miniature book—his nine travel letters. It was not a
heartbreaking experience for him to find out, a bit at a time, that his
series of letters had been very raggedly published, minus a quarter of

its text, all its conclusion, and many key sentences which pulled it together and explained its method and overall sense. He had written a first book, could write others, and did not need to worry. The attitude he showed towards Charles was wholly positive and approving. The idea of an article on Italian politics, Henry said, could not be acted upon but was excellent. Attributing the interest of his travel letters to mere good luck, he said he could hardly have guessed in Dresden that he would meet Garibaldi in Sicily. Again and again, he thanked Charles for his trouble, adding that he rightly ought to be paid. "Give Charles my love," he wrote to their mother, "and tell him to buy a horse and charge it to me."

Yet Henry's plans were not easily settled. He was keeping open the chance of an attractive clerkship in a Boston office. He seemed disposed to postpone final decisions till after the November election. One of his letters from Paris seemed to indicate he might imitate Charles and write anonymously from Washington for the Boston press in defense of their father's actions in Congress. Possibly, for the present, Henry wanted to have no plan at all. The length of his proposed residence in Washington, if anything, grew more indefinite. He only said he would be in the capital for "some time."

Wanting to study, he had rented rooms in Paris, rather cheap ones, and hurled himself into French with greater energy than he had ever thrown himself into German. Guided by some suggestions made by Gibbon in his *Autobiography*, he was working all day every day, and expected to hire two tutors in August, if his current one proved insufficient. Partly for practice, he wrote long letters to his father and Charles in French. *"C'est fatiguant,"* he admitted, *"mais je fais chaque jour de progres."*

By then, he had spent enough money in Europe to draw truly angry comments from his father. To look at him in Paris, however, the fugitive son was not a spender. His clothes were a sight. He was attempting to keep people's eyes distracted from the worn places on his trousers and coats by wearing fine cravats and new kid gloves, bought in Naples for thirty cents. ". . . I calculate that the extras carry off the essentials," he explained, "just as good wine will carry off a poor dinner."

Loo's pianist priend, Theodore Chase, was in Paris when Henry came. So were John Bancroft and Henry Higginson, the elder brother of Jim. Soon Higginson and Bancroft tried to lure Adams away from his studies, urging him to come with them on a three-week trip to Brittany and thereabouts, a part of the world he would have liked to visit. "I thought of going with them," Henry told his mother, "and writing a pastoral description of the tour. . . . But as I came here to work I suppose I'd better stick it out. . . ." As it happened, the amusement offered by Paris itself exceeded his needs. Most often with Henry Higginson, sometimes with other acquaintances, he ate good inexpensive dinners, attended the theatres, which were superb, and looked in the windows of shops. The stand-offishness of the Parisians seemed to him a virtue. Modifying his prejudice against the French, he said contentedly, ". . . I enjoy Paris very much. It's the pleasantest city city I ever was in, for a stranger. The life here is jovially independent and no one bothers me so long as I don't bother them."

Of his seven closest Adams relatives, the most trying to live with were Loo and Brooks. Their mother had described Brooks to Henry the year before as "sweet tempered & tiresome." Mrs. Adams lamented on another occasion, "Poor Brooks, so really good, lovely & bright,— he gets on wretchedly at school. . . ." And more recently, she had specified, "I think Brooks very backward, he cant study close, or read, or spell tolerabley, & I much doubt if he ever goes to college, for he has no taste for books at all, unless boy stories."[9]

The child presented serious problems. An instance of his perversity was the effect of the stamps Henry had sent him from Europe. Formerly dull and inattentive, Brooks now erred on the side of concentration and passion. Hunting stamps wherever he went, he treated everyone as fair targets for his requests. He especially plagued Boston shopkeepers who might correspond with suppliers in other countries. Mary wrote to Henry, ". . . Brooks is always at a person to get him stamps, and you cannot imagine how unpleasant he is to walk and ride with because if he happens to see any store with an East Indian sign or any sign of that kind, he darts in and leaves you standing in the street for five minutes."[10]

Charles Kuhn had returned momentarily to America. Word reached Henry in Paris from Loo in Switzerland that she was unwell and unhappy. He wrote home to their mother, ". . . I am going to . . . propose her coming to Paris and living quietly with me. If she were to accept, I should go down at once and bring her up here and we could keep house together." Loo quickly agreed to his proposal, so he went to Geneva and brought her to Paris, together with a mountain of trunks, bags, and boxes.

In Paris, Loo changed the rules. Where Henry had suggested they live together as equals, she required they live in her way. Taking rooms she liked in a house she had earlier lived in, she summoned friends from all directions, created a salon, and wanted Henry to dance to her music. "Loo loves to have every one about her gay, brilliant and amusing," he wrote, "and dislikes stupid people as she calls them. Unluckily I am . . . particularly fond of being stupid; that is, of sitting still and saying nothing. . . . It makes me blue to feel that I can't be gay and fascinating, and that every one should think me too old and mannered."

Her husband being rich and indulgent, Mrs. Kuhn made a habit of taking captive Henry to great restaurants in Paris—"the Trois Freres Provencaux and Voisin's and Philippe's and the Cafe Anglais"—which otherwise he would never have entered. The experience changed his ideas of the meaning of good wines and good food. When Kuhn himself came back from America, Henry continued to live with them for a while but eventually returned to rooms of his own. Loo in the interval had gone a long way towards learning that efforts to force her brother into a mold were efforts wasted. "As Loo gets used to me and my style of disposition," patient Henry wrote home, "she adapts herself much better to me than at first, not scolding half so much nor bothering me to be like her."

The previous winter, Mrs. Adams had spoken to Mr. Seward about her son Henry in Europe and asked the Senator to sign a copy of one of his speeches so that she could send it to her absent boy.[11] And in July 1860, apparently on his own initiative, Charles sent the New Yorker the published, *Boston Courier* version of Henry's travel letters from Bologna and Florence, mentioning Cavour. Seward read Henry's paragraphs and reacted by writing to Charles, in part, about his own experiences in Italy, where he had gone in 1859. ". . . I saw Count Cavour on his estate in his retirement last year," the senator noted, "and . . . he confided to me his relations towards his King and country."[12]

Increasingly, as each week passed, the fortunes of the Republican Party appeared to rest on Seward's political management. The election had resolved itself into a four-way contest. Two Democratic parties were in the field, a Northern and a Southern; a newly created party of Constitutional Unionists was strong in the border states; and the Republicans were looking to carry most or all of the states in the North, in the teeth of vigorous Democratic opposition. Mr. Lincoln, the antislavery standard-bearer, had chosen to be a silent candidate and let his previous utterances speak the truth about his own opinions. The positive efforts needed to win him an electoral majority would therefore have to be made for him by other Republicans. At least it was assumed that such efforts were indispensable, for the majority to be attained; and the person expected to make most of the efforts was Seward, the very man the Party had preferred not to nominate.

In mid-summer, the ambitious New Yorker began an ostensible pleasure trip. He went to visit some friends, politicians in Vermont and Maine. The trains he took were stopped in almost every town and city by crowds of citizens, demanding he speak. On August 13, in a glare of public notice, he left Bangor, Maine, and started towards Boston. His arrival in the Boston depot was an out-and-out political rally. Senator Henry Wilson and Congressman C. F. Adams escorted him to the Revere House. A dense mass of Republicans had assembled to hear him. Seward's speech that night was the start of the Party's campaign. Its theme was the approaching triumph of the antislavery cause.

He took occasion to speak as well about himself. Remembering his rejection by the convention at Chicago, he said, ". . . it is God's will that we must be overruled and disappointed. . . ." His manner grew very earnest. He spirited his listeners back to what for him was a sacred year, 1838, when, a young politician, unnoticed and unknown, he had traveled to Massachusetts to seek advice from the sage of Quincy, John Quincy Adams. He, the visitor, had discussed with the former president the demoralized condition of the country under Democratic rule. He had been given a needed fund of counsel. Now, twenty-two years later, looking back on all that had occurred, Seward traced his entire political career from that single interview in Quincy at the Old House. Thence, he said, he had "derived . . . every sentiment, that has animated and inspired me in the performance of my duty as a citizen . . . [during] all the intervening time."

He went that night with C. F. Adams to Quincy to start a pleasant visit with the family. He asked to be shown, and saw, the graves of the Adams presidents in the Quincy churchyard.[13] Before departing, he urged Congressman Adams to join him in September on a western speaking tour, also inviting Charles to come.

Mr. Adams liked to think of himself as a modest member of the House. He believed he wished to stay a time in Congress, then retire in favor of his eldest son, whom he expected to enter politics. The elder Adams therefore declined to make the tour with Seward, or, rather, said he would have to think about it.[14]

Seward left. Mrs. Adams wrote to Henry in Paris about the kindly statesman's arrival from Bangor and visit with the family. Her third son would not need to be told that Seward was a masterly politician, direct when possible, devious when not, and that the canny New Yorker would probably succeed in involving the Adamses deeply in his neverceasing machinations. Replying from Paris, Henry told his mother that her political disclosures were "immensely interesting." ". . . your account of Seward's visit is great."

While in Paris, Henry sometimes grew bitter to think that many years might pass before he returned to Europe and resumed his travels. Yet otherwise his feelings were never so positive. His effort to master French was succeeding steadily. He was accomplishing every object which had brought him across the ocean.

On September 3, 1860, a Monday, he allowed himself to become momentarily involved in the troubles of an American family. The story of his involvement, shortly written by him in a letter to his mother, deserved attention, not because of the story's outward facts but because of what they signified. The story's characters included the three religious young women Henry had seen so much of while in Rome. The three women had belonged to an association of persons linked by unusual ties. The association seemed very united. Its leader was a Mrs. Davis, a vigorous, attractive woman in her middle years. Through the deaths of some of her friends, Mrs. Davis had become the guardian of a Miss Cruthers and a Miss Baldwin, together with an eighteen-year-old boy, Leon Baldwin. Another older woman, of sixty or more, a Mrs. Magee, belonged to the group. They were accompanied, too, by an Irish maid. And, when Adams was meeting them in Rome, a Miss Forrest had brought their number to seven.

Going to his bank on Monday to ask for mail, Adams to his surprise was approached excitedly by a young woman. "It was Miss Forrest, but looking like death and the very devil; pale as a corpse; eyes swollen and black, blue, red and green."

She told him that Mrs. Davis had died, instantly and unexpectedly, a short while before in Spezia. Bereft of their leader, the other six in the group had been systematically victimized there by Italians in a way which Adams, after hearing all the details, thought shocking and "horrible."

The six had struggled somehow to Paris. Miss Forrest was expected to join an American family near Orleans, the Butterworths, whom Adams had earlier crossed paths with in Dresden. The others were going to London, where friends had offered to help them. Henry, proposing to assist Miss Forrest in any way he could, "worked hard" for her Monday morning, then in the afternoon called on Miss Baldwin at their hotel. An agreement was reached that he should himself conduct Miss Forrest safely to the Butterworths on Tuesday. He and the young woman would be chaperoned by the Irish maid.

In the account of the matter he wrote to his mother, Henry explained, "To appreciate my conduct it's necessary to recollect that I do not usually arise from my slumbers at seven as I had to Tuesday morning, nor bolt my breakfast and cut my cigar and coffee with the morning paper." He went promptly to the hotel, ushered Miss Forrest and the maid into a vehicle, and rode with them towards the railroad station. ". . . we drove past the Tuilleries and the church of Notre Dame that fine morning, the young woman and the Irish brogue still enlivening my spirits with all the choicest troubles at Spezia. . . ." After a long ride into the country from Orleans, he delivered Miss Forrest to the Butterworths, visited with them a while, and, towing the maid, started back. "The cathedral [of Orleans] was utterly magnificent as I drove through the city at sunset, and it made quite an impression on me."

In Paris again by nine, he left a message for Miss Baldwin at the hotel that he would accompany her and the others to their train on Wednesday. "At five the next morning I was up and kept the appointment at six. . . ." His friends were ready. ". . . I saw them into their omnibus without extra words wasted, and followed them in a carriage to the depot; got their tickets; registered their baggage; received their last commissions and their thanks and promised to see them at London. . . . There was no conversation, nor effusion. I preferred to leave them undisturbed in their troubles [,] and they had the good sense to take my small services as I gave them, without fearing that I should think them ungrateful."

So ended the story, and its moral could not have been simpler. Although he had no wish to say so, he himself belonged to a family in want of a leader. His story did *not* suggest that anything be done to supply the Adamses the leader they lacked. Throwing the question of leadership into the background, it suggested instead that he, Henry, be given the unusual role of family servant or helper; also that no service would be so small or ordinary that he would not try cheerfully to perform it. The suggestion would not be lost on his mother, who had come to adore him, and might be communicated to his father, who painfully missed him. Thus, when read in America, the story might have far-reaching effects.

## 11 / *Just What I Wanted*

C. F. Adams decided to go with Seward on his western tour. Accompanied by Charles, the congressman set out on September 3, 1860, met the senator in Michigan, and campaigned in Wisconsin, Minnesota, and Iowa. At the meetings where they spoke, frequently at night, grand processions were staged by the Wide-Awakes, a sort of Republican Party soldiery, who wore uniforms, carried torches, and marched in formation. If anything, the New Yorker's popularity had grown since his defeat. The cry that he should have been the Party's candidate was voiced on every hand. The crowds behaved sometimes as if a vote for Lincoln would mean a vote for Seward.

The senator's conceptions were often large. At St. Paul, he gave a visionary speech about the future of the Union. Unrolling the map of a better, larger Republic, he foresaw a time when the capital of the United States would be moved from Washington to a site in Minnesota "at the head of navigation on the Mississippi river." He said that the new, permanent capital—the "last seat of power"—would rise at the center of a unified political confederation coextensive with North America. Alaska, he explained, would be acquired from Russia and annexed to the Union, presumably by purchase, like Louisiana. British Canada? His hearers were assured that Canada would follow somehow; that the growth of the United States would proceed to its continental fulfillment.[1]

Mr. Adams was obliged to leave the New Yorker's caravan at Dubuque and return to Massachusetts. Charles continued with Mr. Seward, whose speaking commitments took him southward to Missouri, westward as far as Lawrence, Kansas, then eastward towards the major cities. The leader and his traveling associates were riding on ordinary trains. One such train they took stopped at Springfield, Illinois. A throng was gathered at the station, and Mr. Lincoln was waiting on the platform.

Together with Senator Trumbull of Illinois, the Republican candidate stepped onto the train and entered the car where the New Yorker had been seated with his associates. Seward appeared to be embarrassed; and Lincoln, also apparently embarrassed, seemed perfectly aware that his former rival, not himself, should have been given the nomination. At least this was the impression formed by Charles Francis Adams, Jr., who was standing in the aisle, observing both.

Senator Trumbull chanced to know not only Senator Seward but every one of his companions. Trumbull introduced each in turn to Lincoln, who glanced at Charles and asked: "A son of Charles Francis Adams? I am glad to see you, Sir." Much like his father, Charles had become a Seward extremist. Meeting Lincoln, the son felt attracted and drawn to the man, as a person; but he could not see in Lincoln a potential president, surely not one adapted to a time of stress and trouble. In his diary, when he could, Charles recorded his impressions carefully. He said in part: "Lincoln's face is a good one, and he has proved his skill as a debater; but, if I could judge from a passing glance . . . I should say that his eye never belonged to a great man of action; it is neither the quick sharp eye of a man of sudden and penetrating nature, nor the slow firm eye of one of decided will; but it is a mild, dreamy, meditative eye which one would hardly expect to see in a successful chief magistrate in these days of the republic."[2]

Henry returned from Europe on the Cunard steamer *Arabia*, reaching the Old House at Quincy on October 17. That evening, except for Loo, all the children were at home. Before retiring, C. F. Adams recorded his son's safe arrival, saying: "He has been gone two years and about twenty days. He looks but little altered."[3]

The third son seemed anxious to study law and immediately began to read a copy of Blackstone's *Commentaries on the Laws of England*. His legal studies were just as quickly interrupted by his father. Explaining that his work as congressman had burgeoned to proportions too large for him to shoulder it unassisted any longer, the Chief announced that he would need the help of one or another of his sons in Washington that winter as private secretary, intimating that Henry could best be spared for such a role. It soon grew clear that the duties attaching to the role of secretary—were Henry to perform it— would be numerous and heavy. In addition to copying all outgoing letters into his father's letter books, copying other documents, arranging appointments, and doing various political errands, the son would be expected to join his mother in supervising the servants and running the household, would oversee the education of Mary and Brooks, and, as necessary, would set them lessons. Henry further was expected to continue his legal studies informally by reading Blackstone and other authors. As payment for his labors, he would be granted a suitable extra allowance and would be given room and board.

In what was taken to be a spirit of filial obedience, quiet Henry acceded to all his father's multiple requirements, one excepted. The son believed that little could be gained for the present through informal legal study. He put away his Blackstone and sought occasions to talk with Charles.[4]

On election day, November 6, 1860, the Chief stayed in Quincy. His sons went to Boston to catch the early returns and came back near midnight with word that Lincoln had won sufficient states to be elected. Next morning in the papers, the family read confirmations of the glorious good news. Mr. Adams exulted in his diary, "There is now scarcely a shadow of doubt that the great revolution has actually taken place, and that the country has once for all thrown off the domination of the Slaveholders." He also noted that he had won his own reelection to Congress by a majority "greater even than the plurality I had two years ago."

The family prepared to move from Quincy to Boston. On the eve of their departure, November 9, the Old House became the scene of a Republican celebration. The father could remember other political meetings at the mansion, but none as jubilant as the rally held that night by his constituents and townsmen. The district Wide-Awakes paraded to his door; applause resounded across the hills; rockets ascended, exploded, and disappeared against the sky.

The festivities made the elder Adams reflective. In his diary that night, he reviewed the problem of his political ambitions and seemed to say they were achieved. "My children are grown up good and efficient members of society. What have I to wish? Political advancement?" "I shall never seek it." But he was apprehensive about the president-elect. Lincoln, in his opinion, was not the equal of the country's difficulties. An arrangement was clearly needed to place the new administration in surer hands than Lincoln's until the precarious transition to antislavery rule were completed. Without quite hoping that the western lawyer be barred from active participation in the affairs of the executive branch, C. F. Adams took the view that the responsibilities attached to the presidential office should in this case be devolved upon an "executive council," made up of the Party's "wisest and most experienced" leaders.[5] His opinion was not unusual.

Many Republican leaders in the eastern states were imbued with the same idea. Phrased differently, the proposition could be reduced to an almost innocuous formula: that the president-elect, being inexperienced and perhaps a little less than competent, would do well to seek and follow the advice of those who would later fill his cabinet.

It was generally assumed that the highest cabinet place, secretary of state, would go to Seward. Attention centered in proportion on Senator Seward and, behind him, on Thurlow Weed. But Seward and Weed were interested in all the cabinet places. They prepared a list of members for Lincoln to appoint. In mid-November, Seward communicated secretly with C. F. Adams in Boston, alerting him that his name would be urged upon the president-elect in connection with the cabinet's second place, secretary of the treasury. Mr. Adams had not sought and did not want the treasury appointment. All the same, in view of Seward's wishes, he was prepared to take it, if his services were asked.[6]

The first practical result of the election of 1860 was unexpected and extreme. The South Carolinians, by naming delegates to attend a convention, prepared in earnest to withdraw their state from the Union. Reacting to their intention, Seward went at once to Washington. C. F. Adams lingered in Boston at 57 Mount Vernon Street. Lincoln remained in Springfield, hundreds of miles to the west, and was silent as before.

Kept in Boston, but much concerned about his impending life in Washington, Henry confessed a small ambition to Charles, saying he wished to try his hand that winter as a regular news reporter. Charles approved the notion. The brothers quickly made a behind-the-scenes agreement with Charles Hale, co-editor of the *Boston Daily Advertiser*, that Henry should serve the paper temporarily as its Washington correspondent, without remuneration, as an unpaid volunteer. Congressman Adams was told about the venture and made no effort, or no successful effort, to prevent its being tried.[7]

Father, mother, Henry, Mary, and Brooks started south on Thanksgiving Day, November 29. En route to Washington, they stayed two nights in New York at the Fifth Avenue Hotel. Louisa and Charles Kuhn, back from Europe and anxious to witness the triumph of the Republicans, paid her relatives a fleeting visit. Plans were made for the Kuhns to join them later in the capital.[8]

Once settled in the Markoe House, Henry began to perform his many duties. The one that kept him busiest was his strictly secretarial work. For the purpose, his handwriting was excellent, perhaps a little small, but superbly legible and even. While copying letters and other documents, he progressively grew cognizant of all the aspects of his father's responsibilities and current business in Congress. The duty Henry least enjoyed was tutoring the children.

The private secretary had wanted to circulate in Washington and visit everywhere. For the most part, instead, he kept within a pre-established circle. "I'm a confoundedly unenterprising beggar," he said. " . . . I make no acquaintances except those of the family." Yet it was doubtful whether he would ever again meet so many people in a short time as he met during his first days in the city. The acquaintances of the elder Adamses were legion. No house in Washington was more visited than theirs.[9] Momentary circumstances had made their home even more a gathering place than had been anticipated. Few other houses were providing hospitalities. The election had been upsetting; and a sudden commercial panic, by cutting down the supply of ready cash, had checked the enthusiasms of the socially extravagant.

Henry had known in advance that he would thrive in Washington, if he could only get to stay there. As he was sure they would be, manners in the capital were easy and relaxed. The private secretaries brought there by members of Congress and other ranking government officials were well-thought-of, and he had the added satisfaction of knowing that his unsigned news reports would soon begin to appear in the columns of the *Boston Daily Advertiser*. Everything about his new arrangements, except the problem of the children, seemed perfectly adapted to his wishes. "It's a great life;" he wrote to Charles, "just what I wanted. . . ."

His own good fortune, he soon noticed, stood in vivid contrast with the misgivings of the permanent residents of the District of Columbia. A persistent rumor had gripped the city, that the new administration would emancipate the slaves. Once spread, the idea created fear and agitation. Had he not steadily discounted the frightened conduct of his neighbors, Henry would have been led to believe that the total eclipse of slavery would soon occur before his eyes. " . . . the citizens of Washington are in a most painful position . . . ," he said. "Property is nowhere. All the slaves in Maryland might be bought out now at half-price with a liberal discount for cash."

Setting aside the evident panic in the capital and the reported doings of the South Carolinians, Henry regarded national affairs as entering an enlightened phase. Preferring to think of Mr. Lincoln optimistically, he disagreed with his father and Charles about the president-elect. If his own predictions were correct, beginning with Lincoln's inauguration on March 4, 1861, the country would be governed by a triumvirate. As president, Lincoln would exercise a considerable share of influence. Ultimate authority would rest with Seward, who, as secretary of state and reestablished leader of the Republican Party, would head the Cabinet. C. F. Adams, as secretary of the treasury, would carry the heaviest burdens of governmental management.[10] Speaking of his father, Henry shortly said with confidence: "He will be strongly pushed for the Treasury. . . . Lincoln is all right. You can rely on that."

The topic currently most talked about in Washington was the meeting of Congress. Many persons believed that the occasion would lead to bitter interchanges in both houses, perhaps to scenes of injury and bloodshed. The news from South Carolina was exacerbating old antagonisms and breeding new ones. An astonishing number of people in the capital were avowed disunionists. Listening to their voices, Henry often heard it said in hopeful tones that the Union was as good as dissolved and that Congress would never meet again.[11]

What worried him was fear that the Republicans would split. Although unanimous on the subject of slavery, the members of the Party were of different minds about secession. The subject was a new one, at least as a practical matter, needing actual disposition; and most of the antislavery men in Washington were at a loss to know exactly where they stood.

In the past, the country's politicians had dealt with the slavery question by enacting a succession of legislative compromises, which all good Republicans were honor bound to view retroactively as errors. A possibility now loomed that some of the Republicans in Congress might join with the Democrats in patching together still another compromise. To Henry's way of thinking, the problem of the hour was Republican Party discipline. He sorted the antislavery men in Congress into two categories. Approving of those he judged the stronger, he disdained and criticized the weaker, saying, for example, "The weak brethren weep and tear their hair. . . ." Yet he was far from sure that the strong Republicans could prevail. " . . . there has been no open defection," he explained, "but the pressure is immense and you need not swear too much if something gives at last."

The House of Representatives convened on Monday, December 3, 1860, and the secret Washington correspondent of the *Boston Daily Advertiser* looked on at the proceedings. Except that the Capitol was overrun with visitors, extremely little happened. It was announced that President Buchanan and his cabinet had not yet completed the annual message. Obliged to wait a day till it was finished and could be read, the members merely organized themselves and recessed. For Henry, uneventfulness was welcome. As an untried reporter, it was much easier for him to describe an anticlimax than it would have been to describe a serious debate, not to speak of violence. He quickly began to draft his first report, expecting to continue it when something more definite had happened. His opening lines ran along in a confident fashion. "The members, even those from South Carolina, selected and took possession of their desks and drew their pay and mileage, or as much of it as they could get, as good-naturedly and as quietly as any one could wish. Perhaps the feeling that the struggle was inevitable made all parties the less ready to hurry it, or perhaps the respite of one day on account of the non-appearance of the President's Message, was a relief, and raised their spirits. At all events there was no fight. . . ."

Next day, December 4, Buchanan's message was read. In the House, a member from Virginia introduced a resolution referring the domestic portion of the message to a new, unusual committee, to consist of one member from each state. If established, the new House committee would form a virtual, temporary, second senate. Its function would be to recommend a cure for the country's domestic ills. The ayes and noes were ordered and the resolution passed.[12]

In the voting, the Republicans divided. A vociferous bloc of Southern Democrats, most audibly the South Carolinians, abstained from voting but took the opportunity to say that their states intended to secede. A plainer challenge to the members representing districts in all the other states could not have been devised. Yet the Republicans in the House made no rejoinder. According to young Adams's first report, completed and mailed that afternoon or evening, the antislavery men in Congress had decided to "ignore the whole secession movement as far as possible." " . . . so they sat quietly and listened without any display of feeling, to the declaration that South Carolina is out of the Union."

The reporter's own ideas concerning secession were defiant. To begin with, he believed that disunion was the merest suicide—that secession would not work. Also he believed that the secession of South Carolina could not be prevented. Linking these propositions, he had become a proponent of a rash, aggressive doctrine. On the theory that nothing would better prove its inadvisability than an attempt to put it into practice, he wished to see secession tried.

Protected by anonymity, the correspondent declared his thesis loudly in the *Boston Advertiser*. For fourteen days, in several news reports, he reiterated his contention. "So far as I can learn," he wrote on December 4, "the feeling here [in Washington] is that nothing will do any good until secession has been tried. If South Carolina has got this idea so firmly fixed in her head—that free-trade, and the African slave trade, and an independent government will make her prosperous and happy,—no compromise and no kindness will prevent her from trying it." He repeated, on December 10, "My own belief is that this question has got to be tried on the merits of secession and on that alone. . . ." On December 17, he obstinately said again, " . . . the only sure and final settlement of the whole matter is, to try it on the merits of secession, pure and simple."[13]

When he took this position, young Adams had not met Seward. The precise moment when he first saw the senator is not known. His earliest sustained impressions of the man were formed on Tuesday night, December 4, when Seward visited briefly at the Markoe House, and on Wednesday evening, December 5, when the senator joined the Adamses for dinner "as one of the family." Writing privately to Charles about the latter occasion, Henry remembered: " . . . [Seward] had all the talking to himself. I sat and watched the old fellow with his big nose and his wire hair and grizzly eyebrows and miserable dress, and listened to him rolling out his grand, broad ideas that would inspire a cow with statesmanship if she understood our language. . . ." Words could scarcely express the degree of Henry's fascination. "He is the very most glorious original. It delights me out of my skin to see the wiry old scare-crow insinuate advice."

Henry meant to send the *Advertiser* two reports a week. That same night, December 5, while Seward talked and the reporter listened, the first of the latter's secret communications was on its way to Boston. Complications started for the younger Adams when he began to realize that Seward had a theory of secession apparently similar to his own but in substance very different. In other circumstances, the disparity might not have mattered greatly to Henry; but for the moment, fearing that the Republicans would quarrel among themselves, he wanted all the Republican politicians in Washington, himself included, to follow Seward's lead. Compromising, he so wrote his second report to the *Advertiser*, dated December 7, that it reflected both his own and Seward's ideas.

He later said his second letter had been a "good" one, but added, "I say it because I have my doubts." The report had concerned the secessionists, whose announced designs had grown in scale. "There can be no doubt," Adams wrote, "that a regular plan has been considered, and probably adopted, by the leading democrats of five Southern States, according to which those States will declare themselves out of the confederacy and will set up a confederacy of their own. We may expect to see the whole process unfold itself within the next two months. . . ."

Needless to say, the secession of five states—South Carolina, Mississippi, Florida, Alabama, and Louisiana—and the creation of a new country were much more menacing projects than the secession of South Carolina alone. Yet Adams strove to represent the antislavery leadership in the capital as prepared for any eventuality. "It would be an insult to the great leaders of the party to suppose that their ideas . . . are changed . . . ," he wrote in his doubtful, second report to the *Boston Advertiser*. "Their theory has been declared over and over again that disunion is an impossibility. A mere temporary secession is not disunion nor anything approaching to it. Mr. Seward laid this down very clearly in his great speech in the Senate last winter. . . . Armed coercion has nothing to do with the proposition. . . . He [Seward] has faith in human nature as he has in God, and on this he grounds his belief that sooner or later public opinion must recover its true bearings, and the southern magnetic needle must point again to the North."

Thus confusion mounted. Adams's *Advertiser* reports were sustaining two rival doctrines about secession: his own clear doctrine of defiance—which he would not give up—that secession should be tried; and Seward's vague doctrine of reassurance that secession would only be apparent, that no remedies were needed, that "nature, in such difficulties, is best left to her own resources." If either doctrine were more often spoken in the reports, it was Seward's, which, put in medical terms, seemed to say that secession was a governmental disease which antislavery politicians should examine but not treat. The recommended course for attending physicians was "patience, kindness and forbearance."

On Friday evening, December 7, with his parents and another couple, Henry was a guest at the New Yorker's house on Lafayette Square. "We six had a dinner, at which the Governor caused a superior champagne to be brought out. . . ." Added visitors arrived as the evening continued. One of the many, Senator Anthony of Rhode Island, remarked to the host that affairs were going badly. Slowly Seward countered that affairs were going well. Watching the exchange, the younger Adams realized, with something of a start, that Seward was an actor—that his reassuring optimism was a bluff, so cleverly and steadily sustained that there seemed no way of telling what the man was really thinking about secession, Southern confederation, or other troubling possibilities.

Young Adams had been quick to make this all-important discovery because he was an actor himself, in the *Boston Advertiser*, not in relation to his ideas, but in relation to his age and knowledge of the capital. Readers of the paper would not want to be told that its editors were accepting news reports from a Washington correspondent who was not yet twenty-three, and whose only previous, direct experience of the capital had been a visit, or two visits, very brief, years before. Inescapably, Henry's reports were being worded as the writings of an older person, a veteran Republican of the Massachusetts school, accustomed to the sights and manners of Washington and long acquainted with its politicians.

The reporter was not lowered in his own eyes by his continual dissembling, nor did he think the less of Seward after perceiving that his deceptive pronouncements and assurances were the devices of a leader determined to shape events, or at least affect them. Neither could Henry say anything better about secession and Southern confederation than the things he had already said, or repeated after hearing Seward say, in the *Boston Advertiser*. Such subjects were very hard ones to have improved ideas about. Most Republicans, left to themselves, would not have wanted to think much about either subject. In truth, affairs *were* going badly for the Party's philosophers. As he continued to worry about the plans of the disunionists, the younger Adams grew privately convinced that the withdrawal of five contiguous states and their organization as a new country, even if temporary, would be a momentous occurrence. An applicable phrase formed itself in his mind and came back to him repeatedly: "the great secession."

The diary young Adams had started to keep at fourteen he had continued to keep, and it had grown to many volumes. What he had written in it must have been honest and expressive; for its volumes for 1852 to 1862, when he read them in later life and committed them to the flames, would make his mind reel with reactivated emotions. At a guess, the volumes mainly concerned his ambitions and how he thought they could—or perhaps could not—be achieved. If so, his progress since his fourteenth year had been attributable in part to his private musings in their pages. Surely something had helped him guide himself, and his diary was the most probable something.[14]

From his point of view, the chance to act in secret as the Washington correspondent of the *Boston Advertiser* was politics pure and simple—an opportunity to mold opinion, and thus a lever with which to influence what would happen in the country. Partly written to report the news but mostly written to place a construction on it and promote particular attitudes and courses, his communications to Charles Hale were as much political acts as a senator's speeches, the votes of a member of the House, or proposals or orders devised in the executive mansion. Admittedly, while he was copying letters, filing, and otherwise engrossed in the mere mechanics of his father's congressional business, the private secretary remained a very minor figure in the secession crisis; but when Henry and his father, or better, Henry, his father, and Seward, discussed the public problems currently staring at them like so many lions, waiting to be tamed, the younger Adams was allowed a voice; and when he mailed reports to Boston, the nameless correspondent became an important politician in his own right—a persuasive speaker in a paper widely read.

Wanting *not* to be a politician only, but rather both a politician and a writer, he was still feeling very strongly the inspiration which had come to him in Rome, the discovery that he would one day have to write a great history of the emergence of the American Union as a permanent creation and a power in the world. Now that he was living in the Union's capital, he spied a chance to gratify immediately, albeit in a small, preliminary way, his deep desire to become a great historian. He perceived that, by writing a new series of private letters to his elder brother, he could set down for posterity, not a history of important old events, but a lively record of day-to-day events in a time of severe disturbance. The new series would not be published but instead preserved for reading in a later era. To clear the time for writing its installments, he temporarily broke off his diary.

Rather fancifully perhaps, he conceived his new series in architectural terms, as a "memorial" or monument, erected by himself in Washington. On Sunday, December 9, 1860, stating his purpose to Charles, he said explicitly: "I propose to write you this winter a series of private letters. . . . I fairly confess that I want to leave a record of this winter on file, and . . . would like to think that a century or two hence when everything else about us is forgotten, my letters might still be read and quoted as a memorial of manners and habits at the time of the great secession. . . ."

Charles would be depended upon to do no more than receive and keep the installments, and possibly return them to Henry at some future date. That the elder brother could be trusted to that extent had been shown by his keeping the nine installments of the younger's miniature book of Italian travels, all of which were intact. Secure in the knowledge that his latest scheme was practicable, the third son fell to work in a happy spirit. As soon as he had finished one building block of his Washington "memorial," he started the next, not waiting for his brother to reply. Often writing late at night when his parents and the children were asleep, he added blocks.[15] He could not know it; but his invaluably informative memorial would rise to a height of eighteen installments, all of which would survive, be found, and published in 1930.[16]

While talking in Washington about their eagerness to leave the Union, not a few of the secessionists in Congress also talked freely about conceivable arrangements which might induce them to keep their states within the Union. A favorite proposal was for the country to be dismantled and rebuilt with all its antislavery states left out. Listening to this and similar dreams, Adams was struck by their utter impracticability. Also he doubted that real secessionists—such as Congressman Brown and the two senators from Mississippi—would be satisfied with any arrangement that could be offered. ". . . from the tone of Mr. Brown . . . Mr. Iverson and Mr. Davis," he wrote to the *Advertiser* on December 10, "it seems hardly likely that the South can be appeased by anything but a total, unconditional surrender."

Meeting Jefferson Davis and persons like him at social gatherings in Washington, just after the convening of the House and Senate, Henry at first was pleased, but also astounded and perplexed, to find them very warm and friendly. In his December 10 report, he mentioned that socially the Republicans and the extreme secessionists in Washington for the moment were on "excellent terms." He explained that the latter persons regarded themselves as already "out of the Union." ". . . before leaving this city forever [they] wish to forget all that is past and bear no ill-will." Their sincerity was evident, and their good-naturedness appealing.

Yet Henry could not long return their smiles and listen to their ideas without concluding with alarm that a portion of his countrymen had gone politically insane. Their most extravagant idea was that their future empire would duplicate in modern times the glory and grandeur of Greece and Rome in ancient times. They could prove it with geography. There was an equivalence, in their ideas, between the Mediterranean and the Caribbean. Cuba would be their Sicily, Mexico their Carthage. So overpowering was the rhetoric of their crazy confidence that Henry, months later, would write a record of their December fancies and add, "It was useless to argue with men mad with such ideas. . . ."[17]

The strong Republicans intended that nothing substantial be done to appease the slavepower. Privately exhorting the faithful in letters from Springfield, Abraham Lincoln spoke a language which all true Republicans understood. Writing on December 13, the president-to-be advised: "Prevent, as far as possible, any of our friends from demoralizing themselves, and our cause, by entertaining . . . compromises of any sort, on *'slavery extension.'*" " . . . hold firm, as with a chain of steel. . . ."[18]

In Springfield unhappily, Abraham Lincoln was not as well situated as Henry Adams in Washington to count noses in Congress and determine the actual odds for or against the passage of a legislative compromise relating to slavery. The reporter's opinion soon became that a heterogeneous mass of Democrats, former Whigs, border state Unionists, and weak Republicans would speedily enact a compromise and President Buchanan would sign it into law. In that event, the incoming Lincoln administration would commence its work on March 4, 1861, in the face of an organized, hostile majority in Congress; that is, organized to the extent of having settled the country's policy.

Speaker Pennington had meanwhile announced in the House that the member from Massachusetts selected to serve on the new, unusual "Union Committee"—also known as the "Committee of Thirty-three"—would be Charles Francis Adams.[19] Expecting that his father, being a strong Republican, would find himself as much in the minority as a member of the committee as he already was as a member of the House at large, and Congress at large, Henry wrote to Charles, " . . . our good papa bears up the opposition. . . ." So few did the strong Republicans appear to be in Congress, and so numerous their various opponents, that the sense of Republican victory diminished or even vanished; and Henry was taught to feel that actual victory might have to wait till 1862 or 1864, when the composition of Congress might be changed.

Simultaneously, Henry learned, in deepest secrecy, that Lincoln had offered the place of secretary of state to Seward; that Seward had asked time to consider his response; and that plans were completed to dictate to Lincoln the membership of the entire cabinet. Seward would go to Albany. Weed would journey to Illinois. Lincoln, if all went well, would settle on C. F. Adams as his choice for secretary of the treasury.

Young Adams learned the details of the situation in part from Seward directly, and partly from Seward indirectly through the Chief, but also by watching Seward so closely that he could know what he was doing, despite the man's best efforts at concealment. The Republican leader came again to the Markoe House on the eve of his departure for Albany and Auburn. Henry studied him as the perfection of American political expertise. Itching to tell Charles in private about the future cabinet and the promotion of their father, yet honor bound to keep Seward and his father's secrets, the memorialist contented himself with saying:

> He [Seward] goes home tomorrow. . . . Why he goes home I don't know. *He* says it's not politics that drives him [,] but W. H. S. is not to be sounded by ordinary lines. . . . .
>
> But the Governor will be great; *our* Governor [,] I mean. Hints of any sort are welcome.[20]

Two days were needed, sometimes three, for Adams's reports to the *Advertiser* to travel through the mail to Boston and appear in print. Charles Hale seemed glad to get the reports and published them uniformly on page two under the headings: "LETTER FROM WASHINGTON. [From Our Own Correspondent.]." In keeping with usual newspaper practice, the manuscripts were discarded when printing started. If one may judge from internal evidence, the correspondent's first three reports were published in Boston with only minor changes or deletions, or none at all.

On December 18, 1860, a Monday, opening a copy of the paper in the expectation of seeing his fourth report in print, Adams did not find it. On Tuesday and Wednesday, the report still failed to show itself. He did not like to think that Hale would view the reports as separate entities when they reached the paper's office. The correspondent wished his efforts to be accepted and published as an unbroken series, on the days for which he planned them. Notifying his elder brother that the *Advertiser* had suppressed his fourth report, Henry asked Charles to visit Hale, tell him that the report had been written at a time when everything in Washington "looked fishy," watch the editor, and "mark what he says or looks."

The busy friends of compromise in the national legislature had sifted a variety of schemes and fastened on one put forward by Senator Crittenden of Kentucky. In Henry's words, the proposed legislation would be "the reenactment of the Missouri Compromise as an amendment to the Constitution, with the condition that, as North of that line [36°30′] there should be freedom, so South of that line slavery should be acknowledged, protected and perpetuated if necessary by the active interposition of the Federal Government, not only in all territory now belonging to the United States but also in all that may be acquired hereafter."

For purposes of reconciling the opposing factions in Congress, the Crittenden proposal was worse than useless. Its proslavery tendencies were so decided that the secessionists were able to embrace it as their own. In the House Committee of Thirty-three, they paraded the scheme before the other members as their "ultimatum"—their price for staying in the Union. Watching this new performance, the Republicans on the committee grew very restive. They resented being asked to weigh a "compromise"—the protected and forced extension of slavery in the remaining, and in future, territories—that flew in the face of their Party's first commandment. As Henry said, "No real republican would ever consent to listen to it."

Events were moving faster than the Republicans could realize. It was hard for them to understand why the secessionists, at such a stage, should embrace a compromise of any sort. In fact, the proponents of secession and a Southern Confederacy had not welcomed and endorsed the Crittenden proposal in hopes that it would be considered, much less accepted, by senators or congressmen from Northern states. They hoped that its momentary support by themselves would serve to unify all the Southerners in the Senate and House without exception, whatever their previous opinions and views had been, and thus open the way for the withdrawal and separate confederation of all the Southern and border states, dividing the great Republic beyond the slightest chance of eventual reversal.[1]

The populace in Washington was more alive to the danger than the Republicans. Rumors shook the city like December storms. Residents whimpered that their lives and property would be consumed in a slave revolt, or, failing that, in an attack upon the city by proslavery soldiers, crossing the Potomac from Virginia. Such fears could not seem wholly mad, for the capital was defenseless. In the White House, distracted by the opposing counsels of the Northern and Southern members of his cabinet, old President Buchanan could only urge that the country fast and pray. The regular army was nowhere to be seen, and presumably remained at the disposal of the secretary of war, John B. Floyd, a known secessionist.[2]

A single voice cried out. Andrew Johnson of Tennessee, a Southern Democrat, denounced secession in the Senate on December 18 and 19 as nothing else than treason.[3] As if in answer to Senator Johnson's words, on December 20, the South Carolina convention at Columbia passed its Ordinance of Secession. On the same day in Washington, the House Committee of Thirty-three prepared to vote on the question of slavery in the territories. The secessionists expected that a majority of the committee would side with them in supporting the Crittenden proposal. At the crucial moment, the member representing Maryland, Mr. Henry Winter Davis, rose and introduced an alternative proposal.

Congressman Davis, having first appeared in public life as a leader of the Know-Nothings in Baltimore, and still a member of the American Party, was known in Washington parlance as a "South American." He was recognized for his loyalty to the Union—and proportionally distrusted by those in Congress who wished the Union were dissolved. Winter Davis pointed out that the territories south of the line of the Missouri Compromise were no longer large. With the exception of the Indian Territory, which could be excluded from discussion, the only area south of 36°30′ which had not been admitted to the Union as a state or group of states was New Mexico, including Arizona. He suggested that Congress might better admit New Mexico to the Union as a slave state as soon as possible. If that were done, he urged, no territory would remain to have disputes about.

When he was seated, the other Southern members of the House committee whispered to one another, retired to an adjoining room, and held a long consultation. They returned with the announcement that the Maryland Congressman's suggestion was unacceptable. Yet their faces clearly showed that their unanimity was shaky. Winter Davis had found a wedge with which to drive the other Southern committeemen apart. The Southern members who were still loyal to the Union could not help but be attracted by his idea, which seemed to offer hope of a genuine solution. They could not persist in opposition to his idea without negating the loyalty they sincerely wanted to express.[4]

The younger Adams was following these developments as closely as anyone in Washington. He also was growing nervous. He could not escape anxiety about the future cabinet. That his father did not want the treasury appointment did not diminish Henry's craving for the Chief to learn to want it. The father's indifference only made it imperative that the son quickly think, write, or do something, anything, to increase his father's chances. Seward was still in Auburn. Weed had gone to Springfield. And a bugbear had taken hold of the younger Adams's mind. It seemed to him that his father could lose the treasury appointment were he to raise his voice in the Committee of Thirty-three and make himself conspicuous.

The son had mentioned a few days earlier that his father, attending the meetings of the committee, had decided to be silent and "do nothing." Henry had subsequently realized that this could not go on forever. Debate in the committee would sooner or later require, in all conscience, that C. F. Adams take an active part. The intervention of Winter Davis on December 20 at first seemed to ease the situation. Henry wrote to Charles that their father's safety was assured. " . . . [Congressman Davis of Maryland] is assuming the decided course of breaking with the south[,] and he will bear the brunt of the battle." Henry added, "I am not sorry. . . ." As if he were his father's keeper, he remarked protectively, " . . . I don't care to have him expose himself now."

Next morning, December 21, a new *Advertiser* came from Boston. Looking into it, the younger Adams saw that publication of his reports had been resumed. His fifth report had been published with reasonable speed, more or less as written. Later in the day, the swaying struggle in the Committee of Thirty-three began again, and the Chief did precisely what his private secretary wished he would not do: he made a speech. Rejecting the Crittenden proposal, he told the other members of the committee—in Henry's paraphrase—that "rather than consent . . . to see a constitution which did not countenance slavery and was made for freemen, turned into an instrument discountenancing freedom and protecting slavery, he would see the Union dissolved and endure the consequences whatever they might be."

As instruments for saving the Union, Congressman Adams's words were ill-advised. His speech could only tend to push the Southern members of the committee back together.

Congressman Winter Davis spoke a second time, and several Southerners present showed interest in the New Mexico idea. The secessionists perceived that their majority had vanished.

No vote was taken. By general agreement, the committee recessed for a week, to give time for "reflection and consultation." C. F. Adams and H. B. Adams looked back and were shocked to see what had occurred. Without their help, Davis, an independent Southerner, had broken up a deadly secessionist attack. Henry sent the *Boston Advertiser* a long report, his sixth, which he regarded as important—"the most so of any yet." The report involved a deliberate omission. Although its subject was the struggle in the House Committee of Thirty-three, it failed to mention that Congressman Adams, the member of the committee representing Massachusetts, had made a speech.

That same evening, December 22, Henry wrote to Charles and touched the sensitive question of their father's elevation to the cabinet.

"I hoped yesterday," the third son explained, "that our M. C. for the 3d. would get through quietly, without rubbing, but it may not be so." The message needed to be decoded. Their "M. C. for the 3d." was the member of Congress for the Third Massachusetts District, C. F. Adams, and the trouble was that his appointment as secretary of the treasury now was seriously jeopardized. Affairs had reached a crisis. The fire of secession was burning more fiercely every moment. Within the past few hours, the Chief had formed a secret alliance with Winter Davis. Mr. Davis and Mr. Adams were both opposed to compromise. The difference could seem slight, but they intended to bring about a "settlement."

As a beginning, C. F. Adams would prevail upon the other Republican members of the Committee of Thirty-three to join with him in the adoption of Davis's proposal as a Republican Party measure. The main step would be taken on December 28, when the committee resumed its meetings. Mr. Adams would then present the "settlement" to the entire committee for approval.[5]

Henry understood the necessity and value of the secret alliance and the impending counterattack. He knew that the so-called settlement would not be put forward in the hope that it would be acceptable to the secessionists. Its authors, in the son's words, were determined to "unite the North and divide the South."[6] At a minimum, they intended to keep four border states, Maryland, Virginia, Tennessee, and Kentucky, permanently within the Union. If that could be accomplished, as many as nine states could secede and confederate but no mortal damage would be done. Much the greater part of the Republic would cohere. But Davis and the two Adamses were also hopeful that the fire could be extinguished—that no more than five states would secede, and all would eventually drift back.

Earlier, mixing news and comments, Henry had written reports for the *Advertiser* which most Massachusetts Republicans would relish both for style and doctrine. He had said forthrightly that he saw in compromise "only a postponement of an inevitable struggle, which every new concession makes more disastrous." The actual secession of South Carolina on December 20 forced upon him—and upon his father—an immediate decision about priorities. He had to answer a question: was the extinction of slavery to be placed ahead of the preservation of the Union?

In his speech before the Committee of Thirty-three, the chief had seemed to say it was.

After Winter Davis spoke a second time and the committee agreed to a week's recess, both C. F. Adams and H. B. Adams supported the opposite answer, that it was not.

Henry omitted the matter of his father's speech in the important sixth report he sent to the *Advertiser* on December 22 mainly in order to simplify the work of publicizing the New Mexico expedient. The key report sang the praises of Winter Davis and explained in detailed fashion the possibility of a settlement. It bears repeating that Congressman Davis was a Know-Nothing and "South American." In no sense could he be taken for a Republican—although he later became one. The *Boston Advertiser* was a leading Republican organ. Yet its Washington correspondent was sure that the newspaper would be willing, for a time, to print remarks and explanations favorable to Davis. The paper had earlier done so. In his two "Pemberton" reports, published in the *Advertiser* the previous February, Charles had copiously lauded the man from Maryland.

Tragically for the Adamses who had gone to Washington in the crisis, few Republicans in the capital besides themselves, and even fewer in other places, had yet begun to sense the degree of the Union's peril. Lincoln, for example, was continuing to choose his cabinet on the now out-dated assumption that he should try to make selections that would unite the Republican Party, as distinct from selections that would unite whatever might remain in March of a swiftly dissolving Union. The vice-president-elect, Hannibal Hamlin, asked Lincoln in mid-December about the chance of a cabinet place for C. F. Adams. The question as Lincoln viewed it was bound up with the facts of former political loyalties. The Republican Party was mostly comprised of former Whigs, former Free-Soilers, and former Democrats. The president-elect wished to balance these different breeds of Republicans against each other within the cabinet and at the same time choose men from different regions of the North. Remembering that Mr. Adams had been a Conscience Whig and a Free-Soiler, Lincoln answered Hamlin on December 24: "I need a man of Democratic antecedents from New England. I cannot get a fair share of that element in without. This stands in the way of Mr. Adams."[7]

Thurlow Weed had received a similar reply to inquiries he put to Lincoln personally in Springfield in mid-December and had reported to Seward the disappointing news that the president-elect was tenaciously resisting their direction.[8] On December 24 and for two days thereafter, the Adamses in Washington remained in ignorance of Lincoln's course.[9] At the time, father and son were much absorbed in other matters. In private meetings, C. F. Adams was gaining Republican converts to the New Mexico settlement within the Committee of Thirty-three. H. B. Adams was worrying about the impressions his father would make on Republicans in Boston and its environs, if he persisted in the effort.

The Republican Party, divisible into the weaker and stronger brethren with respect to compromise, was best viewed in connection with the New Mexico proposal as divisible into the weak, the strong, and the "ultra men." A fair specimen of an "ultra" Republican was Charles Sumner. In better health, Mr. Sumner had resumed his duties in the Senate, remained a kind friend and frequent guest of the Adamses at dinner, and was hoping to shift to diplomatic work, preferably as secretary of state, or alternatively as minister to England.

As Henry knew, Sumner's friendliness towards the family made him an exception among the Massachusetts ultras. There were ultras in New England who were spoiling for an opportunity to attack Charles Francis Adams for being nothing better than a strong Republican. As soon as the news got out in Boston that Congressman Adams had gone along with a suggestion put forward by Winter Davis that the government in Washington should admit another slave state to the Union, also that Mr. Adams wanted other Republicans to follow his example, a headlong attack on the chief would be launched in Massachusetts.

First a small attack was directed against Henry. His reports so far published in the *Advertiser* had failed to measure up to the requirements of C. F. Adams, Jr. On Christmas Day, Henry received from his irritated brother a private letter "almost wholly occupied with criticisms" of his reports in the paper.

Cheerfully, on December 26, the volunteer correspondent replied to Charles: "What you say is perfectly true. . . . Naturally it is hard at first for a beginner . . . to strike the key note; still I think I can manage it in time; and meanwhile criticise away just as much as you please."

The reporter's cheerfulness was caused in part by new reflections concerning the prospects of his father. While Seward had stayed in Washington, Henry had grown aware that his father was trapped within the magnetic field of the New Yorker's domination. The discovery had not been one that the private secretary could find agreeable. During the senator's long absence, Henry also grew aware of something hugely pleasing. Compared with the other members of the House of Representatives, and even most of the members of the Senate, C. F. Adams was a paragon of competence. Moreover, the congressman was growing in political stature. Calm, well-informed, deliberate, and willing to listen while others spoke, he made very good impressions.

Reversing himself, Henry no longer hoped his father would hide his light under a bushel. Indeed he wished the Chief would do the opposite. A delusion seemed almost to grip the son, that the father could outgrow his subordination to Seward and recover his former independence. "Our good father stands in a position of great power," he wrote to Charles. "Crittenden says that he is the greatest block in the way of conciliation, and some one else says that his speech . . . in the Committee will prevent his confirmation as *Secretary of State,* which is rather a wild remark in more ways than one. Now he will have to bear the brunt of all attacks from the ultra men. But he can stand that well enough, and it may even do him good."

Seward reappeared in Washington, spoke to C. F. Adams on December 27, and told him that his appointment as secretary of the treasury had been resisted by Lincoln in Springfield. The elder Adams was just as glad. He had rather feared the appointment, which seemed to him "gigantic."[10] But the New Yorker had no intention of permitting present or future chief executives to run the executive branch of the federal government. He had come from Auburn more than ever resolved to guide the actions of both the outgoing and incoming administrations, with or without the consents of Presidents Buchanan and Lincoln.

That Seward would succeed in dominating Buchanan seemed entirely possible. A rift had opened within the cabinet concerning the conduct of an officer of the regular army. The officer was Major Robert Anderson, commander of the garrison at Fort Moultrie, in the harbor of Charleston, South Carolina—also, it may be mentioned, an uncle of Henry's friend Nick Anderson at college. On December 26, Major Anderson had quietly transferred his men from Fort Moultrie, easily attacked on its landward side, to less accessible Fort Sumter, on an island in the harbor. The major had acted on his own initiative.

Learning what Anderson had done, the secretary of war, John B. Floyd, had confronted President Buchanan with a demand that all regular army forces be withdrawn at once by sea from South Carolina. The president refused, and Floyd resigned. Other members of the cabinet quit for varied reasons. Embezzlements and frauds were discovered in the Interior Department. The little dignity that still attached to the Democrats surrounding the bewildered Buchanan completely fell away.[11]

Charles wrote to Henry in some alarm on December 27 that the attack on the Chief had started. Republican ultras, maverick radicals, and extreme abolitionists were chanting in unison that C. F. Adams had trafficked with Southern men in Congress and was guilty of a "back-down." How well on onslaught could be repelled was far from certain. Explaining to otherwise intelligent Republicans that, to extinguish slavery, they first must save the Union and its government and then use that government to free the slaves would not be easy.

Meaning to discomfort his father's enemies, Henry wrote a lying, seventh report to Hale, dated December 28, which assigned responsibility for the promotion of the New Mexico idea among the Republicans in the House, not to C. F. Adams, but generally to the Republicans serving on the Committee of Thirty-three. A more complete misstatement of the facts could not have been invented. Where the Chief had led the way, persuading other men to join him in support of Winter Davis's saving tactics, Henry depicted Congressman Adams as a merely passive spokesman whom the other Republicans had saddled with the onerous task of announcing an unlooked-for adaptation of accepted Party strategy. In the bargain, as if the speech any longer represented his father's views, the anonymous reporter coolly explained that, far from being guilty of a "back-down," Mr. Adams had made a defiant speech against the Crittenden proposal.

Lies were flowing from other pens than Henry's. That same day, December 28, Seward wrote to Lincoln consenting to serve in his cabinet as secretary of state.[12] The New Yorker's consent was not consent. It was the first move in a new campaign to bring about the selection of a cabinet by Lincoln adapted to national, not just Republican, requirements—and suited also to Seward's wishes and convenience. As a second move in the campaign, the New Yorker approved the New Mexico expedient and himself brought the Davis proposal before an emergency committee of the Senate, working in parallel with the House Committee of Thirty-three.[13]

In good faith, on December 31, Lincoln accepted Seward's agreement to serve. Taking a second step of his own, the president-elect attempted to keep a promise his managers had made at the Chicago convention by offering a place in the cabinet—either as secretary of the treasury or as secretary of war—he had not yet decided which—to Senator Simon Cameron, the Republican boss of Pennsylvania.[14] Word of Lincoln's offer got out. A mistaken rumor spread in Washington that Lincoln had offered Cameron the treasury outright.

Consternation ensued. Howls arose from the Massachusetts Republicans. According to Henry's private letters, they soon were "raving" that Massachusetts was "left out in the cold." Like it or not, Charles Francis Adams was publicly rushed forward as a proper person to serve in the future cabinet. In Congress, the Massachusetts delegation "united in a memorial recommending C. F. A. [to Lincoln] as the New England member." Seward meanwhile, through Leonard Swett, a friend of Lincoln's, had again recommended that a cabinet place be given to Mr. Adams. The Massachusetts delegation, wanting to press his candidacy with all possible vigor, called on Mr. Swett and induced him to telegraph the future president "to hold off a day or two until they could be heard."[15]

The *Boston Advertiser* published its Washington correspondent's dishonest seventh report only one day late. Pleased with the result, the anonymous reporter passed a "jovial" New Year's Day. All things considered, it seemed to him that affairs were going beautifully. Writing to his elder brother on January 2, 1861, Henry rejoiced: " . . . our good father is becoming a very Jove in his committee. . . . I consider that the unity of the Republicans is due in a very great measure to him, as well as the unity of the entire north, and I believe that his action alone may turn the scale in the border states."

To all appearances, the problem of secession had been solved. Of the thirty-three states that comprised the present Union, only one had gone out. In strident tones, young Adams crowed: "South Carolina has got to eat dirt. . . . I doubt if any other State goes so far, but all the cotton states may go and welcome[,] if we can keep the border ones."

Yet Henry could not avoid returning in his private letters to the peculiar behavior of the ordinary citizens in Washington. He studied them and saw that they were truly panic-stricken. He had never seen a spectacle quite like it. "The terror here among the inhabitants," he noted, "is something wonderful to witness."

Seward had resumed his visits to the Adams house on I Street. To watch them, one might have thought that the New Yorker and the younger Adams were now good friends. The Governor had taken a liking to the excellent cigars that Henry never failed to offer him. After dinner, smoking two while the gentlemen lingered in the dining room and talked, the never-hesitant statesman would gladly pocket a third, to smoke later while walking home. In fact, the two men were friendly rivals, different in age, rather similar in ability. As politicians went, both were honest enough, whenever honesty was possible. Both, too, were very deep. "He's a precious foxy old man," the younger said about the elder after his return, "and tells no one his secrets."

Among the questions that could be asked concerning their relationship that winter, none at present seems harder to answer than the question whether Seward had been told that Henry was writing the biweekly reports from Washington in the *Boston Daily Advertiser*. Positive evidence one way or the other has not been found, and inferences from their behavior could easily be wrong. Yet the question had a certain importance, at least for Henry, if not for Seward, and may have been entangled with another question which for Henry was very pressing.

On January 2, reading the *New York Times*, he had come across a passage from his own sixth report to the *Boston Advertiser*, reprinted "with copious italics." Such borrowings by one newspaper from another were part of the stock in trade of the American press in those years, but young Adams in this instance had cause to fear. The reporters of the *Times* were known for their persistence and success in ferreting out the information they thought would serve their needs. If they tried to learn the name of the *Advertiser's* Washington correspondent, whose reports they were clearly reading, they might not be long in finding out that a young Adams was their man.

The situation grew more curious the more one studied it. The famous founder-editor of the *New York Times*, Henry Jarvis Raymond, a youngish man whom Adams had not met, was very close to Seward.[16] Either Raymond or someone high on his staff was reading Adams's reports to the *Advertiser* with "particular respect." The reason could be that the reports seemed strangely well-informed. It could also be that their authorship had gotten out. "I don't like this," Henry said. "Can they suspect[,] or have they been told whence they come?"

# 13  /  *The Union Party*

As a New Year's vacation, Adams had omitted one report to Hale. When he might have wanted to resume his correspondence, the unpaid reporter came down with a "violent cold which completely upset me." Although apparently not long confined to bed, he put off the day of resuming his communications. During the interval, he changed his attitude towards the press. Where earlier he had worked in the partly self-distrustful, partly confident spirit of a comparative beginner, he now felt almost ready to act as correspondent for better papers than the *Boston Daily Advertiser* and, moreover, write for money.

Protests decrying the appointment of Senator Cameron of Pennsylvania to the cabinet had meanwhile continued. The objections were shrill because the senator's name, fairly or not, had become synonymous with political chicanery and suspected graft. Yielding to the bombardment on January 3, the president-elect retracted his guarded offer of December 31. Lincoln wrote to Cameron, ". . . things have developed which make it impossible for me to take you into the cabinet." On his side, the senator was willing to give up the treasury but unwilling to be ejected from the cabinet entirely. He lodged a counterprotest which eventuated in his securing the place of secretary of war.[1]

Young Adams learned of Cameron's disappointment. To his surprise, the reporter also was told that the Pennsylvanian, a comparative stranger to the family, had suggested the Chief to Lincoln as the best replacement for himself in the Treasury Department. This new endorsement seemed unlikely to make a difference. Henry wrote to Charles in Boston: ". . . Lincoln seems jealous of C. F. A. as too Sewardish. He wants someone [in the Treasury] to balance Seward's influence."

An idea had taken hold in the younger brother's mind that, when it came to keeping secrets and holding firm to a purpose, Mr. Lincoln might be interchangeable with Mr. Seward. It seemed to Henry, too, that the power to select the cabinet rested by rights with Lincoln, no one else, and that the man would assert it. "... what will be the end, he knows. I do not," the third son remarked. "At all events it is not so sure that C. F. A. may not come in after all."

When he restarted his reports to the *Advertiser*, on January 7, 1861, Adams wrote as if the period when he was silent had been a time of blessings. "The plot is thickening...," he said. "There is the sound of war in Washington. Troops are concentrating here; the militia is organizing; officers are ordered off, and we hear no more of that weak hesitation which lasted up to the retreat of Floyd."

Between the lines of this new beginning, a discerning reader could have seen the figures of two men in the capital sufficiently great in reputation and decisive in action to effect a quiet *coup d'etat*. One was Seward, who, stretching his hand into the shattered Buchanan administration, picked up its pieces, arranged them to suit himself, and established what he described as a "dictatorship."[2] The other was Lieutenant General Winfield Scott, the ranking officer of the regular army, a Virginian and loyal Unionist. He had taken personal responsibility for the defense of Washington.

The strength of Seward and Scott's exertions was most apparent at the White House. James Buchanan was on his feet again, it seemed, and the country had a busy president. In the *Boston Advertiser*, without going into the reasons behind the change, Adams reported: "Mr. Buchanan is redeeming himself. ... Wonder of wonders, he is supported by the republicans and is now to most intents and purposes as good as a republican."

An altered tone was audible in the correspondent's January 7 report. He threw out a comment intended to draw, not discourage, the scrutiny of the *New York Times*. Disdainfully contradicting a statement he had seen in a newspaper concerning Seward, he said, "I believe there could not be invented a story crazy enough not to be snapped up by the New York reporters."

Just as Illinois had big Chicago and, to the south, the small city of Springfield, so Massachusetts had Boston and, to the west, its own city of Springfield, famed for its remarkable newspaper, the *Springfield Republican*. Henry Adams only said what others said when he remarked that the *Republican* was "the best paper in the State and carries most weight." Its editor, Samuel Bowles, knew the Adamses and was well-disposed towards them. Henry shortly wrote to his elder brother that, in addition to serving the *Advertiser* as a volunteer, he wanted an opportunity to arrange with Bowles to become the Washington correspondent of the *Republican,* as a paid assignment. Were he to get the place, young Adams presumably would use it partly to taunt the papers in New York.

Until January 7, ambitious Henry continued to suppose that the border states, including Virginia and Maryland, could be kept in the Union and that the terror of the year-round inhabitants of the District of Columbia, while understandable, was needless. Between January 7 and 8, during the hours of a single night, he learned a truer opinion. His father and Seward were similarly affected. The cause of their distress was a tidal wave of disunion sentiment, which, advancing with resistless force and fearful sped through North Carolina and Virginia, flooded Maryland and the capital. Henry wrote at once to Charles that Seward and the Chief despaired of everything. Virginia might secede. Maryland was insecure.

What most appalled the strong Republicans in Washington was their own conviction that the secessionists would attempt to seize the capital by force of arms. Henry said the blow seemed sure to fall "before the 4th of March," in time to prevent the inauguration of an antislavery president at the Capitol and his occupying the White House. In the younger Adams's mind, the prospect was not made less terrible by his believing that military forces loyal to the Union would strike back and undo the secessionists' design. "If Virginia and Maryland secede," he wrote in his private letters, "they will strike at this city, and we shall have to give them such an extermination that it were better we had not been borne [*sic*]. I do not want to fight them. . . . They are mad, mere maniacs, and I want to lock them up. . . . I want to educate, humanize and refine them, not send fire and sword among them."

All the greater Adamses were terrific fighters. Each, too, was passionately interested in making peace. A person bent on sketching his career in the fewest possible words could say that John Adams began his career by starting a war with England and ended it by making peace with France; also that John Quincy Adams in youth made peace with England and in old age started the antislavery conflict; and that Henry Adams, as much as they, would probably move in both directions.

The sense that war might begin at any moment brought Henry's deepest feelings into play.[3] War was one thing; civil war was quite another; and he wanted it not to start. Moreover, he proposed to remain an optimist. "I am confident," he assured his elder brother, "that if an actual conflict can be kept off for a few months, there would be none. . . . But if Virginia goes out, I do not see how it is to be avoided."

He felt a profound attachment to the capital. Because the hour seemed to call for personal decisions, he declared his own: ". . . I intend to remain in this city. If there is war [,] I intend to take such part in it as is necessary or useful. It would be a comfort if such times come, to know that the Massachusetts regiments are ready, and if one can be formed on the Cromwell type, I will enrol myself."

The disunion flood somewhat receded. In Maryland, Governor Hicks failed to act on his sympathies and bring about his state's secession. In Virginia, the citizens decided to wait four weeks and learn the outcome of their state elections, set for February 4.[4] But hesitancy near Washington went hand in hand with intransigence in the cotton states. One after the other, Mississippi, Florida, and Alabama left the Union. The Alabama ordinance of secession called upon the people in every Southern and border state to send representatives to a convention in Montgomery, with the object of creating a Southern government. The convention would meet on the same day as the crucial elections in Virginia, February 4.

Following Seward's lead, the strong Republicans in Washington had begun to temporize. Intending to complicate and protract its business, Congressman Adams brought new resolutions before the Committee of Thirty-three. In the Senate on January 12, Seward gave a long-awaited speech.[5] The chamber was packed to the verge of suffocation. He spoke about two hours and puzzled everyone. Writing about the speech in the *Boston Advertiser,* the younger Adams said, ". . . the concessions which Seward does make are very guarded, and it is rather hard to see what he does mean about the Territories."

By then, at least for Henry, the stuggle had lost its appalling aspect and become exhilarating. Thinking hard about his own affairs as well as the divided country's, he had worked out a plan for his future which completely satisfied him. "I feel in a continual intoxication in this life," he wrote to Charles. "It is magnificent to feel strong and quiet in all this row, and see one's own path clear through all the chaos."

The Adamses were hosts at Sunday dinner on January 13 to two senators, Charles Sumner of Massachusetts and Preston King of New York. After dinner, when the ladies had gone upstairs, a spirited conversation, almost a quarrel, began between C. F. Adams and the senators. Silent Henry, looking on, regarded King as an "amiable, fat old fanatic." King and Sumner were clinging to the doctrines favored by the Republican Party's "ultra men"; but Sumner, in the younger Adams's observation, was showing signs of mental or emotional disturbance. It seemed to the reporter that the senator was the "most frightened" man in Washington. His fright seemed rooted in blind credulity. Henry described him as "believing and repeating all the reports and rumors" that were echoing through the city.

King and Sumner, taking turns, objected to the New Mexico stratagem and tried to tell C. F. Adams that "the South must be made to bend." According to Henry's later account, the congressman at one point replied: "Sumner, you don't know what you're talking about. Your's [sic] is the very kind of stiff-necked obstinacy that will break you down if you persevere."

Leaving the dining room, Henry was gone for a brief moment, came back carrying a book, and, interrupting his elders, read aloud some lines from Francis Bacon's essay "On Seditions and Troubles." The lines served as an apt but rather crushing rejoinder to Sumner's views particularly. There was a pause. Sumner appeared uncomfortable. King and C. F. Adams talked a short while longer. Both Senators left.

H. B. Adams was pleased with his little coup. To use his own expression, Henry had "squenched" a senator. He soon remarked that Sumner could "no more argue than a cat."

The Kuhns had arrived and were staying in the house. Guests in increasing numbers flowed in and out the door. More than ever amused, Henry indulged his taste for exaggeration. He wrote, in one of the stream of private letters he was sending to Boston: ". . . Lars Anderson dined here. . . . He has been in Charleston [, South Carolina], has seen his brother [at Fort Sumter] and had all the talk with him he wants. . . . He says they are all crazy down there, but polite and chivalrous. Every one is a soldier, but no one hold any rank lower than that of a Colonel, of whom there are five thousand."

The Adamses' favorite guest continued to be Seward. On one occasion, after taking off his boots in the parlor to dry his feet, the irrepressible New Yorker patted Mrs. Adams on the head as if she were a girl. Then he invited all the Adams children to come to his house for dinner without their parents. He conceded that their mother, too, could come to visit *after* dinner, if she were lonely.

The invitation was genuine, and the children accepted it delightedly. On January 16, although Louisa was ill and had to leave her bed to do it, she, Henry, Mary, and Brooks all dressed and gaily went. "... we had the funniest little party," Henry later explained to Charles. "The Governor was grand. No one but his secretary Mr. Harrington was at the table with us, but he [Seward] had up some Moselle wine that Baron Gerold [*sic*] had sent him and we managed to be pretty jolly."

The party at the house on Lafayette Square bore some resemblance to a family dinner at the White House. Seward's power in Washington had grown to incalculable proportions. In perfect earnest, Henry wrote to his elder brother about the future secretary: "He is now, as perhaps you do not know, virtual ruler of this country. Whether he is ever made President or not, he never will be in a more responsible position than he is in now, nor ever have more influence."

Georgia seceded.

A cluster at a time, as their states left the union, disloyal senators and congressmen were resigning their seats and leaving Washington. At the Capitol, where committee work was giving way to general debate, Adams moved back and forth between the House and Senate, listening to speeches and widening his acquaintance. His anonymous *Advertiser* reports were mostly filled with descriptions of the speakers and comments on their views. He increasingly mocked the resigning Southern statesmen. "... Jefferson Davis made another last speech; this time positively the last; and so, like Cataline [*sic*] and his friends, these men are vanishing from the capitol to find their own ruin, I hope, without the need of ... civil war, in some obscure village in the South."

Louisiana seceded.

On reflection, Adams was giving up the idea that he should continue to write for the *Boston Daily Advertiser*. Feelings, expressions, and attitudes that were acceptable in Washington were often unacceptable in Massachusetts. Hale was trimming Henry's newest reports, attempting to make them look more grave and dignified.

Without desiring to leave the newspaper until it had served his uses to the full, yet growing irritated and impatient, the dissatisfied correspondent wrote and mailed a communication to Hale intended as a challenge. Henry alerted Charles on January 28, "I have written a letter to the *Advertiser* chaffing the five wise men of Boston. . . ." Presumably the report spoofed such extreme abolitionists as Wendell

Phillips and William Lloyd Garrison. Its author predicted—correctly—that Hale would suppress it. ". . . he always cuts out the spicy parts of my letters . . . ," Henry grumbled to Charles, later adding: "Chaff seems to be his horror [,] and he promptly expunges all that I write of an unfavorable personal character. . . . So it is with all our Boston papers."[6]

The falling away of six states was not fatal to the nerve and courage of Seward, Scott, the Adamses, Winter Davis, and other persons momentarily occupying positions of extraordinary influence in the capital. Yet it was extremely damaging to faith in the Republican Party as an instrument of national salvation. Although they would not say so, indeed would deny it, Seward and his closest associates had ceased to be Republicans and had turned into something else.

They had a name for what they had become. Simply, they were a new Union Party. The purposes of their organization were the preservation of the Union and the reversal of secession. It was hoped that the organization could be built up with explosive speed to include all persons in national and local politics who were loyal to the Union.[7]

H. B. Adams was evidently one of the secret new Union Party's inventors. Unlike its other inventors in the capital, he was free to do something more than talk privately about the embryonic organization's potentialities. He began to fold information about its intended development into his newest regular report to the *Boston Advertiser*.

C. F. Adams simultaneously was preparing to deliver a speech in the House about disunion on January 31. The *Advertiser* needed a copy for early publication. The labor of making the copy fell to Henry, as private secretary, and he completed and mailed it on January 30.[8] The next day, before his father spoke, the son also mailed the report containing information about the nascent Union Party. He had so worded the report that it could be read as if no desertion of the Republican Party would be incurred, were a good Republican to become a Unionist. Rather broadly, the nameless correspondent explained: "The measures which Mr. Adams proposed [in the Committee of Thirty-three] . . . the speech of Gov. Seward . . . and the course of the South Americans . . . Andrew Johnson, and others . . . tend to show that the effort of the republican leaders now is to change the front of battle; to settle the slavery question in a way that all honorable men can acquiesce in [meaning the New Mexico expedient], and with a united North behind them, and a strong and able minority in the South with them, to stand up as the *Union* party, and maintain as their one great and all-important object, the Union, the Constitution, and the enforcement of the laws. . . ."

The anonymous writer's explanation was nothing more, and nothing less, than a feeler. The recent effort to teach other Republicans to swallow the New Mexico idea without complaining had been so successful, on the whole, as to encourage hope that the much larger idea of a total replacement of the Republican Party with something greater and better might possibly take hold. Departing from his usual style, the correspondent both revealed the larger, new idea and gave it his own endorsement. He ended his report: "The movement is a bold one, only justified by the greatness of the danger. . . . Being in Washington, and seeing what the feeling all over the South really is, I believe that this is a wise and far-sighted policy; the only one that great statesmen could follow. We shall be anxious to learn what you in New England say to it."[9]

## 14 / *Business That Shall Suit Me*

Henry Jarvis Raymond was William Henry Seward's staunchest backer in the New York City press. The editor and part-owner of the *New York Times* appeared in Washington and, while doing other things, learned about the secret, developing Union Party idea and met Henry Adams. The likeliest place of their meeting was the family's house on I Street. Its most probable date was Monday or Tuesday, January 28 or 29, at the beginning of the week in which Charles Francis Adams was scheduled to speak. Raymond's newspaper wanted an accurately transcribed, advance copy of the speech. Henry, already burdened with making a copy for the *Boston Advertiser*, evidently found the hours and patience that week to make an added copy for the *Times*.

The New York editor and the secret Washington correspondent no sooner met than they became confidential associates. Looking back on their meeting, Adams later said that of all the men he met that winter in the capital, Raymond was the one to whom he "took most kindly."[1] That they should have struck it off so well was natural. Alike in energy and appetite for information, they had done things which were very similar. When the War of Italian Liberation broke out, in June 1859, Raymond had been in Paris. He had rushed to Italy and written for the *Times* an extraordinary news report—his "journey to the Seat of War"—about the victory won at Magenta by Napoleon III. His long report and Adams's account of his dash to Palermo in June 1860 were journalistic twins.[2]

The current Washington reports appearing in the *New York Times* were uniformly signed "Observer." Whoever the reporter was, his communication to his newspaper on January 31, 1861, the day of Congressman Adams's speech, contained information which Henry Adams alone, one would imagine, could easily have supplied.[3] And a startling change occurred in the younger Adams's reports to the

Boston *Advertiser*. He began to supply them twice as frequently as in the past. These indications appeared to mean that the secret association of Raymond and Adams already amounted to a positive alliance; and the latter, pleased and excited, was working in the capital with a sense that his political advancement was hurtling forward at an unheard-of rate.

C. F. Adams's speech, on Thursday, January 31, was listened to with rapt attention, not only by the members of the House but also by many senators and an applauding crowd in the galleries. The speech conformed to Seward's temporizing strategy and was adapted to conciliate Virginia. One of its features was a convincing plea in favor of state's rights. When he had finished speaking, Mr. Adams was "perfectly overwhelmed with congratulations." He himself was very pleased. The elder Adams noted in his diary that his ambition—"which never was great"—had "reached its culmination."[4] Henry was present, watched his father, and could not remember having seen him so affected.

The speech coincided with new sensations of alarm in Washington. In his reports to the *Advertiser*, the younger Adams said: "We see the troops parading and hear the bugles morning and evening. Houses here and there are turned into barracks, with, at night, a sentry before them, bayonet and all. I should almost think it was some European town. . . ." The troops were too few, "not a thousand men." While conceivably numerous enough to hold out within the city for a time, they could not possibly prevent its being encircled and besieged. The correspondent warned his readers in New England, "If the news comes to the North some fine morning that the telegraph wires are down, and the railroad interrupted between here and Baltimore, you may take it for granted that the war has begun and that we are shut up here like so many rats in a trap, to work our own salvation."

For many years, going back as long as Henry could remember, Charles Sumner had joined the Adamses for dinner every Sunday in Boston; and he had done the same in Washington. It had been noticed that Sumner was not among the senators who visited the House to hear Congressman Adams give his speech. The full text of the speech was printed in both the *Boston Advertiser* and the *New York Times* on Friday morning, February 1. Copies of the latter paper reached the capital by train on the same day. Sumner evidently saw the speech and scanned or read it. He may have noted that it contained quotations from famous authors, including one from Francis Bacon.

On Saturday, news reached the Adamses that Sumner was publicly and heatedly denouncing the congressman as an apostate from the antislavery cause. Henry watched his father to see what he would do. C. F. Adams, on the assumption that Sumner's rage was caused by jealousy of Seward's augmented influence in Washington and the New Yorker's not-yet-announced but much-expected nomination as secretary of state, believed he had to choose between an old friend and a new. Mr. Adams chose the new one, Mr. Seward, and made the choice in silence.[5]

Early on Sunday, intending to have a healing talk with him, if he could, Henry went to Sumner's lodgings and begged the senator to come that day and dine as usual with the family. The senator was closeted with a noted journalist, Count Adam Gurowski. The visitor's presence made it impossible for Henry to engage his older friend in any but the briefest interchanges.[6] The senator seemed to give assurances that he would appear, as wished. Doubting that Sumner meant it, the younger Adams went home to I Street and waited anxiously. To his great distress, the statesman did not appear, and the family dined without him.

Desperate, the son tried another way to bring him back. Sumner had no idea that Henry was writing the Washington reports in the *Boston Advertiser*. On Monday, February 4, in a new report to Hale, the son laid down the axiom: "Mr. Garrison and Mr. Phillips may scold as much as they please, but no power on earth can prevent a greater evil from swallowing up a lesser; and disunion has just now swallowed up everything." The sentence made precisely the point that Sumner—who thought that slavery had swallowed up everything—had not been able to grasp. Pressing on, Henry gave a dozen lines to the speech by Mr. Adams in the House, calling it a "great triumph." "By the way," the correspondent continued, "I see various rumors [in the press] about a quarrel between him and Mr. Sumner. . . . The whole story [is] . . . very unfair to Mr. Sumner . . . [and is] only one more example of the evils of 'sensation reports.' There has been no quarrel between these two gentlemen. . . . They disagree in their ideas of treating present affairs. So they have done many times before; but nothing but newspaper reporters could have made it a quarrel."

The hour was late, after midnight, when Henry finished his report. Rather than go to bed, he stayed up and wrote a letter to Charles, dated February 5. Warning him that Sumner had quarreled with their father, he attributed the quarrel to a misunderstanding half-knowingly created by another man, a congressman from New

Hampshire. But the younger brother also said, or at least implied, that the senator's enmity had been incurred by what he, Henry, called "our speech."

So late an hour was not the best time for making accurate predictions. Two things weighed especially on Henry's mind. The secessionists had started their convention at Montgomery, Alabama. The Virginians had held their state elections. Morning would bring word of the Virginia results, and he supposed they would be bad. In truth, he expected that the Old Dominion would secede and Washington would be abandoned. "I'm afraid the game is up," he told his brother, "and that we shall have to make a new Capital on the Mississippi, for a new Northern Union."

Morning brought such news to Washington as the third son could not have wished for. The Virginians had voted against immediate secession! Buoyed up by the event, the secret journalist swam away from gloom and doubt onto the tropic seas of systematic optimism. Hours later, on the same day, February 5, he mailed a fresh report unprecedented in its cheer. " . . . [the Virginia voting] is our first beam of light," he declared, "and we enjoy it." Since only a month remained before the president-elect would be inaugurated and the new administration set in motion, the correspondent took it for a certainty that the secessionists would never capture Washington, much though they might want to. He felt assured as well that the secessionists would keep clear of armed attacks on areas and persons loyal to the Union. Indeed, if his newest ideas were right, the mad creators of the projected Confederate States of America could do their worst in Montgomery, but any nation they might produce would die in infancy of natural causes. In his ebullient report, he said in sweeping terms, " . . . it seems conceded that the capital is now safe, and war no longer to be feared."

The violent swings in Adams's predictions were indications of intelligence and awareness of what was going on. Precisely like a scales, events were sure to tip decisively to one side or the other depending on the last small weights put into either pan—depending, that is, on the choices soon to be made by undecided citizens, half-loyal, half-secessionist, in the border states. Such persons could not be wooed towards loyalty in large numbers or with ease by the Republicans if they remained Republicans. Were Seward and other Republicans to join, publicly and at once, with such Southern Democrats as Andrew Johnson and such South Americans as Winter Davis to found a Union Party and some Virginians came in, swift progress towards a general, peaceful resolution of the country's difficulties could be made, it seemed.

Young Adams's February 5 report, then going through the mail, did not explicitly repeat the phrase, *"Union* party," which had appeared in his January 31 report. The newer communication merely said, " . . . Governor Seward . . . hopes that this step [the voting of the Virginians against immediate secession] will so strengthen the Union men in the border states that a month hence secession will be one of the night-mares of the past." By then, apparently, a decision had been made in secret by Raymond and the younger Adams that the newspaper best suited for sending up trial balloons about a possible Union Party was not the Boston *Advertiser,* circulated rather narrowly in New England, but the *New York Times,* sold in all the nation's major cities and read assiduously by most of the newspaper editors throughout the country. Moreover, the Union Party idea, while more than ever alive, was being subordinated to a still more sweeping and adventurous idea.

The change was visible the following morning, February 6, in an editorial in the *New York Times.* Presumably the work of Raymond himself, the editorial reprinted the paragraph in Adams's January 31 report about the *"Union* party." Also it suggested that the country's peril would be best reduced, not so much by the creation of a party, but instead by the giving of unlimited power to a single leader. The leader meant was Seward. In the opinion of the *Times,* the Governor had shown abilities commensurate with the crisis, had asked to be given a free hand, and deserved a chance to "save the Union in his own way."

Henry studied the editorial—and his own reprinted paragraph— with understandable relief. Earlier, in December, while Seward had been in Albany and Auburn and the Adamses in Washington had been watching the course of Henry Winter Davis, the younger Adams had experienced anxiety so extreme that a moment would later come when he would simply have to rest. His respite started on February 6 and 7. Its first effect was augmented optimism. After listening to more of Seward's private talk, which had never been so sanguine, weary Henry wrote to his elder brother, on February 8: "We shall keep the border states. . . . The storm is weathered."

That same day, February 8, 1861, Congressman Adams learned belatedly that his private secretary not long before had put out a feeler about a possible Union Party movement in the Boston *Advertiser* and that the *New York Times* had reprinted the risky paragraph in an editorial. For Mr. Adams, the moment was not an easy one. He was learning that Senator Sumner's denunciations had had a practical effect. For fear of bringing down the Senator's rage upon themselves, the other Massachusetts men in Congress were not responding as before to Mr. Adams's opinions. Henry understood the trouble and doubted that it was curable. He confided to Charles: "As for Sumner, the utmost that can be expected is to keep him silent. To bring him round is impossible. God Almighty couldn't do it."

If he wanted to damage C. F. Adams badly, all Sumner needed for the purpose was knowledge that the congressman's son was writing the Washington reports in the *Advertiser* and was responsible for a paragraph in one of them, since reprinted in the *New York Times*, about a Union Party and a new policy which "great statesmen" ought to follow. Perceiving that his own situation had become precarious, yet reluctant to interfere overmuch in his sons' activities, Mr. Adams spoke to Henry about his work as a secret journalist and cautioned him not to write "too freely."

Just then, Charles Hale turned up in Washington. The editor had welcomed the younger Adams's frequent, newer reports and had printed them as fast as they reached Boston. It may have surprised and disappointed him a little that, when they met and talked, young Henry asked him, Hale, to assume the entire responsibility for reporting the Washington news to his paper. So they parted, contributor and editor agreeing to a friendly separation; and the worry of the elder Adams, which Hale may or may not have been told about, was as fully as possible relieved by the younger.

Glad to be dissociated from the *Boston Advertiser*, yet not forgetful of the power it had given him, Henry reviewed the work he had done as a secret correspondent. One could say that he had written and sent to Hale three series of reports, totaling nineteen communications, seventeen of which were published more or less intact. By way of an epitaph for all three series, Henry wrote privately to Charles: " . . . I am on the whole tolerably well satisfied with them and their effect. They have had some good influence in shaping the course of opinion in Boston, and the *Advertiser* and the *New York Times* have both profited by them."

After making inquiries now impossible to trace, the third son had accepted a clerkship in the office of Horace Gray, Jr., an extremely able Boston lawyer. Except that Henry was to remain in Washington till after the inauguration, go to Boston with the family, and then appear at Gray's office and start his training, the details of the arrangement are unknown. Whether the son should continue at the office during all the months his father was *not* in Washington, but leave the office and accompany his father to the capital as private secretary whenever the congressman went back, was a question which the Adamses themselves may not yet have tried to answer. Henry's training as a lawyer, however, was regarded as indispensable; and he could not have found a mentor more respected than Mr. Gray.

Like Winter Davis and Raymond, Gray was a man of forty or so. At twenty-three, the younger Adams could easily be mistaken for being somewhat older, but hardly for being one of their contemporaries. Yet he was showing a tendency to align himself with such men as if he were their age. His doing so was partly a result of rapidly increasing revulsion from the company of men still older.

Adams later said that his experiences in Washington during the first winter he spent there ended in making him a "harsh judge" of the men who had taken themselves to be his "masters."[7] As he saw them at the time he broke off his correspondence with the *Advertiser,* these men—including his father, Sumner, Seward, Cameron, Lincoln, Douglas, and the absent Jefferson Davis—had a talent for getting into quarrels, and not much talent for getting out of them. Much as Henry could blame himself for provoking Sumner and bringing on the senator's fulminations concerning C. F. Adams's alleged apostasy, the private secretary believed that much the worse deserter from the antislavery cause in recent weeks had not been adaptable Mr. Adams but inflexible Mr. Sumner. Nothing had hurt Henry Adams so much in Washington as the Senator's behavior. To use the words that Adams himself would later use about the hurt, Sumner's "defection" had "struck home."[8]

From one point of view, the biggest quarreler in the United States was Seward. As Henry had been quick to realize, the New Yorker, by asserting his "dictatorship," had initiated a struggle with Lincoln, not merely about the cabinet appointments but instead about every major aspect of the federal government's business. Compared to Sumner's petty feud with C. F. Adams within the Massachusetts congressional delegation, the contest of Seward and Lincoln was clearly huge.

Since he was simultaneously locked in another struggle with the secessionists for favor in the border states, the New Yorker appeared to have his hands full. His visits to the Adams house had stopped. In tones astonishingly altered and detached, Henry observed to Charles: "I've not seen Seward. . . . He is hard at work I suppose, and I don't like to go down and interrupt him. . . . Between Lincoln and the secession-ists he must have a hard time. . . .''

During spare hours, in place of writing news reports, the third son was rereading Shakespeare's *Hamlet*. In other circumstances, he might merely have run through the play again in an objective frame of mind. Things being as they were, he yielded to an impulse to take the prince's part, memorize his lines, and saturate himself in the Dane's shifting moods.

Not long before, the Virginia legislature had approved a plan for an elaborate "Peace Convention," to be held in Washington.[9] The meeting's deliberations, now in progress, were being chaired by a man still older than those from whose company Henry was in flight, one of Virginia's eldest statesmen, ex-president John Tyler. As a pleasurable diversion, the younger Adams attended a grand ball at the home of Senator Douglas. While roaming through the "wildest collection of people I ever saw," Prince Henry came upon the former president, surrounded by admiring devotees. Next day, imitating some of Ham-let's lines, he wrote to Charles: "Ye Gods, what are we, when mortals no bigger—no . . . not so big as—ourselves, are looked up to as though their thunder spoke from the real original Olympus. Here is an old Virginia politician, of whom by good rights, no one ought ever to have heard, reappearing in the ancient cerements of his forgotten grave. . . .''

Never pleased with Henry's performances in the *Boston Adver-tiser*, and as sure as ever that the third son should be a writer, Charles had been badgering him again to write an article for the magazines, this time on American politics. Falling in with the advice, and half-mocking some of Hamlet's lines, while half-repeating them word for word, Henry responded on February 13: " . . . I for one am going upon the business or the pleasure that shall suit me, for every man hath business or desire such as . . . it is, and for my own poor part—look you—I will go write an article for the *Atlantic Monthly*, intituled 'The great Secession Winter of 1860-61'.''

Independently three days earlier, on February 10, Charles had gone to Cambridge and seen the editor of the *Atlantic*, James Russell Lowell. The second son had told the editor that he was leaving for Washington and wished to supply the magazine an article on national affairs. Professor Lowell had encouraged him to write one and send the manuscript to Cambridge but probably had not unconditionally guaranteed its publication.

While preparing to take the train, the second son received the third's announcement that *he* intended to write an article for Lowell's magazine. The younger brother's proposal did not improve the elder's state of mind.

Charles reached Washington on February 20. The house on I Street had grown so crowded that Henry had moved to Jost's, a hotel on Pennsylvania Avenue. The second son was expected to share the third's accommodations. As he unpacked, or soon thereafter, Charles told Henry about the clash of their plans and his own agreement with Lowell.

Probably, but not certainly, Henry answered by saying that his own article needed to be written but undoubtedly would not be good enough to publish. When finished, the third son's manuscript would tell the inside story of the winter's politics, as well as Henry had been able to trace it, and in the process would explain how Washington had been saved. Writing the story would not be easy, but he intended to work steadily at the task.

When he was only getting under way, on February 23, Henry took his unhappy elder brother with him to dine with the Lees in Arlington, at their house on the hilltop overlooking the broad Potomac and the capital. Exactly who was present at the table is now unknown. Rooney may not have been there. His father, Colonel Lee, was away. Perhaps the dinner was a very small one, bringing together the Adams brothers, Mrs. Lee, and some other women belonging to the Colonel's family.[10]

Henry liked the Lees and thought them well-meaning people. He had learned to regard the women of the family as passionately Southern. They seemed capable—should Virginia secede—of driving the colonel from the service of his country to the service of his state.

The greater Adamses were not mere sons of Massachusetts. In any final reckoning, they were not New Englanders but belonged to all the Union. By going to visit the Lees in Arlington, sitting at their table, and eating their food, Henry Adams began to suffer a revulsion much stronger than any he earlier had felt. The thought that Colonel Robert E. Lee might resign his commission, leave the national service, and fight on the side of rebels against the Union, once ignited in Adams's mind, moved him to ever-increasing indignation. Such a fury could never go away. When fifty years had passed, in 1911, a visitor at Adams's house in Washington would be amazed at hearing old Adams say that General Lee, when the Civil War was over, ought to have been hanged. The visitor shortly recorded what he had heard. "It was all the worse," excited Adams had said, "that [Lee] was a good man and a fine character and acted conscientiously. . . . It's always the good men who do the most harm in the world."[11]

## 15 / *Appointments*

Jefferson Davis had taken the oath of office as president of the Confederate States of America on February 18 at Montgomery, and the wheels of a Southern government had been set immediately and energetically in motion. Texas was added to the six states earlier included in the new American republic.

Abraham Lincoln reached Washington during the very early hours of February 23, the day the Adams brothers visited the Lees. The president-elect put up at Willard's Hotel. Two private secretaries had come with him to the capital, an elder, John Nicolay, and a younger, John Hay. An Illinoisian and a graduate of Brown in the Class of 1858, Hay looked younger than he was and to that extent was the opposite of his exact contemporary, Henry Adams. Moving about in the limited room of Washington politics and society, Hay "lighted on the Markoe House," brimming with gaiety and fun, and was introduced to Adams, who was more than glad to meet him. Adams later said he knew that he and Hay would become extremely close, practically from the instant he first saw him.[1]

John Quincy Adams II had also come to the capital, and all the Adamses were united to await the inauguration. Henry tried to seize the occasion as an opportunity to relax. As if Washington were Rome, which in some respects it seemed to be, especially with spring in the air and the trees about to bud, he explored the neighboring areas on horseback, sometimes taking Mary with him. He invited Charles to go, but when possible Charles avoided Henry at the time, preferring to keep company with Mary, John, or Boston friends then visiting the city. Besides, the second son was writing news reports, not many, for unsigned publication in the *Boston Advertiser* and *Boston Transcript*. Charles also contemplated sending a letter about Senator Sumner to the *New York Times*.[2]

Seward had learned that Lincoln had chosen Salmon P. Chase of

Ohio, the weightiest of the ultra Republicans, to serve as secretary of the treasury. On March 3, the eve of the inauguration, making still another effort to impose his own cabinet choices on the president-elect, Seward retracted his consent to head the State Department. Lincoln talked with him, the New Yorker again agreed to serve, and their long contest to all appearances was ended. Next day, Lincoln took the oath of office and made public the names of all his cabinet members. His inaugural address had healing effects on wounded feelings among the politicians then in Washington. It approved the settlement proposals that C. F. Adams had placed before the Committee of Thirty-three on December 28. Mr. Adams was pleased, as was Mr. Henry Winter Davis. Lincoln was a stranger to so many people in Washington that curiosity about his character was general. Seward told his closer associates reassuringly that the president had an unexpected trait, a vein of feeling and sentiment, which might more than compensate for any errors which his newness to elevated public station might lead him to commit.[3]

While reading and hearing much about the man, Henry Adams saw Lincoln only once, at the White House on the night of March 4, 1861, at the inauguration ball. Henry saw what he expected, a figure long and awkward, and a "plain, ploughed face." The president was wearing huge white gloves, brand new, which appeared to worry him. He seemed neither self-confident nor strong. What Adams most noticed was outward mildness—"lack of apparent force."[4]

On Sunday, March 10, Charles Francis Adams, Jr., went to Senator Sumner's lodgings, waited until some other people left, and invited the senator to join the family that same day for dinner. Sumner came with perfect willingness and grace, and his affectionate relations with all the Adamses were restored. Their meal served somewhat as a reminder of former days, in 1848, when young Sumner had allied himself with C. F. Adams and a few other Conscience Whigs, and they had started the Free Soil Party. The swirling currents of American politics had turned the Free-Soilers into Republicans; but in the hour of triumph, when the Republicans took charge of the executive branch of the diminished Union's federal government, the Adamses and Sumner were mindful that certain old Free-Soldiers might be overlooked in the division of the spoils. They especially wanted to secure a large reward for a writer-politician in Boston, John Gorham Palfrey, author of a large-scale *History of New-England,* successive volumes of which were gradually appearing. The reward they wanted to secure for Palfrey was the place of postmaster in Boston, competition for which would probably be fierce.[5]

While Sumner angled for the desired appointment, on March 13, the Adamses started back towards Boston and Quincy. Preparations were needed for the wedding of J. Q. Adams II and Fanny Crowninshield, set for April 29. Henry, it seems, traveled north with his relations.

Presumably on Monday, March 18, the third son reported at the office of Horace Gray, Jr., and entered upon the rights and duties of a legal apprentice. Before the day was over, Henry read again the opening pages of Blackstone's *Commentaries.* He wished nothing better than to stay where he had come to rest, under what he would later term Gray's "fostering care."[6] On Tuesday morning, the third son went again to Court Street and passed the day in Gray's office, but Henry's second day there bore no resemblance to his first. That same morning, while the family was eating breakfast at 57 Mount Vernon Street, his father had read a telegraphic announcement in a Boston newspaper that he, Charles Francis Adams, had been appointed minister to England.

The news had burst among the members of the family with the shattering force of a grenade. Mrs. Adams was inconsolable. If her husband accepted the appointment, she would have to cut the hundred cords that tied her to relatives and friends in New England, New York, and Washington. Her husband could not relieve her sorrow. Such an honor was not refusable. The English mission was a very high appointment, in fact the highest in the Foreign Service, but what affected C. F. Adams was the historic truth that both his father and grandfather had occupied the same position.

The congressman sent word at once to Washington that he would accept the English mission. His metamorphosis from legislator to diplomat lacked only confirmation by the Senate for its completion. But the elder Adams did not want to be a diplomat. He would have much preferred to stay in the House of Representatives.

True, in Washington not long before, Seward had urged the president to give Adams the English mission. Lincoln had wanted instead to give the post to William F. Dayton of New Jersey. That the president had since changed his mind, shifting Mr. Dayton to the French mission and giving the English to Mr. Adams, seemed a calamity to the latter. At such a time, with the Union rent in halves, the city to which an American patriot would want to turn his steps, at least in the elder Adams's judgment, was Washington, not London. In effect, President Lincoln was sending him into "comparative retirement.''[7] The father consented to go abroad but did so with the feeling that his new role had "too much the aspect of a withdrawal from the great theatre of action.''[8]

Henry's two-year absence in Europe had taught the Chief the conscious lesson, that, if he could help it, he would never again be without his third son's company. Their experiences together since the son's return had also taught the father an unconscious lesson, that while his son was with him he leaped ahead in politics without much effort—or at least without much added effort—on his own part. The father was not about to become aware that the combination of himself and Henry in politics was a very different thing from himself alone in politics; but the father liked political advancement—liked it hugely—even while telling himself he did not want it or like it. Mr. Adams was affected, too, by the unforgettable fact that, only five years earlier, in 1856, another politician, James Buchanan, had risen to the presidency directly from the English mission. If the Democrat's experience meant anything, it meant that one way upward in American politics was eastward to London, however real might seem the urgency of going southward to Washington.

The son, incomparably quicker in intellect than the father, was abreast of all these family and political realities but had a difficulty to contend with. The resentment Henry had come to feel towards his country's older, ruling office-seekers and professional politicians was not a slight one. He had not turned against his father, to all appearances, but he had surely turned away from him. As far as Henry was concerned, prospective Minister C. F. Adams and his former private secretary had parted company. Albeit in hated Boston, not in friendly Washington, Henry was steering his own course. He meant to continue.[9]

On Tuesday evening, March 19, Horace Gray visited C. F. Adams.[10] The lawyer may have wished to extend congratulations. He also may have wanted to discuss his apprentice, H. B. Adams. Copies of the the morning's *New York Times* were being read in Boston. On page one, they said that Henry Adams would "probably" be named to serve as his father's immediate subordinate in the English mission, getting the appointment as secretary of legation. The relevant sentences, printed in the midst of a general news report from Washington concerning appointments, said simply: "The Secretaries of the several legations above named, are not yet settled. Mr. Adams' son will probably accompany him to London, however." That the son meant was Henry, not John or Charles, would be evident even in Boston.

That same Tuesday evening, it seems, at the family's house on Mount Vernon Street, the son was subjected to a memorable "talk about diplomacy" by his father.[11] The matters at issue were not simple. The outcome of the talk partly hinged on certain facts.

The yearly salary of the U.S. minister to England, set by law, was $17,500. The minister was provided only two important aides, a secretary of legation, paid a substantial salary of about $2,500, and an assistant secretary of legation, paid a subsistence salary of about $1,500. The expenses of ministers to England much outran their salaries. Partly for this reason, it had grown customary in the State Department for sons and other young relations to be added to the payroll. The current minister, George M. Dallas, whom C. F. Adams would replace on reaching London, had been aided throughout his four-year term by his son, Philip Dallas, as secretary of legation. That Seward approved of the appointment of sons could be seen in his own behavior. He had obtained for his own son Frederick the appointment as assistant secretary of state. It was a foregone conclusion that serving in England would be very expensive for the Adamses, as for their predecessors. Alarmed by the cost, Henry later wrote that his father, to perform his diplomatic duties in a creditable manner in London, would have to incur annual expenses of at least $40,000.

C. F. Adams had made no effort to get the English mission. If he had made such an effort, he might also have made another and positively asked, at once, by telegraph, that the place of secretary of legation be kept for his son Henry without fail. Alternatively, had the government asked Mr. Adams whether he would want the place of secretary of legation awarded to his son John, the father might have encouraged the appointment. In the father's mind, eldest sons in the Adams family, like John, and only surviving sons, like himself, were entitled to political careers. Henry was a third son, and the idea of Henry's taking office apparently had not occurred to the father, even though he was a third son himself, and had just received a high appointment. So he felt no impulse, none at all, to insure that the probable appointment of Henry as secretary of legation, predicted in the *New York Times,* be turned into a certainty.

The elder Adams was disinclined to welcome, much less seek, the assistance of strangers. The only assistance he desired was Henry's, wherever the government might send them, and on whatever errand. The father's need for his third son's support had grown so constant and unchanging that he felt he had a right to require it—of course in his son's best interest, as well as in his own.

Henry had a tendency to know more about any subject that might come up than he would be expected to know. He recently had shown small interest in American diplomacy, but he had visited several United States legations abroad, met several ministers, and knew a little about what a secretary of legation might look like, do, and be called upon to do. It went without saying that the legation in London was normally the busiest in the Foreign Service. To thrive at the head of the legation there, Minister Adams would need to have extremely capable assistants. There could be no doubt that C. F. Adams was going to London. Yet, to Henry's silent amazement, his father—in the son's later expression—"made no effort to find efficient help."[12]

The third son absolutely did not want to go to England with the minister. At the moment, the son did not want office, power, or influence. His exclusive wish was to go on in peace as Gray's apprentice. But if the minister needed persons of ability in London to assist him and would not exert himself in Boston to recruit them, who was there left to act on his behalf, if not the only grown son of the family who was taken seriously in Washington as a politician?

On Wednesday, news reached the family by telegraph from Sumner that the Senate had confirmed the minister's appointment.[13] Also on Wednesday, in a state approaching desperation, without his father's consent or even knowledge, Henry wrote Sumner a letter and telegraphed it to the Capitol, asking that the place of first secretary in the English mission be reserved for himself.[14] Unhappily, too, the son advised Horace Gray that this, the third day of their association, would be the last—that he was going to England with his father. Henry consoled himself by thinking that his sudden rush into diplomacy would be merely temporary.

Before any reply could come from Sumner, on Friday, March 22, 1861, Henry read in the newspapers that the new secretary of legation at London would be Charles Lush Wilson, editor and part-owner of the *Chicago Daily Journal*. The new announcement threw the younger Adams's affairs, already turned upside down, into chaos.

Henry's predicament was partly ugly and offensive. The appointment of Mr. Wilson on its face was the merest tossing away of a four-year, well-paid appointment to a political hanger-on.[15] It was a brutal reminder that all American political parties, the Republican included, habitually corrupted themselves by giving offices and salaries to adherents who intended not to work. In London, Secretary Wilson might sometimes want to save his self-respect by working a small amount. If so, the impulse might only make him all the more a nuisance and encumbrance.

In Washington two weeks before, Henry had made fun of a tendency Seward had shown to offer people ill-paid government posts as if they were large, richly-paid bestowals. At the time, the younger Adams had not expected to become the butt of such an offer.[16] Now, however, without the slightest hesitation, he could predict what Seward was going to do. Having deprived the Adamses of a greater salary and position they could have felt was theirs by right, he would attempt to cover up the deprivation by reserving a lesser position and salary for the family without their asking it. In short, Henry was as good as appointed to the place of assistant secretary of legation in the English mission, and no one else could get the place.

The son already knew, or somehow learned that day in Boston, that the current holder of the place of assistant secretary in London was a Pennsylvania Democrat named Benjamin Moran, a protege of President Buchanan's. With this fact in mind, Henry drew his father into a second talk about diplomacy more decisive than their first. Its main result was a decision that Henry—to use the father's phrase— would go to London as "private Secretary."[17] The capital letter was significant. The Adamses had decided to foot the bill for keeping the minister's chief assistant in London. Henry would not go to England as an official diplomat in the eyes of the State Department, the president, or the Senate. Yet he would go to England as an official diplomat in the eyes of Minister Charles Francis Adams. His pay would be private. His duties would be confidential. His rank would be that of leading—in fact, only—secretary. Intruding Charles Wilson would be ignored, so far as possible. Expert help would be sought from Mr. Moran, who, if the State Department were willing, would be retained as assistant secretary.

The plan was anomalous and fraught with ironies, some obvious, some very subtle. No other arrangement seemed possible. Aware of its ironies, drawbacks, and advantages, its principal creator wrote and mailed a new letter, dated Friday, March 22, 1861, to Sumner in Washington. Speaking in his father's absence, writing a letter his father would not see, yet acting for them both, Henry said, with all possible diplomacy:

> We see the nomination of Mr[.] Wilson by today's papers. As I suppose this to be one of Mr[.] Lincoln's selections, of course there is no use in commenting on it. Indeed my father

seems rather pleased that the burden of deciding is taken off his shoulders.

Without troubling you further[,] I will merely state that I write to express the hope that Mr[.] Moran may be retained. It is my father's wish also, though this is not an authorized assertion. You will see at once what a position the Embassy would be in if another freshman were put in, especially if he were an incompetent Westerner. . . . If Mr [.] Moran remains[,] we shall have every reason to be grateful.

Excuse this meddling, of which I know you have too much already. I should not do it except that I fear the appointments will much affect me . . . if I am to be Private Secretary, and may throw a lot of work on me that I have no capacity for nor knowledge of.

Although raised to eminence as chairman of the Senate's most prestigious committee, Charles Sumner would have much preferred becoming secretary of state or minister to England. Susceptible to envy, he was certain fairly soon to suffer new, profounder feelings of hostility towards Charles Francis Adams.[18] The senator was capable, however, of maintaining separate relations with different Adamses. On Wednesday, when he received the first, telegraphed letter from Henry, understandably requesting that the place of secretary in the English mission be held for himself, Sumner had been disposed to help the son, if possible; but, as it happened, the letter had come too late. All chance to help was lost.

Four days later, on Monday, March 25, at his desk in the Senate chamber, Sumner received a second letter from Henry and wrote at once in reply. The senator explained that the State Department's "nomination (of Mr. Wilson) for 1st Secy was sent to the Senate the day I recd your first letter. Several Senators insisted that it was an improper nomination, &, before reporting it, I proposed to the Secy of State to withdraw him. *He* [Seward] *insisted;* & the Senate confirmed." Sumner added, "Wilson lost the Post Office at Chicago, & the Secretaryship was given him instead."

Responding also to Henry's second letter, suggesting that Mr. Moran be retained in London as assistant secretary, Sumner said he had tried his best. "I have done what I could; but I know not the result."

The senator's kind reply did not say so, but Sumner that same Monday had forwarded young Adams's second, Friday letter to Seward at the State Department, first writing on the top if its front page the helpful words: "Please read this letter—from Henry Adams—asking that Mr[.] Moran should be retained as 2d Secretary at London. C. S."

On the decisive day, Friday, March 22, 1861, Minister to England C. F. Adams had written in his diary: " . . . the government has given me a Secretary of legation without the courtesy of a question. I do not on the whole regret it, as it saves me the necessity of determining two questions that might have embarrassed me." The two questions he meant were the names of his first and second secretaries in London. If he had been asked to name the first, Mr. Adams would have had to endure the extreme embarrassment of improperly setting aside his two elder sons, John and Charles, in the process of arranging a federal appointment for their younger brother Henry; and if he had been asked to name the second secretary also, Mr. Adams—merely for the sake of filling a vacant post—would have had to endure the embarrassment of suggesting a stranger whose assistance he would never welcome.

As the father understood that day's developments, an incompetent Westerner, President Lincoln, had indulged one of the Republican Party's office-seeking journalists with a political plum. The action was a flagrant but entirely predictable abuse of the power to distribute places and salaries. Henry had made the intelligent suggestion that the incumbent assistant secretary in London could be retained, somewhat as an offset to Lincoln's harmful act. Commendably, too, the third son had consented to serve in London as "private Secretary," at least until some different arrangement might be possible. Thus, in the father's mind, the problem of appointments was wholly solved.

The one remaining awkwardness for Minister Adams was a choice he had to make between two urgencies, one public, one familial. The pretended government of the so-called Confederate States of America was expected to seek approval and support from foreign powers, beginning with Great Britain and France, but possibly including Spain and Russia. As president of the attempted Southern government, Jefferson Davis might send envoys to London and Paris very soon. In short, an early appearance by Minister Adams in the British capital was clearly recommended. All the same, he elected *not* to hurry. John, his eldest son, was getting married. The date, April 29, was five weeks or so in the future; weddings in Boston were extremely serious; the date could not readily be advanced; and his own absence from the wedding was not to be imagined.[19]

Although the third son had said in his controlling Friday letter to Sumner that Charles Lush Wilson had presumably been "one of Mr[.]Lincoln's selections," Henry had suspected it was probably Seward's choice. Moreover, the son perceived that his father would continue to think of the Wilson appointment as Lincoln's work, whatever the facts might prove to be. The issue was not merely differing estimates of Seward and Lincoln. One of the gulfs that separated the greater from the lesser Adamses was the gulf that separated open-minded willingness to learn from the mere persistent will to believe.

As soon as possible, without waiting for Sumner to answer, Henry set out alone for New York and Washington. The day of his departure is uncertain. It probably was Monday, March 25, the day that Sumner wrote to him from the Capitol and sent his request about Moran to Seward at the State Department. The third son's pretexts for going south were apparently both practical and familial. Five Adamses—the parents, Henry, Mary, and Brooks—would have to be moved from three places where their possessions were scattered— Boston, Quincy, and Washington—to another place across an ocean. One person charged with responsibility for many details would be Henry.[20] The difficulty of moving seemed so great that the minister described the process as similar to "pulling up an oak."[21] While in Washington, if he wished, Henry could stay with his sympathetic aunt, whose helpful company he was now again to lose. He and "Mrs. John" would want an opportunity to say good-bye.

Customarily, when going to Washington, the Adamses stopped overnight in New York. Judging from all that later happened, Henry took advantage of his stopover in this instance to visit the office or home of Henry J. Raymond. He told the editor that he was going temporarily to London as his father's private secretary. He asked to be appointed to the post of regular London correspondent of the *New York Times*, on a paid basis, at the rate of compensation usually given by the newspaper to its trusted correspondents. Were Raymond to agree, absolutely no one in the United States Government—not Lincoln, not Seward, not C. F. Adams—was to know of the appointment. If possible, no one in the office and printshop of the *Times*— other than Raymond himself—was to know of it. The rule of secrecy would be relaxed only to the minimum extent required to permit the sending of the secret reporter's pay to his brother Charles by mail, to be deposited by the brother in Henry's Boston bank account.[22]

Raymond saw no reason to refuse the younger Adams's offer to serve the *Times* and good reason to accept it. The newspaper at the moment had a regular correspondent in Paris but none in London. The vacuum in the British capital was regrettable and crying to be filled. An inflow of reports to the *Times* from London would not disturb the paper; on the contrary, it would enhance the paper's claims to authority and completeness.

The editor understood the seriousness of Henry's requirements concerning secrecy. Raymond was capable of seeing that his own pledges of secrecy were kept. That the editor of such a newspaper would enter into a deeply secret arrangement with the son and confidential secretary of the country's leading diplomat abroad to write professionally for the paper without his father's knowledge—an arrangement involving the continuous deception not only of the U.S. minister to England but also of the State Department and the White House—might have astonished some of the editor's friends, if they had heard about it, but not his enemies. Horace Greeley, editor of a rival paper of importance, the *New York Tribune*, formerly Raymond's employer, thought he understood the man and once called him the "Little Villain."[23]

In this instance, of course, the question could be asked, if Henry J. Raymond were a villain, what was Henry B. Adams?[24] But if the question had been put to Adams that same day, after he and Raymond had completed their agreement with perfect satisfaction on both sides, the newly appointed correspondent would have answered ironically that he was *not* an officeseeker![25] Admittedly, he was on his way to Washington. True, he was another of the many Republican politicians, and interchangeable to that extent with Lincoln, Seward, Sumner, C. F. Adams, John Gorham Palfrey, and Charles Lush Wilson. Yet when he got to Washington, instead of accepting the place of assistant secretary of legation in the English mission—an ill-paid foothold in the Foreign Service, but still a foothold, which many an office-seeker would have rejoiced to get—he would give the place away. Seward would try to force the place upon him; but he, Henry Adams, would prevail on Seward to give the place instead to a Democrat, a Pennsylvanian named Moran.

If the ironic answer that he was not an office-seeker seemed insufficient, Adams would also be ready with a second ironic answer, that he was not a diplomat! When he arrived in Washington, he took no interest in the most important diplomatic envoy stationed in the city, the British minister, Lord Lyons. His lordship was a hard-working bachelor and an able man, often well-informed. But the younger Adams had long since learned that the British mission in Washington—like the French—was "thrown in the scale against the Union," and that Lyons himself has "no faith in the success of the national government, or in its professions."[26]

What most concerned the younger Adams in Washington was the chance of getting good information about his probable difficulties in London. Evidently, while again in the capital, he ascertained for a fact—assuredly from Sumner—that Mr. Charles L. Wilson was one of the personal adherents of Seward, not of Lincoln, and that Seward mainly was responsible for the Chicagoan's appointment. The information perhaps was not important, but the son absorbed it. To that extent, he moved ahead of his father. He made positive inquiries and showed himself to be a learner. By getting one item of information, he prepared his mind for possible, later accretions, more serious and disturbing.[27]

By all odds, the foremost newspaper in the English-speaking world was *The Times* of London. The foremost news reporter in the English-speaking world undoubtedly was one of that paper's employees, William Howard Russell, a gifted Irishman. Russell had grown famous for his reports to his paper during the Crimean War in 1856. His chief, John Thaddeus Delane, editor of *The Times*, had recently ordered him to America as roving correspondent, to look into the dissensions which apparently had divided one large Union into two lesser ones, a United States and a Confederate States. Deciding first to visit the Northern government, before traveling to inspect the Southern, the correspondent had appeared in Washington on Tuesday, March 26, and gone to his room at "Willard's Menagerie." Passing through the lobby, he had found himself among a swarm of office-seekers. Never in its history had the capital been so overrun with deserving politicians, crying for their dues.

On Tuesday evening at the home of Henry S. Sanford, the newly appointed U.S. minister to Belgium, W. H. Russell was introduced to Secretary of State Seward. The following morning, Sanford and Russell went together to Seward's office, where it had been arranged that the visiting "Special Correspondent" should have a word or two with President Lincoln. When the president appeared and they had shaken hands, Lincoln said, as nearly as the reporter could recall: " . . .

I am very glad to make your acquaintance, and to see you in this country. The London *Times* is one of the greatest powers in the world; in fact, I don't know anything which has more power, except perhaps the Mississippi. I am glad to know you as its minister.[28]

That same Wednesday morning, two political Adamses, H. B. Adams and C. F. Adams, were either present in Washington or arriving. They perhaps were approaching on the same train from New York. More probably, the son had preceded the father, both to New York and Washington, by one-day intervals. In that case, Henry was already in the city.

On Thursday, the elder Adams called on Lincoln at the White House and, during a hasty interview, was merely told that he owed his appointment as minister to England entirely to Secretary Seward.

In the course of a separate meeting of their own at the State Department, Seward apologized to C. F. Adams for the appointment of Wilson as secretary of legation and gave his word that the Chicagoan would prove an "unobjectionable" helper.[29] Seward also advised the minister that his second secretary in London would be Henry, of course, and the appointment would be sent to the Senate for confirmation as soon as Henry learned of it and agreed to serve.

The minister relayed Seward's offer of the place to his son, and Henry rejected it. Speaking to his father, or possibly to his father and Seward together at another meeting—if indeed the whole process was not compressed into one meeting at which all three men were present—Henry used the following words or their near equivalents: " . . . [I would not be] acting in the best interests either of the [diplomatic] service, or of the Minister, or of myself in accepting any official position in the Legation."

Seward already knew, from Henry's second letter to Sumner, that the son proposed to serve in London as "Private Secretary"—to use the son's curious doubled capitals. That the younger Adams was in earnest could be seen from his behavior. On Friday, March 29, in Washington, he copied one of his father's outgoing letters into the minister's letter book, to create the usual, necessary record.[30]

One may presume that he said his good-byes and left Washington that same Friday, slept in New York, and went on to Boston on Saturday, to press ahead with his arrangements to move five Adamses to London.

On Saturday morning, the *New York Times* printed some interesting news concerning William Howard Russell. Somehow detailed word had been brought from Washington to New York about the

Wednesday meeting in Seward's office between the British correspondent and President Lincoln. Raymond's paper knew that Lincoln had called Russell the "minister" of *The Times* of London and had placed a very high estimate upon that paper's influence. The result was an editorial in the *New York Times* which expanded the president's single word into a virtual journalistic creed. Raymond, the probable author of the editorial, put forward the idea that modern countries should be represented in one another's capitals, not only by diplomatic envoys, necessary though they were, but also, and with equal necessity, by highly trusted correspondents.

If Henry Adams were not the person who brought the news from one city to another, and if the editorial in the Saturday *New York Times* did not arise from a new conversation between himself and Raymond, it was nonetheless a probability that the secretly appointed London correspondent of the foremost newspaper in the United States read the editorial and appreciated its application to himself. Looked at from his point of view, it was especially notable for expressing two ideas: that newspaper correspondents were quite as important as official diplomats, and that a correspondent stationed in a foreign capital was put there with the object of reporting, not merely to his paper, but to his country's *people*. Developing the second idea, the editorial drew an invidious comparison between the reports sent home by journalists, which were instantly published and made the basis for action by both people and government, and reports sent home by diplomats, which the *Times* said scornfully were mostly "filed away in dusty pigeon-holes, and kept sacred from sight or knowledge of men, until they have lost all their importance."

Left behind in Washington, C. F. Adams conferred with Seward about the place of assistant secretary of legation and a paradox without a parallel in the current experience of the United States Government: a federal appointment rejected by a Republican nominee. After thinking about the matter, the secretary of state and the minister to England found they differed. Believing that Henry might change his mind, Seward suggested that the appointment of an assistant secretary in London could be kept open till mid-April. Sure that Henry would *not* change his mind, C. F. Adams suggested that someone else would have to be selected. He seconded his son's earlier-communicated opinion that the needed person was Benjamin Moran.[31]

April Fool's Day for the younger Adams had become an anniversary. The year before on April 1, Henry had heard a concert at Dresden which marked the beginning of his journey to Italy and "book of life." During the evening of April 1, 1861, he secretly wrote a news report to Raymond on the subject of Massachusetts politics. The report was published in the *New York Times* on April 5 under the headings: "FROM BOSTON. The Federal Appointments for Massachusetts." The correspondent announced: " . . . Boston may hope to slumber again. The appointments have been made. . . . "

The theme of the news report was that some former leaders of the Free Soil Party in Massachusetts had at last been given the rewards of virtue. Out of five outstanding federal appointments in the state, three had gone to old Free-Soilers. Criticizing one of the other two, which in his opinion ought also to have gone to a Free-Soiler, the nameless reporter observed ironically that, "since we can't get all we want, we are willing to take all we can get."

The principal appointment of the five had been that of Congressman Adams as minister to England. In its connection, the report flattered Senator Sumner. " . . . Massachusetts has been much pleased at having the English mission. . . . The great body of the people were indifferent whether it was given to Mr. ADAMS or to Mr. SUMNER; either would have suited them, and either would have been excellent; all they wanted was that it should be offered to one of them, and since Mr. ADAMS was the one, they are perfectly satisfied." Sumner had brought about the appointment of John Gorham Palfrey as Boston postmaster. The report praised the choice, saying it did "honor to the Government."

The need for such gestures was very pressing. While C. F. Adams and H. B. Adams were both in Washington the week before, Sumner had immured himself in his lodgings on the excuse that he was "troubled with a severe affliction of the eyes."[1] News also had reached the Adamses that the senator was leaving for a vacation and lecture tour in the West and might not get home to Boston in time to bid the minister good-bye. Henry's father had had enough of Sumner's envy and was content that he and his former friend should forever separate, but the son acted pertinaciously to save his own relationship with the senator.[2]

That same evening, the younger Adams wrote a new letter to Sumner at the Capitol. In it he disclosed that a news report about the Massachusetts appointments, written by himself, might soon appear in the *New York Times,* adding pointedly, " . . . no one is to know who wrote it." Explaining that he would steer a course in England independent of his father's, Henry went so far as to claim that he would be "outside of the Legation and unconnected with it." He closed by asking Sumner for letters of introduction to editors in London. "As I may have occasion in England to make some little use of the press now and then, I want to know whether you can put me in the way, or can suggest a way, of getting an entrance into some of the English papers."

The April issue of the *Atlantic Monthly* contained an article, "The Reign of King Cotton," by Charles Francis Adams, Jr. It was well-received in Boston.[3] Sight of his elder brother basking in applause encouraged Henry to accelerate his work on his own article, "The Great Secession Winter of 1860-61," not with a view to its being published, but merely to get it written. The five departing Adamses would not sail for England until May 1, so the third son had a month to work in, and much of the time would be his own.

Not long after he started working with renewed determination, in the first days of April, a fleet of Union ships sailed from New York on an undisclosed mission. It was alleged in the press that the ships were carrying reinforcements and supplies to two isolated outposts, Fort Sumter at Charleston, South Carolina, and Fort Pickens near Pensacola, Florida, on the Gulf of Mexico. Uncertainty about the true mission of the fleet had given rise to extreme anxiety and tumultuous excitement, in both the Northern and Southern states.

On April 11, vessels belonging to the fleet were sighted near the entrance of Charleston Harbor. Deciding not to wait, lest additional ships should come with forces sufficiently strong to storm ashore, the Confederate officers at Charleston ordered their batteries to open fire on Fort Sumter at dawn on April 12. Once fired upon, the Union garrison holding Fort Sumter opened fire in reply.

Detailed news of the outbreak of civil war appeared in the New York and Boston papers on the morning of April 13. That day, C. F. Adams wrote laconically to Seward in Washington that Henry would go to England as "my private Secretary only" and that the place of assistant secretary of legation was indeed best given to Benjamin Moran—a plea that Seward quickly granted.[4]

H. B. Adams all the while was pushing forward in his article. He meant it to provide a dependable, accurate history of the United States during the past ten or eleven months, written without regard to Republican Party interests. Specifically, he wanted to tell the unknown story of how the city of Washington had happened not to fall into the hands of the disunionists. Portions of the narrative, when finished, would be surprising. For instance, it would partly praise a politician whom he in many ways despised, asserting that Senator Stephen A. Douglas, at an early moment when all the rest of the politicians in the North had been fast asleep to the Union's danger, had learned about and wrecked the deepest scheme of the secessionists, a design to capture Washington in November 1860, just after the election, were the Republican candidate to win.

On Monday, April 15, 1861, President Lincoln issued a proclamation declaring the existence of an armed rebellion and calling for 75,000 three-month volunteers to strengthen the government's military forces. The proclamation brought on an outburst of patriotic fervor throughout the North such as no one had anticipated. Certainty of speedy truimph on the battlefield was exultantly proclaimed in every Northern town and city. Throngs of men and boys sought ways to join the army.

It was not to be supposed that any of the Adams sons would be present in any of the expected battles. John would soon be married. Charles had been entrusted with supervision of the family's investments and properties. Henry was going to England. Just as easily, the family's holdings could have been entrusted to John, releasing Charles for military duty; but the second son had failed as a lawyer, drawn no clients, and stood in danger of not acquiring business habits, if no business were given him to perform. So all the older sons were occupied, and the family's needs were fully met, at least in the minds of both the parents.

After a two-week silence, a letter came to Henry from Senator Sumner, written in New York on April 18. Alluding to the fact that he had "differed from others this winter in my interpretation of events," the senator claimed to have been a true prophet. "What I have foreseen is now upon us. . . ." He seemed satisfied that the outbreak of war justified his former opinions and conduct in all particulars. Yet his letter was fully as cordial as Henry could have wished. The older man continued: "I enclose a brief note to a gentleman (in England) who knows well the *Times, Examiner, Spectator, News, Globe,* & can help you. . . . But you will meet Mr[.] Delane[,] editor in chief of the *Times* at Lord Palmerston's, Lord Granville's, and generally in society— except that people in earnest are afraid of him."[5]

Sumner's helpfulness was more or less simultaneous with some advice to Henry about his opportunities in London. John Gorham Palfrey knew young Charles and Henry well and was aware that both were would-be writers. Apropos of articles for magazines, Palfrey took advantage of a visit at the Adams house to put Henry in possession of an interesting tip. The historian had had occasion to study the activities of Captain John Smith, the founder of Virgina, who, it happened, had published several books. Palfrey's attention had been caught especially by the Captain's *Generall Historie of Virginia, New England, and the Sumner Isles,* first printed in 1624, and especially by the passage in which Smith recalled being captured near Jamestown by the Indians. Condemned to death by their ruler, the Emperor Powhatan, and prepared for execution, Smith had been rescued by Powhatan's daughter, the Princess Pocahontas, who—according to the Captain's *Historie*—dramatically interceded and secured his release. But Palfrey told Henry there was reason to believe Smith's story might be false. Palfrey noted that one of Smith's associates, Edward Wingfield, had kept a diary at Jamestown which made no mention of Smith's capture or of the saving Pocahontas. The historian suggested that the captain's escape from certain death had been invented from thin air during his later years, after his return to London, by his publishers.

At the Adams house, the historian emphasized his idea that the captain's rescue—in Henry's words—was presumably "of London Grub Street manufacture." The truth or falsity of the story, Palfrey said, could be conveniently investigated in London at the British Museum, where the requisite books, some of which could not be found in Boston, were undoubtedly waiting on the shelves. He further mentioned that Pocahontas was claimed by several leading families of Virginia as one of their distinguished ancestors. He therefore hinted that an ambitious Northern writer, merely by visiting the British Museum, could collect explosives for an article on Smith and

Pocahontas which, in addition to unmasking an old imposture, might injure a large amount of Southern pride.[6]

Charles was of several minds about himself. He wanted not to admit his failure as a lawyer. His success in the *Atlantic*, not to mention his various news reports in the Boston papers, inclined him more than ever to want to be a writer. He also had a feeling that he should become a soldier.

The second son had earlier joined the state militia. On April 24, his battalion was ordered to temporary, active duty at Fort Independence in Boston Harbor. The state militia was something less than a true military force, but Charles proposed to use his five-week tour of service to learn some lessons in military science. While with his unit, he showed uncommon willingness to drill, parade, sweep floors, wash dishes, and wheel coal.[7] The third son visited Fort Independence and glimpsed soldier Charles in action.[8] Stories were coming Henry's way about classmates of his at Harvard and acquaintances in Boston who were rushing to the colors. It was said that some had received commissions as lieutenants, even captains. He could not himself join the army. His commitment to his adventure in England had been made in earnest, and he would not try to withdraw it. All the more deeply on that account, part of him yearned to "go into the army with the other fellows."[9] His feelings became divided as they had never been before. Illness set in. He tired easily, felt irritable, and—possibly—experienced severe indigestion.[10]

Like a great many other well-informed politicians and journalists, Henry had learned not long after the inauguration of Lincoln on March 4 that Seward's acquiescence in the matter of the president's cabinet choices had not meant that the New Yorker's struggle to control the new administration had reached an end. In late March and early April, Seward had become identified in many people's minds with a policy that looked towards the restoration of the Union *without* resort to arms. Resisting Seward's attempts to control all the departments of the executive branch, Lincoln had seemed in the same people's minds to have identified himself with a policy which looked towards armed coercion as the remedy of Southern independence. This was not to say that Lincoln had favored war, nor that Seward would not have fought under any provocation. It just happened that Lincoln's continuing resistance to Seward's attempted usurpations had created a feeling that war was not to be avoided.

Because the first shot fired at Charleston on April 12, 1861, had come from a Confederate cannon, the younger Adams had found it easy to support the president completely. All along, since the previous December, Henry had agreed with Andrew Johnson that secession was treason. On that assumption, war against the traitors was simply a meting out of justice. It seemed to Adams that the appropriate punishment could be inflicted and the Union restored during the months of spring and summer.

The outbreak of war had not affected his progress, working on "The Great Secession Winter of 1860-1861," and had not altered his ideas. He apparently labored upon the pages of his manuscript until the last possible day, striving to improve it. On Sunday, April 28, the day before their brother's wedding, he mailed the manuscript to Charles at Fort Independence. By the time Charles received and read it, Henry would be as good as gone for England with their parents and the younger children. A note appended to the manuscript pronounced the article a failure. It also explained to Charles that, for all its faults, the work was a present to himself, and possible raw material for a second article in the *Atlantic*, should he wish to submit a second. " . . . parts of it . . . might be put to some use," Henry suggested. "If you ever feel like taking the labor necessary to rewriting it at more length and in a better form, you are welcome to all the honor you can get from the result."

Throughout its length, the narrative the third son had written in Washington and Boston was terse, passionate, and philosophical. Henry had told in detail how, in December 1860, the efforts of the secessionists had been resisted, renewed by the secessionists, again resisted with increasing determination on either side until, in January and February, under Seward's leadership, the capital had been secured. The impression of the Republicans given by the manuscript was unflattering and harsh. Henry said that Seward had been the "only" Northerner in Congress who had traveled to Washington in November or December prepared to meet the designs of the secessionists with a coherent policy and readiness to attempt its execution—that the senator, by temporizing, had saved the Union single-handed.[11] Without exempting his father from this general verdict, the son gave him credit for a minor share of saving leadership. The three men whom the manuscript praised unstintingly, William Henry Seward, Andrew Johnson, and Henry Winter Davis, belonged to as many different parties.

The narrative was put together with extraordinary deftness and assurance. Its overall effect was relieved and even joyous. In its later pages, Henry had told how Lincoln, resisting pressures from every side, had successfully formed a cabinet which Seward would not be able to control. The writer's attitude towards Lincoln was loyal and sympathetic. Clearly familiar with the many complaints that had been urged against the president, young Adams came close at one point to charging Lincoln with an error.[12] Yet Henry really shied away from close discussion of the president's character and actions, in order to stress that Lincoln, arriving in the capital, had had to deal with "men and measures that would have taxed the patience of Washington and required the genius of Napoleon."[13] The essential subject of the narrative was not persons but the Union. In the writer's view, the greatest battle to save the Union had been already fought and won. The rescue of the capital from the secessionists had been effected, made the necessary difference, and would mean in the end the surrender of the South.

Henry packed his trunk, the same one he had unpacked the previous October, when he had come back from Paris.[14] He attended John and Fanny's wedding. At East Boston on Wednesday, May 1, 1861, he went aboard the old Cunard steamer *Niagara* with his parents, Mary, and Brooks.[15] The other passengers included the newly appointed U.S. minister to Russia, Cassius Clay of Kentucky, and several members of his family. In honor of the two American ministers, the vessel was brightly trimmed with colors. At half past twelve noon, flying her British union jack, the *Niagara* sailed for Liverpool.

Except to notice that the Adamses and Clays seldom spoke, and that Henry was seasick in a manner so injurious as to prove that his divided feelings were far from being reunited, there was little to be said about the voyage.[16] A more deserving subject was a secret. Possibly at the last moment in Boston, or at Fort Independence when he went there, Henry had told his brother Charles in deepest confidence about the arrangement worked out earlier between himself and Raymond in New York. Charles sympathized, at least to the extent of being willing to accept and deposit Henry's pay.

The manuscript left behind by the younger brother as a present to the older was not a failure. Its closing lines may possibly have been written after the body of the narrative was finished. The lines were rather somber. The third son had asked himself afresh how long the civil war would last. As before, he thought it would be short. Yet, if such a challenge were not to be prevented, he was content to see the Union undergo a long and tragic test. He had written: "It is said very generally among our people that our theory of Government is a failure. We know that it has been the subject of long controversy and stands now as an experiment. As with all other governments, so with this, it was to be expected that time would bring its trials, and until they came, and the fact of their having been endured and surmounted was patent to the world, this experiment . . . could never be called a complete success."

# 17 / *True Americans*

Benjamin Moran seldom tasted happiness. As a printer's devil in Pennsylvania, an itinerant poet and artist in cities as far apart as New Orleans and Boston, a correspondent in Europe for American newspapers and magazines, he had struggled from one adventure to another until in London in 1854, as a temporary employee of the U. S. legation under Minister Buchanan, he had found the trade that suited him and become a diplomat. Briefly he seemed to prosper. When Buchanan was installed as president in 1857, Moran received the assistant secretaryship in the English mission; but his new chief at the legation, Minister Dallas, conspired with the first secretary, Philip Dallas, to prevent the second secretary's being invited, as he should have been, to diplomatic social functions. Ostracized Moran at the same time suffered the lingering illness and death of his English wife.

In 1861, a widower of forty, lonely, impecunious, and more than ever troubled by dreams of failure and success, the assistant secretary had resolved if possible to stay at the legation. He had written to friends in America, asking them to intercede on his behalf with the Republicans. Waiting to hear of his reappointment or dismissal, he had become extremely apprehensive. American news reached England along two far-from-speedy paths. Urgent bulletins were sometimes telegraphed to Halifax in Nova Scotia, brought by ship to Ireland, and retelegraphed to England. Ordinary news, mostly in the form of newspapers, was simply carried by ship from New York, Boston, and other American ports to Liverpool or Southampton, sometimes arriving in eleven days, but more usually in twelve.

Moran was keeping a detailed private journal. When word reached London that the new minister to England would be Charles Francis Adams, the assistant secretary recorded in his journal approvingly, "This gentleman is the son and grandson of Presidents, & both his grandfather and father were Ministers at London." Two days later, when another ship had come, the journal-keeper less happily continued: "There is news in town this morning that Charles L. Wilson of Chicago has been appointed Secretary of Legation here and that I am to be retained. This last I doubt, and have pretty well made up my mind to be displaced."

Inquiring in London about the wealth of the family, Moran was told that the Adamses were nabobs. Four added days confirmed his gloomy expectations. "The American papers contain a rumor of my removal. . . . " The papers said the new assistant secretary would be a son of Mr. Adams. Moran had prepared himself for failure, but the thought of being hurt again by the combination of a father and a son was hard for him to bear. In his journal, he exclaimed about the younger Adams, " . . . what he wants with my place, God only knows." The careless son in Boston who had stolen his place in London was understood to have a private income of $12,000 a year!

Still other steamers brought indisputable information that Moran was reappointed. In the usual course of things, he, a Democrat, could have looked for nothing better from the Republican administration than qualified hostility. American politicians were not supposed to love their enemies, much less retain them in the diplomatic corps. Yet his retention had occurred.

Thrilled by his rare good fortune, the assistant secretary became elated and positively buoyant. He looked afresh at his surroundings, busy London, the legation on Portland Place, his duties in the office, and brimmed with satisfaction and eagerness to work. "The Legation is an exciting place . . .," he wrote rejoicingly. "No sooner does one exciting theme pass than we have another, and the tension of mind is thus kept up continually."[1]

Early on May 10, 1861, Moran received a telegram saying that Charles L. Wilson would be in London that same morning and would be pleased to see him at Morley's Hotel. The assistant secretary went to Morley's, met the secretary, and found him a "pleasant, gentlemanlike person, rather short, stout and good looking, with a fine dark beard and moustache." Another message three days later said that Minister Adams had arrived at Liverpool and was coming straight to London. That evening, May 13, at half past nine, at Euston Station, Wilson and Moran greeted the minister and his family as they came from their train. Moran was fond of analyzing people, was a judge of character, and knew phrenology. He was "rather favorably inpressed" with C. F. Adams and also with his wife. He recorded that the eldest of their children, a son named Henry, was "about 25."

The assistant secretary's observations were interrupted by an emergency. The London "season" was at its height, and rooms at good hotels were in very great demand. Accommodations for the Adamses at Maurigy's Hotel had been arranged by Joshua Bates, an American banker in London, a senior partner in the firm of Baring Brothers. No similar arrangements had been made for Cassius Clay and his family, a party of eight people. Strangers to the city, Minister Clay and his dependents had already driven off with their trunks in four cabs to make belated inquiries.

Hoping to be of service, Moran and Wilson escorted the Adamses to Maurigy's, then pursued the Clays along a trail that led through five hotels, all full. When they overtook him, in the lobby of the Westminster Palace Hotel, the minister to Russia was pacing up and down beneath the gaslight like an irritated god. Further inquiries secured a scattering of rooms in which the Clays could pass the night. Moran had meanwhile received an unforgettable impression of Cassius Clay, a tall, handsome figure, dressed in a uniform apparently of his own design, half-military and half-diplomatic, including a "blue dress coat with gilt buttons." The minister was surrounded by his secretaries, "tall, sharp faced Kentuckians," and looked very much like "a man to be avoided."[2]

Secret correspondent Henry Adams was not intimidated by the duty of reporting authoritatively about the English. Two fleeting visits to England in 1858 and 1860, together with much reading of English authors and random dips into English periodicals, had given him an acquaintance with English life and politics which he thought would serve for a beginning. Besides, with luck, he might be able to start his reports the easy way, by confining them to subjects which would not lead him into deep or troubled waters.

In passing in one of his reports to the *Boston Advertiser,* Henry earlier had mentioned that England was "more anti-slavery" than the United States.[3] A generation before, the British Whigs had made great reputations for themselves as emancipators by effecting the abolition of slavery in Great Britain and all its dependencies. From the point of view of an arriving strong Republican, English politics since then had become less edifying. The English politicians were grouped in Parliament as members of two parties, Whigs and Tories, also known as Liberals and Conservatives. The division in the House of Commons was very even. The Liberals were in power but not expected to stay so very long. Viscount Palmerston, the prime minister, although amazingly vigorous, even youthful, was seventy-seven years of age. His colleagues in the cabinet were known to disagree on many issues.

Reporter Adams accordingly had arrived at Euston Station, gone to Maurigy's Hotel at the foot of Regent Street, and slept in his room protected by two wholly logical assumptions. One was that a well-known American antislavery leader such as C. F. Adams would be unreservedly welcomed by Lord Palmerston and the Liberals as a body. The other was that any Confederate envoys who might have hurried across the Atlantic to the British capital would be shunned by the prime minister and more especially by the foreign secretary, Lord John Russell.

Downstairs at breakfast the next morning, Tuesday, May 14, a failure of communication seemed to show that H. B. Adams, while not yet entirely at home among the English, was surely more so than C. F. Adams. A waiter approached the table and, speaking to the minister, asked in a London accent, "'amhandeggsir?" While Henry started laughing, his uncomprehending father asked that someone tell him what the waiter could have said.[4]

Reading newspapers at Liverpool, or on the train, or in London the night before, Henry had begun to learn about a strange development. The English, it appeared, had grown interested in two recent occurrences in America. On April 17, in hopes of strengthening the naval power of the Confederacy, President Davis had issued a proclamation offering letters of marque and reprisal to owners of ships who would venture to operate as Confederate privateers. On April 19, in reply, President Lincoln had issued a counterproclamation declaring that rebel privateers would be seized as pirates and that all the ports of the disloyal states would be closed by a rigorous blockade. The texts of both proclamations had since been published in England, where, beginning on May 1, they had caused much worry and concern.

Voices had been raised in Parliament urging the ministry to take effective measures for the protection of British ships at sea. Two men had stepped forward in the House of Commons as champions of America's warring sides. The champion on the side of the Union was Mr. William E. Forster, a Liberal elected two years earlier from Bradford in Yorkshire, a young man, able and ambitious. The champion on the Confederate side was Sir William Gregory, the member from Galway, a Conservative not esteemed for ability or brains but well supplied with the courage of his convictions. Mr. Gregory had attempted to introduce a motion calling for the immediate recognition of the Confederate States of America as an independent power.

His attempt had been thwarted, but Gregory had announced it would be repeated.

Serious difficulties started with the fact that Jefferson Davis had long since ordered three Confederate commissioners—William L. Yancey, Ambrose Dudley Mann, and Pierre A. Rost—to meet in London and seek the full support—political, military, financial, and commercial—of England, France, and Spain. The three Southern envoys had met in London two weeks earlier, on April 29. Since that day, as nearly as Henry Adams could determine, the commissioners had arranged to call at the Foreign Office and had been granted at least one interview by Foreign Secretary Russell. As if this untoward procedure were not a sufficient challenge to the secret reporter's comforting assumptions, the Liberal cabinet, guided by Lord John Russell, had readied a proclamation of its own.

The British action seemed very hasty. It had been known in London that Minister Adams would arrive on Monday evening, May 13. Yet that same Monday, in advance of his arrival, Queen Victoria had issued a Proclamation of Neutrality with respect to the American conflict. The document appeared in the London press on Tuesday morning, May 14, the morning the Adamses ate their first breakfast in London, at Maurigy's Hotel.[5] Henry closely studied the queen's imperative command. In its main clauses, the Proclamation of Neutrality forbade all forms of assistance by Her Majesty's loving subjects to either of the contesting parties in America. While abstaining from recognizing the Confederacy as an independent country, the British government recognized the Confederate government as a belligerent.

When he had mastered these disclosures, the younger Adams did not know what to think. His first reaction was one of dazed perplexity. It appeared that the Liberals, in defiance of their reputation as foes of slavery, had half-befriended the Confederate States and half-betrayed the Union! The act stood opposite to reason.[6]

Minister Adams's instructions, while friendly to England, said that he should try as far as possible to prevent the slightest recognition of the Confederacy by the British government. For the purpose, he had arrived in London a week or more too late. Without declaring the independence of the South, the Liberal ministry had hastened very far in that direction.

C. F. Adams lost no more time. He started work on his first day in London. During his second day, he asked to be presented to Queen Victoria. During his third, he was received by the queen at Buckingham Palace and took charge at the legation, relieving George M.

Dallas. The day after, he wrote his first despatch to Secretary Seward; and on its morrow, May 18, a Saturday, he drove nine miles from London to Pembroke Lodge, Lord John Russell's country house, and told the foreign secretary that, "in case there was a disposition here to favor the pretended Confederated States, he would have nothing more to do in England," and would arrange to leave. Acting as he did, the new minister created distinct impressions. On Friday at the legation, copying Mr. Adams's first despatch, Moran was pleased to learn that his chief, in addition to being an "accomplished man of business," displayed "surprising knowledge of English politics." On Saturday at Pembroke Lodge, Lord John Russell perceived that the U. S. minister was a "calm and judicious man."[7]

With equal or greater energy, H. B. Adams had started working as a minister of the journalistic sort. His method of operation was the simplest possible. He wrote a thorough news report, much longer than any he had written for the *Boston Advertiser*, addressed it to editor Raymond of the *New York Times*, affixed the needed postage to the envelope, and slipped it into a London mailbox. He synchronized the mailing of his reports with the weekly departures of Cunard steamers going to New York. Since the ships left Liverpool each Saturday but stopped at Queenstown in Ireland on Sunday, a report mailed in London as late as Saturday afternoon would normally be in time to catch its ship. In the present instance, taking no chances, Henry finished and mailed his report on Friday, May 17.[8]

He led off with a paragraph about the curious habits of the English, who chose the lovely weeks of May, not to flee the city as Americans would do, but instead to congregate in London for their social season, which lasted till July. This gently mocking preface accorded with the new London correspondent's apparent character. At scattered points in his report, the writer supplied a sketchy but unhesitating picture of himself. He was an American resident of Europe, a Republican, with "a pretty long experience of English-men," who, after a stay in France, had just arrived from Paris. These lies, when printed in the *New York Times*, would appear beneath a subheading, "From Our Own Correspondent." Seeing the heading and believing all the lies, readers would assume that nameless Henry Adams was a veteran journalist not less than thirty-five years of age and very possibly somewhat older.

The impression would be confirmed by the news he had to tell. His report said that several loyal, active, able Unionists, himself among them, were on the scene in London and Paris. They had begun an effort to reverse any harmful developments that might already have occurred in Europe in connection with the rebellion in America. Vigorous measures would be needed. Three days earlier, his report admitted, Americans adhering to the Union had been called upon by Queen Victoria to swallow a bitter pill, "a proclamation on privateering" which placed the Union and the Confederacy on an all-but-equal basis in their dealings with the British government.

To say the least, the Proclamation of Neutrality had been a disappointment. In his role as a veteran journalist, anonymous Henry would be expected to account for its being issued. But the conduct of the Liberal ministry remained astonishing to him. He had not learned an explanation of the British action which he could thoroughly believe. He therefore chose in his report to view the matter lightly. Lord Palmerston and his associates, Adams volunteered, had "done a silly thing." If they had used their heads, the members of the Liberal ministry would have remembered, not forgotten, that British interests required an early victory for the Union land and naval forces in America, if only so that trade between the countries, at present much curtailed, should flourish as in the past. English politicians were human and had erred. The Liberals had issued a proclamation, a "timid half measure," which would be of "little practical use" to the Confederate States, yet promised to "alienate" the Union.

Energetically as well, Henry had started work as "private Secretary." New quarters were needed for the legation. Beginning on May 18, temporary space for the legation offices was obtained at No. 7 Duke Street, at Duchess Street, "an obscure locality off Portland Place."[9] The address was inappropriate, the rooms were cramped, and the need for proper quarters both for business and residence purposes was very urgent. Henry has been sent to find a house. While his father was consulting with the "usual crowd of old buffers," as the son described the minister's visitors, English and American, and while Mrs. Adams conferred with Madame Bates about the multitudinous exactions of etiquette at the queen's Court, the unofficial secretary of legation inspected London mansions. One he saw on Grosvenor Square could be had, he was told, for three months at $500 a month, a figure he regarded as extortionate.

Returning at intervals to Maurigy's Hotel, where the five Adamses would have to live till he found a house, the third son wrote to Charles in Boston that his health was not restored, the hotel was poor, and London food intolerably bad. Diplomacy seemed not to interest the conscripted, privately paid, much wanted and trusted "Secretary." Yet he also seemed envious of the official secretaries, Wilson and Moran, as if he wanted their duties and could not have them. "I pass my time in doing errands," he complained to his brother, "and am not sure that this will not be my duty and only duty always. I can assure you, my own share in matters in general will be very small."[10]

Cassius Marcellus Clay had risen to prominence as publisher of *The True American,* a weekly newspaper devoted to the expansion of a free United States and the ruin of the slavepower. He had supported Lincoln and aspired to membership in Lincoln's cabinet. Knowing his talents to be chiefly military, Mr. Clay had proposed himself as the man to head the War Department. Told it had been given to another aspirant, Clay had offered to take a commission as a general in the army, and, if arranging his commission took time, to serve in the interval as minister to England or minister to France. Denied all three honors, he was next denied the place of minister to Spain. He accepted the post of minister to Russia and started for St. Petersburg but felt a stronger interest in the nearer capitals, London, Paris, and Madrid, to which he had asked to be assigned.

His wishes considered, his conduct on reaching London was understandable. At a glance, he perceived that American affairs were "not at all understood in London and on the Continent." He arranged with American friends in the city to have "a frank talk with members of the House of Commons and House of Lords, and also with Lord Palmerston." Then he wrote a "popular article" for immediate publication in the British Isles and on the Continent, translated into French. On Friday, May 17, 1861, he mailed the article—actually a long, signed letter to the editor of *The Times* of London.[11] Of course, he could not know that another American in the city, Henry Adams, was simultaneously mailing an anonymous news report to the editor of the *New York Times* at home.

The letter sent by the U. S. minister to Russia to John Delane, editor of *The Times,* was partly helpful and constructive. Clay posed three well-chosen questions about the Americans loyal to the Union. The questions were: "What are we fighting for?"—"But can you subdue the revolted States?"—"But can you govern a 'subjugated' people and reconstruct the Union?" The answers the Kentuckian provided were optimistic Union answers of a kind which till then had not been publicized in England. Briefly and simply, he explained the Union cause.

He went on to lecture the English people about their true interests. Asking rhetorically whether Great Britain could "afford to offend" so strong a power as the United States of America, he raised his eyes above the limitations of the present and foresaw the dimensions of the reconstructed great Republic. He prophesied—and underlined the words—that the Union would soon have a population of *"one hundred millions"* and would be furnished with railroads laid "four thousand miles upon a single parallel"—these railroads to have the purpose of "binding our empire, which must master the Atlantic and Pacific Oceans."[12]

*The Times* was mostly run by two men only, its manager, Mowbray Morris, and its editor, John Delane. The dissensions in American found both men predisposed to distrust and fear the Union government. As early as April 19, advised that President Lincoln and his cabinet intended to collect the federal revenues in the seceded states even if doing so should provoke a civil war, Morris had written, " . . . they are not statesmen but executioners. . . ."[13]

Delane was similarly affected when he received a letter on May 18 from one of Lincoln's diplomatic envoys, a certain C. M. Clay, the federal minister to Russia. The Northern envoy not only favored the armed subjugation of the South but aired a bragging dream of future Yankee wealth and power. On Monday, May 20, 1861, *The Times* published both Clay's letter to the editor and an editorial rejoinder. The result in London was a sensation.

Learning what C. M. Clay had done, H. B. Adams could not avoid the feeling that the Kentuckian's letter was a gross intrusion upon his father's diplomatic province and, worse, a violation of the rules of the Foreign Service, which explicitly forebade communications by official diplomats to the press. [14] But the younger Adams also saw that Clay has stumbled into a den of British lions. *The Times* had offered the minister to Russia some experienced advice. Clay was told that he and his Northern countrymen should drop their gaze from "long visions" of future things "which no man now alive will ever see accomplished," the better to fix their thoughts on the present, where they would find sufficient troubles to "occupy their attention."[15]

To Adams's mind, Delane's rejoinder was stingingly insulting. No choice existed between *The Times* and the minister to Russia. Henry sided with Mr. Clay. Especially he believed all Clay said about the future of the United States.

Adams mailed his second report to Raymond on Saturday, May

25. The report was quite complex. If skimmed, it would seem to many readers a mere routine account of the week's events in England. While dealing with more serious matters, Henry mentioned the approach of Derby Day, an amusing controversy in the field of literature and morals, the impending debate in the House of Commons about the budget—also throwing in a passage about the pleasures of musing upon the "magnificence of London" and of sitting in Hyde Park to watch the "display of wealth and horseflesh in Rotten-row."

To other eyes, the report would be curious for its loud complaints against the English press. Hitting in two directions at once, Henry called *The Times* of London a "sort of aristocratic New-York *Herald.*" He listed the sins of the English papers against the loyal citizens of the United States. " . . . the *News* is almost the only paper whose editorials are sound and determined on the right side. The *Times* is against us. . . . The *Morning Post* is with us, but not reliable. The *Herald* is better, but not firm. The *Standard* is against us. The *Globe* is on the fence. A great Southern success would throw them all over, and they merely indicate a similar state of feeling among their readers."

Next Adams attacked the British people. He termed the struggle in America a contest between "medieval barbarism" and "modern civilization." Looking on at the struggle, the citizens of the United Kingdom had made it their pride to choose neutrality. To him their choice seemed completely retrograde. "Neutrality in a struggle like this is a disgrace to their great name."

He went on to undercut and threaten the Liberal ministry. His main grudge against the British leaders was that they had written and issued the Proclamation of Neutrality. Their misdeed appeared to lie within the range of reprisal. He pointed out that Lord Palmerston's cabinet was lacking in cohesion. "There is no homogeneity, no warm union at the bottom of it." Thus an opportunity existed for President Lincoln and Secretary Seward to "make serious trouble" for their counterparts in London. Adams explained, underlining what he wrote: " *If our Government forces the evil to a head by resenting the course the Ministry have taken, it will infallibly create trouble here; may even make a question on which the Ministry would divide and break up.*"

It was hardly usual for Americans in England to write home for publication that the British ministry could be so sternly challenged from Washington that it would crumble and fall from power. Adams had lost his balance. His resentment of the Liberals in Parliament had carried him outside the harbors of common sense onto the open seas of unrestrained imagination. He remembered an idea he had earlier heard discussed in the Union's capital. It was *not* that President Lincoln and Secretary Seward should topple the British Liberals from power. It was that the United States, as a means of pulling its loyal and disloyal parts back together, would do well to start an immediate war with England.[16]

Adams believed that the option of immediate war lay squarely before the loyal citizens of the United States. ". . . we have cause enough to quarrel upon, if we want to do so." He confessed himself uncertain whether a majority of his loyal counterparts at home would wish to enter such a quarrel, yet seemed inclined to guess that they indeed would choose to fight. To him, the benefits of immediate war were manifest. If entered into with energy and spirit, the contest for the Americans involved would revive patriotic feelings, even in the deepest South. The disaffection of the cotton states would end. The broad river of the nation's life would return to its proper channel. The Union would expand, acquiring part or all of British Canada.

For him, three thousand miles removed from Washington, true predictions of the American response to England's strange misdeed were very difficult to make. Hoping that the news from the Union government, when it came, would have a welcome shape, the correspondent said that many shrewd Americans in London were "waiting in great anxiety for the 1st of June." But, rather than wait in silence, he wished to ruminate in print about the probability of war.

At points his second report assumed that war with England would merely carry existing Republican Party policies to their logical conclusions.[17] If that were true, he asked himself, by whom might the war best be started? He wrote that Mr. Adams as minister to England would "take no step without due care." The war, then, would have to be started by the minister's chiefs at home. Really Lincoln would have to begin the war himself. "The stroke, if it comes at all, must come from Washington and the President. . . ."

On the assumption that Mr. Lincoln might attempt the "stroke," Adams looked forward hypothetically in his report to an era of immense confusion and general conflict in the North Atlantic world. He half-expected the fall of the British Liberals, a peaceful solution of the quarrels in America, and great naval battles on the ocean. It pleased him to think of the English in their astonishment, when they found themselves at war. " . . . if the Government at Washington should take this matter up with a high hand, and in the hope of uniting America against England," he theorized, "I am convinced that this country would be taken completely by surprise, and it might cost the Whigs their ascendancy, though in the embroilment that would ensue it would need a rash man to foretell what good would result from their overthrow."

After expressing his resentment, Adams somewhat ceased to feel it. As before, he told himself that British politicians, being enemies of slavery and friends of freedom, ought logically to support the Union. But he fully realized—what he had always known—that the English were disbelievers in democracy and incredulous deriders of large-scale, federal republics, which they scorned as chimeras increasingly unreal in proportion to their size. Thus, on second thought, Henry satisfied himself that the Unionists could expect a fraternal welcome in London only from a small proportion of the more enlightened Liberals in Parliament.

One such person, John Bright, the member of the House of Commons representing Birmingham, had called the week before at the legation and offered his good offices and friendship to Minister Adams and his aides.[1] Since then, Bright had hurried to cement a firm alliance between the Union envoy, himself, and several like-minded men in Parliament, notably William Forster, Richard Monckton Milnes, and the Duke of Argyll. The alliance was not without its risks. Wide notice of its existence could easily augment ill will in the United Kingdom towards the United States. The British in recent decades had not much liked Americans and particularly had disliked their boasting about their novel form of government. Being the English leader who most evidently shared American ideals and admired American institutions, John Bright was shunned in England as a revolutionary radical. Antipathy to him might flare at any moment into aggravated hostility towards Mr. Adams, or, behind him, Mr. Seward and Mr. Lincoln.

Ill will towards Americans displayed itself in the House of Commons on Monday evening, May 27, 1861, during the debate about the budget. C. F. Adams selected the occasion to make his first appearance in the halls of Parliament and went accompanied by his official secretaries. Henry did not go but learned from his elders that a Liberal member, Sir John Ramsden, intending to injure Bright, had ridiculed the United States, saying triumphantly that the British were "now witnessing the bursting of the great republican bubble which has been so often held up to us as the model on which to recast our own English constitution."[2]

Ramsden's words provided a test of sentiment in the House of Commons towards the Union. Moran noted that they were "ve.y warmly cheered by the Tory side, and not much disapproved of by :he Liberal."[3] When closely studied from the Union point of view, these reactions could have a truly dismal meaning.[4] It was even possible to show that the Union had no friends at all in Parliament. After hearing Ramsden announce the demise of the great Republic across the seas, a scattering of Liberals had deplored his manner and wished his words unspoken, but none believed his words had been untrue. Cassius Clay might plead the contrary in a letter to John Delane; the members of the legation might try to teach more sanguine views to their warmer Liberal friends; but every British politician, in May and June 1861, was sure that the cleavage in American into two lesser unions was final and irreversible. No sympathizer, not Bright, not Forster, could as yet conceive a glimmer of a hope that the American Union, with effort and sacrifice, might someday be restored.[5]

The main comfort the Unionists in England could draw from such an atmosphere was thinking that their case could only alter for the better. Several excitements meanwhile were going on at once. The budget debate brought on a crisis. The chancellor of the exchequer, Mr. Gladstone, angered the Irish members, including several Liberals. The Conservatives tried to use the disaffection of the Irish Liberals as a lever to hurl Lord Palmerston from power. The prime minister dexterously escaped defeat by postponing the vote on the budget until a later evening.

Tuesday, May 28, changed the face of things at the legation. A house had been obtained, at No. 17 St. George's Place, at Hyde Park Corner. Well-located for official purposes, the building had a pleasing exterior, permitted splendid views across Hyde Park, but inside was neither spacious nor conveniently laid out. C. F. Adams took it only from month to month. Further inquiries by Henry, it was assumed, would subsequently permit another move into a larger, better structure.[6]

The five Adamses prepared to leave their hotel, and the official secretaries made ready to shift their work from Duke Street. Each passing day brought the secret correspondent closer to his weekly deadline, the last mail to catch the steamer, and involved him more deeply, too, in the affairs of the legation. The reporter, going with the minister, witnessed the continuation of the budget debate in the House of Commons on Thursday evening, May 30. After a rush of errands, evidently on Friday evening, the younger Adams completed a third report to Raymond.

He provided in it what would seem to be a first-hand account of the losing bets, inebriation, and fearful traffic incident to the joys of Derby Day—based, no doubt, on a conversation with Charley Wilson, who had attended the races. To judge from a full account he gave of the debate on the budget, Adams's first impressions of the House of Commons at work had been extremely vivid. It met, he mentioned, in a chamber oddly small, long, and crowded. Six hundred members sat on benches on either side of a narrow passage partly blocked by a table for the clerks. "Across this table Mr. GLADSTONE and Mr. DISRAELI, the Treasury Bench and the leaders of the Opposition, glare in each other's eyes, or, as is more common, loll with their legs stretched out and their hats pulled down over their foreheads, and listen to bitter attacks with an air of the most utter imbecility."

The Conservatives had again attempted without success to bring down Lord Palmerston. The treasury bench had taken steps to discourage further slurs against the United States. " . . . it is a matter of some significance," Henry wrote, "that both Lord JOHN [RUSSELL] and Mr. GLADSTONE attacked Sir JOHN RAMSDEN, and commented severely on the language he had made use of towards America."

To end his communication, Henry offered some reassurance. The champion of the Confederacy in Parliament, Sir William Gregory, had set a date, June 7, when he would take the floor, make a speech, and again urge the House of Commons to vote upon his motion to recognize the independence of the Southern republic in America. Behind the scenes, John Bright's alliance of champions in favor of the Union was working out a plan to block the threatened motion. Being his father's confidential assistant, the younger Adams knew about the plan. Without so much as hinting that he knew of it, he coolly spoke in his report about Sir William's measure as a thing already killed. " . . . as for Mr. GREGORY'S motion, if he can make much out of it now, he must have some secret power unknown to men. My own belief is that he will be choked off."

The Adamses moved into the house at No. 17 St. George's Place on June 1. Presumably C. F. Adams and H. B. Adams shared one room as an office and study. During the day, Wilson and Moran drove about the city leaving cards for the minister, his wife, and themselves at the houses of the British cabinet ministers and at many embassies.

H. B. Adams, wanting not to be invited to such affairs as Lady Palmerston's At Homes, surely not for the present, refused to be ensnared in the proceedings. Moran, after the social famine imposed on him by the Dallases for four years, was vengefully delighted to foresee that a second secretary, himself, working for the salary of a clerk, would soon enter some of the greatest houses of the Empire.

The mail shortly brought an invitation for Moran to Lady Palmerston's next At Home. Profoundly gratified, the assistance secretary recorded in his journal: "This settles the Dallases as liars and shows they wilfully deprived me of my social right. . . . Jealousy and envy were at the bottom of it. . . ."[7]

Cassius Clay had gone to France. In Paris the previous Thursday, May 30, at the Hotel du Louvre, in company with Colonel Fremont, William Dayton, the U. S. minister to France, and Anson Burlingame, the U. S. minister to Austria, later reassigned to China, Minister Clay had taken part at a breakfast organized to cheer resident American Unionists. The three envoys and Fremont were called upon to speak. Dayton and Fremont's words were not inflammatory, but Clay took issue once again with the British Proclamation of Neutrality and threatened England with bold reminders of the War of 1812 and Napoleon I. Burlingame indulged in similar expressions hostile to Great Britain. In effect, they recommended war with England as the best reply to the Proclamation.

A full account of the breakfast, including verbatim texts of the speeches, was published in *Galignani's Messenger*.[8] Widespread excitement began to show itself. While steamers took copies of the account towards New York and Washington, a copy found its way to the desk of John Delane in London. On Monday, June 3, under the heading, "The Americans in Paris," *The Times* reprinted the long account, adding a comment that the speeches were "worthy of perusal, because they show the spirit in which the Northerners are inclined to look upon the neutral attitude of England."

Suspicion grew in London that Clay and Burlingame's remarks in Paris had been inspired by orders sent to them from Washington by Seward. Afraid the suspicion pointed towards a fact, the duke of Argyll wrote on June 4 to a friend in Washington, Charles Sumner, urging him to "use your influence and official authority to induce your government, and especially Mr. Seward, to act in a more liberal and a less reckless spirit." The duke explained to the senator: "I find much uneasiness prevailing here [in London]. . . . So far as I know, this uneasiness is founded rather on things said than on things yet actually done. But Mr. Seward knows Europe less well than you do; and . . . many of us . . . fear that he may be disposed to do high-handed and offensive things. . . . There is a great fear here that he has got it into his head that the English people can't and won't take offense at anything the American government may do to their ships or their people."[9]

At the legation, Minister Adams did not even slightly share the fear of his firm ally the duke of Argyll concerning Seward. To Henry's father, the noises made by two Union ministers in Paris were wholly unrelated to the secretary of state in Washington. C. F. Adams regarded Clay and Burlingame as persons incapable of common sense and silence. The elder Adams later wrote to Clay in Russia and informed him that in London and Paris he had roundly proved himself a fool.[10]

The younger Adams perused the account of the Paris breakfast printed in *Galignani's Messenger* and reprinted in *The Times*. The account affected him directly. He himself, five days before the breakfast, had outlined a scheme for an immediate war between the United States and England in a several-sided news report. When he was confronted with the selfsame scheme, outlined in print by other men in different words, lightning struck.

The folly of his second report to Raymond, mailed on May 25, smote him in the face. War with England, far from "uniting America," as his mad report had said it would, instead would overstrain the naval and military capabilities of the Union, immediately guarantee the independence of the Confederacy, and possibly disintegrate the much-diminished Union into petty fragments, similar in their impotence and jealousies to mere European Saxonies and Bavarias! And his report was now arriving in New York, to be published undoubtedly within the next three days.

Danger did not end there, for a fatal question had arisen. If three loyal Unionists in Europe, H. B. Adams, C. M. Clay, and Anson Burlingame, had been guilty of rousing their loyal compatriots to suicidal lust for war with England, was it not to be predicted that much-trusted men at home, including officials high in the government, would compound their blunders? Would not Lincoln and his cabinet attempt the stroke which would forever break the Union and cast its pieces in the dust?

Another question was personal. If he were to continue writing for the *New York Times*, what could H. B. Adams do to minimize old damage and prevent himself from perpetrating more? As a start, he could tell a helpful lie, pretending to his readers in America—possibly also to himself—that his second report had been soothing, quiet, and devoted to peaceful concord between Great Britain and the Union. As if nothing at all had happened, he could send his reports each week with perfect regularity. He could use his future reports to unsay all the rash, mistaken offensive things his second report had volunteered.

The private secretary went with the minister and the official secretaries to see what would happen to Sir William Gregory's motion in the House of Commons on Friday evening, June 7. The four Americans were shown to seats on the Liberal side of the gangway. Across from themselves, seated with the Conservatives, they spied one of the three Confederate commissioners, Dudley Mann. Mr. Patten, a Conservative member, obtained the floor and somewhat startled the House by asking Sir William *not* to speak—indeed to withdraw his motion. The suggestion was loudly cheered. Finding himself opposed by the members generally, Gregory consented to keep silent and withdrew his motion *sine die.*

Assistant secretary Moran, watching the Confederate commissioner across the gangway, saw the face of Dudley Mann distorted by a scowl.[11] Mr. Bright spoke next and asked Sir William to withdraw his motion altogether. Gregory refused. Mr. Forster, too, asked Sir William to withdraw it altogether; and Gregory again refused. The matter was concluded, not as a Union victory so much as a Confederate unsuccess.

H. B. Adams found a time and place to work and quietly wrote a corrective fourth report. Mailed on Saturday, June 8, his newest communication was a thorough turnabout. Without explaining what he was doing, he recanted all the errors in his evil second communication.

He made excuses for the misguided London newspapers. "It is natural enough," he said, "that Americans should feel somewhat sore at the way the English Press talks about American affairs, and yet it is certain that they have treated us with much more fairness and candor than they have ever shown towards the Continental Powers. . . . Even the *Times,* which never was known to acknowledge an error . . ., deprecates the effects of its own policy, instead of acting the bully, as it naturally prefers to do."

He further made excuses for Parliament, the Liberal ministry, and Foreign Secretary Russell. Recalling an important announcement made by Russell the previous Monday night about the closing of English and French ports to all American privateers, whether confederate or federal, Adams said that the closing of the ports meant "practically nothing" to the Union, "while to the Southerners it is everything, and knocks their plan of privateering directly in the head."

The correspondent wished to give a strong impression that events had stabilized. The last lines of his report were if anything overdone, for he drew a picture of Union victory in England which left nothing to be desired. "The Southern Commissioners have been driven out of the field. . . . Our own representatives never had more weight and influence. . . . Everything is sailing on quietly and peacefully. Only the death of CAVOUR has thrown a gloom over the country, as though some great Englishman were being carried to-day to his grave."

Moran had recently been afflicted with inordinate nervousness, occasional hot fevers, and a recurrent sore throat.[12] He might better have avoided the debate in Parliament on Friday night, in order to seek his bed and rest. He had not only attended the debate but gone afterwards with friends to hear a program of dramatic readings by an American lady actress, Mrs. Frances Key Blunt, a daughter of the Baltimorean who wrote "The Star-spangled Banner."

In 1858 and 1859, the assistant secretary had twice met Henry J. Raymond, when the distinguished editor had visited the legation.[13] Moran may have noticed that the *New York Times* lacked a regularly contributing London correspondent. Being an officer in the Foreign Service, he was barred by law from writing for the press. But the severe anxiety created in recent weeks for persons like himself by the presence of three Confederate commissioners in the British capital had blessedly lifted. Besides, in youth, he had made his living as a foreign correspondent.

Secretly, on Saturday, June 8, 1861, Moran wrote and mailed a news report to Mr. Raymond for publication if desired. The diplomat's illegal report set forth the pleasing story of the withdrawal *sine die* of Sir William Gregory's motion and the resulting angry scowl on the face of the traitor Dudley Mann.[14]While showing that its author retained his skill as a journalist, the report also showed his inward misery. In seven paragraphs, the assistant secretary treated the entire subject of Anglo-American relations and disparaged ten people he disliked, including Confederate Commissioners Mann and Yancey in London; President Davis, then reportedly moving to the new Confederate capital at Richmond, Virginia; Mrs. Frances Key Blunt, who was a traitress devoid of talent; and Thornton Hunt, an English journalist, who owed Moran some money.[15]

Composing his song of victory and vengeance exhausted the diplomat's vitality. On Saturday, his worsening sore throat forced his retirement to his lodgings and prevented his attending Lady Palmerston's At Home. His fever rose alarmingly on Sunday, and the infection spread to his arm. On Monday, under orders from his physician, he stayed away from work.[16]

If a higher income could have made him happy, the younger Adams should have become a happy man. In addition to a regular allowance given to him as a son of his parents, and an additional allowance for his labor as his father's chief assistant, he was enjoying free room and board. Then, too, he had the income from his inheritance and the money going into his bank account in Boston from his associate in journalistic politics, silent Raymond in New York.[17] But Henry was far from being happy. After a despondent weekend, on Monday, June 10, he began a letter to Charles in Boston by finding fault with London prices. He next complained that the labor of getting into English society was "repulsive."

Not being invited, he had not gone to Lady Palmerston's At Home two nights before. Their father and mother had gone, and he had learned from them what it was like. The function, held at Cambridge House in Piccadilly, had presented formidable terrors to any guest who was new to London. "You arrive at eleven o'clock. . . . The lady or ladies of the house receive you and shake hands. You pass on and there you are. You know not a soul. No one offers to introduce you. . . . No one knows that you're a stranger."

Charles was the only person to whom Henry could speak with anything approaching freedom about the deeper causes of his depression and unhappiness. In his letter, the younger brother touched upon the possibility of a new war between the United States and Great Britain, to match the War of 1812 and the War of Independence. Lying outright, he said that favoring a new war against the British had always seemed to him "the extreme of shallowness and folly." Lying again, he said, " . . . I did my best in my letters to the Times to quiet rather than inflame." He contrasted himself and the Chief with "those noisy jackasses Clay and Burlingame"—as if his second report to Raymond had not resembled their speeches at the Paris breakfast.

Henry tried to interest Charles in a scheme to plant an editorial in the *Boston Advertiser*. The drift of the editorial would be that the Union needed friends, not foes, abroad. Not unlike Moran, the younger brother seemed possessed by a blind need to make an extra effort, if possible in the daily press at home.

A terrible idea crept into the third son's lines. He said that no adventures into general North Atlantic conflict would pull Americans back together. Patriotism in the Southern states had died. "The cotton states would rather annex themselves to England or Spain than come back to us."

Before he could finish what he was writing, the younger Adams was interrupted. New instructions had reached the minister from the State Department. The instructions, "Despatch No. 10," dated May 21, 1861, had been slow in transit. They had taken twenty days to arrive from Washington. The elder Adams read them and grew extremely puzzled. They seemed to involve an utter contradiction. C. F. Adams could only assume that W. H. Seward, as secretary of state, had written or at least approved them, before affixing his signature. Yet the instructions were intended to bring about immediate war between the United States and England. The minister recorded in his diary: "I scarcely know how to understand Mr. Seward. The rest of the Government may be demented for all I know, but he surely is calm and wise."

Charles Francis Adams had no intention of starting a war with any country, certainly not with England. In his diary, he assured himself, "My duty here is . . . to prevent the mutual irritation from coming to a downright quarrel." Were he able to find one, he would welcome an honest way to evade his new instructions. But there was a little he could do at first, other than look at the strange despatch and wonder where it really came from. He could see that the pages had come from Seward's department. He supposed that the ideas on the pages could *not* have come from Seward—must necessarily have originated in the mind of some other member of the cabinet or possibly the president. At least that supposition, the minister reasoned, would account for their demented tendency.[18]

He showed the despatch to Henry, who read it and experienced twin reactions. The son was partly terrified. He knew that Seward on May 21 could very well have wished to start a war with England. It was instantly clear to the private secretary that Seward had drafted "Despatch No. 10" and that, at his suggestion, Lincoln and the cabinet had agreed to make as many wars as possible!

The strange despatch did not end with two wars, one against the Confederate States of America, the other against the United Kingdom. It embraced a third with France and maybe others against additional powers in Europe.

Henry also was partly calmed. Till then in England, ever since that first breakfast at Maurigy's Hotel, when he had read the queen's illogical Proclamation of Neutrality, he had needed an explanation of what was happening within the British Government. Now he saw a pattern in events—a combination of human actions which a thinking person could understand.

In his mind, the explanation of what had recently occurred was about as follows. The previous March, or even earlier, in Washington, saying nothing to the foolish Adamses, deceptive Seward had matured a daring scheme to start a general war of the most spectacular description. While sleeping H. B. Adams and C. F. Adams had gone to Boston, learned of the latter's appointment as minister to England, returned to Washington momentarily, then lingered in Boston for a month to attend a wedding, and finally inched to Liverpool on the slow *Niagara*, other people had been awake. Accidentally or otherwise, Englishmen in America—Henry could not be sure which ones—had caught wind of Seward's design and secretly alerted the ministry in London. Palmerston and Russell had heeded the alarm. Augmented distrust of Seward, grounded on correct intelligence, had become the unchanging theme of British policy, accounting for all that had seemed unaccountable, including such a precaution as the Proclamation of Neutrality.

Knowing that he could see, H. B. Adams also felt that he could act. He said nothing to C. F. Adams about his own conviction that the author of "Despatch No. 10" was W. H. Seward. Quarrels between himself and his father about the comparative sanity of the various Republicans in charge of the executive branch of government in Washington would not do any good. The next morning, Tuesday, June 11, 1861, taking a step unusual for him, Henry gave the minister some urgent, positive advice.

In words of the younger man, the elder was to "make an energetic effort and induce the British Government to put us so much in the wrong that we couldn't go further." In plain English, Minister Adams was to evade his instructions by deliberately and skillfully bungling their execution.

Turning about, in great need of an outlet for his brimming knowledge, the son resumed his interrupted private letter to his

brother. " . . . I let you know what I've no business to," he said to
Charles. "A despatch arrived yesterday from Seward, so arrogant in
tone and so extraordinary and unparalleled in its demands that it
leaves no doubt in my mind that our Government wishes to force a war
with all Europe. . . . I have said already that I thought such a policy
shallow madness. . . . I cannot tell you how I am shocked and horrified
by supposing Seward, a man I've admired and respected beyond most
men, guilty of what seems to me so wicked and criminal a course as
this."

Confident that he had thought and acted rightly, the third son
looked ahead. His terror diminished sufficiently to permit his entertaining rival notions of what the future had in store. He half-supposed
that Seward would get his way, a gigantic war would start, and an
effort would be made at home to conquer Canada. He also half-
supposed that the government in Washington might quickly reverse
its policy and the crisis might blow over.

Even so, the shock of reading "Despatch No. 10" had been so great
that, studying himself, Henry concluded that he was—or should be—
in a panic. He said to Charles: "I do not think I exaggerate the danger.
I believe that our Government means to have a war with England; I
believe that England knows it and is preparing for it; and I believe it
will come within two months—if at all."

# PART THREE

## 19 / An Unsettling Intuition

In later life, Adams sought fuller information about the events in which he had been caught when he went to England with his father. He learned a number of things which should be repeated here for the sake of clarity. It was true that the U.S. secretary of state had tried to start "a war with all Europe."[1] Traces of Seward's design had shown themselves in his behavior and conversation as early as January 26, 1861.[2] The New Yorker had not attempted to act decisively until April 1, when he secretly drew up a paper titled "Some Thoughts for the President's Consideration" and placed it in the hands of Lincoln.

The secret paper had suggested that executive authority should be shifted permanently from Lincoln's hands to Seward's; also that the administration should remove the threat of civil war by contriving a vast emergency. Without exaggeration, the secretary of state had sought responsibilities greater than those thrust onto General Washington three generations earlier.

Seward's "Thoughts" outlined a two-part procedure to foment the desired cataclysm. The U.S. Government was to send political incendiaries to Canada, Mexico, and Central America with the purpose of firing a "vigorous continental spirit of independence." Simultaneously, the administration would send messages to the four empires of the old world—England, France, Spain, and Russia—which continued to hold possessions in North and Central America. These empires would be required by the messages to send back "explanations" of their continued holdings which they could not with honor give. Because the demanded "explanations" were not forthcoming, the United States would declare war on some or all of the empires.

Lincoln had dealt with the "Thoughts" by reading them, pigeonholing them, and turning back to his current presidential business, which then had mainly related to the course best taken by the administration in the matter of Fort Sumter and Fort Pickens.[3] But Seward, too, had been concerned about Fort Sumter. All along, he had hoped to arrange the surrender of the installation to the South Carolinians, in the interest of gaining time. In early April, Lincoln had rushed preparations to supply and hold Fort Sumter, even at the cost of blood. Boldly, Seward had tried to interfere. Despite him, supplies for the garrison had left New York; the Union supply fleet had been sighted approaching Charleston; Confederate guns had battered Fort Sumter until Major Anderson surrendered; war had begun; and the first casualty was Seward.[4]

At tragic cost, it seemed to him, the administration had spurned his advice. He wrote in confidence to his wife in Auburn that the endangered Republic, after "so largely relying on my poor efforts to save it," in the crucial days had "refused me the full measure of confidence needful to that end." "I am a chief," he explained, "reduced to a subordinate position, and surrounded with a guard [the other members of the cabinet], to see that I do not do too much for my country. . . ."[5]

Some other important particulars may never have become wholly clarified for Adams. It was a fact that the British had early learned the truth concerning Seward's grand design. Lord Lyons himself, the British minister in Washington, had seen that the New Yorker's attitude towards the United Kingdom, although friendly on the surface, was actually menacing and warlike.[6] At the same time, the British envoy made an error which would have far-reaching consequences. Underestimating Lincoln, he failed to realize that the president—even more than the secretary of state—would decide the policies of the Republican administration. Thus, when Seward lost his primacy on April 12, and just as much thereafter, the New Yorker was believed by the Liberal ministry in London to have kept his primacy.[7]

Expecting the worst, yet trying to avert it, Foreign Secretary Russell assured Lord Lyons: "I rely upon your wisdon, patience, and prudence, to steer us through the dangers of this crisis. If it can possibly be helped[,] Mr. Seward must not be allowed to get us into a quarrel."[8] As quietly as they could, while new alarms concerning the American's war plans continued to reach them, Prime Minister Palmerston and Foreign Secretary Russell initiated defensive measures. The British leaders thus continued to prepare for a crisis which had already passed. Seward, one could say, had lost his war with Lincoln, could make no wars with foreign powers, and would have to content himself with being what he was: something less than a president, yet something more than a leading member of the cabinet.

The defensive measures initiated by Great Britain revived the no-longer-existing but much-dreaded danger they were intended to allay. On May 1, Russell ordered naval reinforcements to American waters; and, on May 3, he talked with Confederate Commissioners Yancey, Mann, and Rost informally.[9] News that the foreign secretary had spoken with the rebel envoys was carried by steamer to New York, telegraphed to Washington, and shown to the Union secretary of state. Apparently on the assumption that his personal adherent, C. F. Adams, now accredited in London as minister to England, would act as told by him to act, Seward tried again.

This time he wrote no "Thoughts for the President's Considera-tion." Instead, on May 21, 1861, he drafted peremptory new instruc-tions for Mr. Adams, and sent them to President Lincoln for approval. As Seward wrote them, Mr. Adams's new instructions left no doubt that war between the United States and several European powers was both expected and desired, even though a civil war was now in progress. The U.S. minister to England was directed to call on Foreign Secretary Russell and read to him a statement—which Seward sup-plied—demanding that Russell cease all contact with agents of the pretended Confederate States of America. The language of the state-ment was so imperative that Lord Russell would have to demur, and Mr. Adams thereupon was to terminate relations.

Rather than pigeonhole the New Yorker's ultimate, attempted stroke of political mastery, Lincoln modified what Seward had writ-ten. The president made changes in the new instructions, approved them as amended, and returned them to the State Department for final copying and speedy sending—as "Despatch No. 10"— to the Union envoy in London.

The modifed instructions, altered by Lincoln, but copied in a uniform handwriting, assured C. F. Adams that the United States did not intend to menace any foreign power. Mr. Adams was *not* required to follow a set procedure. It was stated explicitly that he was to consult his own discretion. But whole segments and portions of Seward's original war-creating orders were allowed to stand unchanged, with the result that the two Adamses in London were sure to be astounded and momentarily frightened when "Despatch No. 10" first came into their hands.[10]

Just so, for many hours on June 10 and June 11, 1861, C. F. Adams and H. B. Adams had focused their attention on the war-creating passages. Gradually they realized that the instructions were very complicated. In the last analysis, the strange document they had received was not belligerent at all. It merely indicated that Minister Adams could take a higher tone, if he desired. So the father arranged at once to meet with Foreign Secretary Russell and have "some plain talk" with him of a kind that would help to clear the air.[11] Satisfied with his own performance, on June 14, he wrote serenely to Charles in Boston, "My position here thus far has not been difficult or painful."[12]

Much enfeebled but recovering, Moran returned to work. He noted in his journal that relations between the United States and England were "more satisfactory than they were a week ago."[13] Concerning the minister's new instructions, which had come while he was absent, the second secretary made no remarks of any kind.

For H. B. Adams, "Despatch No. 10" remained a thing to be remembered. He could see that the instructions had been nothing more nor less than a bomb from which the detonator, but not the massive charge of gunpowder, had been removed. He continued to believe—what his father would die before conceiving—that the bomb had been made by Seward, no one else, with every intention of its being used in London.

Henry believed as well that someone, *not* Seward, and presumably Lincoln, had rendered the weapon harmless. True, the evidence that the younger Adams had to go on was treacherously incomplete. Many details of American and British policy and action were concealed from him. Yet it remained a fact that he alone among the Unionists in Europe had understood the situation, and he was fully alive to his advantage.

Reconsidering, the secret correspondent perceived that, in the course of a hidden but terrific crisis, three men had each exhibited a strength and a shortcoming. C. F. Adams had been calm but blind. W. H. Seward—after a heroic beginning in the first phases of the secession crisis—had taken stock of the alternatives available to the government and chosen one as ruinous to the Union as the course of the Confederate leaders would prove to the luckless South. Lincoln had wisely counteracted Seward's error but seemed himself to lack a foreign policy.

The president's apparent lack of such a policy, as Henry thought about it, could be neatly linked to something else. Raymond, long a friend and ally of Seward's, was gradually becoming more supportive of Lincoln.[14] The editor's behavior had a meaning which the younger Adams till then may not have appreciated. Seward and Lincoln were reading the *New York Times*. Moreover, they were reading his reports.

A one-way speaking tube had been permanently put in place between the anonymous correspondent of Raymond's newspaper and the rulers of the Union. Without their guessing who he was, the London correspondent every week could speak a helpful message in their ears.

Next day, June 15, 1861, Adams sent a long, fifth report to the dependably secretive Raymond in New York. Ostensibly an innocent and competent account of the latest English news, it was ingeniously adapted to serve a hidden purpose. Henry offered his country's leaders a saving lesson in foreign policy. Since Lincoln's knowledge of English politics presumably was slight, the reporter made the lesson simple and insistent. He described the English Liberals and Conservatives, explaining that the Liberals, who were in power, should be maintained in power. "I see that many of the articles in American papers on the Queen's Proclamation, speak of the overthrow of the present English Ministry as if it were an object for Americans to wish . . . ," he wrote in placid tones. " . . . but . . . to keep England on our side, where she undoubtedly new stands . . . the maintenance of the Liberal Cabinet ought to be our policy."

The English Liberals, he averred, had proved their friendship towards the Union. The proof was the failure of the Confederate commissioners in London. " . . . Mr. DUDLEY MANN, it seems, thought a month ago that his Confederacy would be recognized. But he was, as usual, too sanguine, and he can hardly be of that opinion still."

The Conservatives were openly hostile to the Union cause. " . . . if we truly want peace and sympathy, there is no use in flattering ourselves in finding it in the Earl of DERBY, probably the man . . . in [English] public affairs who most profoundly dislikes and distrusts republicanism in every form, nor in Mr. DISRAELI, who likes it no more than his chief."

Thus, by turning from one subject to another, the correspondent reiterated what in the end was a single proposition. "If then we really mean to remain on good terms with England, the very last means to do it is to declare hostility to the Liberals and tear down Lord JOHN RUSSELL. . . ."

In the same report, for Seward's particular attention, Adams noted in his opening paragraph that the U.S. Government might wish to start "a war with England, France and Spain." Further along in the report, mentioning that Lord Palmerston had ordered troops to Canada, Henry pretended the action seemed illogical to him. " . . . it is hard to understand why the [British] Government should have taken a step which would irritate our people. . . ." Then he gave a detailed account of a conversation he said he had had with an acquaintance in London's financial district. Of course, the conversation was a figment of Adams's every-ready imagination, as was the acquaintance also. But the fictitious conversation was so written as to disclose Seward's war plan, unravel its more important details, explain why it was wrong, and alert its author in Washington to the fact of its being known to the Liberal ministry in London. If he would merely read the words of the London correspondent of the *New York Times*, the secretary of state was thus given a chance to see his error clearly and make a new beginning.

Etiquette required that lesser diplomats be presented at court to Queen Victoria. At Minister Adams's request, on June 15, second Secretary Moran—who had been presented years before— applied to the queen's officials at Buckingham Palace for the presentation of first Secretary Wilson and Mr. Henry Brooks Adams, "private Sec. & son of the Minister," in the diplomatic circle at Her Majesty's Drawing Room on Wednesday, June 19.[15]

With regard to Wilson, the application was necessarily acceptable. The Chicagoan was a commissioned secretary of legation. Differently, H. B. Adams was not a commissioned secretary. It did not help matters that he was his father's "private Secretary," for in England persons serving as private secretaries were not invariably well-thought-of and often were classed as menials.[16] But he *was* his father's son, and a rule at court permitted accredited diplomats of ministerial rank to present their sons or other gentlemen in the diplomatic circle if they wished.

A further question was that of dress. One did not approach Her Majesty except in the perfect, appointed costume. If left to their own devices, the queen's officials almost certainly would have ruled that H. B. Adams, being a private citizen, should appear in the Diplomatic Circle in the costume of a private citizen.[17] Minister Adams took the different view that his confidential aide, although not possessed of a commission, was a member of the legation and should appear before the Queen as a member of the legation, wearing its chosen uniform. As a courtesy to him, the American minister was permitted to have his way, and his son was told he would appear at Buckingham Palace in the uniform of an official secretary.

A last question concerned the designs of the uniforms to be worn as court dress by Minister Charles Francis Adams and his three secretaries. Lamentably, in recent years, the official representatives of the United States in London had worn a court dress resembling the usual costume of a butler. C. F. Adams, not wanting to appear in such habiliments, had decided that the legation, during his tenure, should revert to an earlier mode of dress still approved of in the British capital.[18]Three elaborate uniforms had therefore been ordered for Henry Adams, Benjamin Moran, and Charles Wilson—to name the minister's aides in the order of their importance and dignity, as determined by their chief. Each uniform consisted of a blue naval coat, decorated with gold buttons and gold embroidery on the cuffs, lapels, and stand-up collar; a white vest; white knee-breeches with bold buckles; white silk stockings; white gloves; a white cocked hat with gold ornaments; and a fine, gilt, eagle-headed sword.

Wearing a very similar but more lavishly embroidered uniform, on June 19, Minister Adams led his three secretaries to the drawing room. He presented his son and Wilson to Queen Victoria with faultless courtesy. The American uniforms were admired as entirely successful. According to Moran, the minister, "altho' a small man, made an excellent appearance, and Mr. Wilson & Mr. H. B. Adams looked exceedingly well."[19]

Since reaching London, Henry's irritability and tendency to tire had abated gradually until he was nearly better. Shortly after returning from Buckingham Palace, he experienced a sudden, violent recurrence of his difficulties. Their onset apparently was unexpected, very alarming, and mercifully brief. Looking back on his scare when it was over, he said it had been triggered by his presentation to Queen Victoria. He wrote to Charles that his appearance at Her Majesty's drawing room had "caused a relapse for me, which frightened me nearly to death."[20]

Three predecessors of his in the Adams family, his father, grandfather, and great-grandfather, had been accredited, commissioned diplomats at the Court of St. James. Now all three had appeared there in full diplomatic uniform. And he, a fourth Adams, had appeared there in full diplomatic uniform—but *without* a commission. Was he an accredited diplomat? He was, and he was not. Was he a member of the legation? The same answer would apply. Was he entitled to wear the legation uniform? The same answer could again be given.

Thus, an obvious explanation of his upset could be suggested. By putting on the uniform of *an official secretary* and appearing in it before Her Majesty, only to be introduced to Queen Victoria as *a son of the minister,*the younger Adams had participated in an acting out—a real-life dramatization—of the irony and anomalousness of his residence and service at the legation. But he had known in advance that, in London, while he stayed with his father and shared his father's work, he would have the role of a walking, breathing contradiction. More than any other person, it was he, the son, who had made the arrangement which had brought *four* Americans before the queen, not only his father, Wilson, and himself, but also Benjamin Moran. So the apparent explanation was *not* the explanation.

Everything considered, it was better to suppose—as perhaps he came to do himself—that his "relapse" after going to Buckingham Palace had nothing at all to do with the visit and everything to do with a strong, unsettling intuition. If this explanation were correct, the intuition struck first as a seeming physical shock unaccompanied by ideas. The intuition struck Henry Adams, not another person, because, during four generation, the Adamses had developed their genius for apprehending political trouble until the faculty, in him, had become a barometer capable of the most unerring, uncanny, occult, and eerie foresight and foreknowledge. On June 20, 1861, there was nothing the matter with the younger Adams. Just the opposite, he was a perfect instrument for politics in perfect working order. The breath of future trouble had touched his sensors. He had violently reacted and for a time supposed, in error, that he had been briefly ill.[21]

The anonymous correspondent sent a fresh message to Lincoln and Seward through the *New York Times* in a sixth report on July 22, 1861. Adams suggested that the administration should offer inducements to cooperate and be friendly to "every foreign nation." Applying this broad rule to England, he urged, would not be difficult. Two causes, the civil strife in America and the tariff imposed by the U.S. Government on products imported from the United Kingdom, seemed to be blighting English industry. By giving rise to the federal blockade of Confederate ports, the strife had cut off the flow of American raw cotton to the Lancashire spinning mills; and the tariff was just too high. So he asseverated that by "relaxing our tariff a little, and giving also any favor in the way of obtaining cotton that did not conflict with the laws, our statesmen have it in their power to effect the firmest alliance with the people of England that ever yet has existed."

A letter had reached the minister from Charles asking permission to join the army and turn the management of the family's properties over to John, who was willing to assume the burden. The matter was one Henry might well have stayed away from. He chose to become involved. Writing to the second son on July 2, the third gave it as his opinion that parental permission to join the army could be dispensed with. The best thing, Henry advised, would be for Charles to hold off till the state of Massachusetts began to raise another regiment, obtain a commission in the regiment from Governor Andrew at the State House, and then announce the fact to the minister in London. " . . . when the time comes," the younger brother said, "just write and notify him. He will consent to that as a 'fait accompli' which he cannot take the responsibility of encouraging himself."

Henry went on to say that in the interval, while Charles was waiting for his commission, the two of them could work cooperatively in London and Boston as secret journalists. Such work was needed. The newspapers in the United States had taken and were sustaining a very angry tone towards the European powers. The arriving papers from the cities of the North contained a flood of editorial comment hostile to England, France, and Spain. "America seems clean daft," the younger brother told the elder. "She seems to want to quarrel with all the world. . . ."

In his weekly reports to the *New York Times,* one of the brothers was already attempting to excuse and explain the neutral attitude of England, in hopes of soothing the angered Unionists. If the other were to excuse and explain Union anger to English readers by sending news reports to a London paper, the two Adamses between them might do more than double good. Supposing that Charles would gladly help, Henry allowed himself to say: "I am looking round here for some good paper to take you as its American correspondent. I don't know that I can get one. . . ."[1]

The younger brother had predicted on arriving in London with their parents and the children that he would seek admission to a club and try to "slide into the literary set."[2] Within the short space of two months, the minister had been fully admitted to the literary set in England, as well as the political. Summarizing the impression he was forming of the English, C. F. Adams shortly wrote: "I have seen most of the men of any reputation, literary or political. . . . But I have not yet been to a single entertainment where there was any conversation that I should care to remember. . . . The general aspect of [English] society is profound gravity. People look serious at a ball, at a dinner, on a ride on horseback or in a carriage, in Parliament or at Court, in the Theatres or at the Galleries."[3]

The minister could adjust to English gravity and make the most of it. The secret correspondent and private secretary mostly wished that he could get away from England altogether. For Henry it was the old story of being in terrible Berlin or strait-laced Dresden, while longing in every instant to leave for paradisical Italy. In his eighth report to Raymond, he digressed from politics enough to say: "You see, no doubt, by the London journals, the announcement of Mrs. BROWNING'S death. She has been long a helpless invalid, and banished from England nearly all her life. Indeed, neither she nor her husband were made for this country of fogs and etiquette, and awkward stiffness. They were both of warm and expansive natures, and England is hard and unimpulsive. They took refuge, therefore, in

Florence, and became almost Italian, so that her poetry . . . came round to express . . . the warm Italian sympathy of to-day."

The Confederate commissioners had gone to France. Their absence coincided with a phase of Union self-assurance. Everywhere the Unionists had taught each other to assume beyond a doubt that the rebel army would be crushed in a sort of Waterloo, a single victory. They had warned themselves, of course, that the triumph would have to be prepared for. But now much time had passed, and millions of patriotic citizens of the United States were waiting for the battle.

Waiting with the rest, H. B. Adams anticipated victory in the battle but also took a larger view of the situation. He saw that the Southerners were doomed in any case. The attempted Confederate States of America was helplessly dependent on aid from Europe. He reported to his newspaper: " . . . it is not for us of the North to say that all who are not with us are against us. It is for the South to say this, for without active aid she is lost."

So far, active aid from Europe had eluded the grasp of Messrs. Yancey, Mann, and Rost. The most the Confederacy could hope for in the way of early help from abroad appeared to be a potential trickle of war supplies. During the permissive reign of President Buchanan, the flow of British arms to the Southern states in America had purportedly been considerable. If Moran could be believed, Minister Dallas himself had helped the Virginians surreptitiously by "arranging with Lancaster . . . to supply them with 5000 stand of arms"—more than enough to supply a regiment.[4] With the arrival of Minister Adams, and more particularly with the issuance of the British Proclamation of Neutrality, the shipment of munitions for Southern purchasers from British ports had ceased. But it was known that special Confederate agents empowered to purchase arms and hurry the shipments somehow to the rebel army were on the scene in England. It was assumed that these shadowy figures would try to effect their object by double shipment and smuggling. The younger Adams said in his eighth report to Raymond: "The Secessionists expect to get their supplies in by way of Mexico, I am told. This is, of course, all in the air as yet. . . . A cargo of arms might be smuggled into Texas very easily, one would think. They [the Confederate arms agents in England] are an active set of people and will leave no stone unturned."

On July 9, 1861, a secret message was delivered at the legation from the U.S. vice-consul in Liverpool, Henry Wilding. An Englishman but a faithful servant of the Union, Wilding was a man of unusual ability and energy. He had succeeded in learning that Fraser, Trenholm & Company—the English branch of an old American firm in Charleston, John Fraser & Company—would soon send a ship, the *Gondar,* to sea with a "pretended cargo of salt; but in reality of arms, wh[ich] are to be [re]shipped . . . in small craft to Carolina." Wilding indicated that the transfer of the arms from the *Gondar* to the small craft would occur in the Bahamas.[5]

His message was disconcerting. The route selected for the movement of the arms was the directest possible. Moreover, the shipment would be protected all the way to the Bahamas by the British flag!

Adams said nothing in his next report to the *New York Times* about the ominous supply ship or the startling route the Confederate agents had selected. Apparently afraid that his writing about such subjects would stoke the fires of anger already burning against Great Britain in the editorials of Union newspapers, Henry wrote instead about a subject only slightly less disturbing. Both in America and Europe, thinking people were wondering what would happen when the Lancashire spinning mills became completely starved for Southern cotton. Inventive British newspaper editors were fabricating arguments to prove that a British fleet, intent on reopening the old channels of the cotton trade, would one day steam into the harbors of Charleston and Savannah, or up the Mississippi to New Orleans, in defiance of the United States Navy and the Union blockade.

In his tenth report, on July 20, 1861, Adams attempted to counteract such vivid imaginings. He reasoned that the cotton shortage would not become acute in Lancashire for another eight months or so, until the spring of 1862. Thus a period of immunity existed, during which the Union Army could fight its Waterloo with the rebel forces, march on to Richmond, and put an end to the Confederacy without risk of British jostling. "I only repeat to you the optimist's view of affairs," he added. "There is here also [in London] . . . a pessimistic party, who are by no means so sanguine."

As for British politics, he was changing his ideas. He had decided, after all, that whether the Liberals remained in power was *not* the question on which loyal Unionists should center their attention. The differences separating the British Liberals and Conservatives were mostly theoretical, not practical; and the cabinet ministers charged with running the government, whichever party they belonged to, had very little freedom to indulge their political enthusiasms. " . . . the Tories," he declared, "are forced to be liberal in office, as the Liberals are forced to be conservative."

What it came down to was that British leadership was more a matter of weaknesses than of strengths. The British politicians did not get on well with one another, and truly capable men appeared to be in short supply. "... it is hard to see how any homogeneous Cabinet can be formed, capable of commanding the general sympathy of the nation. Mr. GLADSTONE is distrusted and unpopular with the landed interests. He is considered flightly and unreliable, as well as too deeply mixed up with the Radicals. There is no leading man except Lord PALMERSTON. . . ."

As would happen when a great event impended but did not come, a portion of the Unionists at home had entirely lost their tempers. Angry editors were demanding in their newspapers that General Scott move the great army he had been readying onto the roads towards Richmond without additional delay. So noisy was the din in the Northern press that control of the Union forces appeared about to pass from the country's generals to its journalists. On July 23 at the legation, Moran wrote anxiously, "The day of battle is drawing nigh, & the fight, if it takes place soon, may well be charged to the brawling newspaper generals." The second secretary seemed fearful that a battle hastened might prove a battle lost.

The only recourse of Minister C. F. Adams and his secretaries, official and unofficial, was to wait for the coming of more steamers from America, hoping the news they brought would be good. Three days later, on July 26, Henry wrote quietly to Charles at home, "It won't be long before something happens, I suppose."

Charles had sent the family a letter which stirringly described the departure of the newest Massachusetts regiment from Boston for Virginia.[6] The description had driven Henry to honest reflection about his physical attributes. It was not the easiest thing to admit, but his small physique and nervous sensitivity required that he be exempted from military service. "You say you wanted to go off with Gordon's regiment," he wrote to Charles. "I tell you I would give my cocked hat and knee-breeches to be with them at this moment. . . . My own task however lies elsewhere and I should be after all hardly the material for a solder. . . ."

The current of the third son's life appeared to have stopped or even be going backwards. He was trying to study law at odd moments and again had opened Blackstone's *Commentaries*. "... as I invariably go to sleep over him," he confessed, "my progress is not rapid." His thoughts turned often towards the past and things forgotten. He had found himself remembering his Harvard classmates and imagining their present and future activities. Musingly, while writing to his brother, he announced, "My good old Nick Anderson is a Lieut. Colonel . . . ," then went on in the tones of a person talking to himself: "How I'd like to see him. I suppose Rooney Lee has some command also, so it's as likely as not that he and Nick may come in contact [in a battle]. There never was any friendship between them. Indeed they always hated each other. . . ."

The much-needed better house for the legation had been obtained on a one-year lease. Located at No. 5 Mansfield Street, a short block from Portland Place, the house was in a highly desirable and less noisy neighborhood. The Adamses moved into it on July 31 and had the pleasure of being shown their new abode by its owner, a good-natured Irishman, Mr. Seymour Fitzgerald, a Conservative member of Parliament. He drew his tenants' attention in the principal rooms to the Adam ceilings, handsome furniture, and superior paintings, especially a full-length portrait of Napoleon I, dressed in his imperial robes, by Gerrand.[7]

The private secretary's quarters in the new house were two large rooms on the top floor.[8] His front windows looked over Mansfield Street down the length of Duchess Street. Viewed from their transparent panes, the British capital more than ever seemed to him a bastion of privilege and caste. In his secret capacity as a minister of the press, he had had to write detailed accounts of current English politics in recent weeks, and the subject had proved dispiriting. Try as he might, he could not think of the English system of life and government as fair or equitable. It chanced that Lord Herbert had died, when only fifty. Writing his twelfth report on August 3, 1861, a wet, dreary Saturday, Henry philosophized about the dead English politician: "That he was laborious and faithful all parties acknowledge. But a foreigner is forced to the conclusion that his high position and prospects were due rather to his family claims than to his personal genius. England is governed now, as she always has been, by a few great families. . . . Had Lord HERBERT been a commoner without high connections, his abilities alone would never have made him [a Cabinet] Minister; but he was the political head of his family, wielding the influence of the Duke of Pembroke, his brother, and to him all things were possible."

## 21 / *Very Well As I Am*

Early Sunday morning, August 4, 1861, newsboys went about the London streets hawking extras containing a Reuters bulletin summarizing the American news just received at Cork in Ireland. The telegraphed bulletin alleged that the Union Army had marched towards Richmond, met the Confederate Army at a place called "Bull's Run" near Manassas Junction in Virginia, and there had broken, panicked, and fled towards Washington.

Henry Adams read the bulletin. He imagined that the Union troops, although beaten and disgraced, would be reorganized and would then engage the Confederate foe in a second, much larger battle. The miscarriage of the effort in Virginia dismayed him deeply. What was more important perhaps, it revived his all-but-stifled military longings. He thought he understood himself; and he believed that what he really wanted, now that the much-anticipated battle had been lost, was a commission as a lieutenant in a new Massachusetts regiment, in a company whose captain would be his brother Charles. He presumed that Charles would feel as he did: that two Adams sons should join the military forces and hope to be sent where the danger was the worst.[1]

His presumption about his elder brother was mistaken. The following day, Monday, August 5, a letter from Charles arrived at the legation. The second son knew about the debacle in Virginia. Yet he stated flatly, "I no longer see my way clear."

In a spirit which Henry could only find confusing, Charles surveyed the situation. It seemed to him that the Union Army's panic in the battle had been "disgraceful and disastrous." He laid the blame on Mr. Lincoln. "The impression here is very general," the elder brother wrote, "that Scott's policy was interfered with by the President in obedience to what he calls the popular will & at the instigation of Sumner, Greely[*sic*] & others. . . ." In consequence the Union forces had been "demoralised" and the Confederate forces "in the same degree consolidated." It seemed to Charles that the government of the Confederate States in Richmond now was certain to obtain full diplomatic recognition from the European powers, and further that the rebels in the South had as good as won their freedom. " . . . their ultimate independence is I think assured. . . ."[2]

The Monday mail also brought American newspapers containing detailed information about the battle. The accounts were partly corrective, saying that the action, while it lasted, had been so injurious to the Confederate forces involved that they had not been able to take advantage of the Union panic.

Such comfort as could be drawn from this modification of the news was offset by a hostile clamor in the English press.[3] As Henry had predicted, the English editors, with few exceptions, took up the battle of Bull Run as a club with which to strike resounding blows at the United States and at democracy. Noisiest in the clamor was John Delane. In Adams's words, written a few days later, " . . . [The] Times at once came out in tone so needlessly insulting and so wantonly malignant, that no one could worry any longer, even if there ever had been any doubt, on which side its sympathies lie."

Amid the uproar, the third son remained convinced that he wanted to go home and join the army. His only worry concerned the time and circumstances of his going. He saw that his best course might be to pack his things, tell his parents he was leaving, take the train to Liverpool and a ship to New York, and make arrangements himself in Boston for a commission in a Massachusetts unit. Equally, however, he could remain in London, write to Governor Andrew asking the promise of a commission, and start back the moment the promise came. Still another alternative was open. He could stay in London and write to Charles, suggesting that *he* obtain two commissions from helpful Andrew. The last alternative, assuming that Charles would cooperate, had the advantage of increasing the likelihood that the brothers could serve together as captain and lieutenant.

After some hesitation, that afternoon or evening, August 5, Henry elected to stay in London and write to Charles. Saying nothing to their parents, the third son began a letter which would take him, he believed, to Boston and thence to a Virginia battlefield. In the letter, he made the error of contrasting himself outspokenly with his elder brothers. "I am the youngest and the most independent . . . ," he said to Charles. "If you and John are detained from taking part in the war, the same rule does not apply to me."

The third son contradicted the second about the probable effects of the disaster at Bull Run. "... I do not see that this check necessarily involves all the serious consequences that you draw from it. ..." Henry doubted especially that England would recognize the Confederate States of America. "... I still believe that England will prove herself more our friend than we suppose."

The body of Henry's letter was clear and practical enough. He explained: "I wish you, then, on receipt of this, to go to some one in authority and get a commission for me, if you can; no matter what; second, third Lieutenant or Ensign if you can do no better." He candidly expressed his dream of serving as lieutenant under Charles as captain. He insisted on proper speed, saying that if Charles would obtain the promise of a commission and send word to London by ship and telegraph, he, Henry, could leave London before September 1.

Although the letter was completed, Henry did not mail it. Hour by hour, the ground was reeling under him. He had prophesied in the letter that English hostility towards the Union would subside, but it was possible to view the matter differently. A doubt existed about the underlying meaning of the outbursts in the London press. Through the pages of their newspapers, one sometimes glimpsed a vision of the English people and government preparing in their hard, deliberate way to administer the blow which would shatter what was left of the great Republic beyond imaginable repair.

Moran, who could claim to know the English better than the Adamses did, saw trouble in the making. That same day, August 5, the assistant secretary recorded in his journal: "English inherent hatred of us is being expressed unmistakably to-day, in sneers and chuckling over our misfortune. ... The [English] nation secretly longs for the dissolution of the Union. ... "

Parallel ideas were at work in Henry's mind. The private secretary was in a box. If Great Britain were truly hostile and he succeeded in returning to Boston and joining a Massachusetts regiment, it might develop that he had fled the greater foe of the United States of America, in London, in order to face its lesser foe, the mad Confederates, in Virginia.

Attempting to settle his ideas, which were growing more and more unsettled, the conscientious son paced back and forth all night on a floor situated directly above his parents' bedroom. At breakfast, he told his elders that he was going home to join the army. His mother contented herself with objecting to sons who paced all night above parental bedrooms. His father mentioned that if he went Henry would reach America too late to "take part in the actual compaign." Neither parent tried to bar the way of his departure.[4]

After breakfast, Henry added a postscript to his already completed letter to his brother. In the postscript he threatened that, if Charles would not assist him, he would write directly to Andrew at the State House. Indeed the postscript was important. Overnight the third son's views had darkened and even turned around. He had entertained the black idea that the Union Army might lose the second, larger battle. He was tempted to believe that Charles was right and that the civil war could not be won by the Union side. Such ideas greatly hardened his own resolve. "If we must be beaten," Henry told his brother in America, "and it looks now as though that must ultimately be the case, I want to do all I can not to be included among those who ran away."

He mailed the letter, with its postscript, but his thoughts remained disturbed. Something had been published that morning, August 6, which he had read and mentioned in the postscript. It was a British news report from the battlefield in Virgina. Sent to London from Washington by William Howard Russell, the report was a practically unexampled feat of journalistic enterprise. It filled more than eight whole columns of *The Times*.

"Special Correspondent" Russell had witnessed the flight of the Union Army along the Virginia roads from a point near Bull Run to the safety of the capital.[5] His report, written in animated terms and at such length as to create indelible impressions, banished any thought a reader in London might have cherished of proper courage or discipline among the Union soldiers. That morning, reading the British reporter's columns, H. B. Adams had writhed in shame—until a passage struck him funny. In his postscript to Charles, he had confessed: " . . . I could not help howling with laughter over a part of Russell's letter. Such a battle of heels. Such a bloodless, ridiculous race for disgrace, history does not record."

Henry continued to think about the achievements of W. H. Russell, his enterprising counterpart in journalism, and especially thought of one of their more frightening consequences. Russell's history of the battle of Bull Run, as printed in the London *Times*, was now in the mail, would soon reach New York, and would be delivered to other cities across the North. Once received in America, the long report, a masterpiece which Russell could hardly have improved, would stir up a perfect cyclone of anti-British and anti-Russell execration.

As Adams studied it, the situation revealed a clearer and clearer face. From his point of view, the printing of Russell's communication in *The Times* on August 6, 1861, was an event of the first importance. By being where he should have been, and by writing vividly and fully what his eyes had seen and his ears had heard, the British journalist had given added power for good or evil to a class of men whom Henry Adams, in his confusion, had latterly proposed to desert: the world's reporters and especially its "foreign correspondents."

Changing his mind with new and absolute finality, the correspondent of the *New York Times* in London admitted to himself that he had made a foolish error. He ought never to have sent the letter and postscript seeking a lieutenancy. The American Civil War and the international unrest to which it was giving rise were going to be affected to an unheard-of degree by what was done with printer's ink in daily newspapers. In the North Atlantic world, while writing and publishing the news, journalists would also in part decide the course events would take. The rule applied with special force to Henry Adams, who, secretly planted within the U.S. legation in the British capital, commanded sources of information which a William Howard Russell could not boast.

These things considered, late on Tuesday, August 6, 1861, Adams gave up his initial career as London correspondent on the *New York Times* in order to start a new career in the same capacity. The difference between the careers was that the second was undertaken in deadly earnest.

He later wrote about the denizens of the house on Mansfield Street that "the curious and unexpected happened to the Legation, for the effect of Bull Run on them was almost strengthening."[6] Surely he was strengthened. The report he sent to the *New York Times* on Saturday, August 10, 1861—his thirteenth—was easily the strongest he had written.

As short as W. H. Russell's report had been long, Adams's effort consisted of six terse paragraphs. It began with a plea to the loyal citizens of the United States on behalf of his British rival. Anticipating the uproar which would follow the reprinting of Russell's fine history of Bull Run, the American correspondent said: " . . . I confess that I cannot see the justice of the anger that would punish him for telling merely what he saw. If it was so [the panic of the Union Army]—and his account bears all the marks of truth—we ought rather to own up fairly, and to see that such a disgrace never occurs again. Often a man's own angry pride is cap and bells to a fool. It ought not to be so with us."

The news that Adams had to tell the readers of the *New York Times* in the rest of his report was neither good nor bad. Scenting opportunity, the Confederate commissioners had returned from France to England and were busy in London attempting to impair the security of the Union by funneling misinformation about the financial history of the great Republic into the inkwells of John Delane and his helpers on the staff of *The Times*. Henry doubted that the labors of Yancey, Mann, and Rost would hurt the Union cause. Happily, in his opinion, by declaring its Confederate sympathies, *The Times* had sacrificed its old appearance of impartiality and thus had "partly destroyed its own power for evil."

The British government was immobilized. Parliament had adjourned, and the Liberal ministry showed no wish to act. The only English news that Unionists would have to bear in mind was that the Admiralty was constructing an armored navy. Several huge iron-clad ships were being built, of which one, the *Warrior,* had left its dock and would "soon be ready for active service." Otherwise, it seemed that affairs in England would remain as they were until affected by fresh news about the American conflict. " . . . the action of England depends on events," Adams said. "You on the other side of the water, will be able to predict it before we can, according as the war progresses ill or otherwise." Thus the sufferers for the present were the adherents of the Union in Europe, whose only resource was patience. " . . . there is nothing to be done here but to wait with an anxiety that devours every one, for the arrival of the steamers that never before seemed to come so seldom."

That same Saturday, August 10, the private secretary left London with his parents and the children for a vacation at Derby; that is, a vacation for the others and for himself a change of scene.[7] Although at Derby he might appear to be doing nothing more than reading British newspapers, and although he had said that the Unionists in America would be better able to predict events than those in Europe, he was studying and restudying the news in an effort to penetrate the future. Nominal charge of the legation had been conferred upon first Secretary Wilson during the minister's absence. Actual responsibility had devolved on second Secretary Moran.

In former years, Moran had been a beneficiary—like Wilson— of the "spoils system" practiced by American political parties in connection with public offices. His retention in office by the Republicans had given him the honorable status of a nonpartisan civil servant and career diplomat. The change had made the Pennsylvanian acutely sensitive to the comparative suitabilty of other federal appointees for their allotted tasks. In his journal, he set down his estimates of the many Union ministers and consuls who stopped at the legation. On the one hand, he said that Carl Schurz, the new minister to Spain, was "a man of mark, and will represent us both to his own and our credit," and, on the other, that Anson Burlingame was "only ordinary and totally unfit for any Diplomatic Post."[8]

That Moran was fit for important work was a truth he was spoiling to see subjected to stern tests. As if to provide a test, a warning came to the legation on August 14 from Wilding in Liverpool that the Confederate agents, in effect, had taken full charge of a British steamer, the *Bermuda*. Fraser, Trenholm & Company had chartered the ship and loaded it at West Hartlepool with "70 tons of powder, quantities of cartridges, arms & other munitions of war[,] together with 4 guns on deck."

It was pretended by the firm that the *Bermuda* was bound for Havana and that the cargo was wanted by the Cubans. In fact, the vessel, under its British flag, would attempt to steam directly into Charleston, Savannah, or another deep-water Confederate port with the double object of bringing munitions to the Confederate Army and demonstrating to the world that the Union blockade was ineffective. Needless to say, the Union Navy might intercept the ship and seize it, proving instead that the blockade was effective. But it was infinitely preferable from the Union point of view that the ship not be allowed to sail.

Moran immediately sent Charles Light, the legation's messenger, to Derby with a note to Minister Adams concerning the *Bermuda* and the urgent necessity that the ship be prevented from leaving port. The second secretary also telegraphed the American consul nearest West Hartlepool, Albert Davy at Leeds, asking him to watch the ship and make reports. C. F. Adams returned to London, wrote to the Foreign Office requesting that the *Bermuda* be detained by the British government, and received an answer from Earl Russell that the matter would be promptly taken care of. The minister went back to Derby believing that the foreign secretary's assurances were honest.

Oppositely, Moran construed the foreign secretary's reply as a deception and predicted that the ship would not be detained. Sure enough, on August 18, the heavily-laden *Bermuda* went to sea—in

Moran's words—"without any apparent attempt on the part of the [British] authorities here [in London] to stop her." Since the ship mounted four guns on deck and thus was capable of attacking and sinking Union merchant ships, the resourceful assistant secretary telegraphed a warning to the captain of an American merchant vessel at Falmouth, where the *Bermuda* was expected to call. He hastened also to send full particulars concerning the Confederate operation to New York, directing that they be relayed to Washington by telegraph, so that the Navy Department could alert its blockading cruisers in time to hunt the *Bermuda* off the Southern ports.[9]

A note from Foreign Secretary Russell was delivered to the legation about a different matter, an arduous negotiation which Minister Adams, acting on instructions from Secretary Seward, had been attempting to complete ever since his arrival.[10] The United States had offered to become a signatory to the Treaty of Paris, an international agreement dating from 1856, which outlawed privateering. Undertaken by C. F. Adams in good faith, the negotiation had encountered obstacles and delays, of which Earl Russell's latest note was a maddening example.

At bottom, the attempted negotiation had been a series of mutal misunderstandings.[11] What mattered was that Russell had been more or less driven to the conclusion that Seward's offer to give up privateering was a "trap"; that Russell saw the trap as fresh evidence of Seward's concealed hostility to Great Britian; that Moran thought Russell had acted in this instance with "the cool effrontery of a footpad"; and that C. F. Adams, when he returned from his vacation a week later, on Thursday, August 22, resented Russell's conduct throughout the negotiation, which the minister saw in retrospect as less than honest.

The legation's difficulties mounted. On August 24, using impassioned language, Mr. Adams broke off the negotiation concerning the Treaty of Paris, even though to do so meant that the initial chapter of his career in London had closed in sudden failure.[12] The following Saturday, August 31, a letter to him from Thomas Corwin, the U.S. minister to Mexico, provided decisive evidence that England, France, and Spain were contemplating the seizure of Mexico, in aggressive violation of the Monroe Doctrine, and would try to establish a Mexican monarchy. Before two added days could pass, a special messenger from the secretary of state appeared at the legation carrying written proofs, obtained by Seward's secret agents in New York, that the governments of England and France, acting together, had surreptitiously made official contact with the government of the Confederate States in Richmond though a chain of intermediaries, notably the English and French consuls at Charleston. Simultaneously, a new State Department regulation concentrated such crowds of persons at the legation seeking passports and visas that Wilson and Moran at times were literally run down.[13]

While at Derby, the younger Adams had omitted writing one report to the *New York Times*. Back in London, he resumed his secret correspondence. His fourteenth communication, dated August 24, and his fifteenth, dated August 31, were peculiarly forward-looking. Henry announced with strange assurance that the "next struggle" of the loyal Unionists in London would not occur until late autumn or early winter; also that, when it came, the struggle would be ferocious. " . . . I can say with knowledge that we look forward to the months of November and December with an anxiety that it would be hard to over-estimate."

On September 2, a personal telegram reached him from America. The message, wired by Charles to Halifax, had crossed the ocean on a steamer in care of a friend of the Adamses in Boston, John Lothrop Motley, the historian. Replacing Anson Burlingame, Motley had been appointed minister to Austria and was hastening to his post. The message from Charles to Henry instructed him to stay in London.

Four days later, on September 6, the third son received an emotional letter from the second, developing the same idea at considerable length. Charles expressed himself as willing to get Henry a commission, but in the United States Army regulars, if the younger brother insisted on entering the military service. Charles, however, was very anxious that his brother *not* come home. " . . . I think decidedly you ought to . . . remain with your father & mother." Abusively, calling the third son a "coward" and saying—as if Henry had not previously said the same thing himself—that his brother was "not particularly well fitted for the army," unhappy Charles repeated, "You fight our battle in England & let us alone to fight it here." Yet fighting battles of a military sort was something that the second son apparently was loth to try. He took the attitude that the right to be an officer in a Massachusetts regiment was a privilege reserved for himself which Henry should not infringe. He said that he would wait until he was near to being drafted before asserting the privilege. " . . drafting will have to begin before long[,] & then I have made up my mind to go. . . . "

In his most galling vein, Charles went on to lecture Henry about his opportunities and proper course.[14] The lecture was extended in a second, longer letter, so that the younger brother would be provided with a full program of things to keep him busy. The program was erected on wrong assumptions: that Henry till then had been completely idle in London; that he would be content in life to be an author, nothing else; and that he could be persuaded to pattern his future writings after an article by Charles Francis Adams, Jr., "The Reign of King Cotton," in the April *Atlantic Monthly*.[15]

The lecture could be forgiven. The important thing from Henry's point of view was that his mistaken impulse to go home had came to nothing. He thus was able to reply to Charles with composure and affection.

So serious had the legation's troubles become that competent secretaries would be needed all the time, to keep abreast both of routine and urgent business. "I could not go home now if I would," the younger brother told the elder, "nor would I if I could." As quietly as possible, Henry ended his interchange with Charles by saying: "No I am very well as I am. I shall gradually make way and worry along. London does not satisy all my longings, but *enfin* it an exciting, hard-working life. . . ."

The best room in the house Minister Adams had rented for a year on Mansfield Street was an attractively furnished study. Like his library on Mount Vernon Street in Boston, the room occupied the entire front of the house on the parlor floor and was lit by three large windows. Had the windows faced south instead of east, C. F. Adams could almost have called himself at home in such a space, and he liked it well enough to use it as his and Henry's place of work.

His private secretary, who presumably had found the house and arranged the lease, appeared to like the room much more than the minister did. The father tended to complain that it grew too dark in the afternoons.[1] The son rejoiced that he and the minister were permitted by the furnishings to work in close proximity—possibly at a large table or an elaborate, two-sided desk. Describing the arrangement in a letter to Charles, contented Henry said, " . . . the Chief and I are as merry as grigs, writing in this delightful old study all day long, opposite to each other."

The official secretaries occupied a room on the ground floor near the entrance.[2] Their relegation to a lower story did not impair the zeal and efficiency of Moran, who worked hard from morning to evening, always acquiring a strengthened appearance of diplomatic mastery and vocational permanence. Wilson understood that he was being scorned. While upstairs a private secretary was functioning unhindered as the minister's favorite and confidant, downstairs he himself, the secretary of legation, was kept away from serious duties and responsibilities.

The Chicagoan responded in ways which promised to reinforce his banishment. During office hours, he partly idled. Remembering that he was still owner of the *Chicago Daily Journal,* he openly used his desk to write illegal news reports for publication by his paper in Illinois.[3] He continuously read American and English newspapers and, when done with each, threw it carelessly on the floor. Meanwhile H. B. Adams and Moran were dividing a larger and larger part of the secretarial work between them, until it seemed that Wilson was capable of no work whatever, even if asked and encouraged. His good qualities went unnoticed and his bad were held against him. "He . . . seems a very quarrelsome man," Moran recorded on September 9. "His manners are coarse, and he has a way of speaking by no means respectful."

The discrediting of the offical secretary progressed so far in September that Moran and the minister, riding across London and back on an errand, had a conversation about his uselessness. C. F. Adams told the assistant secretary how Wilson had chanced to come to the legation. Omitting or at least not stressing the central fact that Wilson was a friend of Seward's, appointed at Seward's insistence over senatorial protest, the elder Adams attributed the appointment to Mr. Lincoln. The minister explained that the president had no idea of the purposes and needs of the Union's diplomatic outposts. As Moran remembered their talk, C. F. Adams said of the chief executive: "He has a book, in which all foreign posts are noted down, and when hard pressed for a place for a partisan at home [in Illinois], calls for his book[,] and if there is a vacancy, be it Mission, Sec. of Legation, or Consulate, no matter where, gives it to the applicant if he will take [it]. This was the way Wilson was appointed."[4]

For diplomatic purposes, the two Adamses and Moran made a formidable team, but the new situation they were placed in after receiving Corwin and Seward's messages was extremely difficult to analyze. The minister wrote early in September, " . . . the direction of things in Europe [is] almost impossible to foresee."[5] At about the same time, the private secretary asked in a fresh report to the *New York Times:* "What on earth does all this mean? It is enough to puzzle the brains of a conjuror."

The legation's most immediate worry was the movement of British arms on British ships towards Southern ports. According to the best intelligence the Unionists could obtain, the Confederate Army lacked munitions, clothing, and other requisites of modern warfare. The Confederate Navy, for lack of ships, was mostly composed of men ashore. Understanding what their needs were, the rebel authorities were attempting to outfit both their land and sea forces by a single means. The younger Adams—while being careful not to name the vessels he meant—had reported to Raymond on August 24: " . . . there is more than one armed vessel fitting out in English ports, and intended to be run under the British flag till they have escaped the blockade and landed their cargoes. Then they will become ships of war, no doubt, and cruise as the Southern national fleet."[6]

Command of the Union Army charged with the capture of Richmond had passed from old General Winfield Scott to young General George B. McClellan. It was assumed that the new commander, once his forces were reorganized, better trained, and better equipped, would advance towards the rebel capital and precipitate the war's decisive action.

Rumors persisted in London that the English mills needed cotton. Truly reliable information concerning the reserves of raw cotton held in warehouses by the Liverpool cotton lords seemed impossible to get. The younger Adams's earlier estimates had been superseded. He now feared that the famine might begin, not in several months, but rather in several weeks; that a cry would indeed be raised in England against the Union blockade; and that a crisis would arise in which the ministry would have to act. But how the ministry would act remained in doubt. In his August 24 report, Adams had said, "The reaction towards conservatism here is strong, and is likely to be stronger. . . . "[7] He had warned on August 31: "England is not to be trusted. She will get her cotton if we give her the shadow of an excuse." While he wrote, the subject turned about before his eyes, showing dissimilar aspects. He said also in his August 31 report, " . . . the British people, and, as I feel confident, the British Government, are still hesitating, and making up their minds. . . ."[8]

Having sketched two visions, one of England poised to strike and one of England hesitating, Adams went on to sketch a third of England adrift and mute. In his September 7 report, he admitted: "Where the English are drifting to, it is hard to say. The cotton merchants keep their eyes steadily on Earl RUSSELL, but Earl RUSSELL remains in a sphynx-like silence."

Reporter Adams perceived at length that his own worry of worries was one whose source he could not learn. He wrote privately to Charles on September 7, "I am myself more uneasy than I like to acknowledge in my public letters. . . . " Henry did not go into details, merely saying, "Things have taken a turn which make[s] it every day more probable that we must sooner or later come into collision with England. . . ." The younger brother did not mean that the "collision" would necessarily be an outright war between Great Britian and the

United States. The event he felt approaching was one whose outlines he could not distinctly fix. He only knew he felt it coming.

With each added day, the streets of London's aristocratic West End became more vacant and deserted. It appeared that everyone had gone to places far removed from the capital's empty pavements. The members of the legation regretted the absence of their allies among the Liberals in Parliament. Not having seen Mr. Bright, Mr. Forster, or any equally sympathetic English politician for many weeks, the secret correspondent invented an imaginary English friend on paper.

Adams announced in his reports that Foreign Secretary Russell was "a very honorable, straightforward man." In the same breath, he declared that Prime Minister Palmerston was an old-style opportunist who had formed his views in the time of the Napoleonic Wars and the reaction that followed, "when CASTLEREAGH, TALLEYRAND and METTERNICH played ducks and drakes with Europe, and cared as little for nation's rights as it is the fashion now to make much of them." Henry did not believe these statements. If asked his real opinion, he might probably have answered that Russell and Palmerston were English politicians of the standard sort, neither honest nor dishonest.[9] It had merely occurred to him that, as a means of promoting the Union cause, high opinions of the younger foreign secretary and low opinions of the septuagenarian prime minister might yield advantages; and he accordingly expressed them.

He had just resorted to the expedient when the causes of distrust between the Union and Great Britain seemed to evaporate. News of the abrupt and sweeping alteration appeared in Adams's eighteenth report. A memorable communication, mailed on September 21, 1861, the report combined an outline of the things which had recently alarmed the Unionists in London with an outline of the things which had now removed their fears.

> On the news of the Bull Run affair, the whole [British] Press whirled round against us, and began to take a tone which looked anything but encouraging for our blockade. Very grave rumors found currency that the Ministry were thinking of recognizing the Southerners; rumors probably set afloat by [the Confederates] themselves. . . . It was said, too, that there was difficulty in France; that the Emperor now favored the South, and was pressing the English Government to interfere. It was announced that more troops were to be sent to

Canada. It was understood that armed intervention in Mexico, by the three Western Powers, was decided upon. All these stories evidently tended to one conclusion, and men began to dread some great and unknown evil.

Now, however, matters have much brightened up. The Government here has declared plainly that it does not mean to recognize the South, nor does it mean to interfere with our blockade. . . . On the other hand, we received yesterday, from France, an official announcement that the blockade was to be respected. . . . This leaves no more doubt about France. Still further it appears that the dispatch of more troops to Canada has been countermanded. The troops will not go. The Mexican matter remains, it is true, and seems to be the worst part of the whole business. But this is rather a mercantile affair on the part of the British Government than a political move. . . . The colonial system of Great Britain is already so vast that they do not want to multiply their vulnerable places. . . .

Although cheering for a day, the irruption of good news failed to rescue Adams from his anxiety, which paradoxically grew worse. He sought new explanations for it and found one in the weather. Autumnal fogs had descended on Mansfield Street and Portland Place.[10] He wrote to Charles: " . . . the streets look as no streets in the world do look out of England. Berlin was never so gloomy as London."

Then, too, the correspondent believed he might be anxious merely because the secret of his arrangement with the *New York Times* might be learned and suddenly exposed. The likeliest beginning of that calamity, he thought, would be an accusation by one or the other of the official secretaries daily appearing for duty in the legation office.

The saying went that one should set a thief to catch a thief. In the mysterious case of the unnamed London correspondent of the *New York Times*, no setting was required. The thief was directly in the midst of other thieves. Downstairs, in continual defiance of the law, Secretary Wilson was scribbling letters for publication by his paper in Chicago. Moreover, as Adams had detected, second Secretary Moran was not above supplying illegal news reports to the press. In July, reading issues of the *Times* in search of his own reports, and with a view to studying their effects on Raymond's editorials and general policy, Adams had found his June 8 report as expected but also had found an additional report of the same date from London. Published under the heading "FROM ANOTHER CORRESPONDENT," the additional report had inspired reflection and investigation. In a manner which cannot now be reconstructed, Adams had ascertained that the other correspondent was diligent Moran.[11]

Thus a problem had arisen. If H. B. Adams could read one report by "Another Correspondent" and identify that person as Moran, could not Moran read report after report from the writer described in the *New York Times* as "Our Own Correspondent" with increasing certainty that the writer was H. B. Adams? Raymond's *Times* was read at the legation with more care—certainly by Moran— than any other newspaper, not excepting *The Times* of London.[12]

When one considered, too, that Adams had based his entire correspondence in considerable measure on legation secrets, including Earl Russell's notes from the Foreign Office and Seward's never-slackening despatches from the State Department, the wonder was not that Adams had grown afraid that his authorship of the correspondence would be perceived and in some disastrous way divulged. The wonder was that he should have the cool temerity to think of going on with his reports for an indefinite period. For nerve, there may never have been another Adams to approach him. His nerve was all the greater because his continued use of inside information was steeply heightening the probability of ruin. He told himself he most likely would be caught and plainly wrote to Charles, "I doubt if I can carry it on much longer without being known."

Earl Russell was in Scotland, at Albergeldie Castle. Although the business they would discuss was not especially important, the foreign secretary had asked Minister Adams to come north and meet him there. It seemed an inconvenience, but C. F. Adams had made the journey, departing on September 23.[13]

H. B. Adams meanwhile had decided that he would have to defend himself against esposure by the official secretaries, especially intelligent Moran. The theme of journeys took on a helpful meaning in the younger Adams's unsleeping brain. Beginning soon, both Wilson and Moran would be absent from London on brief vacations. So Henry decided to take an imaginary journey, in advance of their real ones, which were expected to start on October 1.[14]

At the house on Mansfield Street in London, Adams wrote a news report to the *New York Times* which pretended to be written from Leamington, a well-known watering place northwest of the capital, on the way to Liverpool. As he later said, the report exercised his "inventive powers." He larded it with particulars, explaining that, on the way to Leamington, he had passed a day at Oxford.[15] "The old buildings look perhaps still older and more ragged than ever. . . . I walked again through the quadrangles. . . . ADDISON'S Walk is as pretty as ever, and the deer are still grazing under the old trees in the park."

His "Leamington" report went back to the subject of British public opinion concerning the United States. He described encounters he had had with Englishmen. He said they were aggrieved by the defiant tone of the Union press, the bite of the Union tariff, the threatening want of cotton in Lancashire. He emphasized that the British simply could not understand so needless and impossible a thing as a single Republic spanning half a continent. They believed there should be several Americas. " . . . the vast majority of the English people, however much they may dislike the North, are still more hostile to the South. The first remark always is, Why not let them go?"

It pleased Adams to know that his report could both concern an important subject and provide "a little wrong scent." In about a month, the report would come back in printed form to the legation and be read by Moran. The second secretary by then would have completed a journey of his own away from London.[16] Reading in the *New York Times* about the pleasant ramble of its correspondent in the British Isles, Moran would know for a fact that he and the authoritative correspondent of the *Times* had been simultaneously vacationing, while H. B. Adams, in his father's study at the legation, had been drudging.

In his own June 8 report, Moran had mentioned Thornton Hunt, an English journalist. In his wrongly scented "Leamington" report, Adams took pains to mention a writer for the *London Telegraph*, "Mr. THORNTON HUNT." The insertion, one imagines, was meant by Adams as the signature of genius, giving Moran occasion to feel obscurely threatened. A new Prince Hamlet, endangered in a London Elsinore, had whispered a knavish speech into a foolish ear.

The fictitious city from which Adams claimed to mail his next report was "Glasgow." While he was writing it in London, a confidential message arrived at the legation. The message concerned a suspicious ship, the *Fingal,* about to be loaded with Confederate war supplies at Greenock.[17] Here was a new legation secret, and Henry was quick to use it. He explained in his report that, en route to Scotland, he had stopped at Liverpool and there discovered that Confederate agents and sympathizers were "very active." He named a British firm,

"FRASER, TRENHOLM & CO.," which earlier had sent "one vessel armed and freighted with large supplies to some Southern port." Now, he said, the firm had a second vessel "nearly ready to follow."

Feeling that his security against accusation by Moran or Wilson was approaching completeness but could not yet withstand the severest strains, Adams took the precaution in his "Glasgow" report of withholding the names of the *Bermuda* and the *Fingal*, while otherwise divulging everything about them. Similarly, in a fresh report he sent on October 12, he avoided the subject of ships entirely. Word by then had come to the legation that the *Fingal* had finished loading and gone to sea, but the canny reporter merely described the slackness of British trade, affirmed the "renewed cordiality" between the governments of the United States and Great Britain, and reverted to the question of Mexico.[18]

According to his October 12 report, the London correspondent of the *New York Times* had ended his vacation and returned to the capital. " . . . there seems to be not much to tell at this time of year," Adams reported quietly. " The [English] newspapers contain, principally, accounts of murders which have not even orginality to lend them interest. . . . Several nobles are dead. . . . London is still deserted as ancient Thebes. . . . "

Wilson came back from a holiday in Paris and Moran from a stay at Great Malvern in Worcestershire. Immediately thereafter, on Thursday, October 17, 1861, announcements appeared in the London press that the *Bermuda*, loaded with British arms, had steamed unhurt and undetected through the Union blockade directly into a Confederate deep-water harbor at Savannah, Georgia. The news was a shocking setback for the Unionists abroad. An instance was the suffering of Moran. " . . . this is simply disgraceful," he moaned in his journal. ". . . I wrote home [that] she would go to a Southern port, but it [his message] seems to have been disregarded."[19]

Adams could absorb the shock more easily than Moran, for he had perfected his own blockade. Sure that the official secretaries could not get through his protective screen, he wrote and mailed a report to the *Times* about Confederate energy in which he adopted an altered style. He named names and places in an uninhibited manner which gave his paragraphs heightened interest and markedly greater impact. He boldly said:

> . . . we see it announced in all the [London] papers that a steamer, called the *Fingal* . . . has left . . . for America. I

mentioned in my letter a fortnight since that . . . such a vessel was getting ready, and now here she is. . . . Nor does one such steamer, or two such, end the matter. . . . The Secessionists . . . are in no want of money. . . . This accounts for the fact that they . . . have freighted two steamers with cargoes, which, in the case of the *Fingal,* is stated at $300,000, and in that of the *Bermuda* could hardly have been less; that they have bought the steamers themselves . . . and . . . are preparing to continue this process. . . . Indeed, they must do so, for their purchases of arms and munitions in England are enormous, and amount, in Birmingham alone, if the newspapers are to be believed, to $100,000 a month. It stands to reason that all these arms and accoutrements must be sent off somehow [to the Confederacy]. . . . It stands to reason, also, that every such cargo run in [at a Confederate port] represents an army to them, and to us the lives of thousands of men, and, perhaps, the loss of the contest, and the final destruction of the Union.

As Adams had foreseen, William Howard Russell's long account of the flight from Bull Run was widely reprinted and read by the Unionists at home, and an eruption of hatred had resulted. The "Special Correspondent" was attacked most furiously for his supposed Confederate sympathies.[20] Yet there were citizens of the United States who were willing to defend him in the newspapers of the Northern cities, and one was Charles.

In late August, Henry's brother had persuaded the *Boston Advertiser* to publish an article on the folly of Russell's American critics.[21] Once started along this path, the second son had shown new signs of energy and decision. He wrote two articles called "English Views," arranged their publication in the *Boston Courier,* and sent a supply of copies to the minister and Henry in London. Charles suggested that Henry might possibly induce the editor of an English newspaper to read them and publish extracts.[22]

The elder brother's "English Views" had arrived at the legation while the younger was making his fictitious journey to "Leamington" and "Glasgow." At the time, Henry had been working very hard on legation business. He had also started making efforts to become acquainted with English editors sympathetic to the Union. His efforts now permitted him to speed his brother's articles to Samuel Lucas, editor of the *London Star,* and Meredith Townsend, editor of the *London Spectator.* A few days later, Henry reported to Charles that the

*Star* had published an article of its own which took note of his opinions.

On October 15, Henry, too, wrote an article, in the form of a pretended personal letter, and sent it posthaste to Boston. Charles was to plant it, if he could, in the *Boston Advertiser*. The feeblest of Henry's journalistic productions, the pretended letter was a failure. When it arrived in Boston, Charles rightly declined to take it to the *Advertiser* office.

All the third son's newest activities in London showed that his anxiety, while ended with respect to his secret work as a reporter, was mounting in connection with the "great and unknown evil" which he for a time had mocked as imaginary. Now even more than earlier, the evil seemed real and looming in the future, and he was attempting to meet or diminish it by making extra efforts.

On October 20, a Sunday, although he had sent a report to Raymond the day before, he wrote an extra one to catch a Monday steamer. In it he spoke again about the armored fighting ships built and building in British yards. The subject was a grim one. "Within a year or two England will have a fleet of these enormous iron vessels, and there seems to be no reason why they will not be able to defy all the ordinary river and harbor defenses.... The *Warrior* might walk up the Hudson or the Mississippi without paying the least regard to the few shot or shell that might be fired at her as she passed."

Each extra effort led immediately to a greater. Remembering what John Gorham Palfrey had told him in Boston the previous April concerning a possible article about Captain Smith and Pocahontas, Adams sought admission to the reading room at the British Museum. Once inside, he asked the keepers to help him search for evidence to prove that the captain's rescue by the Princess was not good history but a lie. After pressing the inquiry vigorously for "several hours," Adams became persuaded that Smith's story was true and proof against all criticism!

The reverse led straightway to an important consequence. Henry had gone to the reading room expecting to arm himself with munitions for an article suited to the *Atlantic Monthly*. When the evidence he saw turned against him, so to speak, he at once foresook all hope of an immediate article on Smith but grew determined to find evidence on some other subject that would interest readers of the *Atlantic*. It was a case of his fighting instincts coming into play. Once in February and now again in October, he had been thwarted in schemes to rush potentially explosive articles into the hands of editor Lowell. Hurt by two defeats, Adams would *have* to send an article to Lowell quickly, possibly in time for publication in the magazine's December issue.

As October drew towards its close, and the two deadly months approached, November and December, which he had prophesied would bring on the "next struggle" for the Unionists in London, Adams's mood appeared to divide into several strands of feeling.

He wrote good-naturedly to Palfrey on October 23 about the disappointing details of the evidence concerning Smith at the British Museum. " . . . I give it up," Henry confessed to the historian, "but would like to know if you think a case is still possible." Adams indicated, too, that his brief researches had affected his sensibilities. While at the reading room, he had seen some astonishing records pertaining to Powhatan. " . . . long conversations of his with English people are extant. . . . Some of his conversation is very touching and strangely life-like."

In the worst humor possible, on October 25, he wrote to Charles and for the first time spoke evil of Abraham Lincoln. The third son asked the second rhetorically: "How do you suppose we [in London] can overcome the effects of the New York press [on England]. . . . How do you suppose we can shut people's eyes to the incompetence of Lincoln. . . . Here we are dying by inches."

Impatience and harshness were creeping into the younger brother's lines. "My one hope," he said to Charles, "is now on McClellan[,] and if he fails us, then as I say, I give it up." Events had taken the Unionists around an ironic circle. Once again, they were waiting for the battle. Looking forward a second time to the American Waterloo, the younger brother said with very little hope: " . . . if we are utterly without honor then, as we promise to be, I mean to come home and be a lawyer until I have money enough to go to Paris again and become an Epicurean hog, a Sardanapalus, by Jove, and drown our disgrace in absynthe and women. The North is a nation of shop-keepers."

Nevertheless, on Saturday, October 26, he wrote a calm report to Raymond which said that nothing had changed. " . . . things remain in the same position in which they have stood for a long time."

Having made a fictitious journey and reported it in the *New York Times* as a fact, Adams felt he should soon make a real journey, *not* report it in the *Times,* and write a true account of it for anonymous publication in the *Atlantic Monthly.* He told his father he wished to visit Manchester and obtain accurate information about the cotton famine. Of course, he omitted all mention of writing anything for publication anywhere. The minister saw no objection to the plan. Free to go but preferring not to leave at once, Henry took pains to insure his trip's success. Possibly through Samuel Lucas—or through Mrs. Lucas, the sister of John Bright—he secured an invitation to stay in Manchester at the home of an American resident and ardent Unionist, William Shorter Stell.[1] Also Henry began collecting a quantity of letters of introduction to leading Manchester businessmen.

The errand he had proposed for himself was a sufficiently serious one. The city he would visit was the center of the English cotton spinning trade. If he could talk to several of its most knowledgeable men, he might be able to estimate with helpful precision the danger of British action against the Union blockade. Deliberately circulated falsehoods had so muddled the subject in London that clarification had become a virtual necessity. As Adams said, "The truth is what is wanted, and here people are wandering in a wilderness of lies on both sides."[2]

He did not say so, but he intended if possible to get the truth as well about another subject. He was interested in the British working class. When he had first crossed England by train, in October 1858, he had been fascinated and appalled by glimpses of Birmingham and the Black District. His eyes had been opened to something new in the world, an "unknown society of the pit," a place where human beings labored in "weird gloom," submerged in "darkness lurid with flames."[3]

Recently, thinking about John Bright, who counted in English politics as the chief representative of the disenfranchised industrial workers in the Midlands, Adams had seen that Bright's political safety might be imperiled. Henry said in his November 2 report to Raymond: "If the operatives of Manchester and elsewhere suffer from the cotton trouble, as is expected, no doubt the secession agents here will work on them to create a popular demonstration in favor of breaking our blockade, and then Mr. BRIGHT will be brought into direct conflict with that very popular power which created him. . . . Such is the plan of the Secession party in England, and it is one which promises well to them."

To increase its claims upon the attention of the European powers, the Confederate administration had appointed James Mason and Benjamin Slidell—former U.S. senators from Virginia and Louisiana—as special commissioners to England and France respectively. As a ruse, the Confederate press reported that Mason and Slidell would run the blockade and travel to Europe on the diminutive rebel paddle steamer *Nashville*. The Union Navy hurried several warships in search of the rebel steamer.[4] On November 2, 1861, a Saturday, one of the warships, a converted merchant vessel, the eight-gun *James Adger*, appeared in English waters and put in at Falmouth for coals.

English inquirers at Falmouth were freely told that the Union warship had been sent across the ocean from New York in hopes of seizing the *Nashville*, removing the envoys from the vessel as prisoners, and getting both the vessel and the captives back to a Union port. The following Wednesday in London, Moran and Wilson encountered the paymaster of the *James Adger;* and the next day, November 7, her commander, Captain Marchand, called on C. F. Adams and showed the minister his orders.

H. B. Adams may well have been in the study when fat, good-natured Marchand came to visit. The captain showed little fighting spirit. Having failed to catch the elusive *Nashville* and its supposed passengers, he seemed inclined to abandon the chase and run for home.[5]

His unpromising explanations coincided with the arrival of grim news from Virginia about a Union defeat in a small battle at Ball's Bluff. Massachusetts units had taken part in the repulse. Henry wrote to Charles, "You can imagine I trembled when I ran down the list of losses."

The idea that Charles become connected with an English newspaper as its American correspondent had originated with Henry, writing privately to his brother four months earlier.[6] Recently, by sending copies of the *Boston Courier* containing his "English Views" to their father, with the suggestion that Henry show the articles to an English editor, Charles had involved the minister in the project. The Chief had taken up the idea, hinting to Charles that the London press could surely use a more sensible contributor than the mischievous scribblers who at present were wrongly informing its editors and readers.[7] C. F. Adams hoped especially that his discontented son in Boston could counteract the bad effects of George Sumner. Brother of Charles Sumner and a person not admired by the Adamses, George— in Henry's words—had been supplying "weekly vile letters" from Boston to the *London Morning Post.*[8]

On the night of November 7, 1861, while writing to Charles about the losses at Ball's Bluff, Henry touched the question of the elder brother's possible service as a transatlantic journalist. "As for . . . your becoming a correspondent for some paper here," he said, "I have had it always in my mind. . . . " He mentioned having visited two men who might be helpful, Meredith Townsend and Thomas Hughes, but held out no hope at all that the desired connection could be formed. Indeed he hinted that no arrangement would be made. " . . . the difficulty is that every paper here has already one or more American correspondents."

In oracular language, the younger brother warned the elder that the fate of the Union had ceased to depend on public opinion and had become exclusively a question of governmental action. He declared about Great Britain: " . . . it is the most wretched folly to waste a moment over what this or any other country *thinks*. We must induce them not to *act*. . . . "

Whether Charles would be able to guess the meaning of Henry's utterance could be doubted, but the younger brother had something very definite in mind. In his reports to the *New York Times,* the third son had been predicting since August that a crisis would occur in November, December, or as late as the New Year.[9] Now his prophecies had hardened into convictions. Time, he knew, had entirely run out. If a way were opened for Charles to send continuous reports to an English newspaper, any effects they might have would be too late. The outcome for the Union would already be decided.

For Henry himself, it was not too late. The next day, November 8, he would write and mail his weekly report to Raymond. At five in the afternoon, he would catch his train for Manchester at King's Cross

Station. " . . . my great gun is the Manchester one," he said to Charles. "Tomorrow evening I start with a pocket-full of letters. . . . "

Although he had first conceived his visit to Manchester as a way of getting material for an article capable of winning immediate publication in the *Atlantic Monthly,* the younger brother had failed to write to Professor Lowell, explain his intentions, and indicate that a manuscript might soon arrive. Henry possibly had been too busy. Also the sense that time was lacking made him wonder whether his article might best be printed the instant it reached America in a daily newspaper. Besides, he continued to feel a strong desire to involve himself and Charles in cooperative enterprises.

Previous experiences should have warned the younger brother to stay clear of the elder in all cases of publishing ventures fraught with risk. Really such experiences *had* warned Henry; but, like Hector in *The Iliad,* he so loved his brothers that he would not heed his own accurate knowledge of their weaknesses and faults. So once again he placed his own fate directly in the hands of Charles. "My present plan," Henry told his brother, "is to report . . . all my conversations and all my observations [while visiting Manchester]. . . . Perhaps it might make a magazine article; except that it should be printed as soon as possible. If I find I can make it effective in that form, I shall write it out and send it to you for the Atlantic. If not, I shall contract it and send it to you for the Advertiser or Courier."

On November 8, a Friday, Henry reversed the game he had played on Moran a month before. He wrote his twenty-sixth report to Raymond under a false dateline: "London, Saturday, Nov. 9, 1861." Moran, a stickler for precise information, would know that on that Saturday, H. B. Adams had *not* been in London.

This expedient permitted Adams to return in the new report to the deadly subject of Confederate supplies and ships for the rebel fleet. ". . . another steamer, loaded with powder, rifles, and blankets, for the Southerners, is on the point of sailing from London. . . . My informant told me, under injunctions of secrecy, that she was to sail on Monday, the 11th. . . ."

Fearing that the Navy Department would neglect its duty in the case, he scornfully burst out: "Here is something for our fleet to do; so many of our fellow citizens' lives to be saved; so many weeks or months of the war to be cut off. If our fleet cannot stop this sort of thing, it would be shorter and safer to wall up every harbor, from Old Point to the Mexican frontier, with granite blocks."

The Great Northern express carried Adams to Manchester by 10:30 that Friday night, and he soon found his way to the home of Mr. Stell. After a bite of supper, tea, and a cigar, he asked his host about "the feeling among the solid people of Manchester towards the North."

Mr. Stell replied that the feeling was "generally unfriendly and even hostile." Their interchange was the beginning of what for Adams proved a long series of conversations. During the next five days, he spoke with as many people in the city as he could contrive to meet. Among others, he conferred with an important commission merchant and his partner; an officer in a cotton-spinning firm; a gentleman and a clerk in a firm that manufactured cotton cloth; a father and two sons in a great firm that printed calicoes; a young expert on cotton fibres at the rooms of the Cotton Supply Association; a newspaperman, probably the editor of the *Manchester Daily Examiner and Times;* and a member of Parliament, possibly Thomas Bazley.

In the evenings, the visitor began to translate the things he had heard and seen into an article about thirty paragraphs long. Written in what would seem a spontaneous way, it was titled "A Visit to Manchester. Extracts from a Private Diary." The article was emphatically not being shortened for newspaper publication. Afire with ambition and self-confidence, Adams was writing it at full length and for publication in Lowell's magazine, nowhere else.

Many miles to the south, fat Captain Marchand had meanwhile made up his mind that the *Nashville* would not be coming to England. Thus freed to return to America, he moved the *James Adger* from Falmouth to Southampton and provisioned his ship for the long voyage. Also he sent a note announcing his departure to Minister Adams.[10]

A second lie had been placed in circulation about the itinerary of the new confederate envoys, Mason and Slidell. Now it was said that they would arrive in England on a British mail packet from the Bahamas, due to reach Southampton very shortly.[11] Taking this lie for a fact, the Liberal ministry became extremely worried about the presence of the *James Adger* at Southampton. Suddenly, on Tuesday, November 12, 1861, Minister Adams was asked to visit Prime Minister Palmerston at his private residence at 1:00 P.M. C. F. Adams shortly wrote an account of their talk, which read in part: " . . . [Lord Palmerston] received me in his library all alone, and at once opened on the subject then evidently weighing on his mind. He said that information had come to him of the late arrival of a United States vessel of war, the James Adger. She had put into one or two places, and finally stopped at Southampton. . . . But the day before [November 11] . . . the captain had got very drunk on brandy, after which he had dropped down to the mouth of the river as if about to sail on a cruise."

So far, nothing had been said which could especially worry Minister Adams, but Prime Minister Palmerston was very serious and apprehensive. His lordship seemed to think that Captain Marchand had accurate knowledge of Confederate plans. As nearly as C. F. Adams could recall, the English leader continued:

> The impression [in Southampton] was that he [Marchand] had been directed to keep on the watch for the [British] steamer expected to arrive Thursday from the West Indies, in order to take out of it by force . . . Messrs. Mason and Slidell, who were presumed to be aboard. . . . All that he [Palmerston] desired to observe was, that such a step would be highly inexpedient in every way he could view it. It would be regarded here very unpleasantly if the captain, after . . . filling his ship with coals and other supplies, and filling his own stomach with brandy (and here he laughed in his characteristic way), should . . . commit an act which would be felt as offensive to the [British] national flag.

C. F. Adams knew that Palmerston was entirely wrong about Captain Marchand, who that same day ordered his ship to sea and disappeared from the story, but the American diplomat was interested to learn what the behavior of the British leader might mean. While Minister Adams continued to ponder his unexpected summons to Cambridge House and the things he had heard in the prime minister's library, on Wednesday evening, November 13, Henry Adams came back from Manchester, was told what had happened, and became as curious as his father. The British leader's gesture could be viewed as friendly and helpful to the Union cause. Alternatively, it could be seen as proof that the Liberal ministry had become irrationally fearful and excited.[12]

The younger Adams did again what he had done at Derby: he fell to studying newspapers, intent on getting at the secret of current happenings. On Saturday, November 16, he found something arresting, a report in the *London Telegraph*. It said that the *James Adger* was moving about near Spithead with the intention of stopping the British mail ship from the Bahamas. According to the report, the mail ship, now two days overdue because of storms, was believed to include Mason and Slidell among its passengers; and the plan of the Union sailors on the *James Adger* was to take the Confederate diplomats from the British mail ship and carry them as prisoners to New York. Henry, of course, knew for a fact that the Union warship—storms notwithstanding—was well advanced on its inglorious voyage homeward. But he had discovered that Lord Palmerston and the *London Telegraph* were supposing very parallel things. He concluded that both had been influenced by Confederate agents and believed their lies.

Pleased, Henry began a fresh report to the *New York Times*—his twenty-seventh—by telling in detail what he had read in the *London Telegraph*. He went on to say that Confederate agents in London, as a means of producing "more irritation" between the United States and England, had spread a lie—an ingenious story that a Union warship was under orders to intercept an English mail ship and take from its decks by force the two rebel special commissioners expected soon to arrive in Europe. "One has to be perpetually on one's guard against the miserable, intriguing spirit of these fellows, who are at the bottom of every contemptible plot."

The mood of Adams' November 16 report was extremely cheerful. He seemed to have put aside his dread of imminent crisis. "A good deal of hope seems now to be felt," he stated, "that . . . the threatened explosion [will] be delayed till Spring. . . . The attitude of England is firm and well understood, and we may rely with certainty on her retaining it at least until the middle of February, when Parliament will meet. . . . " He mailed the report and soon thereafter learned that a British merchant ship from the West Indies had reached Southampton; also that Mason and Slidell were not aboard.[13] Speculation concerning the itinerary of the rebel diplomats accordingly was recommenced in England. The best guess seemed to be that the envoys were indeed aboard the *Nashville*, but that their ship was cruelly tossed by storms. It was possible as well that they were coming to Europe by some circuitous route, rather than a direct one.

Minister Adams left London on November 16 to pass a few days with Speaker Denison of the House of Commons in Nottinghamshire.[14] In the hours immediately following, Henry finished his article, "A Visit to Manchester." Longer than anything he had written till then for publication, it would have been finished sooner, had it not been for the pressure of legation business. The delay was important, for Henry would have liked to mail it that same Saturday,

November 16, in time for the Cunard steamer. Had he been able to do so, the article would have had a chance of last-minute inclusion in Lowell's *Atlantic* for December.

During his stay in Manchester, Henry had found that his ideas concerning the cotton famine and British interference with the Union blockade had been quite inaccurate. The article he completed told a story as new to him as it would be new to readers in America. The Lancashire spinning mills, it said, were not shutting down for lack of raw Southern cotton. In fact, the hoard of cotton fibre stored in Liverpool and other places was far from exhausted. The "real difficulty" at the mills was the "rate of production." Till recently, that rate had been so fast that the Manchester spinners and weavers had created a glut of goods. Even with many mills shut down, the rate was still too fast, requiring the firms to store half the goods they were making. For the glut to be disposed of would require fully "two or three months." Fresh demand would then slowly push prices up again.

At that exact moment, but not sooner, a cry would indeed be heard in Manchester. The owners of the mills would declare themselves "in favor of ending the war [in America] by recognizing the insurgents, and, if necessary, breaking the blockade or declaring it ineffective." Yet the deciding factor again would not be lack of lack of American cotton. It would instead be the lure of profits. " . . . so soon as the mills can again be worked at a profit, difficulty and a hot contest may be expected, which will grow intense in proportion as the prospect of money-making increases."

When large profits could be reaped, the mills would quickly consume whole mountains of raw material. Then the spinners of Manchester and their suppliers, the Liverpool cotton lords, would want more mountains, with which to make more profits. They would do what they till now had not done: take a truly serious interest in obtaining cotton, if not from America, then from new plantations in other places.

To appear in the *Atlantic Monthly*, "A Visit to Manchester" would have to be accepted both by Lowell and by Charles, who would read it before conveying it to the editor. It was a fair assumption that the second son would approve the article; for the third son had so shaped its paragraphs that—without being slavish or over-pliant— they corresponded to a possible article which Charles had outlined for his benefit the previous August.[15]

Similarly, Henry adapted his work to meet the needs of Lowell's subscribers. Although a national magazine, the *Atlantic* was bought and read much more in New England than in other parts of the Union. Not a few of its subscribers were owners and employees of New England's cotton spinning and weaving mills. While in Manchester, young Adams had tried hard to meet such readers half way by learning many technical details of the cotton trade and by acquainting himself with the trade's more disputed, general theories. In his article, he challenged the widespread assumption that the American "Cotton States," by virtue of their climate, enjoyed a "'natural' monopoly" in the raising of superior fibre. He discussed the properties of American, Egyptian, and Indian cotton. He provided information about adjustments in English spinning procedures which permitted the use of inferior and substitute raw materials.

One subject was conspicuous in his article for its absence. Henry said nothing in his pages about possible working-class disturbances in England against the Union blockade. Why he kept away from the matter might be difficult to guess. In its place, he introduced a different theme. He described the city he had gone to see. Manchester, he explained, consisted of "a collection of enormous warehouses, banks and shops," surrounded by a wide ring or margin of "common brick houses, which the lower classes live in."

Because he had reached the city after dark and had spent the night at a private home some distance removed from the city proper, he had first been able to study the city the following morning in daylight. But daylight was not the word. "As we entered the streets, the sun, which had been shining brightly two miles away, became a dull red ball in the smoke and fog, and no one who was not accustomed to the atmosphere would have supposed that it was a fine day."

Almost as smoky as Birmingham, and far smokier than any city he had earlier visited in America or Europe, busy Manchester seemed to Adams a city of a kind that would be commoner in the future. Inside it, people thought and spoke in ways which were foreign to supposed English norms. The visitor was told by several of the persons he spoke with that the English nation at large disliked the city and was "jealous of its growing influence."

It had been enjoyable to Henry to be visiting the future and meeting its inhabitants. The Manchester businessmen were partly peculiar for the lively interest they took in the American Civil War. He remembered in his article one talk with such a man especially. The commission merchant had said that the war across the water was the beginning of a world revolution. Adams represented the merchant as having said: "In the final contest between free and slave labor, which has now broken out, few men are provident enough to be aware that the whole arrangement of the world's relations will have to find a readjustment. . . . The world's balance is shifting. *Gare la dessous!* There can be no settled peace between freedom and slavery, till slavery has gone to the wall.''

The three secretaries at Mansfield Street enjoyed a welcome lull. On Wednesday, November 20, 1861, when Minister Adams returned to London "much pleased with his visit" at Speaker Denison's, the only cloud in the legation's sky was the arrival of a stern despatch from the State Department. The object of the despatch was to terminate the service of the British consul at Charleston, Robert Bunch, one of the intermediaries through whom the Liberal cabinet had secretly contacted the rebel government in Richmond.

On Thursday morning, while C. F. Adams was sweetening the language of Seward's instructions, which seemed "tart in the extreme," a telegram was delivered. Sent to the minister by Captain Britton, the U. S. consul at Southampton, it said that the Confederate paddle steamer *Nashville* was entering that port.[1]

Similar messages sent by other persons from Southampton swiftly awakened excitement in England and on the Continent. That afternoon, when the *Nashville* moored alongside the north jetty in the outer tidal basin, curiosity knew no bounds. Atop her peak, the vessel showed the flag of the Confederate States of America, till then unseen in England. Two passengers disembarked, a Colonel Peyton and his wife. The latter, it soon was learned, had been Lizzie Washington before her marriage and—in the words of the English press—was the "nearest surviving relative of the great General."

Colonel Peyton, replying to questions on the jetty, provided a fund of news. He said that Mason and Slidell had not set foot upon the *Nashville*. Traveling on a miniscule steamer, the *Theodora*, the special commissioners had run the Union blockade off Charleston and steered for the Bahamas. There the envoys learned that the British mail ship in which they intended to proceed to Southampton would make an intermediate stop at New York. Forced to seek an alternative route, they had remained aboard the *Theodora*. Their new plan had been to hurry south to Cuba and catch a different British mail ship, the *Trent,* which could carry them east as far as the Danish island of St. Thomas. The *Trent* connected there with still another British mail ship, the *La Plata.* It was thus a fair assumption that Mason and Slidell would arrive at Southampton on the *La Plata* within the next few days.[2]

Several officials of the Admiralty and the mayor of Southampton boarded the *Nashville* and spoke with her master, Captain R. B. Pegram. To their astonishment, the captain told them that, off the Irish coast two days before, he had captured and burned a Union merchant ship, the sailing vessel *Harvey Birch.* Pegram further said that the officers and crew of the sailing vessel were held aboard the *Nashville* as "prisoners-of-war." They now would be released, to get home to the United States in whatever way they could.

The Admiralty officials asked Captain Pegram to show them the Confederate government's commission empowering the paddle steamer to operate as a warship or privateer. The captain answered that the *Nashville* lacked such a document. He explained that the vessel, although armed with two 12-pound rifled cannon, was not yet a proper ship of war. He had been put aboard the boat only to bring her safely to Southampton, where she was to be adapted in a British dockyard for fuller naval use. But Pegram said he had a document which permitted *his* destroying any Union ships which might cross his path: the commission he held as a captain in the Confederate States Navy. This he helpfully produced.

The Yankee "prisoners-of-war," released, went to Consul Britton for assistance. He telegraphed particulars to Minister Adams and sent the liberated sailors to the Sailor's Home. Captain Nelson of the *Harvey Birch* simultaneously rushed to London and described his misadventure to Minister Adams, Consul Morse, and numerous others. Since at least four persons involved in the affair, Nelson, Pegram, Colonel Peyton, and Mrs. Peyton, were talking freely and sometimes rather wildly, the English newspapers were able to inflate the story to large dimensions. London readers were informed that the Yankee sailors, faced while on the *Nashville* with a choice of taking an oath not to arm themselves against their Southern captors or going into irons, had preferred the irons; but Captain Nelson and some passengers, notably a son of the sailing vessel's owner, had submitted and taken a craven oath of nonresistance to the new Confederate States![3]

The State Department in Washington had decided to support Minister Adams in London and Minister Dayton in Paris by sending

unofficial ambassadors to Europe.[4] Two were clergymen: Charles
McIlvaine, the bishop of Ohio, a much-respected Episcopalian; and
Archbishop Hughes, the hero of the Catholics in New York. Hughes
prevailed on Secretary Seward to appoint Thurlow Weed as a third
emissary; and General Winfield Scott, on sick leave from the Union
Army, and anxious to go abroad, counted as a virtual fourth, although
not formally named to be one.[5]

Archbishop Hughes arrived in Liverpool on the *Africa* on
November 19 and came to London.[6] Expected to concentrate his efforts
in France and Italy, he soon went on to Paris and joined forces with
Minister Dayton. Bishop McIlvaine would not reach England until
some time in December; but General Scott, with his family, and
Thurlow Weed, with his daughter, were known to be coming on the
steamer *Arago,* due in the English Channel very shortly.

Since James Mason, the Confederate special commissioner,
would presumably disembark within three days at Southampton, a
grand contest appeared to be starting in England between two teams of
American representatives. The Confederate team would consist mainly of Special Commissioner Mason and lesser Commissioners Yancey,
Mann, and Rost. The Union team would include not only Minister
Adams, his secretaries, and Consuls Britton and Morse at Southampton and London but also Bishop McIlvaine and, at intervals, Mr.
Weed.

It seemed possible that the Union representatives had already won
the contest. Following his talk with Lord Palmerston about the *James
Adger,* Minister Adams and his wife had twice been asked to dine at
Cambridge House. Again invited there on the evening of the day the
*Nashville* moored at Southampton, C. F. Adams "touched Lord
Palmerston a little on the event of the day, and reminded him of the
connection which the *Nashville* had with our previous conversation."
The prime minister responded in a way which Mr. Adams thought as
friendly and good-natured as could possibly be wished.[7]

Lady Palmerston and Mrs. Adams had meanwhile formed a tie
with one another which promised to blossom into a friendship or
something very near it.[8] The latter was winning acceptance in English
society. She and the minister were wanted guests. An invitation had
come for them to travel to Yorkshire on November 25 and stay a while
with Monckton Milnes at Fryston Hall. A further invitation loomed
for all the family to visit Lord Hatherton in the country, beginning on
December 2.

Henry Adams expected to be deeply involved in the grand contest in London between the two opposing teams of American representatives and thought the outcome of the contest would be settled beyond all doubt about ten weeks in the future, with the convening of the House of Commons in early February. For him, the contest would be partly interesting for the chance it would provide him to meet and study Thurlow Weed. The eldest of the loyal Unionists who would be working side by side in London, Mr. Weed held a place among the politicians of America, past and present, which had no strict parallels. He might loosely be compared with Benjamin Franklin but stood alone as an alleged past master of political subtlety.

The *Arago* stopped at Cowes on Saturday, November 23, and word sped to the legation that Scott and Weed were going on to Paris.[9] It was understood that the latter should divide his time between the French and English capitals. His going first to Paris could possibly indicate that, when done there, he would spend a longer interval in London.

While waiting for large eventualities, the younger Adams devoted his twenty-eighth news report, dated November 23, 1861, to the small drama of the paddle steamer. As Henry viewed it, the affair of the *Nashville* was partly ludicrous. What most amused him was the excitement of the Londoners. He wrote, "It is seldom that great battles [,] where the destinies of nations were decided, have caused more excitement or more alarm among the phlegmatic people of this city than the arrival of this wretched, two-gun, half-manned pirate."

He speculated in his report about the troubles the affair would cause for the Confederate representatives in their office on Suffolk Street. He described Captain Pegram's burning of the *Harvey Birch* as a mere outbreak of folly and insanity, adding that the attack would "outrage" British public opinion, stir the anger of the Liberal ministry, and turn out to be the "most unlucky blow the Confederate agents here have ever received." He averred, " . . . I have no doubt that no one is more thoroughly taken aback by the news than Mr. YANCEY himself, and his associates."

Writing with such bravado, Adams tried to give a good appearance to an ill reality. Europeans judged America as much by Southern strengths or weaknesses as by Northern. In view of this consideration, Captain Pegram was one disgrace and his steamer was another. Pegram had formerly been an officer in the U. S. Navy. He thus belonged to the same species as fat, inebriated Captain Marchand. Thinking of both men but writing explicitly about Pegram, Adams suggested, " . . . a serious question arises as to the character our naval officers must have had, as an average, if he is a fair specimen of the class." As for the fighting abilities of the steamer, Henry described it as "badly fitted out, badly armed, badly officered and badly manned."

Visitors on the *Nashville* were being told by the rebel sailors that they had left Charleston at night and steered their vessel directly "through the blockading fleet," some of the ships of which they "could see in the distance." Such testimony supported an existing suspicion in Europe that the Union blockade of the Confederate ports was thin and ill-conducted. For a Unionist as passionate as Adams, and even more so for one who had made the study of ships and navies a considerable part of his self-education, a naval blockade which could not stop such a craft as the Confederate paddle steamer was something worse than a scandal. " . . . if she is a specimen of the Southern privateer," he wrote bitterly in his report, "it must be either incapacity or treachery that prevents our vessels from catching them."

Wounded by the failures of the Union Navy, he requested in his report that a Union warship be sent to English waters with orders to remain there. "A United States war steamer in these waters now," he urged, "would be of more service than half the blockading squadron in its present position, where it never has caught one single steamer [,] even when it had the knowledge when such a steamer was to arrive, how she was to come, and what she had on board."

Minister Adams sent a note to the Foreign Office providing information about the *Nashville* and asking that restrictive measures be promptly taken against the ship by appropriate British governmental agencies.[10] In London and Southampton, U. S. Consuls Morse and Britton made preparations to take the case before a British court. The legal position of the Union's representatives seemed an ideally strong one. Captain Pegram had behaved in a manner which, for lack of proper papers, had been the strictest piracy. Moreover, by bringing into Southampton an assortment of prizes—the "prisoners-of-war," a chronometer, and other articles from the *Harvey Birch*—Pegram had violated express prohibitions in Her Majesty's Proclamation of Neutrality. At an absolute minimum, from the Union point of view, the captain deserved to have his ship detained.

On Saturday, November 23, 1861, when H. B. Adams wrote his twenty-eighth report to Raymond, the idea that the *Nashville* could be bottled up in Southampton by the forces of British rule and British law had already become a point of honor among the Unionists in London. People has lost their equanimity. Saying one moment that this time

England would positively help them, saying the next that England conceivably might refuse to help them, the resident loyal citizens of the United States had worked themselves into a state of aggravated curiosity, hope, indignation, and suspense.

The disorder was apparent in Henry's paragraphs. He predicted in the report that the English at last would respond to Union protests. "The opinion among sound men here is that this Government ought to interfere, and there is confidence felt that this time we shall receive the treatment one great nation deserves to receive at the hands of another." But he said as well in different tones, " . . . I feel confident that they will not refuse justice now, when it is clearly on our side, and when the peaceful relations of the two countries depend on it."

In still other passages, he explained that difficulties about the *Nashville* might cause a severance of diplomatic relations. "No one doubts that unless the British Government acts in an honorable and straightforward manner, there will be an immediate rupture. . . ." And he even went on to describe in practical terms what the rupture would entail. " . . . the refusal of redress on their part, would be followed by an immediate suspension of diplomatic relations on ours, and . . . the departure of the Ministers from London and Washington at the earliest moment possible. . . ."

That same Saturday, November 23, 1861, during the evening hours, Earl Russell sent assurances to Mr. Adams that the *Nashville* would be restrained from increasing her armament. The Sunday morning newspapers contained official announcements to the same effect. Indeed, from the younger Adams's point of view, Sunday was "one glowing day" of triumph. A Reuter's messenger came to the legation with word that a Union naval force under Admiral Dupont, supported by troops under General Thomas Sherman, had seized Port Royal in South Carolina as a blockading center for the Union fleet off Charleston Harbor.[11] First reported in London as a Union disaster, the landing turned out in the telegram to have been a thorough victory, intelligently planned and resolutely executed.

As expected, on Monday, November 25, the elder Adamses left for Yorkshire.[12] At the legation, Henry caught the sound of irritating news from Southampton about the *Nashville*. Far from staying neutral, the English in that city were demonstrating Confederate sympathies. He shortly reported about their conduct: " . . . the people of Southampton were showing very active sympathy with the vessel and her officers. It was said that many of the principal men of the city were going on board . . . and were dined and feted by Captain PEGRAM, whom in return they were introducing everywhere as a friend and a hero."

These annoyances were as nothing compared to those that followed. On Monday, the lawyers retained by the Union consuls went before the British magistrates at Southampton, asking for a search warrant against the *Nashville*. Young Adams's account went on to say: "The magistrates, headed by a stupid and wrong-headed Dogberry named *ENGLEDUE*, refused to entertain the motion, and comtemptuously referred it to the Foreign Office. Turned off in this manner at Southampton, our lawyers came back to London, and PEGRAM and YANCEY set up a howl of triumph over their victory, which the *Times* joined in. The next day was Tuesday, and our lawyers at once applied to Earl RUSSELL, at the Foreign Office, for the warrant. . . . They were received with the assurance that Lord RUSSELL had no power to grant such a warrant."

The failure of the English magistrates and foreign minister to help the Unionists in such an hour became a cause of furious rage and thoughts of violence. "It now began to look as though we were refused common justice, and there were no means in England of bringing this case into the courts. . . . These refusals, even to listen to their wishes, produced an anger [among the Unionists in England] such as can hardly be described. All sorts of propositions were afloat; to burn the Nashville; to blow her up; to cut her out and sink her. . . . This was the state of mind among all the loyal Americans; a feeling of humiliation and recklessness. . . ."

At the legation on Wednesday morning, November 27, 1861, "nervous as wild beasts," Henry Adams, Benjamin Moran, and Charles Wilson waited to learn what new trouble would befall.[13] At 12:30 P.M., the three secretaries received a telegram from Consul Britton at Southampton informing them that the *La Plata,* arriving early from St. Thomas, brought indisputable reports that Captain Charles Wilkes of the U. S. Navy, famous as one of the discoverers of Antarctica, now commander of the powerful Union sloop-of-war *San Jacinto,* had stopped the British mail ship *Trent* on November 8 in the Old Bahama Channel north of Cuba by firing an explosive shell across the vessel's path. Under orders from Captain Wilkes, a party led by Lieutenant Fairfax had left the *San Jacinto,* gone aboard the *Trent,* and forcibly seized the Confederate envoys, Mason and Slidell, together with their secretaries. The seizure of the rebel diplomats had occurred in the face of protests by the *Trent's* master, Captain Moir, and further protests by a British naval officer, Commander Williams, aboard in charge of mail and government despatches. The four prisoners had been taken onto the *San Jacinto*, which had steamed away in the direction of New York.[14]

Adams, Moran, and Wilson knew at once that the armed capture of the Confederate special commissioners was a Union "declaration of war" against Great Britain. Their nerves abraded beyond endurance, all three secretaries "broke into shouts of delight." The Legation's walls and ceilings resounded with their cheers.[15] Moran recorded, "That the capture of these arch-rebels gave us great satisfaction at the first blush, was natural: & we gave free vent to our exultation."[16]

They sped a telegram of their own to Minister Adams in Yorkshire, advising him that a Union warship had seized the rebel envoys and urging his immediate return to London.[17] During the afternoon, as they considered more fully what had happened in the Old Bahama Channel, their pleasure grew more profound. Since fate intended that there should be another war between the United States and England, it was a joy to them that an American, a great sailor and explorer, should have acted with manly vigor and struck the first blow. For them peculiarly, the blow afforded the double sweetness of aggression and retaliation. By stopping a British ship and insulting the British flag, Captain Wilkes had given the Unionists in London an instantaneous revenge against the ruling of Justice Engledue at Southampton, a reply to the inactivity of Earl Russell at the Foreign Office, an answer to the triumphant talk of Captain Pegram and Commissioner Yancey in the latter's office in Suffolk Street, and a recompense for the failures of the blockade, the disappearance of Captain Marchand, and even the panic at Bull Run.

In the evening, second Secretary Moran experienced a change of heart. He lamented the event and wrote, " . . . it seems as if the demons of darkness were against us." His own ambition had been to stay in England, and now his hope had been defeated. Sickened and all but overcome, he set down an impassioned complaint against the aged leader of the British government. " . . . Lord Palmerston has deliberately determined to force us into a war with England," the injured diplomat recorded.

> With a malicious wickedness his worst enemy could hardly think of charging him with, he has been playing into the hands of the rebels from the first: and with the aid of the *Times* he has been disseminating falsehoods about our en-

mity to England, until he has succeeded in making the people of these realms believe that enormous lie that we are doing all we can to involve them in a war. He is a foe of freedom. . . . His hatred of us is a boyish passion, strengthened by accumulated years. As he was Secretary at War in 1812 [,] he feels that his life and name will not be free from tarnish unless he can expunge us from the earth, and to do so he must be quick.[18]

While Moran went one way, in the direction of distress and accusation, the younger Adams and Wilson went another, towards the extremer regions of "savage exultation." The private secretary and the secretary of legation left the solitudes of Mansfield Street and Portland Place to seek frequented haunts where they could watch the amazed responses of their stolid English hosts. To the full, in Henry's phrase, they enjoyed "the satisfaction of seeing the English suffer under as great a load of bitterness as any under which we have groaned."

The phrase was not too strong, for people everywhere in England were beside themselves with astonishment and painful incredulity. The younger Adams's recollections, sent three days later to the *New York Times*, evoked the commotion of Wednesday afternoon and Wednesday evening. "Never for many years has any event created such an excitement here as this. On 'Change people seemed bewildered; they could not believe what they read, and would not make up their minds, for a time, what to think. Then Consols began to fall. . . . Railroad securities fell alarmingly. The universal cry was war. . . . A few cool men still maintained their self-control, and discouraged all such talk, but all that evening the war fever raged with great violence, and universal confusion and panic prevailed."

How the three Union secretaries passed the later hours of the evening is now unknown. One imagines that Moran went quickly to his lodgings and that Adams and Wilson—whom Adams rather liked—had continued to celebrate.[19] At all events, at midnight, a note from Foreign Secretary Russell was delivered at the legation requesting that Minister Adams call at the Foreign Office for an interview at 2:00 P.M. on Thursday. Both that night and in the morning, Henry Adams disdained to recognize the note's existence. Although the fact was manifest that his father would not arrive from Yorkshire in time to meet Earl Russell at the hour he had selected, the private secretary, in his passion, allowed the note to go without an answer.[20]

London meanwhile endured a night of long-to-be-remembered

chaos. Members of the Liberal cabinet were thrown into varied states of excitement and concern. Typically, Gladstone appeared at a friend's for dinner carrying the newspaper cutting about the seizure of the envoys.[21] Palmerston, according to a story about him later believed by his biographer Philip Guedalla, went to the Confederate office in Pall Mall. There, standing before a map, he discussed with Dudley Mann probable future British naval operations against the eastern seaports of the United States. "New York and Philadelphia were mentioned as points of attack for a British squadron; and there was even talk of some combined operation with General Johnston's [Confederate] army, which would result in the capture of Washington . . . ."[22]

Obliged to attend a funeral mass in honor of the late king of Portugal, Moran did not arrive at the legation office on Thursday morning, November 28, at his usual hour. Asked at the funeral by other diplomats whether there indeed would be a war between his country and Great Britain, the second secretary, in his own words, had "thought it prudent to be quiet." Arriving at the office, he found John Bright—the Union's most heartfelt supporter in the House of Commons—deploring the act of Captain Wilkes. Moran was also struck to notice that Wilson and H. B. Adams were talking indiscreetly to chance visitors about the crisis. Then he learned to his astonishment that an urgent note from Earl Russell to Minister Adams, delivered the night before, had been permitted to lie about unanswered.

Deciding to answer it himself, Moran drove quickly to the Foreign Office and advised the proper officials there of Minister Adams's absence from the city and the unavoidable lapse of time till he returned. When he again crossed the legation's threshold on Mansfield Street, the assistant secretary pressed through a swarm of visitors who were taxing Wilson and the younger Adams with anxious inquiries. Talk of war was unabated. *The Times* that morning had been unexpectedly dispassionate and cool; but other London papers, in the opinion of Moran, were "violent in the extreme, and yet seem in a mist."[23]

Just so, in mists themselves, the Unionists at the legation, visitors and secretaries alike, were groping about in mingled ignorance and impulsive certainty. They agreed, changed their minds, and disagreed, in circles.

Mr. and Mrs. Adams reached London in time for dinner. Because he would be working far beyond his usual hours, Moran stayed with the family and shared their meal. He learned at the table that the telegram sent to Yorkshire the day before had been handed to the minister in tranquil surroundings. The elder Adamses, with several other guests, were being shown by Monckton Milnes around the ruins of Pontefract Castle. C. F. Adams had opened and read the telegram, told the others what had happened in the West Indies, and continued to examine the ruins as before.

After everyone had returned to Fryston Hall, Mrs. Adams had grown acutely miserable. Although disposed to favor the Union against the Confederacy, her host and hostess seemed provoked by what had happened to the rebel envoys. It had been a relief for Mrs. Adams, when she and her husband were summoned away so urgently to London, but her calm husband had not been similarly assisted. The Chief expressed the gravest view of his official situation. Before the meal had ended, he said that orders for his departure might arrive from Washington by Christmas, in roughly thirty days.[24]

Earl Russell had moved the time of his interview with C. F. Adams to Friday at 1:45 P.M. When he faced the foreign secretary, the minister was asked—as he later wrote—"whether I had any information from my Government touching the matter [of the *San Jacinto* and the *Trent*] or was possessed of any light which it might be useful for him to possess." Mr. Adams was also asked afresh about the wanderings of the *James Adger* and the Navy Department's orders to Captain Marchand.

The elder Adams truthfully replied that he could not at all account for what had happened. He supposed that the seizure of the Confederate diplomats had been the brain child of Captain Wilkes, rather than of the government in Washington. Lacking actual knowledge on the point, he could not give strong assurances.[25]

Russell decided that the best way to deal with the problem now besetting the Foreign Office would be exclusively through Lord Lyons. The British minister in Washington was expected to prove a match for Secretary Seward.[26]

In this way, the U. S. minister to England was ejected from the drama. At 2:00 P.M., only minutes after C. F. Adams and Earl Russell ended their brief interview, the British cabinet would meet to decide its ground and plan the communications it would send to the government of the United States. But when the communications were sent, copies would *not* be furnished to Mr. Adams. Other men would conduct all the essential interchanges. He would be required to stand aside.[27]

The younger Adams ceased rejoicing. The affair of the *Trent*, Henry realized, was not as helpful as it had seemed. It placed loyal citizens like himself at the disadvantage of being completely mystified. All alike were at loss to know why the *San Jacinto* had fired a shell and stopped the British mail ship. Had Captain Wilkes been ordered by President Lincoln to seize the rebel commissioners? Had Wilkes contrived the exploit on his own initiative? Had an error supervened, some mistake in understanding orders, or a slip in their preparation? No American in London, whether on the Union or Confederate side, could begin to answer such questions; and, not knowing what to think or say, the Unionists were made to seem contemptible and insignificant.

Contrariwise, the rebel agents gained enormously in stature. Their new importance was further amplified by their purportedly acquiring a two-ship navy. Talk had started in Southampton to the effect that the *Nashville,* after all, would be permitted to increase its armament. And attention was given to a claim, first published the week before, that a similar paddle steamer, the *Pacific,* had been bought by the Confederate States and was in process of conversion for naval use in a Southampton dockyard.[28]

The ministry announced that 10,000 troops were leaving at once for Canada. Reputedly the lawyers for the Crown were agreed that the act of Captain Wilkes—despite abundant English precedents to support it—was illegal beyond a doubt. The London press had thrown off its last hesitations. The newspapers for Friday morning, November 29, particularly *The Times* and the *London Post,* both of which were thought to speak on great occasions directly for Lord Palmerston, were clearly written, according to Henry Adams, in the expectation "that the result of the Cabinet Council held in the afternoon would be an impracticable demand on the American Government [in Washington], and hostilities consequent on its rejection." In plainer language, the English press had said an ultimatum would go to Washington; the United States would defy it; and a war, desired by both countries, would instantly break out.

In stolen moments on Friday, during the night, and on Saturday in time to catch the mail, the younger Adams wrote a long report to Raymond, his twenty-ninth, dated November 30, 1861. While he was writing it, the son was meditating the fateful news that his father would not be permitted to participate directly in the interchanges between the governments of the United States and Great Britain. It is not impossible that Henry regarded his father's exclusion as a help. C. F. Adams was a manifestly honest man, so much so that Earl Russell ought to have remained perfectly sure of it while they talked at the

Foreign Office, but the U. S. minister's honesty was not conjoined to insight and information. Thus handicapped in the midst of so titanic an "explosion" as now had started, the Chief could neither speak nor act with the implicit authority needed to carry conviction and shape events.

The son knew nothing about Captain Wilkes that the father did not know, but the son at least was capable of making fairly accurate judgements of Seward and Lincoln—persons of great importance in the case. Moreover, the son had *not* been excluded from his own business—not at all. To begin his twenty-ninth report, he needed to do nothing more than pick up the narrative he had started about the *Nashville* in his twenty-eighth. This Henry took pains to do, describing in vivid detail what had happened day by day, until he reached the present moment. He brought his narrative to a climax by saying about the government and people of Great Britain: " . . . as it is now evident that the Government means to take a war ground, the overwhelming majority of the people applaud and support the decision. There can be no doubt that war is staring us in the face."

Adams's view of his function as London correspondent of the *New York Times* had never ended, had only begun, with his telling the latest news. His reports had always urged courses, suggested measures, promoted policies. In the present instance, without deserting his former willingness to speak, he seemed to write with extreme deliberation, almost with reluctance. He said in the new report: "It is a state of things much to be regretted. Indeed it is overwhelming."

Yielding to the terrific truth that the mere secession and rebellion of the Southerners at home had brought on a transatlantic conflict, possibly involving not only the United States, the Confederate States, Canada, and Great Britain, but also France and Spain, even Russia, he looked back at the stroke which had ignited the explosion. It seemed to him that the seizure of Mason and Slidell from the deck of a British mail ship, even if defensible under law, was indefensible in every way that mattered. He believed the act to have been a "blunder."

Saying so in his report, he also said that war with England need not have come. The British government, he said, had been opposed to war. He was entirely convinced that the Liberal cabinet, Lord Palmerston with the rest, had meant to avoid a quarrel. He stated categorically, "This Government did not want to have a war, nor would it accept one now, except that it knows that popular opinion demands it, and in the present excited state of the public mind, strong measures are necessary."

He understood the grievances recently stored up by the United States against Great Britain. He explained in his report that a later conflict, begun at a well-chosen moment in 1862, would have given the great Republic an ampler and easier redress. "Six months more would have decided our civil war," he continued, "and then if we liked, we might have taken Great Britain in hand, but as our affairs now stand, a foreign war was neither necessary nor expedient."

Moving on to another topic, he pointed out that a way was open for the Unionists to stop their war with England just as it was starting. The way was simply to encourage the English Radicals and all others in England who cared for freedom and hated slavery. *"If our Government hopes to maintain itself, it must now act with all the vigor or all the violence that can be used. The slaves, wherever we can get at them, must be freed and armed.* Such a measure would still have great effect here, notwithstanding the bitterness of feeling against the North, for no Englishman would like to appear as the upholder of the slave system, and it would give our friends courage to come out again in opposition to the war policy."

Always practical, young Adams knew that his suggestion, although the best that he so far had been able to think of, was far from likely to be adopted by the government in Washington. He allowed himself to offer the impracticable suggestion because he had sincerely favored the emancipation of the slaves in the United States, thought the blacks entitled to their freedom, and would not give up his antislavery principles in any situation, no matter how intimidating.

Really, in the case of his present report to the *New York Times*, his object was not to tell the government in Washington what it should or should not do. It seemed probable to him that the British government was about to make some demands upon the Lincoln administration, that the Republicans in charge of the United States government were already resolved to turn back the British ultimatum, and that the outcome was as good as pre-decided. He therefore reported that the people of London were looking forward to three eventualities. "It is supposed that the first step of this Government [,] on the rejection of its demands, will be to send our Minister his passports; the second, to recognize the South; the third, to raise the blockade. How much of this is really decided upon, I will not venture to say, but it seems to be all a logical sequence, and people here are preparing for the crash."

Adams found energy that same day to write a striking communication to his brother. He bluntly said to Charles about the British, "This nation means to make war."

Whether the war were really fought or not, the younger brother went on to state, the many embarrassments arising for Minister Adams in connection with the *James Adger*, the *Nashville*, the *Pacific*, and especially the *San Jacinto* and the *Trent*, had so undermined the standing of their father as a diplomat that his continuance in England had become impossible. The third son said of the legation, " . . . I consider that we are dished. . . ."

Henry turned to the tragic predicament of John Bright in the Midlands and that of Meredith Townsend and his fellow editors in the office of the *London Spectator*. The latter group, true friends of the United States, had asked Henry to visit them, hoping for consolation, which he had not been able to provide. Their case was worse than his. At least he had a country to go home to, while they, at home already, were facing indefinite obloquy and ostracism.

Again and again in his private letter, restless Henry came back to the mysterious removal of Mason and Slidell from the *Trent*. Obliged to choose between believing that the blunder of seizing the commissioners had originated with Captain Wilkes on his sloop-of-war, with Seward at the State Department, or Lincoln in the White House, he had begun by choosing Seward.[29] On the assumption that the choice was right, he said to Charles about the secretary of state, " . . . if he means war . . . or to run as close as he can without touching, then I say that Mr[.] Seward is the greatest criminal we've had yet."

Were it true, Henry reasoned, that Seward *had* conceived a plan and Wilkes was helping to put it into practice, then the question in Washington had become the plain one of revolution. The Union would have to eject the Republicans from the executive branch by any means that offered. "If the Administration ordered the capture of those men," he declared, "I am satisfied that our present authorities are very unsuitable persons to conduct a war like this or to remain in the direction of our affairs."

As nearly as Henry could know, given present information, the legation in London had been betrayed by its parent agencies in Washington. The betrayal had taken the form of deliberate silence. "The Government," he said, "has left us in the most awkward and unfair position. They have given no warning that such an act was thought of. . . ."

It seemed impossible to guess with exactness what would happen to the family and the official secretaries. " . . . a very few weeks," Henry

conjectured, "may see us either on our way home or on the continent."
But leaving England was a prospect all five Adamses at the Legation
would welcome heartily.

For himself, he absolutely longed to get away. " . . . I feel like
going off and taking up my old German life again. . . . " "I am half-
mad with vexation and despair."

## 25 / *The Bell*

Obliged to follow the course of the British government by buying English newspapers, the members of the U.S. legation read that Foreign Secretary Russell, after two cabinet councils on Friday and Saturday, November 29 and 30, 1861, had drafted an ultimatum to the United States government demanding reparations for the act of Captain Wilkes. The text of the ultimatum reportedly had been sent for review and approval to Queen Victoria and Prince Albert. When given final form, it would be sent to Lord Lyons in Washington by the *Europa*, leaving England immediately, on Sunday, December 1. As yet, the precise severity of the demand set forth in Russell's note remained unknown to the British press—and thus to the legation.[1]

Barred from knowing what he most wished to learn, the younger Adams went back to what had happened in the Old Bahama Channel. The seizure of the rebel diplomats had been viewed two different ways when it occurred, one way by the British aboard the *Trent* and the other by the naval officers and crew of the *San Jacinto*. The account which had reached Southampton by the *La Plata* the previous Wednesday had described the seizure as it had been regarded on the *Trent*. The other side of the story, the *San Jacinto* side, had been only dimly visible. Yet one element of the other side had been known to Adams from the beginning. Lieutenant Fairfax, the American naval officer in charge of the boarding party that carried off the special commissioners and their secretaries, had stated while on the *Trent* that the seizure had been ordered by Captain Wilkes on his own initiative.

In an editorial on Saturday, November 30, *The Times* had taken note of the lieutenant's declaration. "We hear there is a possiblity that the seizure was the act of the American commander, and was not expressly directed by his Government. Lieutenant FAIRFAX, of the San Jacinto, said, we are informed, on board the Trent, that his commanding officer acted on his own responsibility." But John

Thadeus Delane had not repeated the Union lieutenant's words in order to believe them. The English editor had ideas of his own about American affairs, and they were hostile to the Union in a very high degree. In the same editorial, *The Times* looked back upon the recent actions of the United States towards Great Britain as a "series of insults of which the outrage on the Trent is the last and most offensive." Also the editorial adduced a number of reasons for concluding that it had been the "Washington authorities," and *not* Captain Wilkes, who had "secretly planned the outrage for which we are now asking reparation."[2]

On Sunday as planned, the courier entrusted with the British ultimatum sailed on the *Europa*.

On Monday, December 2, Adams received through the mail issues of the *New York Times* through November 20, brought to Liverpool on the *Persia*. From them he learned that, following the seizure of the envoys, Captain Wilkes had ordered the *San Jacinto*, not to New York, but instead into Chesapeake Bay, to Fortress Monroe near Washington. There, while one of his subordinates rushed to the Navy Department with word that Mason and Slidell were captured, Wilkes reportedly had gone ashore and freely stated that he alone had conceived the act.

Adams also learned that Raymond had scored a journalistic coup. Beginning with the outbreak of war on April 12, the editor had been publishing his paper on Sundays as well as weekdays, an innovation in New York City. The news of Wilkes's action had chanced to reach that city too late for its other papers to publish the story on Saturday but in good time for Raymond's paper to publish it on Sunday, November 17, with copious details. The coup, while partly lucky, reflected Raymond's personal qualities. Such an editor had it in him to put his rivals out of business.[3]

Even sooner than Henry Adams, in the very early hours of that same Monday morning, John Delane and his editorial assistants had snatched up the *New York Times* of November 17. After reading it with what they thought sufficient care, they wrote and published a new editorial, this one about the declaration reportedly uttered at Fortress Monroe by Captain Wilkes. The new editorial was almost friendly to the Union. It admitted that "the Captain of the San Jacinto seems to have acted very much on his own responsibility."

Long exposure to *The Times* had acquainted loyal Unionists in England with the melancholy fact that Delane, on a given day, might pour oil on troubled waters, and the next day, if he pleased, set the oil on fire. That the English editor would do just that in the present case was certain; for day after day in New York, in a series of editorials, Raymond had made the seizure of Mason and Slidell the subject of remarks which from the English point of view were themselves insulting.

Adams's political associate and secret employer in America had greeted the behavior of Captain Wilkes as a means of national redemption. Raymond had extolled the stopping of the *Trent* and the forcible removal of the Confederate envoys from its deck as entirely legal and wholly beneficial. On November 17, in his initial outburst, the editor had suggested, in earnest, that the United States of America should consecrate in the captain's honor "another *Fourth* of July."

The meaning of that holiday considered, the phrase the American editor had used could only be understood by English readers as a bragging jibe directed at themselves. Yet, in the same editorial, Raymond had blithely guessed that the English would surely not object to what had happened. "We have not the slightest idea that England will even remonstrate," the New York editor had said. "On the contrary, she will applaud the gallant act. . . ."

After a day of calm, on Tuesday, December 3, using language seldom published in any journal, *The Times* replied in London to the seeming Yankee insolence of Raymond in New York. "It is evident," the great British newspaper exclaimed, "that if England shall be found ready to eat dirt there is no lack of Americans ready to cram it down our throat."

Lest readers should wonder which Americans were chiefly meant, Delane's great newspaper went on to say: "The *New York Times* has not the slightest idea that England will even remonstrate. On the contrary, she will applaud the gallant act. The same journal thinks that the question of the Trent will form a subject for English party politics, the Liberals being in favour of the seizure and the Tories against it."[4]

That Tuesday, Adams compared the errors and excesses of the two newspapers. The moral he evidently drew from the comparison was that troubles were breeding faster than any single person could try to mend them. He might himself be able to teach a measure of common sense to the moonstruck *New York Times,* but he doubted that any mortal could impart good sense and good will to *The Times* of London.

Seward understood the importance of the press. The secretary of state had brought about the appointment of John Bigelow, coeditor of the *New York Evening Post,* as consul general in Paris. Bigelow had not been given consular duties of any usual description. He had been sent to France with the intention that he influence the Paris press in favor of the Union.

Thurlow Weed had not been given a public office and salary, like Bigelow, and was not a man who found such things either needful or convenient. It was Seward's intention, however, that Weed, if possible, should influence the London press in favor of the Union, and that Weed and Bigelow should coordinate their efforts.

Even in the absence of knowing either man, Henry Adams had begun to feel a sense of fellowship with Weed and Bigelow. This sense apparently grew in part from knowledge Adams had of their proposed activities. It also grew from the independent work he had started, attempting to form acquaintanceships with London editors. Some time might pass before he could learn in detail about the first efforts of Bigelow, helped by Weed, in Paris, and before Weed could learn about his own in London.[5]

Weed and his daughter had hardly settled themselves at the Hotel de l'Europe in Paris when he learned that the U.S. Navy had taken four Confederate diplomats from the deck of a British mail ship. Not a person to shrink from acting on his best judgment, the Albany Republican had started writing letters from his hotel room. He wrote especially to Seward, urging that President Lincoln and the cabinet lose no time. Weed said that they should immediately surrender the Confederate captives to Lord Lyons—either that or equally counteract the folly of Captain Wilkes by some other gesture of good will toward the British government and people.

While Weed continued writing, on December 2, John Bigelow called and made a suggestion of his own. The consul general was an optimist. He took the unusual view that Wilkes's act, even if directed by the United States government, could hardly become the start of a general war in the North Atlantic world, an immense conflagration, catching up the Americans, the French, the British, and Heaven only knew how many other nations in its flames. Bigelow wished to write and publish an influential letter denying that Wilkes had been instructed to seize the rebel diplomats, and denying in the bargain that his doing so would end in war. The consul, while anxious to write the letter, was still more anxious that it be made to seem the work of General Scott, and receive the general's signature. What Bigelow wanted Weed to do was get the general's cooperation.

Weed hurried to the Hotel Westminster and persuaded Scott to support the enterprise. Bigelow raced to his office, wrote the letter, brought it to Scott by 2:00 P.M., and read it aloud for his approval. Triumphant, he saw the general sign it.

Bigelow set in motion the arduous process of distributing sufficient copies of the letter, in translation, to meet the needs of the Paris press. Weed had several copies of the original English text prepared immediately. When they were ready, that same afternoon, Tuesday, December 2, he left for England.

In London, Weed promptly distributed the copies to several newspapers. Visiting American bankers in the financial district, he asked them to appraise the situation. To his dismay, they told him that war between the United States and England was a practical certainty. He wrote at once to Bigelow, "If bankers are well informed [,] things are at their worst, with slight chance for improvement."[6]

A Quaker and a deeply religious man, John Bright was unafraid of any contest he might be dared to enter by the designs of Providence. He had reacted to the news from the West Indies by writing urgent letters from London to a friend in Washington, Senator Charles Sumner, entreating the senator to exert himself on behalf of peace. Then, to the regret of the Adamses at the legation, Bright went home to Lancashire.[7]

The weekly mailbag for the legation, sent from the State Department in time to go aboard the *Persia* in New York, was accidentally misrouted in England and did not reach its destination until Tuesday, one day late. Tormented by the delay, the minister and his secretaries were tortured to the limit of their endurance when they discovered that the bag contained not a word about the action of Captain Wilkes. Moran spoke for everyone at the legation when he recorded: " . . . I was sick at heart . . . [that] there was nothing from Washington on this trouble. . . . This is what may be called the extreme of cruel folly."[8]

The second secretary believed that the crisis in England was taking the worst imaginable shape. Control of events in the British Isles had passed from the hands of the government into those of the people. The transfer had been effected by the relentless editors of the daily press. That fearful Tuesday, December 3, the assistant secretary was moved to write: " . . . the excitement in England is truly terrific. . . . By . . . asserting that Capt. Wilkes' act was an authorized and deliberate insult of our Gov't, the journals have lashed the nation into a most indecent rage, and . . . mob rule reigns supreme. . . ."

Although the disturbance shaking London had started in America, where English-speaking persons were engaged in a civil war they partly seemed anxious *not* to wage, the disturbance promised to increase in violence because of disputes in England between Englishmen mortally opposed to one another and prepared to quarrel. On Wednesday, December 4, a two-man war broke out in England between John Bright and John Delane.

Bright spoke that evening at a banquet at Rochdale. His speech was calm, persuasive, and prophetic. He took issue with those English savants—Bulwer-Lytton, for one—who had said in public that "the United States should be severed, and that the North American continent should be as the continent of Europe is, in many States, and subject to all the contentions and disasters which have [disturbed] . . . the States of Europe." The speaker exhorted his English auditors to accept the possibility that the great democracy in the West, far from being broken up, might be extended to embrace the continent, including British Canada. " . . . if a man had a great heart within him, he would . . . look forward to the day when . . . the whole of that vast continent might become one great confederation of States,—without a great army, and without a great navy,—not mixing itself up with the entanglements of European politics,—without a custom-house inside . . . and with freedom everywhere, equality everywhere, law everywhere, peace everywhere. . . ."

The fearless Radical charged *The Times* with doing all it could to "poison" people's minds in Great Britain against the United States. He accused "our great advisers of the *Times*" of having spread the deliberate falsehood that the stopping of the *Trent* was "merely one of a series of acts which denote the determination of the Washington government to pick a quarrel."[9]

As rapidly as Bright could speak in Lancashire, the newsgatherers of *The Times* were scooping up his words and transmitting them to London for publication. All that night, the pressmen at Printing House Square labored to complete the issue of their newspaper for Thursday, December 5. It contained the full text of Bright's speech, a factual account of the Rochdale banquet, and three elaborate editorials, or "leaders," assailing the speaker with destructive epithets and barbs.

While first bundles of the issue were coming onto the streets, in the early hours of the morning, John Delane rode to St. James's Park. One of the finest military units in the empire, Vesey's Battery, was parading there. Knowing that they were leaving straightway for

Canada, the editor watched the superbly accoutred artillerymen with approval.[10] But the editor's enemy in Lancashire was not without resources. Later in the day, Bright would resume and intensify his appeals to Sumner in Washington. In a new private letter, he would urge the senator to begin an effort to have the *Trent* affair submitted to international arbitration. Bright explained that "a courageous stroke, not of arms, but of moral action, may save you and us."

Traces of desperation were discernible in the Quaker's words to his friend across the ocean. Bright cared greatly that the Americans not be hurt. "I dread the consequences of war quite as much for your sakes as for our own." Yet he wrote to Sumner as if his ties to his own people were being severed rapidly. Were war to start between their countries, he told the statesman in Washington, he himself would "retire from public life entirely, and no longer give myself to the vain hope of doing good among the fools and dupes and knaves with whom it is my misfortune to live. . . ."[11]

Very early on Friday, December 6, Thurlow Weed left his hotel and "went down to St. James's Park Barracks to see a regiment of Guards take up their line of march for Canada." Born in 1797, tall and slender, with gray hair, Weed had been a soldier in the War of 1812. Watching the resplendent Guards, he was unexpectedly moved by a surge of patriotic anger. Forgotten British oppressions leapt into the forefront of his awareness. In the words of his own account: "Nearly fifty years had elapsed since I had seen 'British red-coats'. . . . Something of the old feeling—a feeling which I supposed had died out—began to rise, and, after a few moments of painful thought, I turned away."[12]

A few minutes afterwards, the elderly politician was eating breakfast at the Royal Cambridge Hotel in Hanover Square when he was handed the card of the secretary of the U.S. legation, Mr. Charles L. Wilson. Invited to the dining room, the secretary asked Mr. Weed at what hour he could conveniently be visited by Minister Adams. Till then, a coolness had separated the Adamses and the man from Albany—a coolness felt on the Adams side, not on his own. Wanting the separation ended at the earliest possible instant, Weed accompanied the secretary at once to the legation.[13]

Necessarily, his reputation for managing other people, and causing things to happen without revealing how he did it, arrived ahead of him. The members of the legation were prepared to dislike him. They all immediately liked him. Moran spoke their common opinion when he recorded that their newest visitor, with his "marked & intellectual face," possessed the evident advantage of a "strong mind." "I had never seen [him] before," the assistant secretary noted, "and confess myself favorably impressed by him."[14]

Weed talked at length with C. F. Adams in his study. The visitor recorded that the minister—feeling "very despondent"—"saw no possibility of averting war with England except by the release of Messrs. Mason and Slidell." Weed himself, as he well knew, had started out on that precise assumption nine days before, when he began to write privately to Seward from Paris, urging the government in Washington to surrender the captured rebel diplomats to Lord Lyons just as fast as the British minister would take them. The unofficial emissary had wanted the Lincoln administration to sur-render the captives as a *voluntary* act. But a British ultimatum had gone to Washington on December 1, and since then the British press had learned that the ultimatum made the surrender of the captives *compulsory.*

Minister Adams had two observations to make about the demand imposed by the Liberal ministry. First, Mr. Adams gravely doubted that the administration in Washington or the people of the United States could be induced to yield the captives by any agency or suasion whatsoever. Second, he said the British government wanted war in any case.

Part of the secret of Weed's political wizardry was that he could listen. In his report to Bigelow, he summarized the main thing he had heard the elder Adams assert, putting it into a pithy sentence: "The Ministry[,] long believing we meant to pick a quarrel with England, choose their own time, making the *Trent* affair the occasion and pretext."[15]

The unofficial emissary was not attempting, in this summary, to tell Bigelow that the British rulers wanted war. Weed was warning the optimist in Paris that there was a pessimist in London. The Albany politician had gotten at the heart of C. F. Adams's considered judg-ment. If the minister were to be believed, a war *was* being started, not by Wilkes, or Seward, or Lincoln, but by Palmerston and Russell.

Weed and Bigelow, of course, would form their own opinions.

Henry Adams in recent days had written no letters for General Scott to sign, had not distributed copies of an important document to the Paris and London press, had not hurried across the Channel, made a speech, or published editorials demolishing his favorite enemy. He may even have avoided watching artillerymen and guards parading on the drill field adjoining St. James's Barracks. But his newer experiences had had the merit of sharp definition.

More or less from the instant they first shook hands, he had seen that he and Thurlow Weed, despite their difference of more than forty years in age, were fellow spirits and natural friends. It seemed strange, in fact extremely strange, but Weed came closer to fulfilling young Adams's ideal of political ability and address than any politician he had ever seen, his unforgotten grandfather not excepted.[16]

The private secretary may possibly have been absent from the study when the minister and Mr. Weed had their first long conversation. If so, the things that Weed had heard were repetitions of things that Henry had already heard his father say in other interchanges. The son was quite aware of what the minister believed.

It was easy for the younger Adams to forgive the elder's errors, which were palpably the result of personal disappointment. Two days earlier, on Wednesday, the Chief had written a letter to John Lothrop Motley in Vienna which Henry, as a matter of routine, had copied into the minister's letter book. In the letter, the minister to England had told the minister to Austria, "I am here quietly waiting the development of events over which I have no control, and in which I had no participation."[17]

Now, on Friday, the father had written a strongly worded letter to Seward in Washington. Saying that he foresaw a break in diplomatic relations between the United States and England, the minister advised the secretary of state that he and his secretaries were hastening the completion of the legation's ordinary, lesser business, preparatory to departure. Clearly the anomaly of holding an office and not being permitted to perform it had wounded the elder Adams deeply. Needing release from the pain the anomaly imposed, he was shaping his interpretation of events in ways that would assure him that his release was imminent.[18]

The greatest difference the week had made for Henry was not the discovery of a friend but the realization that, after all, he wished to stay in London. This volte-face had been much assisted by his receiving more issues of purblind Raymond's *New York Times*. It was wonderful, the things that were happening in the editor's distinguished newspaper. A quick thinker, Raymond had foreseen that the government of the United States might possibly apologize to the British government for the manner in which Mason and Slidell had had to be taken from the British mail ship in the direction of a Union prison.

The editor had said from the beginning, however, that all good Americans would agree in resolving to "hold on to the prisoners."[19] In never-changing editorials, Raymond was pounding the drum of that one main idea.

With Raymond, Adams had experienced none of the troubles which earlier had terminated his relationship with Hale. What the correspondent mailed in London the *New York Times* was publishing when received, as received, without delays or changes.[20] Something far more important than an editor's willingness and trust could be discerned in this phenomenon. For months on end, citizens, editors, and politicians in the Northern states had been noticing the weekly reports from the nameless American correspondent of the *Times* in London; and the practice had ceased to be an act of curiosity and had become a reliance. The correspondent's voice was being heard, and all the more so because his hearers were *not* concerned to ask whose voice it was.

The British press had ascertained that the ultimatum sent on the *Europa* had demanded not only the surrender of the Confederate diplomats but also arrangement of the surrender within the space of seven days. The stipulation had a meaning for Henry Adams which he could fully appreciate and welcome. Any communication from England meant to be read in America in time to redirect the opinions of the daily press and to influence the decision of the president and cabinet would have to be completed and mailed on the morrow, Saturday, in time to go aboard the Cunard steamer.

In practical ways the most important of all his early writings, Adams's thirtieth report to the *New York Times*, dated December 7, 1861, was also an example of his most effective early style. Less adaptable than Weed, less eloquent than Bright, less guarded than his father, he excelled them in spontaneity and directness; also perhaps in grasp and closeness to the problem. He wrote:

> . . . some strange frenzy, seems to have seized the English nation. The phlegmatic and dogmatic Englishman has been dragged into a state of literal madness, and though not actually riotous, he has lost all his power of self-control. He is seldom well-informed on any but English subjects looked at from a national point of view; he is often sullen, dogged, and unsocial. But in these December days it is worse than all this; it is sheer, downright national insanity, cropping out in

the characteristic forms in which his greatness and weakness always proclaims itself. It is Ajax raving about the lost armor and the slight he has suffered; stupid, brutal Ajax, self-confident and deaf to reason or entreaty.

His December 7 report outlined the events of a "weary, anxious, troubled week." Not yet recognized by the English government, the Confederate States of America had been as much as recognized by the English people. "At present . . . the Confederate flag is to be seen flying side by side with our own on the Adelphi Theatre in the Strand . . . while ragged boys are peddling the glorious emblem of Slavery at a penny a-piece, on the steps of Exeter Hall."

A transformation had occurred at the rebel office on Suffolk Street. " . . . the Secessionists are in raptures," the correspondent reported. "They have cast off even the last appearance of doubt, and swagger up and down, boasting of their certain triumph. The *Nashville* has gone into dock at Southampton, and her commander declares that she will be ready for service about the 1st of January."

War had not begun; yet the British were already waging it in numerous ways. "Every day brings its new list of war-measures taken by the Government, and the workmen in their arsenals are employed day and night. . . . Business men are preparing for the storm; industry is slackened; prices fall; everything shows that the English nation expects a serious shock, and that it will not seek to avoid it."

Most ominous was the monolithic uniformity of feeling. "Never was such unanimity shown in England. None such existed before the war with Russia, nor has the feeling against Austria or France ever compared in intensity or determination to that which now rages against us."

With his utmost strength, young Adams tried to affect the conduct of the president and cabinet in Washington. His suggestion was unusual for its plainness. The problem confronting both the Union-ists and the British had been muddled by the intrusion of legal quibbles. On all hands, writers and speakers were producing real or imagined precedents to show that Captain Wilkes had or had not violated international law and usage. Because the whole legal tradi-tion of the United States, and especially its official stance preceding and during the War of 1812, weighed in the balance against the captain and in favor of the neutral mail ship *Trent*, Adams was able to take the easy side in the legal hostilities.

Thus assisted, he compressed the main ideas of his report into ten sentences. " . . . I must start from the supposition that every American [in England] whose judgment is worth having is wholly against a war." He changed the subject to say in italics: *"Undoubtedly a majority of the British Ministry and of the commercial classes . . . are also against a war.* The apparent hurry in providing for it is partly a concession to popular feeling, and partly to show us that the thing is in earnest."

Claiming no originality for his ideas, he continued: "One proposition has gained many supporters here already. It is that which Gen. SCOTT has proposed, that . . . in strict *accordance with American principles, the four Confederates should be released and given up to the custody of Great Britain.*"

Mainly he spoke in favor of an immediate decision. "It is no business of mine to argue on this question. If these are the best terms we can get, we ought to take them."

That such a decision would rescue the two countries from war with one another seemed probable, and he believed no other decision could. " . . . if we can weather the next six weeks or so in safety, people will cool down and be in a humor to talk common sense. One thing is certain and useless to discuss. The surrender of the men must be the *sine qua non* of any proposition or hope of peace."

He mailed the report in good time, and it went safely aboard the *America* at Queenstown in Ireland.

While his report was carried westward, events implacably advanced. The Union spokesmen in England, their ultimate efforts already made, were required to start new efforts.

Thurlow Weed, during his first day in London, had learned that the duke of Newcastle had told and was repeating a story about the U.S. secretary of state. The story was one which English hearers were accepting as surely true and which loyal Unionists, in their hearts, could not entirely disbelieve. The story went that the duke himself, visiting the United States with the Prince of Wales several months before the outbreak of the secession troubles, had talked with then-Senator Seward at a dinner given by Governor Morgan of New York. Saying that he would probably be raised in the near future to a position of higher responsibility, Seward, according to the story, had said he would use his high position to "insult" the British government.[21]

Weed had brought with him to London some letters of introduction written for him by Seward in Washington. One introduced the unofficial emissary to Foreign Secretary Russell. Addressed to Earl Russell, it began, "Allow me to introduce to you Thurlow Weed, Esq., an eminent citizen of the State of New York, for many years my intimate personal and political friend."

With the help of the letter, Weed secured an invitation to Pembroke Lodge for Saturday, December 7. He talked with the foreign secretary for an hour without material result. They perhaps avoided the touchy subject of the story told by the duke of Newcastle. Not that Weed was slow to understand the story's great importance; for he perceived as soon as anyone that British fury, although roused by Wilkes, was aimed at Seward.[22]

Means of counteracting the duke's testimony, which undoubtedly was honest, were extremely difficult to come by. Would it help much to tell the infuriated English people, while troops were on their way to Canada, that William H. Seward had always been humorously inclined, especially after dinner? Would anything be gained by culling from his speeches lines agreeable to foreign countries and reassuring to Great Britain? American humor could not always be translated into the English idiom; and the secretary of state unfortunately had made speeches in St. Paul and elsewhere in 1860 which contemplated the absorption of Canada into the United States as an object to be desired.

Bishop McIlvaine arrived but brought no positive information about the attitude of Seward or the intentions of Lincoln and the cabinet.

Despatches from Seward came also but contained, in the phrase of the younger Adams, not "one single word as to the present question." The only hint in the despatches of an intended policy or eventual decision was a request that the legation look into a precedent, the case of the ship *Mercury*, from which an American diplomat had been carried off a captive in 1780. Such a request—at least in the judgment of Moran—seemed to indicate a disposition in Washington to confound the *Trent* affair in legal sophistries, a disposition regarded by the members of the legation with abhorrence.[23]

Issues of the *New York Times* through November 22, carried to Europe on the steamer *Edinburgh,* revealed to the secret correspondent inside the U.S. legation that Raymond was printing fervent editorials hailing the seizure of Mason and Slidell with undiminished jubilance.[24]

Coming from Boston, the *Niagara* brought news of proceedings the reverse of anything that loyal Unionists in Europe would want to know about. Captain Wilkes had been directed to move his ship to

Boston, taking his prisoners there for incarceration in Fort Warren. The Bostonians had greeted the captain as a savior. At a banquet held at the Revere House on November 26 in the captain's honor, Governor Andrew had singled out from the list of Wilkes's "illustrious services" one which had crowned "the exultation of the American heart." The captain's greatest merit, the governor declared, was his having fired a shot across the bow of a British ship.

A news report had also arrived on the *Niagara* from William Howard Russell to *The Times*. The "Special Correspondent" assured his readers in the British Isles that Lincoln and Seward could not surrender the rebel captives without disintegrating the government of the United States. "... there is a rumor that Mason and Slidell are to be surrendered. If it be true[,] this Government is broken up. There is so much violence of spirit among the lower orders of the people ... that any honorable concession ... would prove fatal to its authors."[25]

As it was understood by most Unionists in America in mid-November 1861, the story of what happened in the Old Bahama Channel was a story involving three elements only. First was the heroic captain of a warship of the U.S. Navy, a man capable of knowing what was going on in the neighborhood of his ship and willing to act on the information. Second was a collection of traitorous Southerners, attempting to sneak to Europe as pretended diplomats. Third was the ship they were traveling on when they were captured. Incidentally and regrettably, the latter ship had been a British mail ship.

Henry J. Raymond fully shared this conception of the story. He continued to publish editorials daily in praise of the heroic captain, and in derision of the captured rebels, until the *New York Times* had devoted twelve editorials to the subject. The editor then desisted, saying that the captain's achievement could not be further discussed to any positive purposes till news arrived concerning the reactions of the English to the event.[26]

The newspaper's intended interval of silence concerning Wilkes and the captives began on November 28, 1861. At the moment, excitement about the captain was rising in New York. The vaunted hero himself was expected soon to reach the city, and an ovation was being planned for him in appropriate surroundings at the Historical Society.

On its second day of editorial silence about the hero, the newspaper received a news report from its anonymous correspondent in

London. The report began with some extremely startling news which would have exactly anticipated the story of the event in the Old Bahama Channel, had it just not introduced an awkward complication.

The correspondent's startling news involved *four* elements. First was a warship of the U.S. Navy—not the *San Jacinto* but another, called the *James Adger*. Second was the very same collection of traitorous Southerners, sneaking towards Europe as pretended diplomats. Third was a British mail ship—not the *Trent* but another, its name not given. Fourth was *an unnamed, second warship,* belonging to the awesome navy with which Great Britain was said to rule the waves.

The story appeared in the twenty-seventh report sent by the London correspondent to his newspaper. The report had been completed and mailed from the British capital on November 16, long before any news whatever of the seizure of Mason and Slidell near Cuba could have reached that city. The first two sentences of the report said simply:

> A curious paragraph appeared in some of the morning papers to-day—in the *Telegraph,* I think—under the head of naval intelligence, to the effect that one of Her Majesty's frigates[,] which had left Spithead to watch the movements of the United States war-steamer, the *James Adger,* had returned. The paragraph goes on to state that the object of the *James Adger* was supposed to be to intercept the . . . mail steamer now due, with Messrs. SLIDELL and MASON on board, to take those gentlemen out of her and to carry them to New York.

Raymond studied the two sentences and appreciated their relevance to Wilkes's heroic action. But the sentences were followed by a passage in which Henry Adams stated in so many words that, were officers and men from a U.S. warship to take the Southern traitors forcibly from the deck of a British mail ship, the government of Great Britain would be spurred to war. To the editor, the statement seemed an error.

The steamer *Saxonia,* bound from New York to Hamburg, touched at Cowes at 5:00 A.M. on Thursday, December 12. The ship brought issues of the *New York Times* through November 30.[27]

Even before he saw the issues, Henry Adams knew that his reports of the last few Saturdays were in process of falling on Raymond with special weight and force. It was not news to Adams that he and his employer saw things very differently. The correspondent had learned that the positions taken about the *Trent* affair by himself and Raymond were diametrically opposed. Adams was aware as well that he was a mere contributor to the *Times;* Raymond was its famous editor; and thus, in the opinion of readers, were a news report to the paper to state a proposition and were an editorial in the same issue to state a contrary proposition, the editorial might have the greater impact. What was worse, the editor in this instance had reiterated his own position about heroic Wilkes on the *San Jacinto,* the captured Southerners, and the regrettable Britishness of the mail ship until his position had become an article of faith, impossible to change.

Adams obtained and studied carefully the added issues of the *New York Times* carried by the *Saxonia.* He found his twenty-seventh report to Raymond in the issue for November 30. He saw that the report had been welcomed as a startling anticipation of events.

The report appeared under a series of headings in large type:

## THE TRANSATLANTIC NEWS.

### ARRIVAL OF THE MAILS BY THE CANADA.

## *OUR EUROPEAN CORRESPONDENCE.*

What the English Government is Prepared to do in the Case of
Mason and Slidell.

Immediately preceding the report were additional headings, in smaller type, which began:

## IMPORTANT FROM ENGLAND.
An Anticipation of the Arrest of Slidell and
Mason - What the British Government was
Preparing to Do - The James Adger. . . .

Closely studied, the headings showed that Raymond had done more than see the parallels between the news Adams reported and what had really happened in the Old Bahama Channel. Raymond also had understood that, were the *James Adger* to have been rash enough to stop a British mail ship, it would then have had to deal with a watching British warship—"one of Her Majesty's frigates." Henry Adams, in brief, had succeeded in reminding Henry J. Raymond that there *was* a British navy.

Adams did *not* copy each of his news reports in London before he mailed it, so as to have a record. His memory of his writings, however, was very accurate. Reading his twenty-seventh report in printed form, he saw that Raymond—perhaps at the last minute, after the headings were set in type—had entirely deleted a passage warning that the British government would go to war if Mason and Slidell were taken by force from a British mail ship! Also Adams saw that the editor had gone to the trouble of publishing on another page, beneath the paper's masthead, a comment about the newest report from his London correspondent. "As some indication of the temper with which the news of the seizure of SLIDELL and MASON will be received in England, we learn from our London letter, that . . . the British Admiralty directed a vessel of war to pursue the [*James Adger*]. . . ."

The comment amounted to a signal from Raymond to Adams that the mutilation of his report had been deliberate, and was regretted, but had been necessary.

Below the comment, the editor printed a new editorial about the heroic Captain Wilkes. Raymond said in his newest outburst that good Unionists should expect no trouble from the British about the stopping of the *Trent*. He had resumed his briefly suspended editorial campaign. In the contest between the editor and the correspondent, the editor expected to prevail.

Believing that the duke of Newcastle's story would have to be counteracted somehow, Thurlow Weed had decided to take the task upon himself. The means he proposed to use was a letter to John Delane, editor of *The Times*. He spoke of his intention to the younger Adams and second Secretary Moran at the legation. Both at first were partly amused but mostly startled that so astute a man would want to repeat the favorite error of American politicians on reaching London—Cassius Clay being only one example—of writing to *The Times* and affording Delane an opportunity to instruct or condescend.[28]

The letter Weed prepared was quick to say that the reported dinner-table statement made by Seward in 1860 to the duke of Newcastle, if ever made, had surely been intended as "badinage" and deserved to be excused as an "attempted pleasantry." Weed represented Seward as a peaceful man but was careful *not* to say that the secretary of state would arrange the surrender of Mason and Slidell. In opposite fashion, the unofficial emissary predicted that in disputes between the Yankees and the British bad manners might usually be expected on both sides. He warned the editor of *The Times*, "Of the exact nature of the despatch from the English government I am ignorant; but I am constrained to express the opinion that if that despatch has taken the form of a peremptory demand, it will be met by as peremptory a refusal. . . ."[29]

Minister Adams read the letter before it was mailed to Delane and thought that it was perhaps "a little too smooth and deprecating."[30] His private secretary came around to a different opinion. Henry believed the letter would do some good. " . . . even the English," he said, "stupid and slow as they are, can read for themselves, and as they are not all brutes or blackguards, good words will have an effect. . . ."

Friday's mail contained a letter to the minister from his second son in Boston which said that Charles had joined the army and that John and his wife were expecting a baby soon. The letter was intelligent and brave. Charles had wanted to be a lawyer. He confessed forthrightly, "I have completely failed in my profession. . . ." Yet he said he had solved the problem of all his days to come. "My future must be business & literature & I do not see why the army should not educate me for both. . . ."[31]

Henry was shown the letter and rejoiced to see it. That same afternoon or evening, writing a letter of his own to Charles, he said about the expected arrival of a child: "It relieves both of us from the necessity of marrying now and (in case I want one) gives me an excuse for not marrying at all. You can go into the army with a calm conscience and I have a wide margin before me."

It was Friday the thirteenth, a combination of day and date regarded by many Americans as unlucky. The week had been a bad one, and the third son's reactions to its events had been complex. Learning about the behavior of Governor Andrew at the banquet honoring Captain Wilkes, Henry had noticed that his own reaction— "laughing and cursing"—had gone to two extremes. And then he had had to deal also with Raymond's renewed jubilation about Wilkes and the editor's mutilation of his own report.

The conjunction of Andrew and Raymond, as he thought about it, made Henry furious. He erupted to Charles about the Unionists in America: "You're mad, all of you. It's pitiable to see such idiocy in a nation. There's the New York Times[,] which I warned only in my last letter against such an act, and its consequences; and now I find the passage erased, and editorial assurances that war was *impossible* on such grounds. Egad; who knew best, Raymond or I?"

Of all his days till then, this Friday, December 13, was probably the most taxing Henry had experienced. One of his hardships was success. While maddening to him, the issue of the *New York Times* for November 30 had also been exhilarating in the highest possible degree. Even after the main passage of his twenty-seventh report had been deleted, the issue had contained the proof that he had done superbly well. Had many human beings written intelligently and in detail about a great event eleven days *before* they knew about it? Those who had were probably very few. And now he would rank forever among the few.

Equally disturbing was the success of Weed. Much though he liked and admired his new friend from New York and Albany, Henry did not love him. But Henry loved his father quite enough to die for him.[32] These being the facts of the son's emotions, it was terrible for him, day after day, to watch the impotence of his father and the potency of the legation's visitor.

Gloss it over as one might, the unofficial emissary had displaced Minister Adams in London and Minister Dayton in Paris. Weed ranked alone as *the* Union ambassador for the present in the British Isles and on the Continent. A fraction of his preeminence rose from his being Seward's personal and political friend. Most of it rose directly from Weed's own powers of mind and skills in dealing with human beings. No chance existed that Charles Francis Adams could approach such a man in thought or action. If there were an Adams alive who could give the visitor competition, it would be Henry. The medium through which his and the visitor's power would be exerted would be language, spoken, written, and printed. As Henry said, Mr. Weed had been "hard at work on public opinion" since his arrival from Paris. In less perilous circumstances, the younger Adams might have told Weed both about his own relations with editors in London and, in confidence, his hidden tie with Raymond in New York. But Henry had decided *not* to tell the secret to his all-capable new friend. In the eyes of the political master whom Seward had sent aboard, young H. B. Adams would continue to seem a mere promising youth, his father's valued private secretary.

The week had not changed Henry's opinions concerning three important matters. He still believed that England would fight if Mason, Slidell, and their two aides were not surrendered. He had *not* abandoned hope that war between the United States and England could be averted. He continued to wish that the civil war in America were waged. That awful Friday, however, he ceased to think that the Union could do better in the civil war than win favorable terms, in an eventual treaty of peace with the Confederacy. " . . . we must sooner or later yield the matter," he said to Charles. "As a mere question of independence[,] I believe the thing to be settled. We cannot bring the South back."

On Friday, receiving a letter from Mr. Thurlow Weed, editor Delane knew he could safely print it in *The Times* the following morning. The letter might tend to reduce the chance of war between Great Britain and the United States, but two items of news could be trusted to *improve* the chance of war with the Unionists. It had been learned that General Scott was rushing back to America on the *Arago*, the same ship on which he and Mr. Weed had come abroad. Scott apparently desired to enjoy active service in the coming war with England. It also had been learned that Seward in Washington had cosigned the order sending the captured Southern diplomats into prison cells at Fort Warren. One signature, that of Gideon Welles, the secretary of the navy, would obviously have sufficed. The additional signature of the secretary of state appeared to have a defiant meaning.

Delane accordingly wrote for publication in *The Times* the following morning, Saturday, December 14, 1861, a violent attack on the man he took to be "the present Prime Minister of the Northern States of America." The attack reviewed all Seward's crimes, including an alleged proposal to conquer Canada. Summarizing his opinion of the American's recent conduct, Delane asserted that "upon his ability to involve the United States in a war with England[,] Mr. SEWARD has staked his official, and, most probably, also his political existence. . . ."[33]

One of Henry Adams's peculiarities in London was that he would sometimes say discouraged things, then think his way afresh through the welter of confusion to which he was exposed, and arrive at undiscouraged, new opinions. The feeling he had on Friday that the Union could not be saved was displaced on Saturday by an adventurous persuasion that the future of the Union was assured.

In his thirty-first report to Raymond, mailed on December 14, 1861, Adams changed his ground completely. He said that the *British* government had blundered—by demanding that the persons taken from the *Trent* be surrendered by the United States. He said that the authorities in Washington, chiefly Lincoln and Seward, could safely reject the British demand in favor of a different settlement chosen by themselves. Finally, he said that, in such a case the Palmerston regime might well be driven out of office. Implicit in all he said was confidence that the Union leaders, if they kept calm, could deal with all their enemies, foreign and domestic.

This was not to say that Adams absolutely believed his new propositions. Clearly, he was writing on the assumption that, the seven-day limit in Washington having lapsed *without* a decision to surrender the captives to Lord Lyons, the Lincoln administration would need to know the consequences of its course.

All the same, the correspondent stated his changed position in the tones of a person who believed that his newer calculations were more accurate than his old. Without pretending to perfect understanding, he believed he had approached it.

He was right. A little at a time, the world would learn in detail the inside story of the British ultimatum. Here certain aspects of the story should be looked at.

The first reactions of the British leaders to the news about the stopping of the *Trent* and the seizure of the envoys had been extremely rash. Writing to Queen Victoria on November 29, Lord Palmerston had given an account of the event which—without pretending to anything approaching certainty—sketched a vast American design of war. This imagined war plan had embraced not only Lincoln, Seward, and Captain Wilkes on the *San Jacinto* but also General Scott in Paris. Scott was alleged to have come abroad to offer Canada to France, its former owner, as payment for help in the intended war with England.[34]

On November 30, after the second cabinet council, Earl Russell had completed a plainly worded despatch to Lord Lyons instructing him to demand the return of the captured envoys and an apology. A second despatch was contemplated which would bring about the departure of Lord Lyons from Washington, in the event that the surrender of the captives were not arranged in seven days.

At both cabinet councils, on November 29 and 30, Gladstone had urged a more conciliatory course. Overruled, the chancellor of the exchequer had found two sympathetic spirits in Queen Victoria and Prince Albert, whom he visited repeatedly at Windsor Castle.

When Earl Russell's first despatch was sent to Windsor for review and approval on November 30, Prince Albert had held the paper overnight. After much reflection, the prince consort suggested changes, including the addition of a passage expressive of a hope that the action of Captain Wilkes had not been authorized. In its ultimate wording, the passage would read:

> Her Majesty's Government, bearing in mind the friendly relations which have long subsisted between Great Britain

and the United States, are willing to believe that the United States naval officer who committed this aggression was not acting in compliance with any authority from his Government, or that, if he conceived himself to be so authorised, he greatly misunderstood the instructions which he had received.

Queen Victoria strongly supported her husband's views. Palmerston not only adopted the prince consort's conciliatory changes but added others. Sending the ultimatum, Earl Russell accompanied it with private instructions and assurances meant to cushion its impact—meant also to ease the way for Seward, should he need extra time, or should he be able to comply with British wishes in almost every respect, but not in all.[35]

Adams had been suspecting for some time that the British ministry, after taking a war ground, had quickly receded from it. In his thirtieth report, mailed the previous Saturday, he had said that the *"majority"* of the Liberal cabinet regretted the imminence of bloodshed. But Adams could only guess—not know—how rapidly and how far the British leaders had retreated.

His guess was off by two days. He took his new position on Saturday, December 14. So doing, he anticipated an action that Earl Russell would take on Monday, December 16. At that time, writing privately to Lord Palmerston, the Foreign Secretary would say: "I incline more and more to the opinion that if the [American] answer is a reasoning, and not a blunt offensive answer, we should send once more across the Atlantic to ask compliance. . . . I do not think the country would approve an immediate declaration of war."[36]

Still, Adams's calculations had not hinged primarily on the tendency of Palmerston and Russell to initiate important actions they would fail to carry out. The young American had realized that the agency of two other persons in the crisis, the queen and her prince consort, had been far more influential and decisive than had earlier appeared. He said in his new report: " . . . there is one statement [current in London] . . . which has excited great curiosity. . . . This is no less than that *Her Majesty Queen Victoria looks with great aversion and dread at the prospect of war, and has earnestly endeavored to prevent it by every means in her power.* The story at first seems very questionable, but one must bear in mind that the Queen is a woman, kind-hearted, and not given to ambitious dreams of conquest, and that she probably remembers the terrible trials which she endured when her subjects [in the Crimean War] were dying in the hospitals at Varna, and were starving of cold in the trenches before Sebastopol."

The final paragraph of Adams's powerful December 14 report announced the serious illness of Prince Albert and implied that his death was fast approaching. The news of the prince's peril, published in London that very morning, had taken the English by surprise. Albert had earlier been reported to be ill with gastric fever but then had much improved. Now, unexpectedly, he had relapsed.[37]

Rumors were afoot in London that his last official act, performed early on December 1, when he knew he was ill, had been a moderation of the ultimatum sent that day to the Americans.[38] The news of his relapse had been printed in the morning press on December 14 in terms so solemn as to mean that hope for his recovery was lost.[39]

In his report, Adams wrote about the prince consort's peril in a spirit which reflected his own more recent troubles. One should not think that the secret reporter's correspondence had been written lightly or with ease. The burden of speaking in a constructive manner about the relations of the United States and Great Britain had been crushing from the outset; and the mental effort needed to shift from one conception of affairs to another, deeper one—and sometimes to do so overnight, as in the present instance—had frequently been great and had been many times exacted.

Adams was going smoothly forward, making his reports always more skillful, discerning, and important. As a member of the legation, too, he was giving assistance of incalculable value to the Union. Yet his progress went hand in hand with a sense of thanklessness.

He felt a kinship with the German prince, an able man, who, after marrying the sovereign of a great foreign power, and after giving his energies unstintingly to the benefit of England and the betterment of humanity, was dying at Winsor at the age of forty-two. Adams said in his report: "Prince ALBERT had been to England one man in many millions. His influence—all the more efficacious because it was unseen—has done more to contribute to the success of VICTORIA'S reign than that of any other person. . . . If Prince ALBERT had been an Englishman[,] no honors would have been too great, no words of admiration too strong for his royal services. As a foreigner, he has been watched with jealous dislike, [and] forced to hide himself and his influence from public sight. . . ."

As if the prince's death had actually occurred, Adams used his closing sentence to ask Americans to sympathize with Queen Victoria.

"I think there are few persons in America who won't be willing to give the Queen their warm sympathy in this anxious and painful season."

He mailed his report, and at midnight the seldom-heard great bell of St. Paul's Cathedral boomed its sad tones over London.[40] Its peals confirmed to all who heard them that the prince had died and the queen survived, a widow.

Albert's death threw a shadow down England's path to war. The London newspapers on December 16, 1861, printed with black borders, announced that national mourning had begun and would continue for three months.[1]

Adams felt the hurt of the occasion. Beginning immediately and continuing for several days, he gave extra labor to writing a special report on the prince which stood apart from his other contributions to the *New York Times*. The entire text of the special report should be given here, not for what it said about the prince but for indications it contained relating to Adams's past and present efforts; to his ideals and sympathies; and especially to a spirit of indifference—of diminished desire to live—which he attributed to Albert, perhaps correctly, but which certainly was descending upon his own existence.

Presumably all the headings preceding the word "LONDON" were added by the newspaper when the report was published.

### THE DEATH OF PRINCE ALBERT.

The People Taken by Surprise—The Feelings of the
Prince—The Character of his Connection with the
British Government—The Queen in Retirement, &c.

From Our Own Correspondent.
LONDON, Saturday, Dec. 21, 1861

But a few hours after I had mailed my last letter, the great bell of St. Paul's, tolled only at the death of a member of the royal family, struck consternation into the minds of the people of London. They had flattered themselves that the danger was over, and that the Prince Consort would soon be able to continue again his career of usefulness, which they promised themselves to estimate more correctly in the future than they had done in the past. The opportunity has not been granted to them. The main staff of VICTORIA'S reign is now broken. A few words upon the Prince, and we may then return to the troubled current of daily affairs.

It may be wrong to repeat a story whose truth I cannot guarantee, and which, even if true, this would be hardly the time to make public, if it were likely to come back to the ears of that royal family whose feelings every American is as eager to respect as any Englishman can be. As it is not likely to come to their notice, however, I can venture to say that the Prince, on perceiving his complaint to be mortal, is said to have accepted his fate without regret—"I am not sorry to be freed from the whole thing." I will not vouch that these words were really spoken, but such is the current report. Whether they were a result of the long years of self-restraint that he has led in England, or of the new difficulties that threaten the country, or of some accidental domestic annoyance that has broken the course of a private life, known to have been as a rule unusually happy, or a combination of all these causes, this I do not care to guess. Yet no one ventures to deny that the struggle which the Prince has had to acquire and to maintain the position which was his right, has been long and painful. He has been dogged and harassed by the national jealousies of the English people. Naturally reserved and modest, the English nobility from the first, mistook his apparent coldness for pride, and repaid it with haughty disdain. They sneered at his German origin, and at his ignorance of what they call their manly national sports. As he was himself no hunter, they conceived the idea that he was the strong enemy of the fox. They declared that he was avaricious, and accumulated in himself all the posts of profit within his reach. They covered him with arrogant abuse for his supposed German tendencies and friendship for Austria. They begrudged to him even the smallest political influence over the Queen. I remember well how, not many years ago, he was hissed by the London mob in the very face of Her Majesty, nor did respect for her feelings prevent the Press from treating him with a rudeness that was as unjust as it was ungentlemanly. Through this labyrinth of difficulties he still managed to guide himself with a discretion that is astonishing, and now that he is dead, the very persons who so hunted him are the first to acknowledge that his loss is irreparable.

The newspapers are now filled with accounts of his energy and perseverance in the public service. How, under his quiet supervision the arts of design have risen from semi-barbarism to high excellence. How his ambition was to lead the way in agricultural improvements. How he labored to stimulate and elevate, not only every branch of national industry, but every humanitarian reform of the day. With these matters we, as foreigners, have little to do, but there is reason to believe that in ways more direct than these, America has reason to regret the Prince little less than England.

I was in London, some eight years since, when he made his celebrated speech, declaring the duty of the age to be the union of all sorts and conditions of men into a thorough understanding that their interests were one and inseparable, and that he who labored rightly for the improvement of any single class, labored equally for the good of all. I have not at the moment a copy of the speech by me, and do not state his proposition so broadly as it was then laid down; but it made a great sensation at the time, for its results seemed inconsistent with the reputation which he bore of monarchical tendencies. It was his fixed principle, which lay at the bottom of his whole internal policy as regarded England. His religious views were equally broad—unitarian in fact. And in the same mold were framed all his ideas with regard to foreign policy, which looked for their ultimate aim toward the unity and brotherhood of nations and races; "The Parliament of Man; the Federation of the World."

The foreign policy of Great Britain has been usually selfish, insular and short-sighted. The Prince, as a foreigner, brought with him to England broader views and more generous instincts. His uncle, LEOPOLD, King of Belgium, a man also of remarkable powers, exercised a strong influence over both the Prince and Queen, and all this influence was necessarily thrown on the side of peace between all nations, and in favor of the greatest possible development of international relations. This explanation renders at once the truth probable of a rumor which has lately arrived at such distinctness as to make it worth repetition, especially to America at this moment. It is said that when the instructions, drawn up and approved by the Cabinet, demanding of the American Government the release of MASON and SLIDELL, were sent to Windsor and placed before the Queen for her approval, they met with an obstinate resistance. Nothing could induce the Queen to yield to her Ministry, until certain changes of form had been made in the instructions, and even then it is believed that she gave way with reluctance. This opposition is attributed to the influence of the Prince Consort and of LEOPOLD. I repeat the story as it was told me, and as I believe it to be true; and if true, it may explain, perhaps in conjunction with some other reasons, the strange speech of the Prince on his death-bed, and his reported indifference to his fate. At the same time I will not guarantee the truth of either story, for though I believe them myself, I am still more sure that if they should come back here and attract notice, the *Times* and its satelites would give them a flat contradiction.

Meanwhile the nation is in mourning, and this time in sober earnest. Not that the real loss it has sustained is as yet fully appreciated, for it will be some time before that loss is fully understood. But this "nation of shop-keepers" has reason to feel in a humor for grief in a professional way. Christmas is just at hand, and the shops were hoping to make a little money for the first time this year. But now the death of the Prince, coming, as it does, in the midst of the American difficulty, has reduced them to despair. The Winter and the Spring will be the most gloomy known in London for many years. There will be no Court, no gayety, and no money. The proprietors of the mourning establishments may be happy behind their bales of crape, but every one else will lament. Christmas will be saddened throughout all England by the feeling of sympathy for the Queen, and for many weeks the streets will see nothing but black costumes and all the marks of a national calamity.

About the Queen herself, little is known. She is said to have borne the blow better than was expected, but whether she has borne up under it or no, is not stated. Public expectation was so low that it would have been, indeed, hard if she had borne it worse than was expected. After much hesitation and several days delay, she has left Windsor, and gone into retirement at Osborne. Half of her servants have come to Buckingham Palace, and only a portion attend her at Osborne, from

which, it seems natural to suppose that her seclusion will be
as absolute as is possible. I see as yet no reason to suppose that
public fears about her health are not likely to prove well-
founded. My own belief is that the glory of her reign is
departed.

Important news reached the legation in the form of two messages
from Seward to C. F. Adams.[2] One was a private note dated November
27.[3] The other was an official document, "Despatch No. 136," dated
November 30. Both the note and a brief portion of the despatch
touched the question of Mason and Slidell.

The secretary of state mentioned that Minister Adams had not
been furnished—and *would* not be furnished—with "any explanations." Seward described the trouble as a new one, "unknown" and
"unforeseen." He said that he and Lord Lyons had been silent and
inactive in its connection while the latter waited for instructions from
his government. " . . . the discussion if there must be one, shall be had
here [in Washington]."

Three assurances completed Seward's message. He confirmed
that Wilkes had "acted without any instructions" from his superiors
in Washington. He expressed trust that the British leaders would
"consider the subject in a friendly temper." He gave his word that they
could "expect the best disposition on the part of this government."[4]

Different meanings were attached to Seward's assurances by C. F.
Adams and his official secretaries. Although explicitly encouraged by
the secretary of state to read "Despatch No. 136" to Foreign Secretary
Russell, the minister seemed to think that such a course would *not* be
well advised. Moran and Wilson took the opposite view that the
despatch, if read immediately to Russell, might have decisive good
effects. Being very anxious to stay in London, Moran concluded that
Seward's words, though few, were the end of the affair and war had
been avoided. Wilson apparently agreed. Beginning on Tuesday,
December 17, the official secretaries told inquirers at the legation that
there would be no war.[5]

Fear of war continued. British popular conviction that war had
started seemed complete. The ministry's efforts to strengthen the fleet
in American waters and hasten troops to Canada did not slacken. On
Wednesday, when the *Adriatic* and the *Parana* sailed for the St.
Lawrence, the British soldiers aboard the ships believed their true
destination was Charleston and cheered excitedly when a band played
"I Wish I Was in Dixie."[6] England generally was aswarm with

rumors. It was said that Palmerston was ill with gout. The attack was reportedly severe, and some versions of the rumor affirmed that he was dead.[7]

On Thursday, reconsidering, Minister Adams visited Foreign Secretary Russell and read him the new despatch from Washington. Russell was very satisfied with Seward's guarantee of friendship and disclosed to Adams the exact terms of the two despatches which had gone to Lord Lyons on the *Europa* on December 1.[8]

Thurlow Weed, appearing at the legation on Friday, said a rumor was abroad that Minister Adams had received a friendly despatch from Washington and read it to the foreign secretary. On the strength of the rumor, which Russell himself must have started, prices on the stock exchange had "gone up like a rocket."[9]

Henry Adams took a leaf from Seward's book and practiced brevity. He gave his weekly news report for Saturday, December 21, 1861, the uncommon form of a single paragraph. The main thing he reported was that the U.S. minister had visited the Foreign Office and "officially declared the act of Capt. WILKES to be unauthorized, and the action of the United States Government . . . to be still undetermined and open to any proposition." Mr. Adams's declarations, the reporter said, had "caused a return of confidence, and a much less hostile tone towards America." The paragraph mentioned and dismissed John Delane. "The *Times* still thunders, it is true, but the *Times* belongs to the war party, and is likely to become the more bitter in proportion as the prospect of war is diminished." To end his paragraph, the correspondent denied that the prime minister had any "intention of forcing hostilities." " . . . [Lord Palmerston] is no friend of America. On the contrary . . . he honors that country with a cordial dislike, and considers that he has certain debts to pay her in regard to the war of 1812, the Ashburton treaty, the Crampton affair, and the slave-trade; but he can pay off all these debts with interest and yet not make war, and he will do so."

The handwritten originals of Adams's reports to the *New York Times* were evidently being discarded in the usual way after their texts were set in type and printing was begun. If that had happened in the case of his mutilated twenty-seventh report, and if Raymond could not remember the deleted passage word for word, the editor could not publish the report a second time with its missing passage reinserted. But the editor did the next best thing. He waited till a new report arrived from Adams—an astonishing document in itself, full of news about excitement in England concerning the Confederate steamer *Nashville*—and then published both the new report and the opening paragraphs of the old one, with its suggestive story involving a British frigate.

That particular warship had so haunted Raymond's imagination that he had tried to learn more about it.[10] The ship, called the *Phaeton*, had appeared conspicuously, the editor discovered, in another news report, first published in the *Edinburgh Scotsman,* and then reprinted by several other papers in the British Isles which came regularly to Raymond's office. The haunted editor compared the amazing report earlier sent to him by Adams with the report in the *Scotsman* and saw—or thought he saw—what truly was happening inside the minds of the leaders of Great Britain. Raymond did not sufficiently caution himself that the Scottish newspaper's seeming facts might mostly be Confederate lies, entangled with questionable points of law and usage. He swallowed the bait of the lies and jumped to a conclusion in harmony with his preconceptions.

His issue for December 9, 1861, contained both the essential part of Adams's earlier report and the entire text of the report in the *Edinburgh Scotsman.*[11] Also it contained a triumphant editorial in which Raymond said that, thanks to "our London correspondent" and the Scottish report, the United States of America knew in advance what the necessary course of Great Britain would be in the *Trent* affair. The British would do nothing! The editorial announced: "This should settle the matter." " . . . whatever the British authorities may consider it politic to proclaim aloud, we now know what they privately *think.*"[12]

Copies of Raymond's newspaper for December 9 reached England by the *Canada* on Sunday, December 22, but probably did not become available to Adams either that day or the next. The funeral of Prince Albert took place in strictest privacy on Monday. It was memorialized in London by a "cessation of business and empty streets." Moran recorded in his journal: " . . . a gloomier day I never passed. All the shops were closed in London, the sky was dull, the people were in black, and an unusual stillness prevailed in the great city."[13]

Adams presumably studied the evidence of Raymond's detective work on the Tuesday before Christmas, December 24. No record has been found of the correspondent's reactions. He perhaps himself detected contentedly that the editor in New York was forming higher and higher opinions of his hidden associate in the U. S. legation in London.

During the next two days, the Adamses visited a country house,

Mount Felix, at Walton-on-Thames, and shared the Christmas festivities of a wealthy American banker, Russell Sturgis, and his family. On Friday, when he had some opportunity to talk with the elder Adams, Moran was startled by a change in the minister's opinions. The assistant secretary wrote: "There has been the usual anxious discussion between us about the impending war. . . . Mr. Adams is apprehensive that he may have to leave here by the middle of January. A change has come over his views since his visit to Mr. Sturgis . . . ."[14]

No mystery attached to C. F. Adams's new alarms. The date he now assigned to the end of his mission was the anticipated date of arrival in London of the American reply to the British ultimatum. In the British press, this date was being calculated closely. That same Friday, December 27, an English reporter set forth the necessities of the case in the *Manchester Guardian:* "The *Europa* being telegraphed off Cape Race on the 13th inst., her dispatches could not reach Washington before the night of the 16th; and, probably, on the 17th Mr. SEWARD first heard from Lord LYONS, in an unofficial manner. . . . The formal communication of the dispatch would not be made until the 18th or 19th, and seven days from that would render it impossible for the answer to come by the Cunard boat leaving Boston on the 25th. The next boat would be the *Asia,* leaving on the 1st, and due at Queenstown about the 11th or 12th [of January, 1862], and by this [time] the great question will be answered one way or the other."[15]

The younger Adams obtained fresh issues of the *New York Times* through Saturday, December 14, brought on the *City of Baltimore.* They showed that Raymond's editorials about the crisis were unceasing. The editor had received first indications that the British, the instant they learned what Captain Wilkes had done, had been stung with pain and moved to rage. Yet the editor assured his readers that excitement in England about the capture of Mason and Slidell was less tumultuous than expected and was surely dying out.[16]

In his latest editorial, published on December 13, Raymond had said: " . . . we take final stand on the acknowledged rectitude of our position. . . . Of course . . . the rebel emissaries can never be surrendered." One day later, in his thirty-first report, Henry Adams had changed his ground and said that the surrender of the rebel emissaries *could be refused.* But Raymond and Adams had really not agreed. The editor was attempting to defend what he regarded as a Union act of heroism. The reporter had meant that advantage could be taken of a British miscalculation. The editor's impulse had been patriotically defensive; the correspondent's advice had been patriotically aggressive.

Now a new Saturday had come, and the anonymous correspondent was faced with the ultimate question whether he wished to put his country's interests ahead of the broader interests of the human race at large. Adams wrote and mailed a long report, his thirty-fourth, which developed in perfected form a main idea which all his previous reports had tended to approach. The new report presupposed that if neutral nations in time of war had any rights at all, the taking of Confederate envoys from a neutral British mail ship by Union sailors, using force, had been a moral error. The report affirmed that the United States—its people and government—remained completely free to correct the error. The entire affair came down to a choice of hostility or friendship. "I have asserted many times," the anonymous correspondent wrote, "that the English people dislike us, fear us, wish to see our nation crippled, and our free institutions overthrown. . . . But I say with equal positiveness from personal knowledge of people and interests here, that this enmity does not run to the point of a wish for war, whatever bluster the *Times* may talk, or however bitterly the friends of the South may press immediate hostilities. At this moment America holds the balance in her hands. If it is war that she chooses, war it will be. But if we want peace, we can have it at the price of MASON and SLIDELL. . . ."

The point of his statement was not that the Americans would *have* to release the captives—even if his words might seem to say so; it was rather that Adams would be happier if the Union government *would* release them. He wished the surrender of the emissaries because yielding them to the British would be the friendly thing to do; and the peace he wanted with the United Kingdom would be, not brief, but everlasting.

Moran had said early in the week that C. F. Adams sorely needed "some relaxation from the cares of office."[17] The second secretary may not have noticed any outward signs of weariness or strain in H. B. Adams, and would not have thought them important, if he did.

The most visible evidence of strain in the younger Adams was partly baseless alternations of euphoria and hopelessness. The close of his thirty-fourth report was pessimistic. "The year is going out," the correspondent said, "in the midst of anxiety, sorrow and trouble of many kinds. No man dares to foretell what the new year will bring, but it is expected with little hope or confidence in its results."

He did not say so in the report, but he agreed with his father in thinking that their stay in England would soon be over. It seemed to him that events had wedged the minister into a position so untenable that useful diplomatic initiatives by Unionists in the British capital would be impossible to mount. That Saturday, December 28, he wrote to Charles: " . . . I can see no means of preserving our relations with this Court in either the Nashville or the Trent difficulties. For these reasons I think that our stay here is at an end. But I do not believe in war."

In his depression, the son grew all the more disturbed by the discrepancy between his father's abilities and those of Thurlow Weed. He could not deal with such a subject easily. His feelings being what they were, he tried to blind himself to the comparison of Weed and C. F. Adams by instead comparing the masterful visitor with himself. He now had witnessed the old politican's activities through three weeks of stress and anxiousness. In the privacy of his letter to soldier Charles, the third son said about the unofficial emissary: "He's a large man; a very tall man indeed; and a good deal taller than I am. So I can only watch and admire at a distance."

Henry always wanted to be useful. He hoped still to help his father and felt a new, strong impulse to help his elder brother. Acting on the impulse, he gave Charles a large sum of money. The gift took the form of a draft against the money being paid to Henry by Raymond, in care of Charles in Boston. Sending the draft, the younger brother said: "I want you to use this on your [military] outfit; to buy a horse; or equipments; or to fit out your company. It is my contribution to the war and to your start in pride, pomp and circumstance."

The third son had come to England with their father, mother, and the younger children, not intending to stay throughout the four-year term of their father's mission, but intending to stay for a limited time and to perform three tasks. He had wanted to assist in the work of the legation. He had hoped to support the legation indirectly but power-fully by secretly reporting to the *New York Times*. He had meant to complete, energetically and early, the work now being done at last by Weed: cultivating British editors—not to mention businessmen, bank-ers, and financiers—behind the scenes. If he had done all these things, and if his father's mission had seemed sure to be successful, the younger Adams would have been satisfied; but C. F. Adams's position seemed anything but good; and Henry himself had scarcely begun to meet the Englishmen he felt he should have met.

That Weed was doing work he had silently proposed to do himself

only made exhausted Henry surer that he had failed in every way. " . . .
I am tired of this life," he confessed to Charles. "Every attempt I have
made to be of use has failed more or less completely. I stand no stronger
[in London] than the first day I arrived. I cannot find that I have
effected a lodgment anywhere. . . ."

Side by side with the feeling that he had failed in ways for which
he was responsible, he experienced another feeling, a more general
sense of failure, this one a failure for which he would not hold himself
at fault. In sweeping terms, he told his brother that the "strange
madness of the times" had deprived young persons like themselves of
"any chance of settled lives and Christian careers." Peculiarly, their
generation had been shaken and disturbed.

New Year's Day, 1862, brought a false report to London that
Union forces had captured the city of Charleston, South Carolina, and
destroyed it.[18] That the report was believed by either H. B. Adams or C.
F. Adams may be doubted, but the falseness of the story did not prevent
its helping them. Both men threw off their gloom and resumed their
wonted outlooks.

Arriving steamers delivered issues of the *New York Times* needed
by Henry, to keep abreast of his and his editor's contest in New York. It
was already clear that the agile reporter had worsted the dogmatic
editor. Poor Raymond, though, would be the last man in America to
believe the news provided him by his London correspondent. It was
true that the editor was publishing Adams's newer letters intact, in the
most conspicuous places in the newspaper. It was apparent that the
news from England was having very great effects upon the people of
the Union, who seemed very quick to grasp the seriousness of the
*Trent* affair, once its dangers were explained to them in factual terms.
But the editor was loth to absorb the news from abroad and tried
desperately *not* to change his ground.

On December 16, the *New York Times* had had to print the news,
just brought on the *City of Washington*, that excitement in Great
Britain, far from subsiding, had grown to mountainous proportions;
indeed that the two countries were "on the brink of war." The editor
fell back a step and suggested in an editorial on December 17 that the
fate of Mason and Slidell might best be submitted to international
arbitration. But Raymond took heart that day sufficiently to write an
editorial for publication next morning, December 18, which said that
the British ultimatum, when disclosed, would prove a harmless
document. Its contents, he explained, had "doubtless been subjected to
the ordinary sensational exaggeration of the English press."

Later that day, December 18, after a struggle against heavy seas, the *Europa* reached New York, bringing the famous but still mysterious ultimatum, to be carried to Lord Lyons, and Adams's twenty-ninth report to Raymond, the one which said: " . . . it is now evident that the [British] Government means to take a war ground. . . . There can be no doubt that war is staring us in the face."

Raymond honestly confessed, while he was publishing his correspondent's report on December 19, " . . . [the *Trent*] affair has revealed to us a depth of enmity for which we were hardly prepared, on the part of the English public. . . ." " . . . yesterday was altogether a blue day in our calendar."

All the same, for six more days, the editor clung to the wreck of his ideas. "No cause for war exists," his paper said. " . . . a day or two more will prick the bubble which has thrown our people into such a state of anxiety and alarm."

The day or two imparted the frightful news that General Scott was coming back on the *Arago* and that warlike sentiment and preparations in England were unabated. So Raymond wrote in his editorials: "The horizon abroad is evidently clearing up. . . ." " . . . the news is of a cheering character, and in no way justifies the unfavorable inference placed upon it yesterday by the public."[19]

Charles had received from Henry the manuscript earlier sent to him for possible, early publication in the *Atlantic Monthly*. The elder brother may or may not have read it. Distracted by delays relating to his promised commission in a Massachusetts regiment, he also was affected by the article's arriving "just too late" to be considered by Lowell for last-minute inclusion in his magazine's December issue.

It occurred to Charles that he owed a favor to the editor of the *Boston Courier*. Impulsively, he gave the editor Henry's article. The editor gladly accepted the windfall and set about its publication.

More or less immediately, Charles realized that he had made a "mistake." A chance existed that his younger brother had invested a good deal of labor and hope in the article, and surely it would have been better placed in the January *Atlantic*. As things had happened, the *Courier* published it at a time when everyone was so excited about the *Trent* affair that they could not be expected to take much interest in something called "A Visit to Manchester. Extracts from a Private Diary."

Charles sent his brother the issue of the *Courier* in which the article appeared. With the issue, he sent a note of apology and explanation. " . . . I doubt if any one has read it," the older brother remarked, "or any notice will be taken of it. . . ." As nearly as the second son could tell, the matter was closed and done with.[20]

That the writings of Henry Adams should be consigned to the comparative oblivion of the *Boston Courier* had been a favorite idea with one person only, Charles Francis Adams, Jr.[21] Henry had had plenty of warning about his brother's jealousy and would recognize, when he received the dismal issue of the *Courier* and his brother's apology, that he had no one but himself to blame for the miscarriage of his article. But the matter had another aspect.

The elder brother had known that the younger wished that his authorship of the article be concealed absolutely. Charles had failed egregiously to protect his brother in that respect. Henry knew how to read a newspaper. In London, unfolding the *Courier* which Charles had sent him, he not only saw on the front page the "great gun" he had intended for the *Atlantic Monthly* but found on page two an obliging series of sentences written and published by the newspaper's editor:

> The interesting Diary at Manchester, on the outside of to-day's COURIER, we feel at liberty to say, is written by Mr. Henry Adams, the son of our Minister to Great Britain. This accomplished young gentleman has been for some time abroad. The Diary shows that he has by no means degenerated from the hereditary ability of his family,—which now for four generations has either fulfilled high expectations, or, as in the present case, has given promise of future distinguished usefulness to the country.

The publication of his name and kind compliments about his "ability" and probable "distinguished usefulness" thrust the third son into a dilemma. If he wished, he could imagine that the lines on page two of the *Courier* would be noticed by someone who would bring the issue to the attention of the British press or otherwise set in motion a train of horrors for himself. Or he could assume, as Charles did, that the article—and attendant remarks—had gone unread.

Henry elected not to worry.

On Saturday, January 4, he wrote his first report to the *New York Times* for 1862. Putting the *Trent* affair aside as a matter already dealt with, he shifted to the question he had tried to explain exhaustively two months earlier in "A Visit to Manchester": the Union blockade in relation to the British government. He then went on to other topics, until he had written a model news report. He said that the peace party in England was "on its legs again" and "striking out with fresh vigor." Events in other ways were regaining a normal aspect. "The *Times* has . . . returned to its old tactics of quiet irritation. . . . The stock market made a prodigious jump, and the advance has been well maintained. Cotton, too, has advanced a half penny per pound, which is perhaps the best sign of all, as it indicates that the blockade is considered secure."

In one way, the *Trent* affair had worked to the positive advantage of the Union. The Confederate agents in Great Britain, convinced that their enemies had blundered into a suicidal war with England, had ceased their shipments of arms to Southern ports and had allowed the *Nashville* and *Pacific* to lie uselessly in dock, the better armament of the one unstarted and the other uncompleted.[22] Now, waking from their illusion, the rebel agents were resuming their former ways with the energy of desperation. Like Adams, the agents seemed to have turned their minds to one thing mainly: the blockade. " . . . as it is now evident," Henry said, "that the critical moment is here, when the blockade must be broken or the South ruined, the efforts of the Southerners are becoming actually frantic. . . ."

Taking up one of the main ideas of the article he had meant for the *Atlantic*, Adams reviewed the contest in America as a chapter in economic history. Cotton, he said, was being planted increasingly "in India and Africa, and in South America, where cotton never grew before." A single year during which the Confederate States of America grew corn and potatoes while planters in other countries raised cotton for the mills of Europe would permanently deprive the South of the lever which many of the rebels had said would move the world. Their cotton would not be king.

He rounded out his model report with a bit of scandal, the case of a "young man named WINDHAM, the head of the old and famous Windham family, who is accused of being a lunatic." Adams explained: "The scandalous adventures of the young man . . . would do no dishonor to the palmy days of Rome, and to the contemporaries of TIBERIUS and CALIGULA. They reek of the Haymarket and of Leicester-square. Strangely enough the whole evidence is reported in full in the journals, and forms the favorite reading of half the nations of the kingdom, not to speak of the younger portions of society."

He did not know it, but he was writing his last report to Raymond. The lines with which he ended it gave his long series of thirty-five reports an apt conclusion. Adams had many traits, enough to make his behavior at times far from easy to predict, but one of the most decided was sympathy for persons less well-cared for than himself. "The weather," he wrote, "has been remarkably mild. On the Continent there is ice and frost, but in London there is little but fog and mud. It is very fortunate . . . for the poor are now in a very critical state."

Sensational news arrived in London on January 6 that a Confederate war-steamer, the *Sumter,* after burning three Union merchant vessels, had come into port in Spain, at Cadiz. The news was more than matched on January 8 by word that a Union warship, the *Tuscarora,* newly built and heavily armed, had anchored at Southampton.

Moran, earlier very sanguine, had become extremely worried. He recorded, "Our anxiety for news from home about the intentions of the Gov't . . . is still at fever heat." When another steamer came from America without important news, he wrote, "Our suspense amounts to anguish. . . ."[23]

The members of the legation would still have hung in suspense, if they had known in detail what happened in America after the *Europa* appeared in the Narrows and reached its dock in New York. Lord Lyons had not received Earl Russell's despatches till midnight on December 18. The British minister next day visited the secretary of state and acquainted him informally with the terms of the demand: an apology and the arrangement of the return of the captives within a week. The secretary of state, first telling the president about the terms, instantly began to draft a possible reply to the British government. Next Lord Lyons read the ultimatum to Seward officially and completely; Seward continued working on his draft of a reply; and Lincoln, writing independently, started work on an alternative reply.

The president and cabinet planned to meet to discuss the matter and settle their decision on December 24. With Lincoln's consent, Seward rescheduled the meeting for December 25. The paper drafted by the secretary of state was long, and he needed time to finish.[24] Also the Cunard steamer *America* was approaching New York, bringing communications which would reach Washington in time to be consulted before a meeting on that day.

That Seward should wish a postponement was made still more understandable by his having silently resolved to bring about the surrender of the captives and by his knowing that he was outnumbered in the cabinet.[25] The secretary of the treasury, Salmon P. Chase, and the secretary of war, Simon Cameron, were opposed to yielding the captives to Lord Lyons for any reason. Partly on the advice of Senator Sumner, the president had concluded that the prisoners should be kept and their fate submitted to international arbitration, or to British reconsideration.

Sumner was receding day by day from his earlier strong belief in arbitration. He said on December 24 that "in her present mood England will not arbitrate." Lincoln, too, had weakened in his belief in arbitration, to the extent of deciding *not* to place his draft reply before the meeting. Nonetheless, among the persons expected to attend the meeting, a consensus existed that the British demand should be refused.

It seemed to Seward that no one supporting the consensus knew what reasons, exactly, should be given for the refusal. To him, the attitude of his colleagues seemed one of unreasoning determination. In Seward's words, the government "had no idea of the grounds upon which it would explain its action, nor did it believe that it would concede the case."

The meeting on Christmas Day was long and difficult. Sumner attended, as well as Lincoln and all the cabinet. The president's secretaries, John Nicolay and John Hay, later wrote that the meeting involved, among other things, "a general comparing of rumors and outside information."

Sumner read aloud some stirring letters he had received from John Bright and Richard Cobden. One of the former's letters had been written on December 7 and had come on the *America*. Bright had told the senator: "At all hazards you must not let this matter grow to a war with England, even if you are right and we are wrong." "Nations in great crises and difficulties, have often done that which in their prosperous and powerful hour they would not have done, and they have done it without humiliation or disgrace."[26]

Among the items of "outside information" presumably touched at the meeting, or known to some of the persons who took part in it, not the least was a news report in that morning's *New York Times*. The report was published on page one under a headline in large type: "The Question of War or no War to be Settled at Washington." Sent from England by that newspaper's correspondent, it said:

> ... the four Confederates should be released and given up to the custody of Great Britain. ... The surrender of the men must be the *sine qua non* of any proposition or hope of peace.

This being the case, and it being equally true that our own recorded principles are wholly contrary to their retention, it seems to be the part of true patriots to yield the point frankly and fairly, and to call upon England in the same enlightened spirit, to meet us half way.

The bulk of the meeting was given to the hearing and discussion of Seward's long proposed reply. Its beginning pages appeared to sympathize at almost every point with the views of those who wished to reject the British demand and keep Mason, Slidell, and their aides in Fort Warren. By degrees, Seward's argument swung around to the opposite conclusion that the prisoners, having been captured in a manner inconsistent with principles steadily upheld by the United States in the past, should be cheerfully turned over to Lord Lyons.

The president and the other cabinet members would not agree to the adoption of Seward's reply, so the meeting was recessed until the following day, December 26. The discussion in the morning showed that the secretary of state was making converts, the president being the most conspicuous. At last, amid rueful expressions, such as those of Chase, to whom the surrender was "gall and wormwood," and those of Sumner, who was opposed to war but dreaded "compromise," the reply that Seward proposed was formally adopted, with small amendment.[27]

The struggle in Washington had been paralleled by a struggle within the issues of the *New York Times*. Its issue for Christmas morning had presented the spectacle of a newspaper dominated by one of its reporters. Admittedly, on page four, Raymond said in an editorial that English passions would subside; but editorials were not the only contents of the *Times*.[28] On pages one and two, the editor had not only published Adams's all-important thirtieth report but also large masses of information taken from British newspapers and other European sources—information totally consistent with the London correspondent's warnings and, in effect, supportive of his suggestion.

Seward's victory over his opponents in Washington was won at the cost of his having to write a reply to Lord Lyons which was not only long but stuffed with the kind of fustian which the New Yorker had learned to use, in cases when he might need to paralyze or confound an array of politicians who disagreed with him. The long reply, fustian and all, was quickly published. An American steamer, the *Washington*, leaving for Europe in advance of the Cunarder *Asia*, hurried the news across the ocean three days sooner than expected.

On January 8, 1862, at 4:00 P.M., a telegram was delivered at the U.S. legation in the British capital. In Moran's expression, it said that "Mason & Slidell would be given up to Lord Lyons when and where he pleased."

Minister Adams and his wife congratulated one another. Thurlow Weed, who had learned the news independently, came to visit and took part in the rejoicing. Moran drove to the St. James's club and told the news to some twenty diplomats he found there, and they "all sprang to their feet as if electrified." That night in London theatres, when announcements of peace were made, the audiences "arose like one & cheered tremendously."[29]

Just how Henry Adams took the news was not recorded on any paper now in evidence. It was usually his practice to do his best, let others vie for credit, and claim small credit for himself. When he had sufficient time to consider the outcome and satisfy himself that he understood its causes, he would say, " . . . Seward's course and Weed's dexterity just turned the corner. . . ."[30] The remark displayed its author's sometimes startling reticence. The younger Adams was perfectly aware that several persons, not just two, had "turned the corner." He was aware as well that, were he pressed to name all the persons, American and British, who had helped importantly to prevent the *Trent* affair from leading to an expanded war, he would sooner or later have to name himself—and, possibly, admit that, among those persons, he had been not only the youngest and most concealed but also one of the best prepared and informed, and by no means the least effective.

The precise degree of influence that Adams exerted in the crisis may be left for final judgment to historians. His biographers should concern themselves about the precise effect the outcome of the crisis had on him. The decision of his country's government, brought to Europe on the *Washington*, exactly suited his wishes and perfectly accorded with his efforts. What it mainly gave him was a sense of earned contentment. He had won in politics, won also as writer, won at an extremely early age, and won on a scale sufficiently grand to have about it something final.

Seward told Lord Lyons on December 27 that inducing the president and the other members of the cabinet to yield the captives had cost him a world of pains. He said he had gone "through the fires of Tophet."

The phrase marked the beginning of truly cordial relations between the secretary of state and the British minister. They quickly arranged the transfer of special commissioners Mason and Slidell, and their two secretaries, on a tugboat, the *Starlight*, to a British sloop-of-war, the *Rinaldo*, waiting off Provincetown at the end of Cape Cod.

The Confederate commissioners left Fort Warren without enthusiasm. They knew they might never serve their country so well as diplomats in London or Paris as they had served it as prisoners on the *San Jacinto* and in Boston. They were chagrined when the *Rinaldo* turned south, to carry them to remote St. Thomas in the West Indies, there to resume on the *La Plata*, but seventy days behind their former schedule, the journey they had intended to Southampton.[1]

For more than two weeks in England, Henry Adams had been living in two places, instead of one. When the Adamses had gone at Christmas to Walton-on-Thames, their hostess, Mrs. Sturgis, had prevailed on Mrs. Adams to leave Mary and Brooks at Mount Felix for an interval to be with the younger Sturgis children, who somewhat matched them in age. For her part, Mrs. Adams suggested that Henry, by dividing his time between London and Walton, might keep abreast of his work for his father and also help supervise the children. Henry's mother, who herself was momentarily at Walton, defended the arrangement by writing to her husband: " . . . Henry is far better *with* the children & *for* them than I am. They are perfectly happy, & Mary's enjoyment after months of solitude is a pleasure to see."[2]

Although it meant that he would have to work long hours while in London, the useful son and private secretary had welcomed the change and had gone each Saturday afternoon to Walton, returning to the city on Thursday or Friday. Probably, but not certainly, the news of the release of the confederate captives by the Union government had reached him on Wednesday, January 8, at Mount Felix, rather than at the house on Mansfield Street.[3]

Russell Sturgis was one of several Americans who were distinguished London bankers. He was a senior partner in the great firm of Baring Brothers. Mrs. Sturgis, his third wife, a woman of forty, had been Julia Overing Boit of Boston. At Christmas in 1861, she took Henry Adams into her beautiful house at Walton as unreservedly as Lizzie Hooker had taken him into her and her husband's lives in Rome on April 30, 1860. In Mrs. Sturgis, the younger Adams found a friend to whom he could safely impart whatever secrets he might wish to tell, knowing beyond a doubt that she would not reveal them. The presumption is warranted that he told her that he was not in England as his father's chief assistant at the legation, and his mother's partner in managing the household and caring for the children, but on his own initiative, and, further, that he had been serving, without his parents' knowledge, as the London correspondent of the *New York Times*. Till then, he had made no intimate friends, much though he had wished to. Mrs. Sturgis was the first he made, and his stays at Mount Felix were valuable to him for the chances they afforded her and him to get used to being friends and prepare to remain so all their lives.[4]

Moran recorded on Thursday, January 9, that the legation was deserted. The tide of visitors had receded.

On Friday, an elderly Englishman in London read something that excited him. His name was Joe Parkes. A civil servant, he was an ally of the legation and a general busybody and friend of everyone. What he had spied was a long editorial or leader in *The Times* about his friend Henry Adams. It said that a silly article called "A Visit to Manchester," written by a certain "'Mr. H. ADAMS, son of the American Minister in London,'" had been published in a Boston newspaper and was critical of the manners and habits of London society.

Parkes rushed to the office of John Delane to inform *The Times* that the author of the article was not only the minister's son but also his trusted assistant at the legation. Joe then rushed to the legation and told Henry that Delane knew what he really was.[5]

It is not implausible that the younger Adams was waiting for

Parkes, or someone equivalent, to appear with the same or similar news. It was Henry's habit to go through newspapers in quantity. That he had already studied the leader about him in that morning's *Times* when Joe rushed in seems more than likely.

In some manner not recorded, the truth about the publication of "A Visit to Manchester" was imparted to Henry's parents. They presumably were told that Charles had given the article to the *Boston Courier,* that its authorship was to have been kept secret, but something had gone wrong and the newspaper had let the secret out. The truth about the article was learned as well by Wilson and Moran.

The official secretaries were not well situated to criticize the younger Adams for misconduct. They preferred to take the news about the article in the *Courier* and the editorial in *The Times* as a subject for pleasantries and chaff. Moran said about their jokes with Henry, "We have had a little fun at his expense, and have told him that it is not every boy of 25 who can in 6 mo[nth]s residence here extort a leader from *The Times.*"[6]

Henry's elders were not disposed to scold him. They knew that two of their sons, Charles and Henry, had all along been writers and that both had been permitted to publish secretly in the Boston press. The Chief was naturally concerned, however, that the revelation of Henry's authorship of the article in the *Courier* might adversely affect his mission. The father accordingly wrote to Charles: "I see that Henry has got a first rate notice in the London Times today. You must take care about printing on your side, for the disposition is to make me responsible for it all."[7]

The mask that Henry wore that Friday, almost necessarily, was one of complete confession and good-humored entrapment in an error. He appeared to feel he should never have written the thing the *Courier* had published. Since he had, and had been caught in his mistake, he pretended—in his own phrase—to "grin and bear it."

Behind his grins, the son concealed new fear that his authorship of thirty-five important news reports to the *New York Times* might also be brought to the attention of John Delane.[8] The fear Adams now experienced was *not* made great by the fiasco of "A Visit to Manchester" or the leader Delane had published at his expense. Henry's fear built up to very large dimensions because the fiasco and the leader triggered an already latent, existing dread which was proportioned to the magnitude and completeness of his success.

That Adams had succeeded as a journalist could not be doubted.

When he made the secret arrangement with Raymond the previous March to become the "minister" of the *New York Times* in England, that newspaper already had a minister in France. The regular Paris correspondent of the *Times* was Dr. William E. Johnston, an older man and an experienced reporter. His weekly communications were published in New York over a pen-name: "MALAKOFF."[9] For eight months, since May 1861, the reports from nameless Adams in London and "MALAKOFF" in Paris had tended to arrive in New York on the same steamers. Much more often than the contrary, the former's reports had been published above the latter's as more urgent, informative, or important. Because the *Trent* affair had really centered in London, and because his reports throughout the affair had carried conviction and shown mastery of the subject, Adams had outdistanced Johnston altogether. Comparison had become impossible.

A chance existed that Americans, with few exceptions, would never understand the full importance of the *Trent* affair. It might be true that all Americans thought their history had involved two times of supreme danger and crisis. One had been the time of the Revolution, when the Americans had broken away from Great Britain, fought to secure their Independence, and formed their Union. The other had been the time of the War of 1812, when the Americans, fighting many battles, in the course of which the city of Washington was briefly captured and many of its buildings burned, kept their independence and confirmed their Union. But now the Union was sundered, and most Unionists and Confederates were prey to a temptation to believe that their present war with each other was the third great fact of American experience.

Henry Adams was a veteran of the secession winter in Washington and knew as well as anyone alive what it meant for the Union to divide and its members to go to war. Adams also was a veteran of the *Trent* affair. He was one of the few persons who could claim to have known that it was coming, felt its fullest impact, and helped effect its resolution. He might seldom say it, but he would act on the premise that this transatlantic paroxysm—a strange occurrence, in which no one was killed, yet the nerves of thousands were strained to the uttermost—was the controlling event of the mid-nineteenth century for the Americans and the British.

A first consequence of the *Trent* affair was plain enough. Because it was decided that the Unionists and the British would *not* fight, it was also decided that the Confederates were doomed. The rebels in America might fight extremely hard and well. The harder and better they fought, the worse would be their losses. Whatever they did, they would again be in the Union.

A second consequence of the affair was hard to notice. At Christmastime in 1861, when the Unionists surrendered some Confederate diplomats they had seized from a British mail ship, a door was opened for men and women in the United States and the United Kingdom to begin the work of assuring permanent peace between their countries. In the past, the Americans and the British had fought two wars. Now peace between them, perpetual and irremovable, had become a possibility. Adams had helped create that possibility. His work had not been visibly his, but it had been beneficent and effectual, and its anonymity did not detract from its importance.

The first Englishmen to notice an article called "A Visit to Manchester" and publish something relating to it had been persons connected with the *Manchester Daily Examiner and Times*. That newspaper had published extracts from the article on January 4. The leading newspaper in the city, the *Manchester Guardian*, taking an interest in the American article, published longer extracts and some lines of explanation on January 8. In London, seeing what the *Guardian* had printed, *The Times* reprinted all the extracts and lines of explanation on January 9. Thus, off and on, for six days in two English cities, parts of Adams's article were published without injury to its author.

*The Times* for Friday, January 10, 1862, contained on its editorial page no less than three long leaders relating directly or indirectly to the problem of America. In the first, Delane went back to the *Trent* affair and attempted to separate what had been clear in that transaction from what remained obscure. In the second, the editor again discussed the *Trent* affair. He said some very pointed things. " . . . except the actual shedding of blood, we have been for the last month at war with the Northern States of America. We have been spending money at a war rate; we have been moving troops, completing and equipping ships, preparing arms and ammunition, employing our minds and hardening our hearts. . . ." The virtual war had lasted, ironically, through the Christmas season. " . . . and now suddenly Peace is proclaimed, and we are at war no longer. We have to suspend operations, to bring home our forces, and do everything as if after a war of two or of thirty years."

*The Times* asked itself in the second leader what benefits so peculiar an experience had involved for Great Britain, and said it had shown the Americans that the British were in earnest; also that it had served as a useful test of British readiness. But, having said that much, Delane's great newspaper could not resist describing the war that *would* have been fought if it were not now strangely stopped. " . . . [the Americans] may be assured that it has not been a little war they have escaped, even though its actual course has been bloodless and short. In earnestness, in determination, and in magnitude of purpose, it would have been a very great war."

It was the third leader that concerned the sins of Henry Adams, and a better example of Delane's ideal of newspaper utterance would have been hard to find. Like the Aztecs, the English editor and his helpers believed in human sacrifice and needed a large supply of victims. Even longer than its two lengthy predecessors on the page, the third leader filled no less than 195 lines of handsome, well-printed type. The lines explained a curious item of recent history. Sometime the previous autumn, the authorities of the Northern States of America had grown convinced that the millowners of Manchester in England were preparing to demand that the blockade preventing the shipment of cotton from the Southern States of America to Liverpool be forcibly raised by the British Navy. To obtain good information about this dreaded conspiracy in Manchester, the Washington authorities had ordered a "Special Commissioner"—a Union counterpart of Mason or Slidell—to make a visit to Manchester.

The person chosen for the mission had been a "'Mr. H. ADAMS, son of the American Minister in London.'" *The Times* asserted: " . . . young Mr. ADAMS was despatched on a voyage of discovery, and proceeded to take soundings on this unexplored and dangerous coast. He kept a diary of his investigations. . . ." " . . . and the results of this delicate inquiry are published in the *Boston Daily Courier*."

*The Times* wished to differ with the "results" set forth by the explorer in his diary. Failing to explain very clearly what Adams's conclusions had been, the leader also failed to make its replies very plain. A long, turgid paragraph reiterated the favorite idea that the reconstruction of the American Union was a "chimerical object" and ended by suggesting that the Northern States of America would learn that they could not subdue the Southern. But the editorial became extremely clear and effective when it returned to attacking H. Adams and his behavior while on his voyage.

The explorer had had some things to say in "A Visit to Manchester" about the different systems of social intercourse in Manchester and London. In the words of *The Times*, Mr. Adams had drawn "a smart comparison between London and Manchester society, greatly to the disadvantage of the former." The American had listed some amenities which made social life in Manchester pleasing and friendly. He had alluded to what he considered the gloomy stiffness and discomfort of social life in London, calling it a city where "the guests shift for themselves, and a stranger had better depart at once as soon as he has looked at the family pictures."

In reply, the newspaper admitted that London was a mystery to all Americans. "The truth is, that what is called 'society' [in London] is . . . inscrutable to a stranger. . . . Even though he speak the same language and belong to a kindred stock . . . [the American] must ever be an outsider in this kind of intercourse."

It was not suggested that H. Adams cease visiting in London. On the contrary, he was encouraged to return. "He will profess to know less of us when he really knows more."

Later that Friday, January 10, 1862, Henry started a letter to Charles in which he said, " . . . I found myself this morning sarsed through a whole column of the Times, and am laughed at by all England." Leaving it to Charles to realize that he was himself part-author of his brother's embarrassment in London, the victim of British laughter turned to the graver perils that he faced. He said he had decided to interrupt temporarily his work for the *New York Times*. " . . . for the present I shall cease my other wirings as I am in agonies for fear they should be exposed."

So great was Henry's fear that he could not bring himself to do what he had been doing since the previous May: write to Raymond and put the envelope in a mail box. Prevented from doing that, he asked Charles to write on his behalf. "I wish I could get at Raymond, as I don't want to write myself, for fear my letter should get out. Couldn't you write to him and explain without mentioning names why his London correspondent has stopped for a time [?] My connection with him must on no account be known."[10]

The thing most important to Henry was that their father *never* be told—by himself, or Charles, or anyone—about the work his secretary had done for Raymond while a member of the legation. The younger brother told the elder: "The Chief as yet bears this vexation very good-naturedly [,] but another would be my ruin for a long time. I don't want him ever to know about it. . . ."[11]

On Saturday, January 11, still another British newspaper, the *London Examiner*, published something relating to "A Visit to

Manchester." Again, it was a leader resenting Adams's criticisms of London society. Henry had thought of himself as "gently skinned" by *The Times.* He soon remarked that the *Examiner* had "scalped me with considerable savageness."

Omitting a weekly report to Raymond for the first time since his vacation at Derby, Adams that Saturday mailed only his letter to his brother. After doing so, he presumably returned to Walton and to the company of Mrs. Sturgis, whom he would later remember as "the single source of warmth and light" that had shone into his wintry desolation in December 1861 and the first weeks of 1862.[12]

The following Saturday, January 18, afforded Adams a chance to resume his news reports. By then, however, a new prohibition had been raised against his doing so. His father had asked him solemnly not to write again for publication on subjects relating to current events or current politics during the remainder of their stay in England.[13] The son had responded by saying that he would not do so, and for the son the promise was a binding vow.

When still another week had passed, the younger Adams wrote and mailed a news report to Raymond which the editor was *not* to publish. Marked "Private & confidential," it brought the editor up to date in connection with English topics and dissolved the association of editor and reporter in a proper, friendly manner. The letter began by saying, "Circumstances make it advisable that I should, in the present state of affairs, cease to write or do anything that might be made public or that might by any accident bring me into public notice." The correspondent made only one allusion to the thirty-five reports he had earlier supplied. "I . . . only regret that I have been unable to speak so openly as I could have wished."

Charles had joined the cavalry. His regiment in early January went by ship to Port Royal in South Carolina. While on shipboard, during a storm and after a day of seasickness, he wrote Henry an unusually self-important and ill-tempered letter. Since the letter was followed by three months of silence during which he wrote to their father but not to Henry, a certain emphasis attached to the feelings the second son expressed.

His anger was inspired by several things, one being a letter from Henry saying that persons like themselves, what with the "strange madness of the times," were barred from having "settled lives and Christian careers." The furious answer that Charles composed proved abundantly that, if he wished to be a businessman and a writer when the war was over, he might succeed in one of his ambitions. With a genuine writer's sureness and simplicity of expression, he both sketched the general outlines of Henry's life till then and began to name its details.

The elder brother indicated that the younger's career had passed through three phases. He said that the three phases comprised a triumph entire and total. "Pray how old are you," the soldier raged, "& what has been your career? You graduate & pass two years in Europe, & witness by good luck a revolution;—you come home & fall upon great historic events & have better chances than any other young man to witness & become acquainted with them,—you go abroad while great questions are agitated in a position to know all about them, fortune has done nothing but favor you. . . ."[14]

The angry letter was delivered at the legation when fortunate Henry was in the midst of severing his connection with Raymond in New York. The younger brother did not reply until St. Valentine's Day, February 14, 1862—two days before his twenty-fourth birthday.

His reply was a sufficiently loving one. He told Charles he was shifting to a more reflective existence than the one he had earlier known and admitted that a portion of his augmented thoughtfulness was given to "self-contemplation." He said musingly: "You find fault with my desponding tone of mind. So do I. But the evil is one that probably lies where I can't get at it."

Once started in this vein, he mentioned something he *had* been able to get at. "I've disappointed myself," he wrote, "and experience the curious sensation of discovering myself to be a humbug." He did not say so, but the "humbug" he had discovered himself to have been was someone susceptible of objective study. It was the partly fictitious person who had written the reports to the *New York Times,* the last of which had now come back to their author for his perusal, in printed form.

In his letter to Charles, philosophical Henry was most concerned to notice that he could judge himself at all. The ability seemed new, increased, or somehow changed. "One would think," he suggested, rather abstractly, "that the *I* which could feel that, must be a different *ego* from the *I* of which it is felt." Putting the idea a different way, he reasoned that he must be a "double personality." There seemed to be two of him. And so there were, except that the two, respectively, were old and new. The old one had already slipped away and was gone. The new one was beginning life, had had no chance yet to do much thinking, and had only a few settled anticipations.

The emergent Adams expected to be no trouble to others. He would continue to watch over the children, Mary and Brooks. Yes, he would remain for a time with the "parent birds," as he called them. He would stay a while longer in England, where his elders, "afloat on the raging tide," did not yet seem entirely safe or comfortable.

His ideas with regard to one matter were clear and definite. He believed that, for Americans in the months directly ahead, the center of important public events would be American battlefields. So, sending his best wishes to Lieutenant Charles Francis Adams, Jr., of the First Massachusetts Volunteer Cavalry, he was able to conclude: "I think our work here is past its crisis. The insurgents will receive no aid from Europe, and so far are beaten. Our victory is won on this side [of] the water. On your side I hope it will soon be too."

# Notes

The narrative at many points is self-annotating. When it makes an assertion and at the same time fully specifies its source (e.g., a particular letter, a certain day's newspaper, or a given entry in one or another of the Adams family diaries—available in the Adams Papers microfilms), I have avoided the supererogation of notes.

The first five chapters are based on widely scattered sources. I have written notes for these five chapters in a form that requires no special explanations or assurances.

Each of the remaining twenty-two chapters is based on a compact body of *principal* sources and a scattering of *additional* sources. I have begun the notes for each of these later chapters by listing the chapter's principal sources. Then I have added conventional notes directing the reader to the chapter's additional sources. This device has permitted the compression of the notes for the narrative as a whole to a reasonable length; but the device is unusual and requires that the following assurance be given: if a particular assertion made at some point in chapters 6 through 27 is neither self-annotated nor supported by a note directing attention to an additional source or several additional sources, the reader is assured that the assertion is based instead on one or more of the chapter's *principal* sources. Moreover, such unspecified connections between my assertions in chapters 6 through 27 and the particular chapter's *principal* sources should not be difficult to track down.

The preparation of the narrative has involved my looking into thousands of sources which the notes that follow do not mention. My object in supplying the notes is not to indicate the breadth or thoroughness of my inquiries but instead to specify which sources especially made possible my telling the story I have told.

Biographers will be better understood when it is more widely recognized how completely they depend upon three things: evidence, intellectual honesty, and imagination. What the biographer does is tirelessly imagine story after story until a story comes to mind which is in every respect sustained and in no respect undermined by all the available evidence, precisely understood. Then the biographer tells that story. But the matter does not rest there. For the story, when told, is likely to seem—and in one sense is—a mere statement of the facts. Thus the hapless biographer, after an effort of imagination which has to be made to be appreciated, and after developing many stories in the course of finding one, is given the appearance of an unimaginative person, only adept at amassing evidence and exercising intellectual scruples.

Although willing to be grouped with my fellow biographers for the time being as an unimaginative and uncreative writer, I want to mention that the story told in this book did not come easily to mind. The main idea of the story, expressed in the preface, and to some extent in the first two chapters, proved elusive and inaccessible. Simple though it seems, the idea grew clear to me only a segment at a time, and very slowly, during more than thirty years of inquiring, imagining, and—when ideas failed because of contrary evidence—more imagining.

In the last analysis, biographers may be more the beneficiaries than the authors of ideas. The emergence of the story offered here, while perhaps to be credited in part to myself, should mainly be attributed to the silent but devastating reproaches of the evidence, which, by estranging me from many fond but unsound conceptions, left me free to begin afresh with better ones. Despite all I say above about imagining, my experience has *not* been one of inventing a story. Rather it has been that of being given one.

A difficult enterprise, biography ends in persuading the biographer to thank the angels and revere the gods.

# Abbreviations

| | |
|---|---|
| ABA | Abigail Brown Brooks (1808-1889) (married Charles Francis Adams)—HA's mother |
| AHR | *American Historical Review* |
| Anderson | *The Letters and Journals of General Nicholas Longworth Anderson . . . 1855-1892,* NY, Lond & Edinburgh 1942 |
| AP | The Adams Papers, at the Massachusetts Historical Society, Boston—widely available in microfilm |
| *Autobiography* | *Charles Francis Adams / 1835-1915 / An Autobiography,* Bost & NY 1916—in effect a response to HA's *Education,* as privately circulated in 1907 |
| BA | Brooks Adams (1848-1927)—HA's younger brother |
| BAdv | *The Boston Daily Advertiser* |
| BCour | *The Boston Daily Courier* |
| Bemis, I | Samuel Flagg Bemis, *John Quincy Adams and the Foundations of American Foreign Policy,* NY 1949 |
| Bemis, II | Samuel Flagg Bemis, *John Quincy Adams and the Union,* NY 1956 |
| Beringause | Arthur F. Beringause, *Brooks Adams / A Biography,* NY 1955 |
| Bost | Boston |
| BWC | Benjamin W. Crowninshield—Harvard classmate of HA |
| Cater | *Henry Adams and His Friends / A Collection of His Unpublished Letters,* compiled with a Biographical Introduction by Harold Dean Cater, Bost 1947 |

| CFA | Charles Francis Adams (1807-1886)—HA's father |
|---|---|
| CFA2 | Charles Francis Adams (1835-1915)—HA's elder brother |
| CMG | Charles Milnes Gaskell—intimate English friend of HA |
| *Cycle* | *A Cycle of Adams Letters / 1861-1865*, edited by Worthington Chauncey Ford, Bost & NY 1920 |
| *Degradation* | Henry Adams, *The Degradation of the Democratic Dogma* [a title supplied by its compiler, Brooks Adams, who also supplied a long introductory essay, "The Heritage of Henry Adams"], NY 1920 |
| Duberman | Martin B. Duberman, *Charles Francis Adams / 1807-1886*, Bost 1961 |
| EC | Elizabeth Sherman (married James Donald Cameron)—intimate friend of HA |
| *Education* | [Henry Adams], *The Education of Henry Adams*, Bost & NY 1918 [gratuitously, intrusively, and damagingly subtitled *An Autobiography* by its editor, Henry Cabot Lodge and/or the publisher, Houghton Mifflin Company, evidently to lend the book a seeming similarity to *Charles Francis Adams / 1835-1915 / An Autobiography*, issued by the same publisher two years earlier] |
| Ford, I | *Letters of Henry Adams/(1858-1891)*, edited by Worthington Chauncey Ford, Bost & NY 1930 |
| GWA | George Washington Adams (1801-1829)—HA's eldest paternal uncle; died nine years before HA's birth |
| H | Houghton Library, Harvard University |
| HA | Henry Adams (1838-1918)—christened Henry Brooks Adams; dropped his middle name when thirty-two, in 1870 |
| HAP | Henry Adams Papers, 1890-1918, separately boxed at the Massachusetts Historical Society |

| | |
|---|---|
| Hay | John Hay—biographer of Lincoln; secretary of state; intimate friend of HA |
| HMag | *The Harvard Magazine* |
| HMC | Historical Manuscripts Commission, Chancery Lane, London |
| HUA | Harvard University Archives, in Widener Library, Harvard University |
| JA | John Adams (1735-1826)—HA's great-grandfather |
| JQA | John Quincy Adams (1767-1848)—HA's grandfather |
| JQA2 | John Quincy Adams (1833-1894)—HA's eldest brother |
| LC | Library of Congress, Washington, D. C. |
| LCA | Louisa Catherine Johnson (1775-1852) (married John Quincy Adams—1767-1848)— HA's grandmother; decisively influential in his life |
| LCK | Louisa Catherine Adams (1831-1870) (married Charles Kuhn)—HA's elder sister |
| *Letters to a Niece* | Henry Adams, *Letters to a Niece and Prayer to the Virgin of Chartres*, Bost & NY 1920 |
| Lond | London |
| LTimes | *The Times* of London |
| MA | Mary Adams (1846-1928)—HA's younger sister |
| MHA | Marian (or Clover) Hooper (1843-1885)—wife of HA |
| MHS | Massachusetts Historical Society, Boston |
| Moran | *The Journal of Benjamin Moran / 1857-1865*, edited by Sarah Agnes Wallace & Frances Elma Gillespie, Chicago 1948-1949 |
| NY | New York City |
| NYPL | New York Public Library, New York City |
| NYTimes | *The New York Times* |
| Pierce | Edward L. Pierce, *Memoir and Letters of Charles Sumner*, Bost 1877-1894 |
| RWH | Robert William Hooper—father-in-law of HA |
| Seward | William Henry Seward—governor of New York; senator from New York; secretary of state; friend of HA |
| Sumner | Charles Sumner—senator from Massachusetts; friend of HA |

TC  Thoron Collection, meaning the letters, books, photographs, and other evidence relating to HA collected by Louisa Chapin Hooper and her husband, Ward Thoron, originally concentrated in their hands, now mostly at the Houghton Library

Weed  Thurlow Weed—boss of New York; political ally of Seward; friend of the Adamses

## 1 / A FINE BOY

1. It seems possible that, at some date now unknown, HA learned that he was born while CFA was reading *Oedipus at Colonus*. At his own direction, HA and his wife were buried under a memorial in Washington, D. C., which bears no names. To this extent, their burials might be thought to recapitulate the disappearance of Oedipus, and the life of HA may be viewed as ending in a manner somewhat consonant with its beginning.

2. HA, *Education*, 3, 23; CFA2, *Autobiography*, 14-15. The assumption that HA should consider himself as much a Brooks as an Adams is repeatedly evidenced in the letters of ABA to HA, 1858-60, AP.

3. HA, *Education*, 15; CFA2, *Autobiography*, 8, 10; Duberman, 74.

4. HA, *The Life of George Cabot Lodge*, Bost & NY 1911, 10-13—" . . . the . . . boy . . . felt the sea as an echo or double of himself."

5. Explicit reference to Arthur is remarkably absent from the writings of HA.

6. CFA2, *Autobiography*, 5-6.

7. HA, *Education*, 5-6. See also CFA, *Diary*, 3 Dec 1841 through 20 Jan 1842, AP.

8. HA's tendency to react to weather became very evident to HA himself. See especially HA to ABA, 7 Feb 1860, AP—" . . . the weather's beastly and . . . I feel it as I always do feel bad weather." See also *Education*, 7-8—"Winter and summer . . . marked two modes of life. . . ." HA may never have liked the Mount Vernon Street house. CFA2 disliked it intensely. See *Education*, 243, and *Autobiography*, 5-6.

9. Cater, cxvi note 170. See also HA to Hay, 16 Nov 1890, Cater, 219—"my height, or say five-feet-six." Moran, in his *Journal*, II, 1140, says that he himself, at 5'5", was "quite an inch" taller than CFA. Taken together, these indications seem to point towards HA's being slightly taller than CFA.

10. HA, "Henry Brooks Adams," in *Class Book of 1858*, HUA. See also his account of his participation in a snowball fight in *Education*, 41-42.

11. HA to EC, 15 Aug 1912, HAP—" . . . strength seems to be my strong point anyway." See also Louisa Hooper Thoron to James Truslow Adams, 2 Sep 1930, TC—" . . .[HA] had the habit of going downstairs faster than anybody I have ever seen."

12. ABA to HA, 22 Mar 1859, AP.

13. CFA2 to HA, 25 Feb 1907, HAP.

14. The depth of HA's attachment to his elder sister is best evidenced by his reactions to her death. See *Education*, 287-289.

15. Recollections of Louisa Hooper Thoron and Aileen Tone. The latter told me she was almost shocked at times by HA's eager eating and drinking.

16. Mary W. H. Schuyler to CFA, 6 Nov 1870, AP—" . . . [ABA] once told me, that Henry was her most clever son."

17. ABA to HA, 4 Oct 1858, AP—" . . . I . . . reminded him [CFA] that . . . in all your life you had never given us a moment's anxiety, but much happiness & pride. . . ."

18. When BA was a child, CFA read Aesop's fables to him "out of a charming copy bound in blue, filled with engravings, in which I delighted." See BA, "The Seizure of the Laird Rams," MHS *Proceedings*, XLV, 244.

19. HA, "Retrospect," HMag, Mar 1857, 66—the fox and the grapes. See also MHA to RWH, 1 Aug 1880, AP—" . . . the most delicious tapestry with Aesop's fables, which we [MHA and HA] explained to our diminutive guides to their great delectation."

20. HA to CMG, 5 Nov 1872, Ford, I, 234.

21. CFA2, *Autobiography*, 5, 11—describing CFA as "more rigid," "narrower," and "even less companionable" than JQA.

22. HA to Samuel Eliot Morison, 28 Nov 1913, in the latter's "A Letter and a Few Reminiscences of Henry Adams," *New England Quarterly*, Mar 1954, 95-97.

23. HA, *Education*, 15. In the 1950's, granted unusual access to the HA Library at MHS, I chanced upon the book, which apparently had gone unnoticed, and brought it to the attention of the then Director, Stephen T. Riley.

24. Ibid., 14-15. HA's having frequented CFA and JQA's libraries when a child is also evidenced by his later building a library in the front of his Washington house and by his delight in being visited there by children.

25. HA to Louisa Chapin Hooper, 17 Dec 1899, TC.

26. HA, *Education*, 12-14.

27. HA to Mabel Hooper, 9 Feb 1891, *Letters to a Niece*, 41—"After reading about Tahiti since I was a child. . . ." That he similarly read about other distant lands when a child is evidenced in many places in his writings, e.g. a passage in his *Democracy*, NY 1880, 239: "There is little law business in Central Asia, and . . . not enough to require a special agent in Australia. Carrington could hardly be induced to lead an expedition to the sources of the Nile in search of [legal] business. . . ."

28. Beringause, 16-17.

29. HA's dropping his middle name in 1870 apparently sig-nified—among other things—a long-standing desire not to be counted as a Brooks. Yet he did accept an inheritance from his maternal grandfather.

30. HA, *Education*, 11.

31. Recollections of Aileen Tone. The lapse occurred in 1914 while HA was being questioned by the French police.

32. His knowledge that he was already great manifestly underlay all of HA's actions from an early age, is best evidenced by his actions and writings in their totality, and helps explain why he was sometimes thought conceited or self-important.

33. I repeat the story as it was separately repeated to me on different occasions by Aileen Tone, Louisa Hooper Thoron, and Thomas Boylston Adams, all of whom used the words "would have married a blackamoor" to get away from "Boston." Variantly, and I think erroneously, Abigail Adams Homans, in her *Education by Uncles*, Bost 1966, 16, says "get away from Quincy."

34. Typewritten memoir of JQA2 by Abigail Adams Homans, photocopied by me with her permission on 5 Dec 1956, in which she speaks explicitly and at length about her father's "lack of ambiition." See also ABA to HA, 22 Mar 1859, AP—". . . I wish from my heart John had more of Charles and your perseverance & determination."

35. HA to CFA2, 5 Jun 1863, AP.

36. HA to CFA2, 21 Dec 1866, AP—". . . such as I am, the product is unique and positive."

37. HA, *Education*, 52, 243. See also HA to Godkin, 6 Aug 1881,

Cater, 110—"For twenty-five years [that is, since 1856] . . . I have been trying to persuade people that I don't come from Boston. . . ."

38. BA, "Heritage of Henry Adams," in *Degradation*, 13, 35.

39. William P. Lunt, *A Discourse delivered at Quincy, March 11, 1848, at the interment of John Quincy Adams . . .*, Bost 1848.

40. HA, *Education*, 21; CFA2, *Autobiography*, 32.

41. Edward Everett, *A Eulogy on the life and character of John Quincy Adams*, Bost 1848; HA, *Education*, 21-22.

42. CFA2, *Charles Francis Adams*, Bost & NY 1900, 69.

43. HA, *Education*, 25ff—" . . . that his father was running for office . . . dwarfed for the time every other excitement. . . ."

44. HA to Morison, cited in note 22 above.

45. HA to CFA2, 6 Aug 1859, AP—" . . . one person is no more to you than another. A position I was in until I went to College. . . ."

46. HA, *Education*, 243—on "outlawry" as his birthright.

47. ABA to HA, 9 Apr 1859, AP—"fond as you [HA] are of young children."

48. The impulse CFA2 felt to own HA is best evidenced by the elder brother's later, disturbed reactions to the younger's marriage.

49. HA, *Education*, 31.

50. In the memoir of JQA2 cited in note 34 above, the eldest son is quoted as having called HA "a philosopher." See also HA to CFA2, 6-9 Apr 1859, AP—"I'm a philosopher . . . "; HA to CFA2, 6 Aug 1859, AP—" . . . give credit to the philosopher"; and CFA2 to HA, Jan 1862, AP—" . . . You [HA] set up for a philosopher." The appellation may be supposed to have been one of long standing.

51. HA, *Education*, 31. CFA evidently gave HA a set of the resulting volumes. When he catalogued his library after leaving college, HA listed the set as JA's "Life and works, 10 vols."

52. HA to CFA2, 21 Dec 1866, AP—"As for the [question of] suicide, I quite agree with you, having long ago made up my mind that when life becomes a burden to me, I shall end it, and I have even decided the process."

53. Ibid.

54. Originally in TC, the volumes, so inscribed, were given by Louisa Hooper Thoron to the Massachusetts Historical Society in the 1950's.

55. HA, "Henry Brooks Adams," cited above in note 10.

56. Anderson, 13—oral exams. "Six . . . in Latin and Greek, three in mathematics, and one each in ancient history and ancient geography."

57. CFA, *Diary*, 1 Aug 1853, AP—quoted in CFA2 to HA, 15 Nov 1895, HAP.

58. There seems to have been a connection between HA's early thoughts of suicide and his thoughts about school. Both subjects may have been adverted to often in the early volumes of his diary. When he read and burned the volumes at fifty, he wrote concerning their contents, "My brain reels with the vividness of emotions more than thirty years old." He also wrote, "Much is unpleasant and painful to recall." See HA, *Diary*, 23 Sep and 30 Sep 1888, AP. Moreover, HA's definition of "school" may have included his first two years at college. See HA to CFA2, 16 May 1862, AP—" . . . ever since I was a boy at Mrs Storey's in Harvard Street. . . ." If HA did so define "school," his intervals of suicidal melancholia may not have ceased till after he stopped living with CFA2 and, as a college junior, moved into a dormitory.

## 2 / PERILOUS ENDURANCE

1. The view I have taken of the Adams family's history somewhat emphasizes the women to whom a succession of Adams males were married. The same emphasis appears in HA's own writings about his family's history, most obviously in his *Education*, but notably also in two extraordinary long letters, HA to BA, 18 Feb 1909 and HA to BA, 13 Mar 1909, H. The family's history is well told in Bemis I & II.

2. Bemis, I, 85n.

3. Meade Minnegerode, *Some American Ladies*, NY & Lond 1926, 174-175.

4. JA to JQA, 4 Mar 1811, AP.

5. GWA was awarded a part at commencement at Harvard in 1821. His discourse on "The influence of natural scenery on poetry" is in HUA.

6. GWA, *An Oration delivered at Quincy, on the Fourth of July, 1824*, Bost 1824, 4, 7.

7. Bemis, II, 94-85, 116-118.

8. Ibid., 177-184; JQA, *Diary*, 2-6 May 1829, AP; CFA, *Diary*, 2 May 1829, AP.

9. JQA, *Diary*, 7 Nov 1830, AP.

10. CFA2, *Charles Francis Adams*, 15-16.

11. Hugh A. Garland, *The Life of John Randolph of Roanoke*, NY 1850, II, 154.

12. Duberman, 8-11. See also MHS *Proceedings*, 1899-1900, 199, and CFA2, *Charles Francis Adams*, 5—"... French thus became the child's native tongue. ..."

13. I have knowingly departed from historical truth by omitting Elizabeth Adams, daughter of HA's Aunt Mary. There is such a thing as an overcomplicated biographical narrative.

14. HA, *Education*, 5, 44.

15. HA, "Henry Brooks Adams," *Class Book of 1858*, HUA.

16. HA to Mabel Hooper LaFarge, 16 Jun 1901, Cater, 511—"... she [ABA] had the excuse that I was the fourth, and names were getting scarce. ..."

17. See the two extraordinary letters cited in note 1 above.

18. HA, *Education*, 16-19.

19. HA to Mabel Hooper, 9 Feb 1891, *Letters to a Niece*, 44—"I don't mean that the place [Tahiti] is gloomy, but just quietly sad, as though it were a very pretty woman who had got through her fun and her troubles, and grown old, and was just amusing herself by looking on, without caring much what happens. She has retired a long way out of the world, and sees only her particular friends, like me, with the highest introductions; but she dresses well, and her jewels are superb. In private I suspect she is given to crying because she feels so solitary; but when she sees me she always smiles like my venerable grandmother when I was five years old."

20. See the illustrations of this book: the miniature painting of LCA, aged twenty-two, painted by James Thomas Barber in 1797, and the earliest photograph of HA, aged twenty, made for the Harvard *Class Book of 1858*. The suggestion that LCA in old age looked with special interest and pleasure at the face of her grandson Henry is very possibly corroborated by his saying in old age that he when a boy had taken "distinct pleasure in looking at her [LCA's] delicate face"; that is, the grandson's remembered pleasure may indicate that there had been a matching phenomenon, a grandmother's pleasure. See HA, *Education*, 16.

21. The bronze figure made by Augustus St. Gaudens for the memorial erected over the graves HA and MHA was, by the former's direction, shaped by the sculptor to represent both sexes in a single human form. The figure is androgynous. The impulse to have it so made evidently arose from HA's early experience of complete affinity between himself and LCA. Alluding to this affinity in his *Education*, 19, HA says he, like LCA, was "half exotic." This expression could seem a mistake. Ernest Samuels, in *The Education of Henry Adams*,

Bost 1974, 547 note 35, correctly points out that HA by birth was only one-eighth a Marylander. But HA's meaning apparently was that he matched LCA in feeling half-out-of-place in Massachusetts—also that it is feeling, not birth, that really counts in such matchings.

22. HA's poems include several in which he appears to be speaking as if he seriously viewed himself as close to God. See especially his sonnet (translated from Petrarch) beginning "For my lost life . . ." in HA, *Esther*, NY 1884 (or facsimile ed., NY 1938), 108.

23. ABA to HA, 10 May 1859, AP—"Your room [at Quincy] is just as you left it, the little lantern hanging from the wall, the Cologne bottle, & desk. . . . The books in the entry. . . ."

24. The book and letter are in the HA Library, MHS.

25. HA, *Education*, 43-48.

26. Bought by JQA in 1820, the house had a ballroom and was well-adapted to entertaining. See Bemis, I, 275.

27. HA later described himself as "very intimate" with MCA, and I have assumed that their intimacy was of long standing. See HA to CMG, 29 Sep 1870, AP.

28. HA, *Education*, 46-49; CFA, *Diary*, 1-7 Jun 1850, AP.

29. CFA, *The Progress of Liberty in a Hundred Years*, Taunton, Mass., 1876, 22. See also CFA, *What Makes Slavery a Question of National Concern?*, Bost 1855, 25, 38-39.

30. HA, *Education*, 47-48; HA, *Democracy*, chap. 6.

31. HA's account of his announcement in his *Education*, 51, is startingly at variance with an account earlier given by CFA2 to Edward L. Pierce and published in Pierce, III, 244-245. But both accounts make HA the bearer of the great news, for Sumner's delectation. Of the two accounts, I tend to believe the later one, by HA, and suppose it was partly intended as a correction of the earlier, by CFA2.

32. HA, an uncanny judge of character, had enjoyed numberless opportunities when a child to take note of Sumner's qualities while the future senator was visiting CFA in his library. HA's earliest letters to Sumner are all more or less deliberate strokes of conciliation and flattery.

33. Sol Barzman, *The First Ladies*, NY [1970], 56.

34. HA, *Diary*, 23 Sep 1888, AP—" . . . I am reading my old Diaries, and have already finished and destroyed six years, to the end of my college course."

35. CFA, *Diary*, 1 Aug 1853, AP.

36. HA, "Retrospect," HMag, Mar 1857, 63.

37. HA's mother apparently liked to call him "old boy," an

expression inspired, it would seem, by his exceptional maturity. See ABA to HA, 10 May and 3 Aug 1859, AP.

38. The idea of ending a family's history appears explicitly, albeit in a feminized and destructive form, in HA, *Memoirs of Marau Taaroa / Last Queen of Tahiti*, privately printed 1903, 48—"If a family must be ruined by a woman, perhaps it may as well be ruined thoroughly and brilliantly by a woman who makes it famous."

39. The idea of HA advanced in this biography was first suggested to me, in vague outline, by the juxtaposition of Henry Adams and George Washington to be found in BA, "The Heritage of Henry Adams," in *Degradation*. I first read this essay in 1942 and since then have been assisted by it immeasurably.

40. HA to CFA2, 7 Jun 1859, AP—" . . . I, H. B. Adams. . . ."

41. HA, *Democracy*, 124.

42. Ibid., 123.

43. EC to Louisa Hooper Thoron, 18 Feb 1934, TC.

44. That HA was exceptionally conscious of having had a grand-mother who decisively affected him can be glimpsed in his curious remark: "Every American would object that it is untrue to nature [for the hero of a novel] to have a grand-father, but I never yet heard anyone object to a grand-mother." See HA to Hay, 31 Oct 1883, AP.

45. HA's earliest extant writings abound in indications that his four ambitions were already fully formed, and may possibly suggest that he had defined them beyond alteration at fourteen, when he began his diary. Moreover, he later claimed, in effect, to have known and followed his preferences from birth, saying: "I have never varied my course at all. From my birth to this moment it has been straight as an arrow. . . . All the accidents of life have fallen in with the bent of my disposition. . . ." See HA to CFA2, 21 Dec 1866, AP.

46. That the death of his elder sister in 1870 was extremely dangerous to HA will be a chief contention of the second book of this biography.

47. HA's earliest writings indicate knowledge of Shakespeare and a special interest in *Hamlet,* but the catalogue HA made of his library in 1858 lists no books by Shakespeare. The omission may indicate that HA at the time owned no Shakespeare books *in good condition.*

3 / POLITICIAN AND WRITER

1. Kimball C. Elkins, "Foreshadowings of Lamont . . .," *Harvard Library Bulletin,* Winter 1954, 46-47.

2. Compare Robert W. Lovett, "The Undergraduate and the Harvard Library . . .," *Harvard Library Bulletin,* Spring 1947, 222; and HA, "College Politics," HMag, May 1858, 145-148.

3. MHS *Proceedings,* LXIV, 53.

4. *Photographs of the Class of Fifty-eight. College Views and College Faculty,* HUA.

5. *A Catalogue of the Officers and Students of Harvard University for the academical year 1854-55. First Term,* HUA.

6. CFA2, *Autobiography,* 24.

7. HA, *Education,* 67.

8. See note 10 below.

9. CFA, *Diary,* 28 Oct through 30 Nov 1854, AP.

10. All assertions made in chapters 3, 4, and 5 concerning HA's absences, points earned, points penalized, and resulting rank are drawn from one or more of the following records in HUA: (1) *Absences from and Tardiness at Recitations and Lectures,* 1854-1858; (2) *Monthly Returns, Examinations, and Term Aggregates,* 1854-1858; and (3) *Rank Scales/ 1827-58.* Detailed information about the college rules abounds in Anderson, 13-132.

11. HA, "Retrospect," HMag, Mar 1857, 62.

12. Among the friends of CFA2, the one HA seems to have regarded most highly was Henry Higginson.

13. Anderson, 42.

14. Ibid., 23; HA, *Education,* 56-57.

15. HMag itself provides details concerning its founding, management, etc., at various points in its issues.

16. HMag, Nov 1855, 488.

17. Anderson, 45.

18. HA to CFA2, 16 May 1862, AP.

19. Ibid.; HA to CFA2, 30 Jul 1867, AP.

20. CFA2, *Autobiography,* 26.

21. HA, "College Politics," HMag, May 1857, 143.

22. While forming ties with Lee and Anderson, respectively the president and vice-president of the class, HA also retained friendly ties with one of his Boston companions of long standing, Benjamin W. Crowninshield, who was class secretary.

23. *Institute of 1770, Records, 1854-57,* HUA—minutes of meetings on 14 Sep, 26 Oct, and 23 Nov 1855, and 25 Apr 1856. HA's October "Allegory" reportedly concerned the "golden age." His November pieces were judged "excellent" by the institute's secretary.

24. John Langdon Sibley, *Private Journal,* 18 and 23 Dec 1855,

HUA; Francis Ellingwood Abbot, *A Private Diary*, 23 Dec 1855, HUA; *Institute of 1770, Records, 1854-57*—minutes dated 21 Dec 1855.

25. *Institute Records*, same minutes; HA, "Resolutions on the Death of William Gibbons of New York. December, 1855," original MS in HA's handwriting, naming Pond as coauthor, in HA's own bound volume of his college writings, HA Library, MHS. Pond was president of the institute during the term. See also the printed "Obituary," HMag, Dec 1855, 46—which does not name the authors.

26. *Institute of 1770, Records, 1854-57*—minutes dated 4 Jan and 11 Apr 1856. The minutes dated 4 Apr 1856 record that HA and Burgess lost a debate to Allen and Frost while upholding the negative on the question, "Is general reading advisable in a College course?"

27. See note 10 above.

28. CFA2 in old age claimed credit for HA's moving onto the campus as a junior, saying—*Autobiography*, 24-25: "When I graduated [in July 1856], I persuaded him [HA] to live in the [college] buildings. . . . He did so, and it saved his college course." But HA's plan to move into the dormitories was matured months before July, and the elder brother's remarks are apparently an instance of his persuading himself that his advice had caused HA to do something which in fact his advice had been too late to affect, coming well after HA had decided his intentions.

29. Anderson, 76.

30. Ibid., 73.

31. HA, "College Politics," HMag, May 1857, 144-146.

32. HA, *Education*, 57—". . . they [the Virginians in the Class of 1858] and he [HA] knew well how thin an edge of friendship separated them in 1856 from mortal enmity." Yet the emphasis of the passage is less on "enmity" than upon "friendship" and "affinity."

33. Anderson, 31.

34. HA, *Education*, 51—especially the episode of the white crepe.

35. Anderson, 82, 85, 87.

36. Compare HA, *Education*, 42—". . . the sight of Court Square packed with bayonets . . . in order to return a negro to slavery—wrought frenzy in the brain of a . . . boy from Quincy [HA], who wanted to miss no reasonable chance of mischief."; and Anderson, 23—"Anthony Burns has been . . . returned to Boston. . . . This nigger Burns is received with as much ostentation as if he were President of the United States."

37. Anderson, 82; C. A. Allen, "A Plea for Oil," HMag, Sep 1857, 291. My only source for HA's room number is an old undocumented note by Louisa Hooper Thoron in TC.

38. Pierce, III, 441ff.

39. Ibid., III, 462ff.

40 That the injury of Sumner by Brooks was felt by HA almost as an injury to himself is evidenced by the presence of a scene in his *Democracy*, 368-369, in which a senator is struck with a cane, and a line in his *Esther*, 39, in which a person speaks of having "treacherously stabbed him [another person] in the back."

41. Anderson, 87-88. See also Francis Ellingwood Abbot, *Diary*, 14 Jun 1856, HUA—" . . . [Dorr] had fellows in his room till after midnight *drinking;* they left him in apparently good health, but next morning Louis Cabot went into his room to call him to go to prayers, and found him dead on the floor! Cabot rang the bell and fainted away."—"It has made a deep impression on his classmates. . . . "

42. HA's MS of the resolutions in his own bound volume of his college writings, HA Library, MHS; published "Obituary," HMag, Jun 1856, 223.

43. "Catalogue of the Class of '58" in Anderson, 129-131.

44. Anderson, 90 note 3.


4 / ELECTION

1. HA, "Retrospect," HMag, Mar 1857, 61—" . . . unless he wrote regularly for a periodical."

2. Sol Barzman, *The First Ladies*, NY [1970], 49; HA, *Education*, 36.

3. Pierce, III, 509-517.

4. HA to Sumner, 22 Dec 1858, Cater, 1-2—"I believe now, as I said to you two years ago, that you have Massachusetts. . . . "

5. The account I offer of HA's early relations with Sumner is inferred perforce from later evidence, including not only all the extant letters between them but also their known actions towards each other and relevant passages in HA's novels and *Education*.

6. CFA2, *Charles Francis Adams*, 104-105.

7. *Records of ye Hasty Pudding Club;* HUA; *Hasty Pudding Club, Secy's Rep.*, XVII, 1855-58, HUA.

8. *Records of ye Hasty Pudding Club;* playbills in *An Illustrated History of Hasty Pudding Club Theatricals*, Cambridge, Mass., 1933.

9. It should be noticed that HA, writing when a college junior about an "angel in muslin," chose to imagine the "angel" and a Harvard student hunting for "clover"— the alternative name of his future wife, Marian (or Clover) Hooper.

10. *Hasty Pudding Club, Secy's Rep.*, XVII, 6 Mar 1857, HUA.

11. Anderson, 117.

12. All my assertions concerning HA's performance as alligator are drawn from *Hasty Pudding Club—Alligator Records, 1848-1858*, HUA.

13. Undated clipping pasted into E. Arnoult's Term Aggregates, Juniors, Term 1856-57, in *Monthly Returns, Examinations & Term Aggregates, HUA.*

14. HA, "The Cap and Bells," HMag, Apr 1858, 125-26, 129. See also HA to ABA, 6-9 Jan 1860, AP—". . . that ring which you gave me. . . . " My assumption that both sources refer to a single ring may be mistaken.

15. *Hasty Pudding Club, Secy's Rep.*, XVII, 5 Jun 1857, HUA—" . . . we can't remain quite mute/ Regarding *Adams'* Absolute. . . . "

16. HA, *Education*, 59. "Rooney," with an "e," is the spelling used by HA in his early writings.

17. Anderson, 106-107.

18. *Hasty Pudding Library/ Record Book,* HUA—page for "Henry B. Adams." The entries are all in HA's handwriting.

19. Allen's autobiography in *Class Book of 1858*, HUA.

20. Of the three editors elected for the class, Allen, Patten, and Tobey, the first was most a leader, if one may judge from their overall college records. See HMag, Jul 1857, 264.

21. Allen's "Considerations," in Elkins, "Foreshadowings of Lamont . . . , " *Harvard Library Bulletin,"* Winter 1954, 42-45—"This project of a large Club has been discussed in the Senior Class ever since last May."

22. *Harvard College Papers, Second Ser.*, XXIV, 1857, 9; and XXV, 2 (on Holden Chapel), HUA. See also Elkins, op. cit., 45-46.

23. HA's changeover to librarian is noted in an undated Jun or Jul 1857 entry in *Hasty Pudding Club, Secy's Rep.*, XVII, HUA.

24. Anderson, 116.

25. See Allen's "Considerations," note 21 above.

26. Anderson, 111-112.

27. *Annual Scales of College Rank, 1857-71,* HUA.

28. Gerard Curtis Tobey, "The Chronicles," *Harvard Class Book of 1858*, HUA.

29. Anderson, 115.

30. HA adverts to rank lists in his "Reading in College," HMag, Oct 1857, 312, and again in his *Education*, 61, 303. See also ibid., 77—"He had revolted at the American . . . university. . . . "—and 306—" . . .

supposing . . . they [the Harvard students] should have turned on him [HA] as fiercely as he had turned on his old instructors."

31. Index card, "Adams, Henry (1858)," in Catalogue, HUA, summarizing the contents of *Fac. Rec. XIV* as they relate to him.

32. "The Chronicles," *Class Book of 1858*, HUA; Anderson, 115. General scales disappear from the Harvard records in 1858 and only reappear (in a modified form) in 1863-1864. But annual scales were not similarly discontinued.

33. HA to CFA2, 9 Feb 1859, AP.

34. *Hasty Pudding Library/ Record Book*, HUA.

35. Signed by the giver "H. H.," the set is in the HA Library, MHS.

36. Recollections of Louisa Hooper Thoron. In Oct 1854, when a freshman, HA withdrew Poe's works from the college library. See *Library Charging Lists*, HUA.

37. HA, *Education*, 60. See also *Catalogue of . . . Harvard University, First Term, 1857-1858*, HUA.

38. HA Library, MHS.

39. HA played "the argument-loving Sir Robert" in Colman's *Poor Gentleman*. See Anderson, 121.

40 HMag, Apr 1858.

41. Ibid., 133.

42. "The Class Elections," *Class Book of 1858*, 283ff, HUA—the handwriting is Allen's.

43. HA, *Education*,67.

44. Ibid., 56.

45. Anderson, 122.


5 / DEPARTURE

1. CFA2, *Autobiography*, 19—" . . . the proper thing for every young man . . . "—" . . . I should now respect myself a great deal more if I had then rebelled and run away from home, to sea or the Devil." See also HA to ABA, 6 Aug 1859, AP— "The Governor wants us to marry."

2. HA to CFA2, 17-18 Dec 1858, AP—"If Boston hadn't been to me what you describe it . . . I never should have thought of leaving home."

3. CFA2, *Autobiography*, 19.

4. See especially ABA to HA, 26 Feb 1860, AP—" . . . the death of her baby was a great misfortune & yet . . . a discipline. . . . "

5. Crowninshield, 109.

6. See the nine names on the engraved card, Anderson 128. (I wonder why a tenth name, that of Hunnewell, did not appear on the card.)

7. Anderson, 120, 124.

8. The arrangements with Whipple and Black were made by 27 May 1858. See Anderson, 124. Reliable information about HA's coloring is scarce. CFA2 says in his *Autobiography*, 8, that he and JQA2 as boys were "red-headed and freckle-faced." Louisa Hooper Thoron, asked whether HA's hair had a reddish or chestnut tint before turning white, recollected repeatedly that it did have. In the best photographs of HA, his eyes look dark, as if they were brown.

9. *Class Book of 1858*, HUA.

10. References to Italian appear repeatedly in Crowninshield's *Journal*. HA's enrollment in Italian is evidenced in *Absences from the Tardiness at Recitations and Lectures* (also in *Monthly returns . . .* ), HUA.

11. HA, *Education*, 61-63; Crowinshield, 86-87.

12. J. R. Lowell to President Walker, *Harvard College Papers, Second Ser.*, XXII, 318, HUA.

13. HA, *Education*, 61-62; Martin Duberman, *James Russell Lowell*, Bost 1966, 150.

14. Anderson, 123—" . . . a day of gayety and fashion. Feasting, dancing, cheering and singing. . . . "

15. Crowninshield, 147; Sibley, *Private Journal*, 25 Jun 1858, HUA.

16. HA, *Education*, 69; HA, "The Oration," *Class Book of 1858*, HUA.

17. HA, "Henry Brooks Adams," *Class Book of 1858*, HUA.

18. ABA to HA, 10 May 1859, AP—"The whole affair [HA's stay abroad] was arranged here [in Quincy]. . . . "

19. HA to CFA2, 3 Nov 1858, AP—"the two years which are allotted to me here"—"my thousand a year"; HA to CFA2, 17-18 Dec 1858, AP—"a thousand a year"—"the original sum"; CFA to HA, 15 Sep 1859 and 26 Jul 1860, AP—" . . . the gravity of your first proposals to go out only to study and on a thousand a year."

20. HA, *Education*, 71, 86-87—"a Berlin jurist"—"his self-contracted scheme"; HA to CFA2, 3 Nov 1858, AP—"two years studying law in Boston."

21. HA to CMG, 24 May 1875, Cater, 67—"My father and brothers block my path . . . , for all three stand far before me in the order or promotion."

22. *Hasty Pudding Club, Secy's Rep.*, XVII, HUA—a poem mentioning "Old 'Brooks,'" with a marginal note by the secretary: "H. B. A.[,] our efficient Librarian & past Alligator."

23. In addition to departures by older Brookses to Europe, evidenced in the contemporary AP, passim, see HA's being with his cousin Shepherd Brooks on reaching England, in notes from Crowninshield's unpublished *Journal* of his stay abroad, Cater Papers, MHS.

24. CFA to HA, 25 Oct 1858, AP; HA to Sumner, 22 Dec 1858, Cater, 3—"He [CFA] will not come to Europe. . . . "

25. ABA to HA, 10 May 1859, AP— " . . . [I] arranged for your going."; HA to CFA2, 18 Jan 1859, AP—"the fair Caroline"; HA to CFA2, 10-13 Feb 1960, AP—"I wasted a good deal of superfluous philanthropy on her."; HA *Education*, 70—"dread of daughters-in-law."

26. CFA to HA, 25 Oct 1858, AP.

27. HA's subsequent legal studies, more particularly those he carried to extremes while an assistant professor of history at Harvard, were partly undertaken, it would appear, to make good his early promise to become a "jurist"—and thus were testimonies that the promise had been forced, desperate, false, and extremely injurious to the promiser.

28. HA, *Catalogue of the Library of Henry Brooks Adams. Quincy / Massachusetts. August. 1858,* MHS—published in *The Colophon,* Autumn 1938, 483ff.

29. HA, *Education*, 71—mistakenly says "November"; ABA to HA, 4 Oct 1858, AP—"It is a week to day. . . . " On his experiences in New York, see also HA to CFA2, 29 May 1860, AP.

30. All assertions in the narrative about sailing and arrival times of ships in New York are derived from the shipping news in NYTimes.


6 / SIBERIA

*Principal sources*

(1) six letters, HA to CFA2, 3 Nov 1858-9 Apr 1859, AP.

(2) HA, *Education*, 71-81;

(3) notes from BWC's *Journal* of his stay abroad, Cater Papers, MHS.

*Notes concerning additional sources*

1. Letters from ABA, CFA, JQA2, and CFA2 to HA, 4-25 Oct 1858, AP

2. Sumner to HA, 13 Dec 1858, AP.

3. HA to Sumner, 22 Dec 1858, Cater, 1-3.

4. HA, two letters addressed "My Dear ———" and ended "Dresden—May—1859," H, usually known as "Two Letters on a Prussian Gymnasium"—published in AHR, Oct 1947, 59-74.

5. HA to Sumner, 22 Dec 1858, Cater, 1-3.

6. ABA to HA, 30 Jan 1859, AP; HA to Sumner, 28 Jan 1859, Cater, 5.

7. HA, *Education*, 438.

8. CFA2 to HA, 19-23 Dec 1858, AP.

9. HA to Sumner, 22 Dec 1858, Cater, 3.

10. Anderson, 112.


7  /  AN ABSOLUTELY CLOUDLESS SKY

*Principal sources*

(1) six letters, HA to CFA2, 22 Apr-18 Oct 1859, AP;

(2) a letter, HA to ABA, 26 Oct 1859, AP;

(3) HA, *Education*, 82-87;

(4) notes from BWC's *Journal* of his stay abroad, Cater Papers, MHS.

*Notes concerning additional sources*

1. HA, "Retrospect," HMag, Mar 1857, 61.

2. See Chapter 6, note 4, above.

3. HA to CFA2, 9-11 May 1860, AP.

4. HA to CFA2, 15-17 May 1859, AP—the coat may have seemed to him a sort of Adams family uniform, subjected to long service, governmental and diplomatic, on "both sides of the ocean," and *inherited* by him in a worn but usable and even preferred condition.

5. HA, "The Cap and Bells," HMag, Apr 1858, 127; HA, *Education*, 96—"He disapproved of France. . . . "

6. HA to CFA2, 17-18 Dec 1858, AP—". . . if I had found one single young woman who had salt enough in her to keep her from stagnating . . . I never should have thought of leaving home."

7. HA to CFA2, 13 Mar 1859, AP.

8. ABA to HA, 23 Aug 1859, AP.
9. LCK to family, 24 July 1859, AP.
10. ABA to HA, 16 Jan 1859, AP.

## 8 / PLANS AND THOUGHTS OF MY OWN

*Principal sources*

(1) twelve letters, HA to ABA, ca. 30 Oct 1859-10 Mar 1860, AP;
(2) three letters, HA to CFA2, 22 Nov 1859-26 Mar 1860, AP;
(3) HA, *Education*, 87-89.

*Notes concerning additional sources*

1. HA may have been given the same "large ground floor room opening out on an attractive garden" previously occupied by Lowell. See Duberman, *James Russell Lowell*, Bost 1966, 147.

2. CFA2 to HA, 3 Nov 1859, AP.

3. Duberman, *Charles Francis Adams*, 214-215—"The residence chosen looked out over Pennsylvania Avenue. . . ."

4. Many months earlier, on 3 Jun 1859, HA had agreed with BWC that "our language of conversation shall be German"—an agreement the two parties may be presumed to have kept. See notes of BWC's *Journal* of his stay abroad, Cater Papers, MHS.

5. ABA to HA, 16 Jan 1859 and 30 Jan 1859, AP.

6. ABA to HA, 4 Oct 1859, AP.

7. ABA to HA, 17 Feb 1859, AP.

8. The tendency of HA's father and brothers to excel when—and only when—they worked in close association with HA is one of the most striking aspects of HA's life, and equally a striking aspect of their divergent lives. That HA became the leader of the family is attested by this phenomenon, among others, however much he may have wanted his leadership to remain unnoticed and unmentioned.

9. HA, *Education*, 89—"The American parent . . . bitterly hostile to Paris, seemed rather disposed to accept Rome. . . ."

10. The word "book" would appear in the last sentence of his intended work, when finished. HA's idea that letters related to travel could readily grow into books reappears in HA to CFA2, 16 Sep 1863, AP—"my long volume of travels."

11. Often prescient, HA may have anticipated meeting Henry J. Raymond, editor of the *New York Times*, as early as March 1860, and may have known something of Raymond's travels in Europe.

12. That HA was already interested in Weed in March 1860 seems probable, not only because of Weed's newspaper work and his energetic promotion of Seward's claims to the Republican nomination for president, but also because Weed's activities were manifest proof that one could greatly affect the course of American politics without holding office. Yet HA was probably prejudiced against Weed, as possibly too affected by his Wall Street connections, or possibly as dishonest. The very good impression later made on him by Weed, on the basis of first-hand acquaintance, seems to have come as a surprise.

13. The second "Pemberton" letter was published in BAdv on 28 Feb 1860. Both letters appeared on p. 2 under the heading, "LETTER FROM WASHINGTON."

14. On the chance that CFA2 had *not* advised their parents concerning his authorship of the "Pemberton" letters, HA desisted from all talk concerning their authorship for a time in his letters to his relatives in Washington. See HA to CFA2, 26 Mar 1860, AP; HA to ABA, 6 May 1860, AP. This silence in 1860 could be described as HA's first step towards concealment from his parents of his arrangement to serve the *New York Times* in 1861.

## 9 / Something Good and Immortal

*Principal sources*

(1) HA, *Education*, 89-95;
(2) five letters, HA to ABA, 8 Apr-26 May 1860, AP;
(3) nine numbered letters, HA to CFA2, AP, as follows:
No. 1. Vienna, 5 Apr 60
No. 2. Venice, 11-13 Apr 60
No. 3. Bologna, 16 Apr 60
No. 4. Florence, 23 Apr 60
No. 5. Rome, 17 May 60
No. 6. Rome, 29 May 60
No. 7. Naples, [3?-4] Jun 60
No. 8. Palermo, 9 Jun 60
No. 9. Sorrento, 15 Jun 60
With the exception of No. 7, these letters were published—with some deletions—in the *Boston Courier* in its issues for 30 Apr, 9 May, 1 & 29 Jun, and 6, 10, & 13 Jul 60.
All quotations from Nos. 1, 3, 6, 7, & 9 conform to HA's MSS. Differently, all quotations from Nos. 2, 4, 5, and 8 conform to the published texts to be found in the issues of the *Courier* for 9

May, 1 Jun, 29 Jun, & 10 Jul 60. Although these latter quotations differ from HA's originals in punctuation, capitalization, spelling, contraction, and paragraphing, they nowhere differ in wording or sense.

*Notes concerning additional sources*

1. HA to ABA, 6-9 Jan 1860, AP.
2. See especially HA to ABA, 4-6 Mar 1860, AP—"To us who stand so far on the extreme left. . . ."
3. HA to CFA2, 9-11 May 1860, AP.
4. Ibid.
5. HA's conduct in 1888 when he completed his *History of the United States* is the best evidence that he conceived the *History* in Rome in 1860, while retracing Gibbon's footsteps. See HA, *Diary*, 16 Sep 1888, AP—"The narrative was finished last Monday. In imitation of Gibbon I walked in the garden . . . and meditated. . . . The contrast between my beginning and end is something Gibbon never conceived."
6. HA's earliest known efforts to break ground for his *Education* would take the form of an abortive attempt in 1869 to prepare an autobiography of his paternal grandmother by copying long extracts from LCA's surviving papers. The account of her life given in the *Education*, 16-19, is a distillation, in effect, of the abortive autobiography. The account, too, suggests that HA considered his life and hers to be phases or aspects of a single story. His conceiving the *Education* in Rome in 1860—if in fact he did conceive it there and then—might possibly have been inspired by the thought that, in the absence of a book about himself, *she* would be little remembered.
7. The title *A Journey to Italy* would harmonize with one of HA's subsequent remarks: "I am nearly at the point of death from pure curiosity to hear your travels. . . . I think you might entitle your work: 'Journey etc: By various hands. . . .'" See HA to CMG, 26 Mar 1867, AP.
8. HA to CFA2, 19 May 1860, AP.
9. HA to CFA2, [29 May 1860?], AP.
10. Ibid.
11. HA to CFA2, 19 May 1860, AP.

10 / MY SMALL SERVICES

*Principal sources*

(1) a series of letters by HA, published in BCour, signed "H. B. A.," under the following headings and on the following dates:

| LETTER FROM AUSTRIA. | 30 Apr 1860 |
| LETTER FROM ITALY. | 9 May 1860 |
| LETTER FROM A TOURIST. | 1 Jun 1860 |
| Letter from a Boston Tourist. | 29 Jun 1860 |
| LETTER FROM ROME. | 6 Jul 1860 |
| LETTER FROM PALERMO. | 10 Jul 1860 |
| LETTER FROM NAPLES. | 13 Jul 1860 |

(2) five letters, HA to ABA, 1 Jul-7 Sep 1860, AP.

(3) one note and three letters, HA to CFA2, 22 Jun-23 Aug 1860, AP.

(4) HA, *Education*, 96-97.

*Notes concerning additional sources*

1. ABA to HA, 28 May 1860, AP.

2. ABA to HA, 5-6 & 13 May 1860, AP; CFA to HA, 20 Apr [May?] 1860, AP.

3. A contention that it was CFA2 who mainly edited HA's letters would accord with HA's assumptions but otherwise would be conjecture.

4. CFA, *Dairy*, 17 May 1860, AP—see also CFA2, *Charles Francis Adams*, 114-115.

5. The idea that Seward, after his rejection at Chicago, thought and acted as would-be president-in-fact is *not* the idea expressed by his biographer, Glyndon G. Van Deusen, in his *William Henry Seward*, NY 1967, but seems to me to be the idea that best explains Seward's unexampled conduct, and is a concise way of restating a long-held view of the subject, as can be seen in Frederic Bancroft, *The Life of William H. Seward*, NY 1900, I, 546-551, and II, 148-149. How consciously Seward took and acted this role might be hard to determine. Van Deusen quotes him (30, 86) as having remarked in early life, "I am an enigma, even to myself," and, "I am a mystery to myself." HA later wrote of Seward—*Education*, 104—" . . . how much was nature and how much was mask, he [Seward] was himself too simple a nature to know." The relevant idea that Lincoln, after his election, "intended to be President in fact as well as in name" is a leading contention of David M. Potter's great early monograph, *Lincoln and His Party in the Secession Crisis*, New Haven & Lond 1942—and 1962 (with added Preface), 169 and passim.

6. CFA, *Diary*, 17 May 1860, AP— " . . . [I am] no partisan of Governor Seward"; Seward to CFA, 25 May 1860, AP; CFA, . . . *Memorial Address . . . on the life, character, and services of William H.*

Seward. . . , NY 1873, 22-25; Frederick W. Seward, *Seward at Washington . . . 1846-1861,* NY 1891, 454-457.

7. HA to CFA2, 9-11 May 1860, AP—"I wish you would . . . hunt me up an office to enter. . . . I don't feel up to the [Harvard] Law School and would rather have a good office where I can work like a horse."

8. The contents of this letter can be inferred from HA's response, but the letter itself is not in evidence.

9. ABA to HA, 4 Jan and 30 Jan 1860, AP.

10. MA to HA, 20 Aug 1860, AP.

11. ABA to HA, 11 Mar 1860, AP.

12. Seward to CFA2, 24 July 1860, AP.

13. *Seward at Washington,* op. cit., 459-460; Seward, *Works,* ed. by George E. Baker, new ed., Bost 1884, IV, 81-83.

14. CFA2, *Autobiography,* 52, 57-60.


11 / Just What I Wanted

*Principal sources*

(1) a series of news reports by HA, published in BAdv, unsigned, invariably on p. 2 under the headings, "LETTER FROM WASH-INGTON/[From Our Own Correspondent]," as follows:
> [No. 1] dated 4 Dec, published 7 Dec 1860
> [No. 2] dated 7 Dec, published 10 Dec 1860
> [No. 3] dated 10 Dec, published 13 Dec 1860
> [No. 4, dated 17 Dec, never published. MS not in evidence.]
> [No. 5] dated 17 Dec, published 20 Dec 1860

(2) two letters, HA to CFA2, 9-13 Dec and 18-20 Dec 1860, AP;

(3) HA, *Education,* 98-106.

*Notes concerning additional sources*

1. Seward to CFA, 28 Aug 1860, AP; Seward, *Works,* Bost 1884, IV, 330-332; CFA2, *Autobiography,* 52, 60-65; Van Deusen, *William Henry Seward,* NY 1967, 213-234; F. W. Seward, *Seward at Washington . . . 1846-1861,* 460-469.

2. CFA2, *Autobiography,* 60-65. The diary from which CFA2 says he is quoting is not in evidence.

3. CFA, *Diary,* 17 Oct 1860, AP.

4. The details concerning HA's duties as "private Secretary" are best gleaned from his letters, his father's letter books and diary, and his mother's letters from Dec 1860 through January 1862. The exact

amount of his presumed allowance for services is not clear to me. HA conceivably proposed to treat his services as a means of paying off the virtual debts to his father he had incurred while overspending his proposed allowance in Europe.

5. CFA, . . . *Memorial Address . . . on . . . William H. Seward*, 28.

6. CFA, *Diary*, 16 Nov 1860, AP. HA had been looking forward to his father's entering the cabinet for many months, and had written to CFA2 on 25 July 1860 (AP), "Je serais bien content de le voir a la tete de quelque Departement sous la prochaine Administration."

7. That HA and CFA2 made the needed arrangement with Hale in Boston *with their father's knowledge* is evidenced by HA and CFA's later writings, but details concerning the manner, date, and exact place of the negotiation with Hale are now unknown.

8. CFA, *Diary*, 29 Nov-1 Dec, 1860, AP.

9. The social prominence of the Adamses was the greater because Seward's wife and daughter had not accompanied him to Washington. Potter describes the Adams house as "an informal Republican head-quarters." See his *Lincoln and His Party in the Secession Crisis*, 129.

10. Belief in the notion that the country might be governed by a "triumvirate" made up of Lincoln as president, Seward as secretary of state, and CFA as secretary of the treasury seems to have affected HA profoundly at intervals during the winter of 1860-1861, and can be viewed as still affecting him when he wrote the passage about Jefferson as president, Madison as secretary of state, and Gallatin as secretary of the treasury in *The Life of Albert Gallatin*, Philadelphia 1879, 269: "The government was in fact a triumvirate almost as clearly defined as any triumvirate of Rome." HA's fascination that winter with the possibility of his father's heading the Treasury likewise can be viewed as affecting him in a deep and lasting way. See the striking phrase in his *Democracy*, 205, " . . . under the shadow of the Secretary of the Treasury," and the flat assertion, "The Treasury is the controlling political office. . . ," in HA to Godkin, 27 Feb 1885, Cater, 140.

11. HA, "The Great Secession Winter of 1860-61," MHS *Proceedings*, XLIII, 660-665.

12. John G. Nicolay and John Hay, *Abraham Lincoln / A History*, NY 1890, II, 415-416; Potter, *Lincoln and His Party*, 89-90.

13. HA's letter to CFA2 dated 9-13 Dec 1860, AP, may easily be read to indicate that its author believed at the time that the secession of a few states in the deep South would be politically advantageous to the "stronger Republicans" and even essential to their swift political advancement. If he did have such ideas on reaching the capital, HA soon shifted to better considered ones.

14. HA, *Diary*, 23 Sep 1888, AP.

15. HA to CFA2, 2 Jan 1861, AP.

16. The 18 installments were sent as 14 letters—see Ford, I, 62-89. That the "memorial" HA raised in Washington had extraordinary value is manifest in Potter's *Lincoln and His Party*, which makes repeated use of its installments, also draws upon HA's news reports to the *Advertiser*, and lists him (234) as one of the "leading Republicans."

17. HA, "The Great Secession Winter of 1860-61," 661.

18. Lincoln, *Collected Works*, ed. by Roy P. Basler, New Brunswick 1953, IV, 151.

19. Potter, *Lincoln and His Party*, 91 note 57—names all the members.

20. After citing many lines by HA (Ibid., 131-132), Potter says (133), " . . . he [HA] was right that the tide was ebbing, for in December the Republicans exhibited a temper so conciliatory as to have been unimaginable in November."

## 12 / LIES, STRATAGEMS, AND SECRETS

*Principal sources*

(1) three news reports by HA, published in BAdv, unsigned, invariably on p. 2 under the headings, "LETTER FROM WASHINGTON/ [From Our Own Correspondent]," as follows:

[No. 5] dated 17 Dec, published 20 Dec 1860

[No. 6] dated 22 Dec, published 27 Dec 1860

[No. 7] dated 28 Dec 1860, published 1 Jan 1861

(2) seven letters, HA to CFA2, 18 Dec 1860-11 Jan 1861, AP;

(3) HA, "The Great Secession Winter of 1860-61," MHS Proceedings, XLIII, 660-687 (reprinted in HA, *The Great Secession Winter of 1860-61 and Other Essays*, NY 1958, 3-31).

*Notes concerning additional sources*

(1) The explanation of the behavior of the secessionists in Congress, especially in the Committee of Thirty-three, which HA offers in "The Great Secession Winter of 1860-61," 661, 668-670, is corroborated by Potter, who says in the "Preface to the 1962 Edition" of his *Lincoln and His Party*, xvi-xvii: "The papers of Charles Francis Adams have been opened, and I would now use them in my account of developments in the Committee of Thirty-Three, and would not rely so much

on what Henry Adams reported. Yet Martin Duberman's very able biography [of CFA], based upon the papers, does not appreciably alter the story, and it shows that Henry Adams was remarkably accurate."

2. General Scott was in New York and did not arrive in Washington until 12 Dec 1860. See Bruce Catton, *The Coming Fury*, Garden City 1961, 161.

3. It should be noticed that HA did not mention Johnson in his news reports till 11 Jan 1861 [No.9], but then and later praised the Tennessean unstintingly.

4. HA's emphasis on the efforts of Davis to thwart the secessionists in the committee in the "The Great Secession Winter," 671-675, is partly memorable as an instance of HA's ability to rise above family loyalty and pride.

5. The alliance of CFA (and HA) with Davis may have been hastened by the latter's being a cousin of David Davis, Lincoln's manager.

6. HA to BAdv [No. 9], pub. 15 Jan 1861.

7. Lincoln, *Collected Works*, ed. by Basler, IV, 161.

8. Willard L. King, *Lincoln's Manager / David Davis*, Cambridge, Mass., 1960, 166-168. Potter makes much of Weed's conversation with Seward on the train between Syracuse and Albany [on 22 Dec?], saying in his *Lincoln and His Party*, 170, " . . . it is scarcely too much to say that, somewhere along the route, the active leadership of the Republican party passed from Seward to Lincoln. . . ." One can agree with Potter's view and yet add that Seward at the same moment, in deepest secrecy, without relinquishing his claims to being a Republican, was becoming the undisputed leader of what HA would soon be publicizing as the "Union Party."

9. CFA, *Diary*, 27 Dec 1861, AP.

10. Ibid.

11. Catton, *The Coming Fury*, 153-173; W. A. Swanberg, *First Blood / The Story of Fort Sumter*, NY 1957, 109-121.

12. F. W. Seward, *Seward at Washington . . . 1846-1961*, 487.

13. Retelling in more detailed form the story of the "secession crisis" already told by HA three times over (in letters to CFA2, in 19 news reports to Hale, and in his buried essay, "The Great Secession Winter"), Potter goes beyond saying that Seward *approved* the New Mexico expedient, saying instead that the New Yorker probably was *part-author* of the resolutions put before the Committee of Thirty-three by CFA after its recess. See *Lincoln and His Party*, 293: "It appears probable, therefore, that the program formulated by the

Republican members of the House committee was prepared in part by that gifted author of other people's resolutions, William H. Seward." If Potter should be believed, it may be presumed that HA *knew* Seward was helping to write, or alone was writing, an important proposal of which CFA would be made to appear the chief author; also that HA witnessed his father's subordination to Seward in practical operation; and that HA was given a lesson by Seward—whether needed or not—in the uses of anonymity.

14. Lincoln, *Collected Works,* IV, 168.

15. David C. Mearns, *The Lincoln Papers,* Garden City 1948, II, 364, 376. The continued agitation in favor of CFA for a place in the cabinet undoubtedly became a factor in Seward's later success in persuading Lincoln to choose CFA, instead of William L. Dayton, as minister to England.

16. The story of Raymond's replacing Horace Greeley as the great ally of Weed and Seward in the New York City press is told in Van Deusen, *William Henry Seward,* 159-160, and in William Harlan Hale, *Horace Greeley / Voice of the People,* NY 1950, 150-153.

## 13 / THE UNION PARTY

*Principal sources*

(1) a series of news reports by HA, published in BAdv, unsigned, invariably on p. 2 under the headings, "LETTER FROM WASHINGTON/ [From Our Own Correspondent]," as follows:

[No. 8] dated 7 Jan, published 11 Jan 1861
[No. 9] dated 11 Jan, published 15 Jan 1861
[No. 10] dated 13 Jan, published 16 Jan 1861
[No. 11] dated 14 Jan, published 17 Jan 1861
[No. 12] dated 18 Jan, published 22 Jan 1861
[No. 13] dated 21 Jan, published 24 Jan 1861
[No. 14] dated 23 Jan, published 26 Jan 1861
[No. 15, dated 28 Jan? - never published, MS not in evidence]
[No. 16] dated 31 Jan, published 2 Feb 1861

(2) four letters, HA to CFA2, 8 Jan-24 Jan 1861, AP.

*Notes concerning additional sources*

1. Lincoln, *Collected Works,* ed. by Basler, IV, 169-170, 174-175.

2. F. W. Seward, *Seward at Washington . . . 1846-1861,* 491—"I have assumed a sort of dictatorship for defense." See also HA, "Great

Secession Winter," 685—"Under all the dangers and trials, the cares and the triumphs of his dictatorship, he [Seward] maintained always the same self-control and calmness, never parading his importance and never losing his self-command."

3. HA, "Great Secession Winter," 677—" . . . the first days of January came on, the blackest our country has seen since the adoption of the Constitution."

4. Catton, *The Coming Fury*, 193-197.

5. Seward, *Works*, IV, 651ff.

6. HA to CFA2, 5 Feb 1861, AP.

7. Weed had become so alarmed by the secession crisis after Lincoln's election that he printed a suggested compromise in the *Albany Evening Journal* on 24 Nov 1860; and Raymond, similarly alarmed, had warned in the *New York Times* on 7 Dec 1860 that "concessions" were an "absolute necessity." See Potter, *Lincoln and His Party*, 75-78. Seward, constantly in touch with Weed and Raymond, evidently shared their alarm but consistently concealed his fears when in public. During two meetings in Washington in late December, he clearly explained his program to Leonard Swett, so that the latter could report to Lincoln privately on 31 Dec 1860: " . . . the pinch [as explained by Seward] is, not to advance a party but to save a country from anarchy & destruction. . . . A complete union of all patriotic men will be made in the fiery crucible in which we will be tried." See Mearns, *Lincoln Papers*, II, 363-365. By then, Weed, Raymond, CFA, HA, Henry Winter Davis, and others had been recruited as supporters of Seward's program; Seward and Scott were allied; and Seward was reaching out to added persons, most importantly to Senator Douglas. At a large dinner party in Washington hosted by Douglas on January 24, Seward startled the company by offering a toast, "Away with all parties, all platforms, all previous committals, and whatever else will stand in the way of the restoration of the American Union." See Robert W. Johannsen, *Stephen A. Douglas*, NY 1973, 827-828. Alive to these and many parallel developments, and aware that Seward's words at the dinner were said in earnest, HA wrote his sixteenth report to Hale, dated 31 Jan 1861, with full knowledge of the importance of his own action.

8. CFA, *Diary*, 30 Jan 1861, AP.

9. Four days after HA mailed his key news report, Lord Lyons wrote from Washington to his superiors in London that Seward—publicly known to be the future secretary of state—meant within the next ten months to "place himself at the head of a strong Union party,

having extensive ramifications both in the North and in the South, and to make *Union* or *Disunion*, not *Freedom* or *Slavery* the watchwords of Political Parties." See MHS *Proceedings*, XLVIII, 213.

## 14 / BUSINESS THAT SHALL SUIT ME

### *Principal sources*

(1) three news reports by HA, published in BAdv, unsigned, invariably on p. 2 under the headings, "LETTER FROM WASHINGTON/ [From Our Own Correspondent]," as follows:

[No. 17] dated 4 Feb, published 6 Feb 1861
[No. 18] dated 5 Feb, published 8 Feb 1861
[No. 19] dated 7 Feb, published 11 Feb 1861

(2) four letters, HA to CFA2, 31 Jan-13 Feb 1861, AP.

### *Notes concerning lesser sources*

1. HA, *Education*, 101.
2. MS dated Turin, 19 Jun 1859, Raymond Papers, NYPL.
3. "The Political Crisis," signed "Observer," NYTimes, 5 Feb 1861.
4. CFA, *Diary*, 31 Jan 1861, AP.
5. HA, *Education, 107-108; CFA, Diary*, 31 Jan, 2 and 10 Feb 1861, AP; Duberman, *Charles Francis Adams*, 250, 469 note 65. Edward Pierce, Sumner's biographer, said the quarrel between CFA and Sumner was precipitated by "a scene in which Adams resented Sumner's protest against his support of compromise, the details of which are not known." See Pierce, IV, 13. But Sumner's main quarrel evidently was with Seward and had been precipitated both by the public announcements earlier in the month that the New Yorker would indeed be secretary of state and by Seward's "Union Party" activities and "dictatorship." See David Donald, *Charles Sumner and the Coming of the Civil War*, NY 1960, 372-382. The alignment of CFA with Seward gave Sumner a scapegoat for the envy and rage he felt towards his greater rival, and HA may possibly have triggered Sumner's open denunciations; for the mysterious "scene" referred to by Pierce very probably had been the one of 13 Jan 1861 during which Sumner was first scolded by CFA and then "squenched" by HA. See ibid., 375. That scene occurred only one day after Seward gave his speech in the Senate. When CFA also spoke, in the House on 31 Jan 1861, portions of the speech could readily have affected Sumner as a deliberate repetition by the Adamses of the challenges thrown at him

by CFA and the insulting conduct of HA in the dining room of the Markoe House three Sundays earlier.

6. Gurowski, later hired by Seward at the State Department as a translator at Sumner's urging, became a "virtual spy" for Sumner while so employed. See David Donald, *Charles Sumner and the Rights of Man*, NY 1970, 19. HA's visit to Sumner, brief thought it was made to be, may have sufficed to end Sumner's quarrel—if he had one—with the younger Adams. Astonishingly good relations between HA and Sumner continued from that day, 3 Feb 1861, till the latter's death in 1874.

7. HA, *Education*, 113.

8. Ibid., 107-108. Very precise in his use of words, HA could not have said "defection" unthinkingly; but what he meant that Sumner defected from is not clear to me. The senator was in no sense a defector from the Republican Party, and, not having joined, could not be a defector from the ranks of Seward's secretly formed "Union Party." Possibly HA used the word as a means of pointing towards Sumner's betrayal of State Department secrets to Lord Lyons in the later months of 1861, a matter of which HA may have become aware at the time, or later, and which would give the term "defector" a meaning it usually has. But the explanation is not satisfactory to me; and neither is the alternative possibility that HA viewed Sumner as having defected as an adopted relation of the Adamses, for he had not to my knowledge been taken into the family.

9. HA knew the convention had been secretly arranged by Seward and said so in "The Great Secession Winter," 680. Attempting to trace the New Yorker's "extraordinary maneuver" in detail, Potter concludes—*Lincoln and His Party*, 306-309: "Seward's part in the matter was adroitly and deftly concealed."

10. CFA2, *Diary*, 19 Feb 1861, AP; CFA2, *Autobiography*, 40-41, 90-91.

11. Jacob E. Cooke, "Chats with Henry Adams," *American Heritage*, Dec 1955, 44. See also HA's passing suggestion that Rooney Lee did not deserve to be hanged—HA to Henry Lee Higginson, 10 Sep 1863, AP.

15 / APPOINTMENTS

*Principal sources*

(1) seven exceptionally important letters, as follows:

HA to Sumner, 22 Mar 1861, Seward Papers, Univ. of Rochester

Sumner to HA, 25 Mar 1861, Dwight Papers, MHS
HA to Sumner, 1 Apr 1861, H (and Cater, 6-7)
HA to CFA2, 16 May 1861, Ford, I, 90-91
HA to CFA2, 10-11 Jun 1861, AP
HA to Horace Gray, Jr., 17 Jun 1861, H
HA to Seward, 25 Aug 1864, in *Diplomatic Despatches, Great Britain,* Vol. 87, National Archives
(2) an editorial, "A New Minister," in NYTimes, 30 Mar 1861;
(3) the overall spirit exhibited by HA in his reports to the NYTimes listed in the notes for Chapters 16-26 below.

*Notes concerning additional sources*

1. HA, *Education,* 106, 503; Tyler Dennett, *John Hay / From Poetry to Politics,* NY 1934, 39.

2. CFA2, *Autobiography,* 92; CFA2, *Diary,* 29 Feb-12 Mar 1861, AP.

3. James G. Randall, *Lincoln the President,* NY 1945, I, 291; Bancroft, *Life of Seward,* II, 23-24; Lincoln, *Collected Works,* ed. by Basler, IV, 261-262 and 261 note 99; CFA2, *Autobiography,* 96-98.

4. HA, *Education,* 107.

5. CFA2, *Autobiography,* 100-102.

6. The conjecture that HA started working for Gray on Monday morning is just that, conjecture, based on nothing more than usual office practice, and on HA's saying (*Education,* 110) that he studied common law for a "week" in March 1861, until his father was named minister. HA specified that he was with Gray for "three days." See HA to Horace Gray, Jr., 17 Jun 1861, H.

7. CFA2, *Autobiography,* 107-108; CFA, *Diary,* 19 Mar 1861, AP; William Everett, *Address in commemoration of . . . Charles Francis Adams. . . ,* Cambridge, Mass., 1887, 55.

8. CFA, "Reminiscences of his mission to Great Britain," AP (reel 296 in microfilms).

9. The strongly worded ironies in HA, *Education,* 110-114—e. g., " . . . when . . . the young man realized what had happened, he felt it as a betrayal"—can be taken as evidence that the son's determination to part company with his father in March 1861 had been wholehearted.

10. CFA, *Diary,* 19 Mar 1861, AP.

11. HA, *Education,* 293. See also HA to CMG, 3 Mar 1865, AP— " . . . I have not the most distant idea . . . when it will please my father to order me to some new occupation."

12. HA, *Education,* 111.

13. Telegram, Sumner to CFA, 20 Mar 1861, AP.

14. HA's "first letter" to Sumner is not in evidence. I tend to think its author recovered it in Washington and destroyed it. That HA *telegraphed* the letter to the Capitol I infer from Sumner's replying that he received it on the day Wilson's nomination reached the Senate. That HA, in the first letter, asked for the place of secretary of legation I infer from (1) the supposed political norms of the moment, which led the *New York Times* to imagine that HA would get the place, (2) HA's later flat rejection of the assistant secretaryship, and (3) HA's active agency in obtaining the lesser place for a person other than himself, Moran. I further suppose that a striking passage in *The Education*, 322, may have a bearing on the matter: "Adams had held no office, and when his friends asked the reason, he could not go into long explanations, but preferred to answer simply that no President had ever invited him to fill one. The reason was good, and was also conveniently true, but left open an awkward doubt of his morals or capacity. Why had no President ever cared to employ him? The question needed a volume of intricate explanation."

15. A week and a half before, on 11 Mar 1861, Seward had written to Lincoln: "Please hold in reserve [the first] Secretaryships of these legations. They are almost as good as missions and almost as important." See Mearns, *Lincoln Papers*, II, 479. When Lincoln acceded to the request, Seward awarded the most coveted of the first secretaryships, the one at London, to a political satellite of his, Wilson, whom he manifestly considered unequal to an important post and undeserving of it. Seward's words to Lincoln may later have been shown to Adams by John Hay, when the latter was in possession of the Lincoln Papers.

16. CFA2, *Diary*, 11 May 1861, AP.

17. CFA to Seward, 13 Apr 1861, AP.

18. According to Seward, the appointment of CFA as minister to England had been made in the face of "energetic remonstrances" by Sumner. Moreover, Seward attributed Sumner's feud with himself to his own unwillingness to heed the remonstrances. See Donald, *Charles Sumner and the Rights of Man*, 24. Sumner had himself been a candidate for the English mission. See Donald, *Charles Sumner and the Coming of the Civil War*, 381-382.

19. HA may always have considered his father's delay in starting for London an egregious error. Nineteen years later, when James Russell Lowell was made minister to England, HA advised him: " . . . every day you lose after the meeting of Parliament, will be

unfortunate. We [CFA and HA] arrived on May 15th, at least two months too late." See HA to Lowell, 21 Jan 1880, Cater, 97.

20. My conjecture that HA went alone to Washington, in advance of CFA, is consistent with his having taken matters into his own hands, consistent with his writing letters to Sumner which his father did not authorize, and consistent with his returning to the role of private secretary, which, as defined after his father's appointment to the English mission, made HA responsible for the renting of houses, shipping arrangements, packing, etc. The conjecture is consistent also with HA's momentary aversion to his would-be "masters" and, too, with his need to visit Raymond in perfect secrecy.

21. CFA, *Diary*, 23 Mar 1861, AP.

22. That HA meant his work for the *New York Times* as a step in *politics*—rather than mere political journalism—seems indisputable and is consistent with a series of lines he had written six months earlier: "Charles will I suppose . . . write letters to some paper. . . . This taste for politics is a perfect mania in us." See HA to ABA, 7 Sep 1860, AP.

23. Van Deusen, *William Henry Seward*, 159.

24. In his *Education*, 113, HA answered the question defiantly by saying, " . . . in the mission attached to Mr. Adams in 1861, the only rag of legitimacy or order was the private secretary. . . ."

25. The same ironic answer may be found in *The Education*, 110—" . . . he [HA] was less ridiculous than his betters. He was at least no public official. . . . He was not a vulture of carrion—patronage."

26. HA, *Historical Essays*, NY 1891, 259.

27. HA, *Education*, 129— saying that Wilson and Moran were "secretaries of his [Seward's] own selection." The fact that Wilson was a hanger-on of Seward's became a sore point with Sumner, who later threw the secretary of state into a rage by making an issue of Wilson's insufficiencies in London. See Donald, *Charles Sumner and the Rights of Man*, 100.

28. *The History of* THE TIMES, Lond 1939, II, 363-364; John Black Atkins, *The Life of Sir William Howard Russell*, NY 1911, II, 11-14.

29. CFA, *Diary*, 28 Mar 1861, AP.

30. That HA *was* in Washington is plainly documented by this entry in CFA, *Letterbook*, 29 Mar 1861, AP; but otherwise the history of the son's unexpected return to the capital can be reconstructed only by logical inference from collateral data, contemporary and subsequent.

31. That CFA had urged Moran's retention was reported in London on 15 Apr 1861 by *The Times*. See Moran, same date.

## 16 / THE MANUSCRIPT

*Principal sources*

(1) a news report, HA to NYTimes, dated 1 Apr, published 5 Apr 1861;

(2) a letter, HA to Sumner, 1 Apr 1861, H (and Cater, 6-7);

(3) HA, "The Great Secession Winter of 1860-61," and a fragment of a note, HA to CFA2, 28 Apr 1861, MHS *Proceedings*, XLIII, 656-687.

*Notes concerning additional sources*

1. NY Times, 28 Mar 1861, 1. Although unwilling to see CFA, Sumner may have willingly seen HA, who regarded his friendship with the senator as intact.

2. CFA, *Diary*, 27 Apr, 1 May 1861, AP; Pierce, IV 13.

3. CFA2, *Autobiography*, 41.

4. CFA to Seward, 13 Apr 1861, AP— forcing the adoption of a plan essentially designed by HA and made necessary, in part, by his simultaneous, concealed arrangement with Raymond in New York.

5. Sumner to HA, 18 Apr 1861, Dwight Papers, MHS.

6. HA to Palfrey, 23 Oct 1861, Cater, 8-10; Palfrey, *History of New England*, Bost 1859, 89n. In his *Education*, 222, HA shifted this conversation from 1861 to a time after the Civil War.

7. CFA2, *Autobiography*, 116-117.

8. HA, *Education*, 111-112.

9. HA to CFA2, 25 Oct 1861, AP.

10. HA to CFA2, 16 May and 2 July 1861, Ford, I, 90-91 & AP.

11. MHS *Proceedings*, XLIII, 678—" . . . he [Seward] was probably the only man in Congress, on the northern side, who went to Washington prepared for what might happen with a definite policy to meet it. Certainly he was the only one who succeeded in carrying out such a policy and balancing himself and the nation upon it."

12. Ibid., 682—" . . . the mass of the party . . . turned for the decisive word to the final authority [Lincoln] at Springfield. The word did not come."

13. Ibid.

14. HA, *Education*, 110—"Henry packed his trunk again without a word."

15. CFA, *Diary*, 1 May 1861, AP.

16. Albert A. Woldman, *Lincoln and the Russians*, Cleveland & NY 1952, 107; HA to CFA2, 1 May 1863, AP—" . . . how prostrated I was by sea-sickness on that voyage!"

## 17 / TRUE AMERICANS

*Principal sources*

(1) two news reports by HA, published in NYTimes, unsigned, but identified as "From Our Own Correspondent," as follows:

[No. 1] dated 17 May, published 3 Jun 1861, under the headings, "FROM ENGLAND. / London at the Height of the Season—Reception of Mr. Adams—Efforts of the Secessionists—State of English Opinion."

[No. 2] dated 25 May, published 7 June 1861, under the headings, "IMPORTANT FROM ENGLAND. / Position of the British Press on the American Question—Probable Overthrow of the Ministry—The Duty of the Government at Washington—Derby Day—The Essays and Reviews—Mr. Motley's Defence of the Union."

(2) two letters, HA to CFA2, 16 May and 10-11 Jun 1861, Ford, I, 90-91 & AP.

*Notes concerning additional sources*

1. Moran, I, viii-x, and entries 3 Apr-4 May 1861.
2. Ibid., 10, 13, 14 May 1861.
3. HA to BAdv [No. 2], dated 7 Dec 1860.
4. HA, *Education*, 114-116.
5. Ephraim Douglass Adams, *Great Britian and the American Civil War*, NY [Russell & Russell] n. d., I, 76-97; Frank Lawrence Owsley, *King Cotton Diplomacy*, Chicago 1959, 56. The text of the Proclamation is given in Frank Moore, ed., *The Rebellion Record*, NY 1861, doc. pp. 245-247.
6. HA, *Education*, 115.
7. Moran, 14-17, 20 May 1861; HA, *Historical Essays*, 244; Russell to Lyons, 21 May 1861, quoted in E.D. Adams, op. cit., I, 131.
8. It is possible, but not probably, that HA had some of his secret news reports carried for him by the legation's messenger to Queenstown, leaving London each Saturday at 9:00 P.M. See HA, *Historical Essays*, 252-253.
9. Moran, 16, 18 May 1861.
10. Ford, I, 90.
11. Woldman, *Lincoln and the Russians*, 105-107; Mearns, *Lincoln Papers*, I, 612-613.
12. LTimes, 20 May, 1861, 9—also in Moore, *Rebellion Record*, doc. pp. 340-341.

13. *History of* THE TIMES, 1939, I, 362.

14. HA, *Education*, 113.

15. LTimes, 20 May 1861, 8; Moore, op. cit., doc. pp. 341-341.

16. In his "Great Secession Winter of 1860-61," while explaining Seward's policy of conciliating the border states, to delay their seceding, or prevent it altogether, HA had said that conciliation at home was only half of Seward's policy, and that the other half was a "dignified" response to any foreign interference. See MHS *Proceedings*, XLIII, 684—"No infringement of our laws [by a foreign power] . . . would have been permitted, and if attempted, would have been instantly resented."

17. See especially; "Mr. SEWARD'S instructions to Mr. DAYTON [in Paris], to say nothing of instructions much more positive said to have been sent to our Minister here [Mr. Adams], leave no doubt as to the intentions of our Government."

18 / "DESPATCH NO. 10"

*Principal sources*

(1) two news reports by HA, published in NYTimes, unsigned, but identified as "From Our Own Correspondent," as follows:

[No. 3] dated 31 May, published 17 Jun 1861, under the headings, " AFFAIRS IN ENGLAND. / Lively Times in London—The Derby—The Ministry—Mr. Gladstone's Budget—The Paper Duty—Manners in Parliament, &c."

[No.4] dated 8 Jun, published 21 Jun 1861, under the headings, "AMERICAN TOPICS IN ENGLAND. / The Tone of the English Press—Some Excuses For It—The Southern Commissioners—Their Misfortunes."

(2) a letter, HA to CFA2, 10-11 Jun 1861, AP.

*Notes concerning additional sources*

1. Moran, 17 May 1861.

2. Norman B. Ferris, *Desperate Diplomacy / William H. Seward's Foreign Policy, 1861*, Knoxville 1976, 4.

3. Moran, 28 May 1861.

4. HA, *Education*, 114-115—" . . . in May, 1861, no one in England—literally no one—doubted that Jefferson Davis had made or would make a nation, and nearly all were glad of it, though not often saying so."

5. George Macaulay Trevelyan, *The Life of John Bright,* Bost & NY 1913, 311—quoting Bright to Sumner, 6 Sep 1861: " ... I am hoping for something which will enable you [the leaders of the Union and the Confederacy] to negotiate." See also Ferris, *Desperate Diplomacy,* 131-134.

6. Moran, 28 May 1861; CFA to CFA2, 14 Jun 1861, AP.

7. Moran, 28 May-5 Jun 1861.

8. *Galignani's Messenger,* 30 May 1861; also NYTimes, 11 and 14 Jun 1861.

9. Pierce, IV, 31.

10. CFA to Clay, 14 Jan 1862, MHS *Proceedings,* XLV, 128-130.

11. Moran, 8 Jun 1861.

12. Ibid., 17 and 30 May, 6 Jun 1861.

13. Ibid., 23 Jul 1858, 10 Aug 1859.

14. An unsigned news report in NYTimes, dated 8 Jun, published 21 Jun 1861—following the report by HA [No. 3] dated 8 Jun—under the headings, "From Another Correspondent./ Effect of the Seward-Dayton Dispatch—Confederate Recognition Disposed of—Corrupt Agencies Employed by the Southern Emissaries—General Indications of English Sentiment." The suggestion that Moran was the author is my own. I think the evidence in favor of the suggestion is strong and conclusive.

15. Moran, 27 Jun 1864—when Hunt paid him.

16. Ibid., 14 Jun 1861.

17. Exact information about HA's income is hard to come by, at any time in his life; but scattered indications in his writings beginning in May 1861 and continuing into 1867 may be taken to indicate that his annual income from all sources exceeded $2500—and exceeded Wilson's salary.

18. CFA, *Diary,* 10 Jun 1861, AP.


## 19 / An Unsettling Intuition

*Principal sources*

(1) a news report by HA, published in NYTimes, unsigned, but identified as "From Our Own Correspondent":

[No. 5] dated 15 Jun, published 28 Jun 1861, under the headings, "INTERESTING FROM ENGLAND. / The Attitude of the Ministry—the true Policy of the American Press and People—

The French Proclamation—The Ascot Races—What Parliament is doing."
(2) two letters, HA to CFA2, 2 Jul and 26 Jul 1861, AP.

*Notes concerning additional sources*

1. HA may fairly be presumed to have studied carefully chapter 26, "Premier or President?" in Nicolay and Hay, *Abraham Lincoln / A History*, NY 1890, III, 429-449—ending with the disclosure of an "extraordinary state paper, unlike anything to be found in the political history of the United States": Sewards's "Some Thoughts for the President's Consideration." A biographical and historical bombshell, this chapter provided both the text of Seward's paper and the text of a letter, likewise dated 1 Apr 1861, which Lincoln wrote to Seward in reply. The chapter, too, was the first of many that have been written more or less with the purpose of saying that, of the two men, Lincoln and Seward, the president was in the instance of these documents shown to be the superior, both in policy and ability. For example, in his *Great Britain and the American Civil War*, I, 120, E. D. Adams writes of Seward's "insane scheme of saving the Union by plunging it into a foreign war"; and, in his *Lincoln and His Party in the Secession Crisis*, 369, Potter says that Seward "was at the end of his tether, and his proposals . . . indicate . . . the deterioration of his policy."

2. E. D. Adams, op. cit., I, 124.

3. Lincoln's modern editors, after studying Seward's "Thoughts" and Lincoln's letter in reply, reported themselves as having "doubts that the letter was presented to Seward at all." See Lincoln, *Collected Works*, ed. by Basler a. o., IV, 317 note 1—"Having written it, Lincoln may have thought better of rebuking his secretary. . . ."

4. Potter, op. cit., 371-374; Catton, *The Coming Fury*, 271-336; Swanberg, *First Blood*, chaps. 22-30.

5. F. W. Seward, *Seward at Washington . . . 1846-1861*, 575. HA may also be presumed to have studied at least portions of this remarkable book, published—together with two other compendious volumes—by Seward's son Frederick in 1891, in effect as a reply to Nicolay and Hay's *Abraham Lincoln*. After giving the text of his father's "Thoughts" and quoting the essential lines of the president's rejoinder, F. W. Seward pointed out that the policy suggested by his father, far from being rejected, was in its most essential respect adopted. The elder Seward had explained to Lincoln: "My system is built on this *idea*, as a ruling one, namely: that we must change the question, before the public, from one upon Slavery, or about Slavery,

for a question upon *Union or Disunion.*" Both the idea of conciliation of the border states at home and the idea of seeking wars abroad had been subsidiary in the elder Seward's thinking to his "ruling one." With this in mind, the younger Seward was able to assert, 536: "Before the month [of April 1861] passed away, the policy thus discussed had been adopted. . . . The swift march of events, and the Administration's action thereon, soon 'changed the question . . . from one upon Slavery . . . for a question upon Union. . . .'" Writing in this vein, Frederick Seward became the first writer to say, in effect, that of the two men, Lincoln and W. H. Seward, the secretary of state was shown to be the superior, both in policy and ability, in the instance of the two documents. The same idea has recently been forcibly reasserted by Norman B. Ferris. In his *Desperate Diplomacy,* 184, Ferris alludes to the main passage in the elder Seward's "Thoughts" and says that "the foreign policy of the United States," beginning on 1 Apr 1861 and continuously thereafter, "had been based on that principle"; that is, on Seward's "ruling" idea that the government would have to "change the question." Thus confronted with two divergent traditions about the same documents, biographers of HA may be forgiven for wishing that some great historian will combine the two traditions and show that, while Seward lost his "dictatorship" when the confederate forces fired their guns on 12 Apr 1861, Lincoln adopted his secretary's new "system," and, while Lincoln continued to assert his primacy as chief executive, Seward never ceased to exercise a degree of power and influence in the administration beyond the degree associated with mere membership in the cabinet—that is, both leaders won; both lost; they learned to work together; and, in the end, both were unionists; both were emancipators.

6. MHS *Proceedings,* XLVIII, 214-223.

7. Ibid., 224—quoting Lyons to Russell, 9 Apr 1861: "Mr. Lincoln has not hitherto given proof of his possessing any natural talents to compensate for his ignorance of everything but Illinois village politics."

8. Russell to Lyons, 1 Apr 1861—quoted in E. D. Adams, *Great Britain and the American Civil War,* I, 67.

9. Jasper Ridley, *Lord Palmerston,* Lond 1970, 551; Ferris, *Desperate Diplomacy,* 25, 38; E. D. Adams, op. cit., I, 85-86.

10. Nicolay and Hay, *Abraham Lincoln / A History,* IV, 269-276; Lincoln, *Collected Works,* IV, 376-380; J. G. Randall, *Lincoln the President,* II, 35-37; Ferris, *Desperate Diplomacy,* 21-23.

11. Moran, 14 Jun 1861.

12. CFA to CFA2, 14 Jun 1861, AP.
13. Moran, 14 Jun 1861.
14. Francis Brown, *Raymond of the Times*, NY 1951, 218-219, 227.
15. Moran, 15 and 19 Jun 1861.
16. Ibid., 1-2 Mar 1864.
17. Ibid.
18. Ibid., 29 May, 15 Jun 1861.
19. Ibid., 19 Jun 1861.
20. HA to CFA2, 2 Jul 1861, AP.
21. When experience had made him better able to recognize his exceptional ability to sense oncoming events, HA laid positive claim to the ability, saying that what he felt immediately and strongly would be felt as well by others, but later and not so strongly. See his letter to CFA2, 3 Apr 1867, AP— "Depend upon it that what affects me so violently will affect the average man at last."

## 20 / Waiting for the Battle

*Principal sources*

(1) seven news reports by HA, published in NYTimes, unsigned, under varying headings, as follows:

[No. 6] dated 22 Jun, published 4 Jul 1861, under the headings: "AFFAIRS AT LONDON. / Mr. Train's Polemic Dejeuner—What Came of It—The Rebel Commissioners on the Continent—English Politics—Meeting of Convocation—Improvement in American Affairs. / From Our Own Correspondent."
[No. 7] dated 29 Jun, published 15 Jul 1861, under the headings: "FROM LONDON. / The Death of the Lord Chancellor—The Great Fire—The Canadian Reinforcements—Mr. Adams and the New-York Herald—The Rebel Commissioners, &c." ["From Our Own Correspondent" does not appear.]
[No. 8] dated 1 Jul, published 19 Jul 1861, under the headings: "AFFAIRS IN LONDON. / Celebration of the Fourth—No Chance for Privateers Fitting Out in English Ports—The Oath of Allegiance Administered to Applicants for Passports—Lord Brougham, M. Du Chaillu and his Travels. / From Our Own Correspondent."
[No. 9] dated 13 Jul, published 26 Jul 1861, under the headings: "Why Troops were Sent to Canada. / Correspondence of the New-York Times." ["From Our Own Correspondent" does not appear.]

[No. 10] dated 20 Jul, published 2 Aug 1861, under the headings: "FROM LONDON. / Dull Times—The Queen's Health—Discouraging Prospects—Lord Palmerston's Policy—Another Reform Bill Expected, &c. / From Our Own Correspondent."
[No. 11] dated 27 Jul, published 12 Aug 1861, under the headings: "AFFAIRS IN ENGLAND. / Earl Russell's Farewell to his London Constituents—His Parting Bequest to the House of Commons—The Strike among the Masons—Diplomatic Matters, &c. / From Our Own Correspondent."
[No 12] dated 3 Aug, published 15 Aug 1861, under the headings: "AFFAIRS IN ENGLAND. / The Recent Changes in the Ministry—Advancement of Lord John Russell—The Contest for the London Seat—Lord Herbert—Mr. Bright, &c. / From Our Own Correspondent."
(2) two letters, HA to CFA2, 2 and 26 Jul 1861, AP.

*Notes concerning additional sources*

1. When he made this suggestion, HA may already have suspected, or even discovered, that George Sumner, brother of Charles Sumner, was the author of weekly unsigned letters from Boston currently appearing in the *London Morning Post*. See HA to CFA2, 7 Nov 1861, AP; HA to Charles Sumner, 30 Jan 1862, Sumner Papers, H; and HA to NYTimes [No. 26], dated 9 Nov 1861—"... there is a Boston writer in the *Morning Post* who is singularly clever in blowing hot and cold. . . ."
2. HA to CFA2, 10-11 Jun 1861, AP.
3. CFA to CFA2, 18 Jul 1861, AP.
4. Moran, 1 Jul 1861.
5. Ibid., 9 Jul 1861.
6. CFA2 to ABA, 9 Jul 1861, AP.
7. CFA to CFA2, 18 Jul 1861, AP; Moran, 31 Jul 1861. On 28 Aug 1962, permitted to inspect the interior of the house when it was vacant, I learned that practically all of its best interior features, including the Adam ceilings, had been sold and removed.
8. HA to CFA2, 5-6 Aug 1861, AP.


21 / Very Well As I Am

*Principal sources*

(1) three news reports by HA, published in NYTimes, unsigned, but identified as "From Our Own Correspondent," as follows:

[No. 13] dated 10 Aug, published 24 Aug 1861, under the headings: "FROM LONDON. / The Battle of Bull Run, and Its Effect upon European Nations—The Question of the Blockade—The Effort to Break Down American Credit in England—Danger from France, &c."

[No. 14] dated 24 Aug, published 6 Sep 1861, under the headings: "AMERICAN QUESTIONS IN ENGLAND./ British Sentiment upon the Repulse at Bull Run—How English Politicians Stand—The Rebels Send a War Steamer to Sea from England—The British Government Declines to Interfere—The South Lancashire Election."

[No. 15] dated "Sunday, Aug. 31, 1861," published 14 Sep 1861, under the headings: "FROM LONDON. / Payment of Interest on Georgia Bonds—Financial Prospects of the South—Necessity for a Strict Blockade—What England is Likely to Do." [August 31 was a Saturday, so "Sunday" must be an error—possibly by the *Times*—if HA's date, as given, was right.]

(2) two letters, HA to CFA2, 5-6 Aug and 7 Sep 1861, AP.

## Notes concerning additional sources

1. The idea of accompanying CFA2 into battle also appears in HA's account of a snowball fight which he and Charles, in boyhood, had taken part in—an account which directly refers to the Civil War and involves fighters who panicked and fled. See *Education*, 41-42.

2. CFA2 to CFA, 23 Jul 1861, AP.

3. Moran, 5 Aug 1861.

4. HA, *Education*, 128-129. Shifting this restless night from 5 Aug 1861, after the first battle of Bull Run, to a night in 1862 after the second battle at the same place appears to be one of the important, deliberate falsifications implanted by HA in his pages in *The Education* about his experiences in London.

5. In the process, Russell caught sight of "Mr. Raymond, of the *New York Times*,. . . looking by no means happy." See William Howard Russell, *My Diary / North and South*, NY 1954, 230.

6. HA, *Education*, 118.

7. Moran, 10 Aug 1861.

8. Ibid., 24 Jun and 26 Aug 1861.

9. Ibid., 14-20 Aug 1861.

10. Ibid., 19 Aug 1861.

11. HA, "The Declaration of Paris. 1861," in *Historical Essays*, 237-278; CFA2, *Charles Francis Adams*, chap. 11, "The Treaty of

Paris"; CFA2, "The Negotiation of 1861 relating to the Declaration of Paris. . . ," MHS *Proceedings*, XLVI, 23-81; Ferris, *Desperate Diplomacy*, 77-84.

12. E. D. Adams, *Great Britain and the American Civil War*, I, 168-171; Moran, 19 Aug 1861; CFA2, *Charles Francis Adams*, 209; Duberman, *Charles Francis Adams*, 269-272.

13. Moran, 31 Aug-5 Sep 1861; Ferris, *Desperate Diplomacy*, 100.

14. CFA2 to HA, 23 Aug 1861, AP; Moran, 2 Sep 1861.

15. CFA2 to HA, 25 Aug 1861, AP.

## 22 / GREAT AND UNKNOWN EVIL

*Principal sources*

(1) nine news reports by HA, published in NYTimes, unsigned, under varying headings, as follows:

[No. 16] dated 7 Sep, published 24 Sep 1861, under the headings: "FROM LONDON. / The English People and the American Troubles—Explanation of the Apparent Hostility of the Press—Secession Agents Busy—The Cotton Question, &c./ From Our Own Correspondent."

[No. 17] dated 14 Sep, published 26 Sep 1861, under the headings: "FROM LONDON. / Bad Effects of the Defeat at Manassas—Designs of the British Government—Mr. Russell's Letters—The Passport Regulation, &c. / From Our Own Correspondent."

[No. 18] dated 21 Sep, published 8 Oct 1861, under the headings: "MATTERS AT LONDON. / Improvement in the British Tone—The C.S.A. apply for Recognition and are Refused—The Programme for Mexico—Hostility of the London Times—The Incidents of a Week. / From Our Own Correspondent."

[No. 19] dated 27 Sep, published 13 Oct 1861, under the headings: "AFFAIRS IN ENGLAND. / A Trip to Leamington—Oxford—Warwick Castle—English View of American Affairs—Little Sympathy with the South. / Correspondence of the New-York Times." [The dateline falsely reads "Leamington." "From Our Own Correspondent" does not appear.]

[No. 20] dated 4 Oct, published 20 Oct, under the headings: "FROM GLASGOW. / The Scenery of the English Lake

Disticts—Its Tameness, Compared with that of New-England—Opinions of American Affairs—Scotch Sympathy, &c. / Correspondence of the New-York Times." [The dateline falsely reads "Glasgow." "From Our Own Correspondent" does not appear.]

[No. 21] dated 12 Oct, published 28 Oct 1861, under the headings: "FROM LONDON. / Effects of the War in the United States upon the the [*sic*] English Industrial Classes—Probable Suffering—Course of the Government—The Mexican Difficulty, &c." ["From Our Own Correspondent" does not appear.]

[No. 22] dated 19 Oct, published 2 Nov 1861, under the headings: "SECESSION INTRIGUES IN ENGLAND. / Success of the Bermuda in Running the Blockade—Activity and Resources of Rebel Agents in the Great Towns—Manufacture of Arms—The Movement to Break the Blockade. / From Our Own Correspondent."

[No. 23] dated 20 Oct, published 7 Nov 1861, under the dateline, "London, Sunday, Oct. 20, 1861," as a sequel to the letter sent by HA the following Saturday—[No. 24]. [This is the first instance of HA sending two letters in one week.]

[No. 24] dated 26 Oct, published 7 Nov 1861, under the headings: "AFFAIRS IN ENGLAND. / Public Opinion Forming Against the North—Work of the Southern Agents—Liverpool a Hot-bed of Secession—English Annoyance at the Late Visit of the King of Prussia to France, &c. / From Our Own Correspondent."

(2) four letters, HA to CFA2, 14 and 28 Sep, 5 and 25 Oct 1861, AP;

(3) a letter, HA to CFA2, 15 Oct 1861, AP, written for possible publication in BAdv, but not so used;

(4) a letter, HA to John Gorham Palfrey, 23 Oct 1861, Cater, 8-10.

## Notes concerning additional sources

1. CFA to CFA2, 2 May 1862, AP.

2. The positioning of the official secretaries in a room directly below the study occupied by CFA and HA inevitably functioned as a silent but insistent reminder to Wilson and Moran that in some sense they were much outranked by the younger Adams.

3. Moran, I, 796 note 4, and 9 Sep 1861.

4. Ibid., 17 Sep 1861.

5. CFA to CFA2, 7 Sep 1861, AP.

6. HA to NYTimes [No. 14].

7. Ibid.

8. HA to NYTimes [No. 15].

9. With regard to Russell, see HA to NYTimes [No. 11], dated 27 Jul 1861. With regard to Palmerston, see HA to Sumner, 30 Jan 1862, Sumner Papers, H—"... he will be on the winning side, and that is all that can be said of him."

10. Moran, 18 Sep 1861.

11. HA's fear of detection by Moran appears to have been simultaneous with the latter's first strong feelings of disgust with Wilson. See Moran, 9 and 17 Sep 1861.

12. An instance of Moran's interest in the New York press is his *Journal* entry dated 10 Sep 1861.

13. Moran, 21 and 24 Sep 1861.

14. Ibid, 1 and 16 Oct 1861.

15. HA may have visited Oxford briefly in 1860, while journeying from Paris to Quincy.

16. Moran, 16 Oct 1861.

17. Ibid., 5 Oct 1861.

18. Ibid., 9 Oct 1861.

19. Ibid., 16-17 Oct 1861.

20. Atkins, *Life of Sir William Howard Russell*, I, 68-74.

21. CFA2 to CFA, 3 Sep 1861, AP.

22. BCour, 16-17 Sep 1861; CFA2 to HA, 17 Sep 1861, AP.

## 23 / A VISIT TO MANCHESTER

*Principal sources*

(1) three news reports by HA, published in NYTimes, unsigned, under varying headings, as follows:

[No. 25] dated 2 Nov, published 18 Nov 1861, under the headings: "THE ATTITUDE OF ENGLAND. / The Correspondence between the British Foreign Office and Mr. Hayman—The Declaration of the Duke of Argyle—Unpopularity of the American Cause—Its Probable Increase—The Mexican Question./ Correspondence of the New-York Times." ["From Our Own Correspondent" does not appear.]

[No. 26] dated 9 Nov, published 22 Nov 1861, under the headings: "THE AMERICAN QUESTION. / English Opinion concerning Mr. Seward's Correspondence with Lord Lyons. / From Our Own Correspondent."

[No. 27] dated 16 Nov, published 30 Nov 1861, under the headings: "IMPORTANT FROM ENGLAND. / An Anticipation of the Arrest of Slidell and Mason—What the British Government was Preparing to Do—The James Adger—Friendly Understanding Between the English and American Governments—The Speeches at the Lord Mayor's Banquet—Preparations for a New Parliamentary Campaign, &c., &c./ From Our Special Correspondent."

(2) HA, "A Visit to Manchester: Extracts from a Private Diary," written for publication in the *Atlantic Monthly,* but delayed in completion, sent too late, and published instead in BCour, 16 Dec 1861 (reprinted in AHR, Oct 1945, 79-89);

(3) a letter, HA to CFA2, 7 Nov 1861, AP.

*Notes concerning additional sources*

1. For information about Stell, I am indebted to Franklin Brooks.

2. HA to NYTimes [No. 24].

3. HA, *Education,* 72; HA to NYTimes [Nos. 12,13, 16, and 21].

4. Thomas L. Harris, *The Trent Affair,* Indianapolis and Kansas City, 1896, 91-93; Norman B. Ferris, *The* TRENT *Affair/ A Diplomatic Crisis,* Knoxville, 1977, 5-9.

5. Moran, 2 and 7 Nov 1861; extracts from English newspapers, NYTimes, 9 Dec 1861, 2.

6. HA to CFA2, 2 July 1861, AP.

7. CFA2 to HA, 14 Oct 1861, AP.

8. Thinking that George Sumner's letters might be quashed, HA in the same letter (7 Nov 61) urged CFA2 to intervene if possible, adding that the Sumner brothers were "both crazy." Because the offending letters continued to appear in London, HA later tried to quash them himself by writing to Charles Sumner: "It is very generally asserted here that certain letters from Boston in the [London] Morning Post, are written by your brother, Mr. George Sumner. As they are not altogether of a friendly tone and bear internal evidence of some other sources than his, I have taken the liberty to deny the statement. It would however be useful both to him and to you, I think, if some authoritative denial were made or if I had the means of positively refuting it. As I haven't the pleasure of your brother's acquaintance, I make the suggestion to you." See HA to Charles Sumner, 30 Jan 1862, Sumner Papers, H. This artful passage elicited from the senator the sweeping denial: "Of course the whole story is absurd. I doubt if he [George] ever corresponded with a newspaper in

his life—surely never to my knowledge. I know nothing of the letters to which you refer. . . ." See Charles Sumner to HA, 26 Feb 1862, Dwight Papers, MHS.

9. HA to NYTimes [Nos. 14, 15, 17, and 24].

10. Moran, 7 Nov 1861; CFA to Seward, 15 Nov 1861, AP; extract from LTimes, "The Real Mission of the Adger," in NYTimes, 9 Dec 1861, 2.

11. See especially the extract from the *Edinburgh Scotsman* in NYTimes, 9 Dec 1861, 2.

12. CFA to Seward, 15 Nov 1861, AP. HA copied this letter into his father's *Letterbooks*, same date, AP.

13. The *Conway* reached Southampton on 16 Nov. See LTimes, 18 Nov 1861, 5.

14. Moran, 16 Nov 1861.

15. CFA2 to HA, 23 and 25 Aug 1861, AP.


## 24  /  VEXATION AND DESPAIR

*Principal sources*

(1) two extremely important news reports by HA, published in NYTimes, unsigned, but identified as "From Our Own Correspondent," as follows:

[No. 28] dated 23 Nov, published 9 Dec 1861, under the headings: "THE AFFAIR OF THE NASHVILLE. / First Impression Upon the English Public—The Facts—Statement of Capt. Nelson—Uncertainty of the British Government—Speculations."

[No. 29] dated 30 Nov, published 19 Dec 1861, under the headings: "ENGLAND AND AMERICA. / The Case of the Nashville—Hospitalities of the Southampton People—Corruption of the Press—Capt. Nelson Everywhere Denied Redress—Indignation of Americans—The News from the Trent—The Government and the Press for War—An Estimate of the Situation."

(2) a letter, HA to CFA2, 30 Nov 1861, AP.

*Notes concerning additional sources*

1. Moran, 19 and 21 Nov 1861.

2. Extracts from the English press relating to the *Nashville*, NYTimes, 9 Dec 1861, 2.

3. Ibid.; Moran, 22 Nov 1861.

4. HA may never have learned that the sending of unofficial envoys had been inspired, at least in part, by an urgent request to Seward from Navy Captain William M. Walker to arrange "the presence in London of *several gentlemen* altogether in the confidence of the Govt, but ostensibly without any connexion with it, competent to discuss American affairs in conversation or in writing, & occupying such a position in society as would ensure their friendly reception into any circles." See Ferris, *Desperate Diplomacy*, 176-177—identifying Walker as "the State Department's top secret agent in Europe." Walker had visited the legation in August while the Adamses were at Derby, and Moran had said of him, "He moves very mysteriously...." See Moran, 10 Aug 1861. Walker again turned up at the legation at a moment when HA was there but CFA was away in Scotland. See ibid., 24 Sep 1861. The captain's advice to Seward was sent four weeks later, on 20 Oct.

5. F. W. Seward, *Seward at Washington . . . 1861-1872*, 17-22; *Autobiography of Thurlow Weed*, ed. by Harriet A. Weed, Bost 1883, 650-657; Thurlow Weed Barnes, *Memoir of Thurlow Weed*, Bost 1884, 349; Glyndon G. Van Deusen, *Thurlow Weed/ Wizard of the Lobby*, Bost 1947, 275-276.

6. LTimes, 20 Nov 1861, 7.

7. CFA2, *The Trent Affair/ An Historical Retrospect*, Bost 1912, 20-22 (reprinted from MHS *Proceedings*, XLV, 35-76).

8. Moran, 27 Jan 1862.

9. LTimes, 25 Nov 1861, 7.

10. Moran, 22 and 23 Nov 1861.

11. Ibid., 25 Nov 1861.

12. Ibid.

13. HA, *Education*, 119.

14. For convenience, details have been included in this paragraph which could not have appeared in Britton's message.

15. HA, *Education*, 119.

16. Moran, 27 Nov 1861.

17. Telegram, Moran to CFA, 27 Nov 1861, AP.

18. Moran, 27 Nov 1861.

19. HA, *Education*, 111—"... a good fellow, universally known as Charley Wilson...."

20. Moran, 28 Nov 1861.

21. John Morley, *The Life of William Ewart Gladstone*, NY 1921, II, 73.

22. Philip Guedalla, *Palmerston,* Lond 1926, 428.

23. Moran, 28 Nov 1861. CFA attached importance to Moran's visit to the Foreign Office and mentioned it to Seward. See CFA to Seward, 29 Nov 1861, quoted in John Bigelow, *Recollections of an Active Life,* NY 1909, I, 425.

24. Moran, 29 Nov 1861; Ferris, *The* TRENT *Affair,* 42-44.

25. CFA to Seward, 29 Nov 1861—in Bigelow, *Recollections,* I, 425.

26. Russell to Palmerston, 7 Dec 1861, Palmerston Papers, HMC—"I send you Lyon's letter. It all looks like war. Lyons will be quite right [,] as he is now right."

27. CFA did not have another interview with Russell for three weeks, and then, on 19 Dec 1861, while learning the terms of the British ultimatum, was not given copies of the despatches. See CFA to Motley, 26 Dec 1861, in MHS *Proceedings,* XLV, 109. In the interval, CFA was suspected of either ignorant good will or disarmingly cordial dishonesty by both Palmerston and Russell, for reasons lucidly set forth by CFA2 in his *Charles Francis Adams,* 212-226.

28. LTimes, 22 Nov 1861, 7; 26 Nov 1861, 9.

29. Making this guess, HA momentarily aligned himself with the English, with respect to the question of Seward's responsibility. See Ferris, *The* TRENT *Affair, 89—*" . . . few Englishmen doubted that Seward, in some manner, had arranged the *Trent* affair." More particularly, HA shared the thinking of Russell and Palmerston on the same question. See Russell to Palmerston, 11 Dec 1861, Palmerston Papers, HMC—"Every day commits some new person [in America] . . . to the Wilkes side of the question, so that Lincoln will find himself unable to shake off Seward [the supposed author of the affair], even if he wishes it."


25 / THE BELL

*Principal sources*

(1) two climactically important news reports by HA, published in NYTimes, unsigned, but identified as "From Our Own Correspondent," as follows:

[No. 30] dated 7 Dec, published 25 Dec 1861, under the headings: "THE WAR PANIC IN ENGLAND. / The Real English Sentiment Adverse to War—The Free Policy of the United States—Raptures of the Secessionists, &c., &c."

[No. 31] dated 14 Dec, published 30 Dec 1861, under the headings: "THE ANGLO-AMERICAN ISSUE. / The Condition of Public Sentiment in England—A Ground Current toward Peace—Bad Position of the British Ministry—Aversion of the Queen to War—A Plain Course for the United States Government, &c."

(2) an earlier news report by HA [No. 27], as published in NYTimes, 30 Nov 1861;

(3) a letter, HA to CFA2, 13 Dec 1861, AP.

*Notes concerning additional sources*

1. Moran, 2-10 Dec 1861.

2. LTimes, 30 Nov 1861, 8.

3. Raymond's paper had commenced Sunday publication with the news of the firing on Fort Sumter, in mid-April. (See also Hale, *Horace Greeley,* 75.)

4. LTimes, 2 Dec 1861, 6; 3 Dec 1861, 4; and 4 Dec 1861, 8.

5. Bigelow, *Recollections,* I, 365—" . . . not primarily for the discharge of consular duties . . . but to look after the press in France." HA's shifting the whole matter of Seward's unofficial emissaries, and particularly the arrival of Weed in London, from Nov-Dec 1861 to the summer of 1863 is altogether the most spectacular of his knowing distortions of historical fact in the early chapters of his *Education.* But his account—145-146—is accurate in saying: " . . . Weed . . . came [abroad] to do what the private secretary [HA] himself had attempted . . . . Mr. Weed took charge of the press. . . ."

6. *Autobiography of . . . Weed,* 656; Barnes, *Weed,* 350; *Seward at Washington . . . 1861-1872,* 27-32; Bigelow, *Recollections,* I, 385-390, 402.

7. MHS *Proceedings,* XLV, 148-150.

8. Moran, 3 Dec 1861.

9. John Bright, *Speeches on Questions of Public Policy,* Lond 1869, I, 185-187, 190.

10. Arthur Irwin Dasent, *John Thadeus Delane/ Editor of "The Times,"* Lond 1908, II, 38.

11. MHS *Proceedings,* XLV, 151; Trevelyan, *John Bright,* 314.

12. Barnes, *Weed,* 368.

13. Ibid., 350.

14. Moran, 6 Dec 1861.

15. Bigelow, *Recollections,* I, 403; Barnes, *Weed,* 350. See also Weed to Cameron, 7 Dec 1861, in Randall, *Lincoln the President,* II, 38.

16. HA, *Education*, 146—"Thurlow Weed was a complete American education in himself. . . . He was the model of political management. . . ."

17. CFA to Motley, 4 Dec 1861, in MHS *Proceedings*, XLV, 92. See also Duberman, *Charles Francis Adams*, 280—"Throughout the crisis of the next few weeks [Minister] Adams remained a passive and impotent spectator." While true with respect to CFA's feelings, both the elder Adams's statement about himself and Duberman's statement about the minister's passivity and impotence seem overstated, for CFA had a decided effect on events in Washington. One day earlier, on 3 Dec 1861, in a long despatch to Seward, the minister had explained that the release of Mason and Slidell by the U.S. Government would be consistent with the position taken in 1804 by James Madison, then secretary of state, in a dispute with Great Britain and consistent, too, with earlier American policy on such matters generally. Seward made positive use of CFA's suggestion in the decisive document ending the crisis. See Ferris, *The* TRENT *Affair*, 184-185, 246 note 41. When he saw Seward's despatch, after it at last reached London, HA wrote that it was "particularly grateful to me because the ground taken is that which the Chief recommended." See HA to CFA2, 10 Jan 1862, AP. It seems probable that HA had been a participant in early Dec 1861 in the reading of Madison's state papers at the legation, preparatory to the sending of CFA's helpful despatch to Seward. HA's similar but more independent role in providing early *British* state papers to a *British* politician, Richard Cobden, to help ease relations between Great Britain and the U.S. in 1863, will be recounted in the second book of this biography.

18. CFA to Seward, 6 Dec 1861, in Bigelow, *Recollections*, I, 397-399.

19. NYTimes, 17 Nov 1861, 1.

20. This possibly mistaken inference is based on (1) the absence of complaints by HA about the treatment of his reports by the *New York Times*, (2) his strong reaction when one report was tampered with, and (3) the texts of the reports themselves, which read—with the one exception—as if they were printed in full. (HA was presumably not responsible for the headings printed above his reports, and might have found some of them slanted towards Raymond's views.)

21. Bigelow, *Recollections*, I, 402-403, 412; CFA2, *The Trent Affair*, Bost 1912, 33 note 2; Lyons to Russell, 21 Feb 1861, in MHS *Proceedings*, XLVIII, 218; E. D. Adams, *Great Britain and the American Civil War*, I, 80, 113-114, 216.

22. Barnes, *Weed*, 351-353.

23. Moran, 9-10 Dec 1861.

24. Assertions in the narrative about ships' sailing and arrival times in English ports are derived from shipping news in LTimes.

25. CFA2, *The Trent Affair*, 16-17, 33-34; LTimes, 10 Dec 1861, 9.

26. One or more editorials concerning the *Trent* affair appeared daily in Raymond's newspaper from 17 through 24 Nov and on 26 and 27 Nov 1861.

27. LTimes, 13 Dec 1861, 5.

28. HA, *Education*, 146.

29. LTimes, 14 Dec 1861, 7; Barnes, *Weed*, 354-358.

30. CFA2, *Charles Francis Adams*, 233.

31. CFA2 to CFA, 26 Nov 1861, AP.

32. In one sense, HA did die for his father—by later refusing to participate in the writing of CFA's life and by distorting the facts of his own work while in his father's company in Washington and in London in the period from Dec 1860 through the early months of 1868 when writing his *Education*. Together, these actions sufficed to give even the most inquiring authorities on the American Civil War and its near-expansion into a world war a grossly diminished idea of HA's importance and a mistaken idea of his relations with his father, not to mention his relation with his brother Charles. In the bargain, HA's actions lent his father an appearance of having worked without significant assistance from himself, or from Moran. This carefully fostered illusion served successfully to augment his father's stature.

33. Barnes, *Weed*, 358-361. The editorial—concluding with a reference to a phrase of Raymond's: "protracted negotiations"—is scathing evidence that British distrust of Seward had widened and become distrust of three New Yorkers: Seward, Weed, and Raymond. It now appears that the three had been equal sharers in the creation of Seward's Union Party the previous winter, to such an extent that both Weed and Raymond were consulted by Seward on 31 Mar 1861, the day before he wrote "Some Thoughts for the President's Consideration." (See Van Deusen, *William Henry Seward*, 281-282.) If Delane, Russell, and Palmerston had learned between that time and 14 Dec 1861 that Seward had written such a paper, with Weed and Raymond's support, Delane's editorial presumably would have been even more violent than it was. As things were, British distrust of the three Americans was founded only on detailed leaks concerning "Despatch No. 10" and direct knowledge of other, lesser threats to Great Britain by Seward, both verbal and written, gathered for the Foreign Office and the

ministry by Lord Lyons and other persons. Acquiring such knowledge, the British evidently enjoyed the active, secret assistance of Seward's archrival in foreign affairs, Charles Sumner. See Ferris, *Desperate Diplomacy*, 23-26, 57-59, and Ferris, *The* TRENT *Affair*, 102.

34. Bigelow, *Recollections*, I, 404-405; Brian Connell, *Regina Vs. Palmerston*, Garden City, 1961, 345-346.

35. Theodore Martin, *The Life of His Royal Highness/ the Prince Consort*, Lond 1880, V, 418-423; Spencer Walpole, *The Life of Lord John Russell*, Lond 1889, II, 346-348; Morley, Gladstone, II, 73-75; Ferris, *The* TRENT *Affair*, 50-53.

36. E. D. Adams, *Great Britain and the American Civil War*, I, 215.

37. Martin, op. cit., 353-354.

38. Moran, 14 Dec 1861.

39. LTimes, 14 Dec 1861, 6-7.

40. HA to NYTimes [No. 32], dated 21 Dec 1861, on "The Death of Prince Albert."


26 / NEWS BY THE "WASHINGTON"

*Principal sources*

(1) a special news report by HA, published in NYTimes, unsigned, but identified as "From Our Own Correspondent," as follows:
> [No. 32] dated 21 Dec 1861, published 5 Jan 1862, under the headings: "THE DEATH OF PRINCE ALBERT. / The People Taken by Surprise—The Feelings of the Prince—The Character of his Connections with the British Government—The Queen in Retirement, &c."

(2) three regular news reports by HA, published in NYTimes, unsigned, but identified as "From Our Own Correspondent," as follows:
> [No. 33] dated 21 Dec 1861, published 4 Jan 1862, under the headings: "IMPORTANT FROM LONDON. / A Change for the Better in American Affairs—The Act of Capt. Wilkes Disavowed in Advance—Frantic Efforts of the War Party—The Position of Lord Palmerston, &c."
> [No. 34] dated 28 Dec 1861, published 11 Jan 1862, under the headings: "THE SUSPENSE IN ENGLAND. / Uprise of the Peace Sentiment—A Mischievous Error—Its Foundation the Seward-Newcastle Anecdote—Lord Palmerston Expects No

War—Confidence of the Rebels—Funeral of Prince Albert, &c., &c."

[No. 35] dated 4 Jan, published 21 Jan 1862, under the headings: "THE AFFAIR OF THE TRENT. / A Better Feeling with the Opening of the New Year—Confidence in Peace—Stocks and Cotton Up—The Position of France—The Question of the Blockade—Good Effect of Mr. Seward's Correspondence, &c."

(3) four earlier news reports by HA [Nos. 27-30], as published in NYTimes respectively on 30 Nov, 9 Dec, 19 Dec, and 25 Dec 1861;

(4) an article by HA, "A Visit to Manchester: Extracts from a Private Diary," as mistakenly published, with his authorship disclosed, in BCour, 16 Dec 1861;

(5) a letter, HA to CFA2, 28 Dec 1861, AP.

## Notes Concerning Additional Sources

1. Moran, 16 Dec 1861.
2. Ibid., 17 Dec 1861.
3. Nicolay and Hay, *Abraham Lincoln / A History*, V, 32.
4. Harris, *The Trent Affair*, 134-135.
5. Moran, 17 Dec 1861.
6. Harris, op. cit., 144.
7. Guedalla, *Palmerston*, 433.
8. CFA2, *Charles Francis Adams*, 227-229; E. D. Adams, *Great Britain and the American Civil War*, I, 226; Ferris, *The* TRENT *Affair*, 145-147—"But [C. F.] Adams could still feel little confidence in the favorable issue of the entanglement."
9. Moran, 21 Dec 1861.
10. That HA's twenty-seventh report (even with its warning passage expunged) strongly affected readers in America seems certain; for it troubled the columns of Raymond's newspaper for ten days, from 30 Nov until 9 Dec 1861, and elicited from CFA2 a confidential remark to the secret correspondent in London: " . . . your letter in which you mention that the James Adger was watched created a good deal of uneasiness." See CFA2 to HA, 3 Dec 1861, AP. HA had already received this news from his brother when he wrote his brief thirty-third report, dated 21 Dec 1861.
11. In late Nov 1861, CFA and HA had themselves both noticed the article in the *Edinburgh Scotsman*. CFA later wrote about it: "The article . . . attracted my attention immediately upon its publication. It is one of many instances . . . of the uses made of the press in Great Britain from central points and high sources . . . to affect public

opinion. . . . I had reason to know in the case of the *Scotsman* that the information [about Capt. Marchand and the *James Adger*] must have come from authority [i. e. Prime Minister Palmerston]." See CFA to Everett, 27 Dec 1861, in MHS *Proceedings*, XLV, 112-113. From HA's point of view, the article's significance very probably centered in its repeating one principal Confederate lie (also believed by Palmerston and the *London Telegraph,* but explained to Raymond and his readers by HA in his twenty-seventh report) that Marchand was hunting, not a confederate ship, the *Nashville,* but a British mail ship from the West Indies—the one that Mason and Slidell had elected not to board in the Bahamas, knowing it would have to make a stop in New York, a Union port.

12. In the period 17-27 Nov 1861, Raymond had earlier published twelve editorials on the *Trent* Affair. His new editorial, responding to HA and the *Edinburgh Scotsman,* completed an added series of eight editorials on the crisis, published on 30 Nov and 3, 4, 6, 7, 8, and 9 Dec 1861.

13. Moran, 23 Dec 1861.

14. Ibid., 24 and 27 Dec 1861; HA, *Education,* 121-122.

15. Extract from the *Manchester Guardian,* "Expecting the American Answer," in NYTimes, 11 Jan 1862, 2.

16. Raymond was in the process of adding a third series of editorials on the *Trent* affair to those he had previous published. Ten in number, these further editorials were published on 10, 11, 13, 14, and 15 Dec 1861, when they were interrupted by alarming news from Europe, brought on the steamer *City of Washington.*

17. Moran, 24 Dec 1861.

18. Ibid., 1 Jan 1862.

19. In this way, Raymond went forward through still a fourth series of editorials on the *Trent* affair. Eleven in number, they were published at the rate of one or more a day continuously from 16 Dec through 22 Dec 1861.

20. CFA2 to HA, 17 Dec 1861, AP.

21. CFA2 may have been governed in part by the fact that his own two recent articles, called "English Views," had both been published in BCour.

22. HA to CFA2, 31 Jan 1862, AP.

23. Moran, 2-13 Jan 1862.

24. Nicolay and Hay, *Abraham Lincoln/ A History,* V, 32-34; *Seward at Washington . . . 1861-1872,* 24-25; Frederick W. Seward, *Reminiscences of a War-Time Statesman and Diplomat,* NY & Lond

1916, 187-188; E. D. Adams, *Great Britain and the American Civil War*, I, 230 note 2 and 231 note 2; Ferris, *The* TRENT *Affair*, 131-135.

25. That Seward should secretly have attempted in Apr-May 1861 to start "a war with all Europe"—to use HA's expression—and then should secretly have resolved in late Nov 1861 to do his best to arrange the return of Mason and Slidell to British hands could seem an astonishing turnabout. Lord Lyons, one of the first persons to learn of Seward's new resolve, wrote to Earl Russell: "You will perhaps be surprised to find Mr. Seward on the side of peace." Offering to explain the phenomenon, Lyons added: "Ten months of office have dispelled many of his illusions. I presume that he no longer believes in . . . the return of the South to the arms of the North in case of a foreign war . . . ." See Lyons to Russell, 23 Dec 1861 (quoted in Ferris, *The* TRENT *Affair*, 135). But it may be doubted whether Seward had ever had any illusions that office could dispel. His unsuccessful efforts to start a foreign war and his successful effort to arrange the surrender of Mason and Slidell could both be explained as actions by a politician who (1) had been actively in contact with Southern Unionists tragically at the mercy of dictatorial Southern secessionists, (2) understood and recoiled from the peculiar horror of civil war, (3) preferred the different horror of foreign war, (4) was so confident of his own abilities that he believed he could manage a diminished rebellion at home in combination with a great war with other powers, (5) was wise enough to yield when Lincoln would not support so adventurous a course, (6) felt the same fierce animus against Great Britain also experienced at moments in 1861 by HA, Clay, Fremont, Burlingame, Moran, Weed, and numberless other American Unionists, (6) was wise enough to yield a second time when Lincoln altered "Despatch No. 10," and (7) discovered that, after all, he remained a "chief" of sorts, with paramount responsibility for preventing disastrous European interference in the Union's efforts to subdue the Confederacy. Imbued with this sense of retained importance, Seward had written privately to his wife on 31 Oct 1861: "The responsibility resting upon me is overwhelming. . . . I thought that my health would fail, but now I am well and cheerful, and hopeful as ever." See *Seward at Washington . . . 1846-1861*, 627.

26. Nicolay and Hay, op cit., V, 34-39; Pierce, IV, 58-59; MHS Proceedings, XLV, 153; Donald, *Charles Sumner & The Rights of Man*, 31-38; Ferris, *The* TRENT *Affair*, 171-186.

27. Nicolay and Hay, *op. cit.*, V, 37; Pierce, IV, 58-59; Ferris, *The* TRENT *Affair*, 186-187.

28. Raymond, having published five more editorials on the *Trent*

affair on 23, 24, and 25 Dec 1861, thus completed his forty-sixth editorial on the subject without bringing himself into tune with the policy preferred by Seward in Washington and by Weed, HA, CFA, and Moran in London.

29. Moran, 8-9 Jan 1862; Barnes, *Weed*, 379.

30. HA to CFA2, 31 Jan 1862, AP.

## 27 / A DIFFERENT EGO

*Principal sources*

(1) four news reports by HA [Nos. 31, 33, 34, and 35], as published in NYTimes respectively on 30 Dec 1861, 4 Jan, 11 Jan and 21 Jan 1862;

(2) an article by HA, "A Visit to Manchester: Extracts from a Private Diary," as partially reprinted and editorially attacked in four English newspapers, 4-11 Jan 1862;

(3) a "Private & confidential" communication, both a letter and a commentary on recent news, HA to Henry J. Raymond, 24 Jan 1862, Raymond Papers, NYPL;

(4) four letters, HA to CFA2, 10 Jan-14 Feb 1862, AP.

*Notes concerning additional sources*

1. Evan John [Capt. E. J. Simpson], *Atlantic Impact/ 1861*, NY [1952?], 273; Harris, *The Trent Affair*, 225-226; F. W. Seward, *Reminiscences*, 191-193.

2. ABA to CFA, 27 Dec 1861, AP.

3. Returning to London on Thursday or Friday mornings would permit HA to take his usual share in the legation's getting ready to send its despatch bag to the State Department on Saturday night, and was expected by HA to facilitate his continuing his news reports— mostly written, presumably, in his rooms on the top floor of the house.

4. HA, *Education*, 121-122. His close relations with Julia Sturgis will be recounted in the second book of this biography.

5. Ibid., 120-121. See also an unpublished entry, dated 12 Aug 1865, in the *Benjamin Moran Diaries*, Manuscript Division, LC: "Mr. Parkes was an English politician who carried water on both shoulders in our war, and while professing friendship for us to Mr. Adams, got all he could from him and carried it to De Laine [sic] of the *Times*. He was particular to report Mr. Adams' gloomy views during the Trent affair. . . . I always regarded him as a snake in the grass."

6. Moran, 10 Jan 1862.

7. CFA to CFA2, 10 Jan 1862, AP.

8. Writing about the *Trent* affair, an English author later expressed himself as scandalized that HA should have deceived his father. See
Evan John [Capt. E. J. Simpson], op. cit., 197—" . . . Henry was
meanwhile sending a weekly letter to the *New York Times,* and
concealing the fact from his father, whose position he was . . .
jeopardising. He used desperate shifts—even putting GLASGOW and
LEAMINGTON at the head of articles written in London. . . . One
might say that Duplicity could go no farther, and that the testimony of
such a witness is not worthy of a moment's consideration. And yet that
beautifully written book, *The Education of Henry Adams,* remains
good evidence . . . of how he felt, long after. . . ."

9. Brown, *Raymond of the Times,* 167, 320-321.

10. A chance exists that HA's connection with Raymond was
disclosed in confidence by the editor (without HA's knowledge) to
Lincoln and/or Seward. This narrative has assumed that Raymond
made no such disclosure to the president or secretary of state; but the
assumption is based on nothing more than the high probability that
HA had sworn Raymond to total secrecy in Mar 1861 and that
Raymond, in addition to feeling he must keep his word, foresaw later
as well as immediate dealings between himself and the younger
Adams, and thus felt it advantageous to himself to hold strictly to the
pledge he had made.

11. Whether CFA ever learned that HA had written thirty-five
news reports to the *New York Times* is at present unknown to me, but
I strongly incline to the supposition that neither HA nor CFA2 ever
told him.

12. HA, *Education,* 122.

13. HA later went out of his way to tell John Gorham Palfrey:
"There seems to be such a fog over the whole affair [a letter by CFA,
recently published in British and American newspapers] . . . that I
should long ago have explained it in some of our newspapers, if it were
not forbidden ground to me to appear in print on matter connected
with the affairs of the Legation." See HA to Palfrey 29 May 1863, Cater,
17. Because HA was not a secretary of legation, and not, strictly
speaking, an employee of the legation, but instead a private citizen
exceptionally and anomalously given an official uniform, plus room,
board, and a private allowance, federal law against such secretaries
and employees' writing for newspapers did *not* apply to him. It can
therefore be assumed that HA's writing for newspapers had become
"forbidden ground" because someone—CFA—expressly forbade it.

The probable date of the supposed prohibition is Thursday, 16 Jan, or Friday, 17 Jan 1862, after HA again returned to London from Walton-on-Thames, and after CFA had had a few days to mull the "first rate notice" given to his son in *The Times*. All of HA's subsequent behavior in London while his father remained minister supports this assumption that the elder man expressly asked the younger *not* to write for newspapers—and the younger made a promise he absolutely would not break.

14. CFA2 to HA, "Friday, January, 1862," AP. The elder brother's concise summary of the younger's "career" may have made an indelible impression on HA and become a factor in his deciding how to distort the facts of his first life when he wrote an account of it in his *Education*. The main distortions he decided upon were six in number and warrant listing. He shifted his talk with Palfrey concerning Smith and Pocahontas from the spring of 1861 to an unspecified time after the Civil War, four or more years later. He shifted Weed's arrival in Europe from 1861 to 1863. He shifted his own decision to go home and be a soldier from August 1861, following the first battle of Bull Run, to a corresponding moment in 1862, after the second battle of Bull Run. He minimized his secret labors as a newspaper correspondent, giving the impression that his reports to the *New York Times* had been occasional, personal, and unimportant, when they had been systematic, paid, and very important. He expunged his early interest in contributing to the *Atlantic Monthly*. Lastly, he minimized the *Trent* affair, drawing attention instead to the later affair of the Laird rams, in such a way as to humble his own exertions and elevate those of his father. These distortions served to falsify and conceal—from all eyes but those of persons attuned to his deceptions or in possession of corrective knowledge—not only the story of his youth but also his idea of his own era, an idea which centered in the *Trent* affair and the dawn of Anglo-American cooperation and solidarity. Yet so well-managed were his carefully shaded falsehoods that they also worked effectively to disclose the truth. After all, it was *The Education of Henry Adams* that first alerted people to the hidden fact that its protagonist, in addition to going with his father to London as private secretary, had gone in another, possibly more important capacity, as a secret journalist and independent politician, armed with an extraordinary means of affecting public opinion. It was Adams himself who provided the essential, starting clues needed by those in search of better knowledge of his far-reaching young adventurers.

# Index

Adams, Abigail (*nee* Smith), great-grandmother of HA, 34, 42, 46, 49, 400
Adams, Abigail Brown (*nee* Brooks), mother of HA, 19-22, 25, 31, 40, 44, 49, 90, 103-4, 107, 109, 126-7, 129, 133-40, 142-3, 151, 178-82, 185-6, 191, 195, 216, 231, 249, 252-3, 257, 266, 293, 296, 299, 324, 331-2, 337, 379-82, 389, 401-3, 416
  names HA, 20
  declares him her cleverest son, 397
  favors his escape to Europe, 98-101
  praises his letters, 136-7, 175, 178-9
Adams, Arthur, younger brother of HA, 30, 40, 396
  born, 21; dies, 24
Adams, Brooks (*ne* Peter Chardon Brooks), youngest brother of HA, 25-6, 30-1, 40, 107, 125, 133, 136-7, 178, 180, 182, 189-90, 216-7, 238, 249, 296, 337, 380, 389, 397, 402, 412
  calls HA "powerful and original," 27
Adams, Charles Francis, father of HA, 19-35, 39-40, 42, 44-6, 48-50, 64, 68, 70, 88-9, 107, 111-2, 129, 131-3, 136-40, 142-4, 162, 175, 180-1, 186-92, 195, 197, 220-2, 226, 230-8, 241-5, 248-9, 261, 263-72, 283-6, 289, 293-4, 296-8, 301-2, 306, 312-4, 318, 322-4, 326-7, 335-8, 342, 347, 366-72, 379-80, 385-6, 389, 396-9, 402,

408, 412, 415-21, 429, 437, 441, 445, 447-8, 450-2
  gives HA table in library, 31
  takes him to Washington, 45-6
  gives him Bacon's writings, 85
  permits his going to Europe, 98-101
  elected to Congress, 104, 106
  misses HA extremely, 103-4, 136-7
  grumbles at his expenses, 126-7, 153-4, 409
  not a leader, 137
  becomes follower of Seward, 176-8, 184, 187-8
  makes HA his private secretary, 188-9
  permits his writing anonymously for press on politics, 190
  serves on Committee of Thirty-three, 199, 203-10, 214-5
  urged as possible secretary of the treasury, 191-2, 199-200, 203-4, 208, 210, 212-3, 229-30, 417
  enrages Sumner, 215-6, 221-2, 230-1, 236, 243-4, 422-3
  joins secret Union Party, 218, 224-5
  warns HA not to write "too freely" for press, 225
  appointed minister to England, 231
  fails to arrange appointments of official secretaries; orders HA to accompany him to London, 233-4, 424-7
  delays arrival in London; starts

Union Party; establishes "dictatorship," 200, 203, 208-11, 213, 223-4, 419, 421-2

pretends to accept appointment as secretary of state; again tries to impose cabinet choices; resisted by Lincoln; seems to relent, 209, 212, 226-7, 230, 420

implements temporizing strategy to save capital and insure orderly inauguration of antislavery administration, 215, 221

gives party for younger Adamses, 216-7

known by English to be planning war with England and other European powers, 266-7, 273, 278-9, 421

arranges appointment of CFA as minister to England and Wilson as first secretary; fails in effort to make HA second secretary; accepts Moran for place, 231, 234-42, 245, 302, 420, 425-6

continues attempt to dominate administration; suggests government (1) shift to Union policy, (2) start foreign war, and (3) commit leadership to his hands; is viewed as conciliatory towards South; diminished politically by outbreak of Civil War; feels depressed; wins adoption of proposal 1, above, 247, 277-8, 429, 431-2

wrongly imagined by English to be still in full charge in Washington, 278-9

again suggests war with England and other European powers; is thwarted in way that permits HA in London to discover his intentions, 271-3, 279-80

is warned by correspondent of *New York Times* in London that his war plan is well-known there and a mistake best super-

seded by policy of support to British Liberals, 280-2

advised by secret agent in Europe to send unofficial emissaries, 441

sends unofficial emissaries (John Hughes, McIlvaine, Weed, and Scott), 323-4, 443

believed by English to be author of *Trent* affair, 339, 349-50, 354, 357-8, 442, 445

very promptly advised by Weed from Paris to surrender Mason and Slidell, 341, 345

sends brief assurances to CFA (and Weed) in London, 366-7

secretly prepares to arrange surrender of Confederate captives to British custody; suddenly persuades administration to go along with him, 376-8, 380

belatedly understood by English to favor peace, 380

defensible as constructive, consistent, and successful, 449

probably unaware HA was London correspondent regularly published in *New York Times*, 451

Shakespeare, William, 86, 129, 135, 227, 403

Simpson, E. J., 450-1

Slidell, Benjamin, 313, 316-8, 322-3, 328-9, 334, 336, 339-41, 345-6, 349-54, 356, 365-6, 369-70, 372, 377-80, 385, 444, 448-9

Smith, John, 246, 310-1, 452

Sophocles, 68
in relation to HA's birth and death, 19, 396

Stell, William Shorter, 312, 316

Story, William Wetmore, 158-9, 163; Emelyn Story (*nee* Eldredge), 161

Sturgis, Russell, and family, 369, 381

Sturgis, Julia Overing (*nee* Boit), 380-1, 387, 450

Sumner, Charles, 108, 175, 225-6, 229-30, 234-41, 267, 291, 314, 342, 344, 406, 430, 434, 439-40
elected senator, 46-7, 402

BOTH SIDES OF THE OCEAN

has been set in Baskerville by Autopage Book
Composition, Inc., Oceanside, New York.
John Baskerville was one of the great type
designers of the eighteenth century in
England. His typefaces introduced the
modern pseudoclassical style.
Cushing Malloy, Inc., of Ann Arbor,
Michigan, has lithoprinted the book on
neutral pH factor, long-lived paper.
Riverside Book Bindery, Inc., of Rochester,
New York, has bound the book.
Designed by Patricia Bernblum